W9-AZT-970

VISUAL QUICKSTART GUIDE

MAC OS X 10.6 SNOW LEOPARD

Maria Langer

 Peachpit Press

Visual QuickStart Guide
Mac OS X 10.6 Snow Leopard
Maria Langer

Peachpit Press
1249 Eighth Street
Berkeley, CA 94710
510-524-2178
510-524-2221 (fax)

Find us on the Web at: www.peachpit.com

Peachpit Press is a division of Pearson Education

Copyright ©2010 by Maria Langer

Editor: Clifford Colby
Technical Editor: Clifford Colby
Indexer: Julie Bess
Cover Design: Peachpit Press
Production: Maria Langer and David Van Ness

Colophon

This book was produced with Adobe InDesign CS4 and Adobe Photoshop CS3 on a 24-in. iMac with 2.8 GHz Intel Core 2 Duo processor. The fonts used were Utopia, Meta Plus, and PIXymbols Command. Screenshots were created using Snapz Pro X on a pair of Mac Book Pros. Screenshots reprinted by permission of Apple Inc.

Notice of Rights

Notice of Liability

Trademarks

ISBN 13: 978-0-321-63539-6
ISBN 10:   0-321-63539-6

9 8 7 6 5 4 3 2 1

Printed and bound in the United States of America.

Dedication

To my friend
and fellow helicopter pilot,
Jim Van Sky,
with best wishes always.
Fly safe.

Thanks!

To Cliff Colby, for guiding me through yet another addition of our *Mac OS Visual Quick-Start Guide*. I think I whined more than usual this time around; hope I wasn't too much of a nuisance.

To David Van Ness, for his usual excellent job fine-tuning the book's layout. Nudge a pixel here, change a line break there—it's all good.

To Julie Bess, for another great index—this time, with a serious crunch date. I promise to give you more time next time around.

To the folks at ASpeedyNet in Wenatchee and Quincy, WA, especially Dennis and Jayson. Without your help, I would still be stuck on Chapter 20.

To the folks at the Colockum Ridge Golf Course in Quincy, WA, my home away from home, for making me feel welcome there this summer. Now you know what I was up to, cooped up in that little camper.

To Stephen Tonna at Apple Inc., for helping us stay on schedule for the book's production.

To the developers and testers at Apple, for continuing to refine the world's best operating system.

To the folks at Ambrosia Software, for developing and continuing to update Snapz Pro X. I could not have taken the 2,000+ screen shots in this book without this great software program.

And to Mike, for the usual reasons.

Learn more online!

Find more information about Mac OS and other topics I write about on my book support site, www.MariasGuides.com.

And keep checking in at www.Peachpit.com for more articles by your favorite Peachpit authors!

www.marialanger.com

Contents
at a Glance

Table of Contents

TABLE OF CONTENTS

Introduction

Figure 1 The About This Mac window for a computer with Mac OS X 10.6 installed.

✔ Tips

■ The "X" in "Mac OS X" is pronounced "ten."

■ Although this book is almost 650 pages long, it doesn't cover every single aspect of using Mac OS X. You can find additional material that didn't make it into this book on my book support Web site, www.MariasGuides.com.

Mac OS X 10.6 (**Figure 1**) is the latest version of the computer operating system that put the phrase *graphic user interface* in everyone's vocabulary. With Mac OS, you can point, click, and drag to work with files, applications, and utilities. Because the same intuitive interface is utilized throughout the system, you'll find that a procedure that works in one program works in virtually all the others.

This Visual QuickStart Guide will help you learn Mac OS X 10.6 by providing step-by-step instructions, plenty of illustrations, and a generous helping of tips. On these pages, you'll find everything you need to know to get up and running quickly with Mac OS X—and a lot more!

This book was designed for page flipping. Use the thumb tabs, index, or table of contents to find the topics for which you need help. If you're brand new to Mac OS, however, I recommend that you begin by reading at least the first two chapters. In them, you'll find basic information about techniques you'll use every day with your computer.

If you're interested in information about new Mac OS X features, be sure to browse through this Introduction. It'll give you a good idea of what you can expect to see on your computer.

New Features in Mac OS X 10.6

Mac OS X 10.6 (Snow Leopard) combines "under-the-hood" changes to improve performance with a handful of interface and functionality improvements. Here's a look at some of the new and revised features you can expect to find.

✔ Tip

■ This book covers many of these features.

Under the Hood

◆ The Mac OS X installation and upgrade process has been streamlined, making it easier and quicker to complete.

◆ Mac OS X 10.6 takes up as much as 6 GB *less* disk space than Mac OS X 10.5.

◆ The Finder has been completely rewritten to take advantage of modern Mac architecture capabilities, making it faster, especially on newer Mac models.

◆ Macs now start up, shut down, wake from sleep, and connect to networks faster.

◆ Initial Time Machine backups are now faster.

◆ File sharing can continue when Energy Saver settings put the computer to sleep, thus helping you save power when on a file sharing networking.

Figure 2 Exposé is now integrated into the Dock.

Figure 3 Stacks' grid view is scrollable, so you can view all items in the grid.

Figure 4 The services menu now only includes applicable items—and you can determine which ones to include or exclude.

Finder

◆ Exposé is now integrated into the Dock. You can click and hold a Dock icon for a running application to quickly see all of its windows (**Figure 2**) and select the one you want.

◆ Exposé's windows are now arranged neatly in a grid (**Figure 2**), making it easier to see them.

◆ The Grid view in stacks is now scrollable, making it easier to find and select an item in a stack (**Figure 3**).

◆ You can click a folder in a stack to view that folder's content in the stack.

◆ You can now eject disks more reliably, with less of a chance of being warned that a file on disk is in use.

System

◆ You can now draw Chinese characters on a laptop's Multi-Touch trackpad to input them into your computer. (No, this isn't something I have a need for everyday, but if you *did* have a need, you'd probably be thrilled by this new feature.)

◆ Mac OS X can automatically use your Internet connection to find and update printer drivers as needed, ensuring that you always have the latest version of printer drivers for the printers you use.

◆ Your computer can now set your time zone automatically using Location Services, which obtains location information from your Internet connection.

◆ The Services submenu that appears under the Application menu for most applications is now configurable and only includes commands that apply to the current application and/or selection (**Figure 4**).

Applications

- Preview now properly recognizes columns in a multicolumn document, making it possible to select just the text you want to (**Figure 5**).

- QuickTime Player (**Figure 6**) has been rewritten with a cleaner interface, fewer commands, and some of the features formerly available only in the Pro version.

- Safari 's new Top Sites feature keeps track of the sites you visit most and can display a thumbnail menu on command (**Figure 7**).

- iChat video chats now have higher resolution with bandwidth requirements reduced to 300 Kbps (from 900 Kbps).

Figure 5 Preview is now smarter about selecting text in multicolumn documents.

Figure 6 QuickTime Player's interface is now simpler and cleaner.

Figure 7 Safari's new Top Sites feature can automatically display a grid of thumbnail icons for the sites you visit most.

NEW FEATURES IN MAC OS X 10.6

Setting Up Mac OS X 10.6

Figure 1 The currently installed version of Mac OS appears in the About This Mac window.

Setting Up Mac OS X 10.6

Before you can use Mac OS X, you must install it on your computer and configure it to work the way you need it to. The steps you need to complete to do this depend on the software currently installed on your computer.

Use the Mac OS X 10.6 installer to do one of the following:

◆ Update an existing Mac OS X installation to Mac OS X 10.6.

◆ Install Mac OS X 10.6 to replace an existing Mac OS X installation.

Then restart your computer and use the Mac OS Setup Assistant to configure Mac OS X.

This chapter explains how to properly install and configure Mac OS X 10.6 on your computer.

✔ Tips

■ Not sure which version of Mac OS is installed on your computer? Choose Apple > About This Mac. The currently installed version number appears in the About This Mac window (**Figure 1**).

■ If your computer is brand new and you haven't started it yet, chances are you have Mac OS X 10.6 installed. When you start your computer, it'll display the Mac OS Setup assistant. Skip ahead to the section titled "Configuring Mac OS X 10.6" on page 6.

Installing Mac OS X 10.6

Mac OS X's installer application handles all aspects of a Mac OS X installation. It restarts your computer from the Mac OS X Install DVD, then displays step-by-step instructions to install Mac OS X 10.6 from its install disc. When the installation process is finished, the installer automatically restarts your computer from your hard disk and displays the Mac OS Setup Assistant so you can configure Mac OS X 10.6 for your use.

This part of the chapter explains how to install and configure Mac OS X. Unfortunately, since there's no way to take screen shots of the Mac OS X installation and configuration procedure, this part of the chapter won't be very "visual." Follow along closely and you'll get all the information you need to complete the installation and configuration process without any problems.

✔ Tips

■ The installation instructions in this chapter assume you know basic Mac OS techniques, such as pointing, clicking, double-clicking, dragging, and selecting items from a menu. If you're brand new to the Mac and don't know any of these techniques, skip ahead to **Chapter 2**, which discusses Mac OS basics.

■ You can click the Go Back button in an installer window at any time during installation to change options in a previous window.

■ Remember, you can skip using the Mac OS X 10.6 installer if Mac OS X 10.6 or later is already installed on your computer.

Figure 2
When you insert the Mac OS X Install DVD, its icon appears on the desktop...

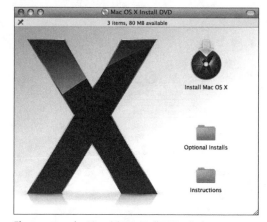

Figure 3 ...and a Mac OS X Install DVD window opens.

Figure 4 The first installation dialog for Mac OS X 10.6.

Figure 5 As you probably expected, you'll have to agree to this licensing agreement before you can proceed.

To install Mac OS X 10.6

1. Insert the Mac OS X Install DVD disc in your drive. A Mac OS X Install DVD icon should appear on your desktop (**Figure 2**), along with a Mac OS X Install DVD window (**Figure 3**).

2. Double-click the Install Mac OS X icon.

3. An Install Mac OS X dialog appears (**Figure 4**). Click Continue.

4. A license agreement dialog like the one in **Figure 5** appears. Read the contents of this dialog and click Agree.

5. The next dialog indicates which hard disk Mac OS X will be installed on:

   ▲ If there's only one hard disk in or connected to your computer, the screen should look something like **Figure 6**. Skip ahead to step 6.

   ▲ If there are multiple hard disks in or connected to your computer, the screen should look something like **Figure 7**. Click to select the disk you want to install Mac OS X on.

Continued on next page...

Figure 6 If your computer has just one hard disk, it will appear as the installation destination...

Figure 7 ...but if you have more than one hard disk, you can choose the one you want to install on.

LAUNCHING THE MAC OS X INSTALLER

Continued from previous page.

6. If desired, click Customize to display a screen like the one in **Figure 8**. You can toggle check boxes to determine which options should be installed. When you're finished making changes, click OK.

7. Click the Install button.

8. A confirmation dialog like the one in **Figure 9** appears. Click Install.

9. An authentication dialog appears (**Figure 10**). Enter an administrator name and password and click OK.

10. Wait while software from the DVD is installed. A status area in the window tells you how much longer the installation should take (**Figure 11**). During the process, your computer will restart at least once.

11. When the installation is finished, one of two things happens:

   ▲ If you are updating an existing Mac OS X installation, a Thank You dialog appears (**Figure 12**). Click Continue. The Mac OS X Desktop appears with your Home folder window and the Mac OS X Install DVD window open (**Figure 14**). You're finished.

   ▲ If you have installed Mac OS X on a hard disk that did not already contain a Mac OS installation, the first screen of the Setup Assistant appears. Continue following instructions in the section titled "Configuring Mac OS X 10.6" on page 6.

Figure 8 You can customize the installation by setting options in this dialog.

Figure 9 The installer verifies that you really do want to install Mac OS X.

Figure 10 Use this authentication dialog to authorize the installation.

Figure 11 A dialog like this indicates installation progress.

Figure 12 A dialog like this appears when installation is complete.

Figure 13 If you want to run Mac OS X utilities on the installation disk on your computer, you'll see this screen with instructions and a Restart button.

✔ Tips

■ It's a good idea to open and read the files in the Instructions folder on the Mac OS X Install DVD (**Figure 3**). They include illustrated instructions for installing and setting up Mac OS 10.6.

■ In step 3, if you want to use Mac OS X utilities from the Install DVD, click the Utilities button. Then click the Restart button in the window that appears (**Figure 13**). When your computer restarts, you can access the utility you need from a menu that appears.

■ In step 4, if you click the Disagree button, you will not be able to install Mac OS X.

■ A note beneath the disk icons in step 5 indicates how much space is available on each disk (**Figure 7**). You can see how much space a Mac OS X installation takes by looking at the bottom of the window. Make sure the disk you select has enough space for the installation.

■ The Customize option in step 6 is provided for Mac OS X "power users" and users who want to minimize the installation options. For example, you can use the Customize option to prevent installation of various language files and related fonts to save disk space. If you're not sure about the options you want to install, stick with the default options.

■ The authentication dialog (**Figure 10**) prevents someone without administrator privileges from installing system software. This is especially important on a computer used by more than one person.

■ The installation could take a while—an hour or more, depending on your computer setup.

INSTALLING MAC OS X

5

Configuring Mac OS X 10.6

When your computer restarts after a Mac OS X installation, the Mac OS X Setup Assistant automatically appears. This program uses a simple question-and-answer process to get information about you and the way you use your computer. The information you provide is automatically entered in the various System Preferences panes of Mac OS X to configure your computer for Mac OS X.

✔ Tips

- Although I'm pretty good at getting screenshots for my book, I was unable to capture images of Mac OS X's Setup Assistant. Try to follow along with the text. As you'll see, the process is pretty self-explanatory.

- If you just bought your Macintosh and Mac OS X is installed, the first time you start your computer, you'll see the Mac OS X Setup Assistant described here. Follow these instructions to configure your computer.

- If the Mac OS X Setup Assistant does not appear, Mac OS X is already configured. You can skip this section.

- If you upgraded from a previous version of Mac OS X to Mac OS X 10.6 only some of the Mac OS X Setup Assistant screens will appear and many of them may already contain configuration information. Follow along with the instructions in this section if you need help entering missing information.

To configure Mac OS X

1. In the Welcome window that appears after installing Mac OS X, select the name of the country you're in. Click Continue.

2. In the Select Your Keyboard window, select a keyboard layout. Click Continue.

3. In the Do You Already Own a Mac? window, select an option and click Continue:

   - ▲ **From another Mac** enables you to use a FireWire cable to connect your Mac to another Mac and transfer configuration settings from the other Mac. If you choose this option, continue following the instructions that appear onscreen. You should be able to skip most of the rest of these steps.

   - ▲ **From another volume on this Mac** transfers configuration settings from another disk connected to your computer. If you choose this option, continue following the instructions that appear onscreen. You should be able to skip most of the rest of these steps.

   - ▲ **From a Time Machine backup** enables you to configure your Mac from a Time Machine backup on an attached disk. If you choose this option, continue following instructions that appear onscreen. You should be able to skip most of the rest of these steps.

   - ▲ **Do not transfer my information now** does not transfer any configuration information. Continue following these steps.

4. The Mac OS Setup Assistant attempts to determine how you connect to the Internet by sensing connections. It then displays appropriate screens for configuring your connection. How you proceed depends on what appears:

   ▲ If the options that appear are correct for your setup, continue following the instructions in step 6.

   ▲ If the options are not appropriate for your setup, click the Different Network Setup button and continue following the instructions in step 5.

5. In the How Do You Connect? window that appears, select one of the options for how you connect to the Internet and click Continue:

   ▲ **AirPort wireless** requires access to a wireless network.

   ▲ **Telephone modem** uses your computer's internal modem or an external modem. (This option only appears if your Macintosh has a modem.)

   ▲ **Cable modem** uses a cable modem connected to your computer via Ethernet or USB cable.

   ▲ **DSL modem** uses a DSL modem connected to your computer via Ethernet.

   ▲ **Local network (Ethernet)** uses an Ethernet network. This option is common at workplaces.

   ▲ **My computer does not connect to the Internet** is for computers that are not connected to the Internet in any way. Skip ahead to step 8.

6. Enter information in the screen that appears to provide information about your Internet service or local area network and click Continue. If you're not sure what to enter, contact your ISP or system administrator.

7. The Enter Your Apple ID window appears. If you have an Apple ID, enter it and your password. If you don't, leave both boxes blank. Then click Continue.

8. In the Registration Information window, fill in the form. You can press Tab to move from one field to another. Click Continue.

9. In the A Few More Questions window, use pop-up menus to answer two marketing questions. Turn on the check box to get information about Apple products via e-mail. Then click Continue.

10. In the Create Your Account window, fill in the form to enter information to set up your Mac OS X account:

   ▲ **Full Name** is your name.

   ▲ **Account Name** is a short version of your name used for networking. This name is also used to label your Home folder. I usually use my first initial followed by my last name: *mlanger*.

   ▲ **Password** is a password you want to use with your account.

   ▲ **Verify** is the same password you entered in the Password box.

   ▲ **Password Hint** is a hint that will remind you what your password is. Don't use this box to enter your password again, since it will appear when you cannot successfully log in to your account.

   When you're finished entering account information, click Continue.

Continued on next page...

CONFIGURING MAC OS X

Continued from previous page.

11. The Select a Picture for This Account window may appear. If you have a built-in iSight camera, it offers two options:

   ▲ **Take a snapshot** enables you to use the camera to take a photo. Frame the subject—you?— in the preview window and click the Take a video snapshot button. Your computer will beep the countdown from three and snap a photo. You can repeat this process if you don't like the results.

   ▲ **Choose from the picture library** displays Apple's library of user icons. Choose the one you like. If you don't have an iSight camera and this screen appears, this is the only option you'll have to select a picture for your account.

   When you're finished selecting a picture, click Continue.

12. The Select Time Zone window may appear. Click on the world map to set your approximate location, then choose a city from the Closest City pop-up menu. Click Continue.

13 If you do not have an Internet connection, the Set Date and Time window may appear. Set the date and time and click Continue.

14. You may be prompted to renew your MobileMe membership (if you have one) or sign up for a free MobileMe trial membership. Follow the onscreen prompts to provide information if requested.

15. Continue following the steps in the section titled "To finish the installation" later in this chapter.

✔ Tips

- If your country is not listed in step 1, turn on the Show All check box to display more options.

- In step 1, if you wait long enough, you'll hear your Mac provide some instructions using its VoiceOver feature. You can also press ⎋Esc to get VoiceOver instructions for configuration. I tell you about Voice-Over on page 591.

- In step 2, you can turn on the Show All check box to show additional keyboard layouts.

- In step 8, if you have a MobileMe account and a connection to the Internet, your contact information may already be filled in based on data stored on Apple's MobileMe server. I tell you about using the MobileMe service with your Mac on page 433.

- In step 8, you can learn about Apple's privacy policy by clicking the Privacy button. When you're finished reading the information in the dialog sheet that appears, click OK to dismiss it and return to the Registration Information window.

- When you enter your password in steps 7 and 10, it displays as bullet characters. That's why you enter it twice: so you're sure you entered what you thought you did the first time.

- Remember the password you enter in step 10! If you forget your password, you may not be able to use your computer. It's a good idea to use the Password Hint field to enter a hint that makes your password impossible to forget.

- The photo feature in step 11 is similar to that in Photo Booth, which I discuss on page 295.

Figure 14 At the end of the installation, the Mac OS X 10.6 desktop appears.

To finish the installation

In the Thank You window that appears (**Figure 12**), click Go.

The Mac OS X Desktop appears with the Mac OS X Install DVD window open (**Figure 14**).

✔ Tips

- If you do not have an Internet connection, you'll see the Don't Forget to Register window instead of the Thank You window.

- I explain how to work with the Mac OS Desktop and Finder in **Chapters 2** through **4**.

- To eject the Install DVD, press the Eject Media button on your keyboard or drag the DVD icon to the Trash icon in the Dock. I tell you more about ejecting discs on page 101.

- The Software Update utility may run right after installing Mac OS X 10.6. If any software updates are available for your computer, a dialog with update information appears. I explain how to use Software Update on page 552.

Finder Basics

The Finder & Desktop

The *Finder* is a program that is part of Mac OS. It launches automatically when you start your computer.

The Finder provides a graphic user interface called the *desktop* (**Figure 1**) that you can use to open, copy, delete, list, organize, and perform other operations on computer files.

This chapter provides important instructions for using the Finder and items that appear on the Mac OS X desktop. It's important that you understand how to use these basic Finder techniques, since you'll use them again and again every time you work with your Mac.

✔ Tips

- You never have to manually launch the Finder; it always starts automatically.

- Under normal circumstances, you cannot quit the Finder.

- If you're new to Mac OS, don't skip this chapter. It provides the basic information you'll need to use your computer successfully.

Figure 1 Basic desktop elements.

The Mouse & Trackpad

Mac OS, like most graphic user interface systems, uses the mouse or trackpad as an input device to manipulate an onscreen pointer. There are several basic techniques you must know to use your computer:

◆ **Point** to a specific item onscreen.

◆ **Click** an item to select it.

◆ **Double-click** an item to open it.

◆ **Drag** to move an item or select multiple items.

✔ Tips

■ Laptop computers use a trackpad instead of a mouse. You can, however, connect an external mouse via USB or Bluetooth and use that as an input device.

■ If you have a MacBook or MacBook Pro computer with a Multi-Touch trackpad, be sure to read the additional instructions on page 15 for more information about how to take advantage of its special features.

■ You can customize the settings for your mouse with Mouse preferences pane, which I discuss on page 550.

■ You can customize the settings for your laptop's trackpad with the Trackpad preferences pane, which I discuss on page 551.

Figure 2 The pointer usually looks like an arrow pointer when you are working in the Finder.

Applications

Figure 3
Move the pointer so the arrow's tip is on the item you want to point to.

To point

1. Move the mouse on the work surface or mouse pad.

   or

   Move the tip of one finger (usually your forefinger) on the surface of the trackpad.

   The pointer, which usually looks like an arrow (**Figure 2**), moves on your computer screen.

2. When the tip of the pointer's arrow is on the item you want to point to (**Figure 3**), stop moving it.

✔ Tip

■ The tip of the pointer is its "business end."

Figure 4
Click to select
an icon...

Figure 5 ...or an item in a list.

Figure 6 Drag to move items such as
folder icons.

To click

1. Point to the item you want to click.

2. Press (and release) the mouse button or
   trackpad button once.

   The item you clicked becomes selected
   (**Figures 4** and **5**).

✔ Tip

- With a two-button mouse, you normally
  click by pressing the left mouse button.
  I cover two-button mouse use on the
  next page.

To double-click

1. Point to the item you want to double-
   click or double-tap.

2. Press (and release) the mouse button or
   trackpad button twice quickly.

   The item you double-clicked opens.

✔ Tip

- Keep the pointer still while double-
  clicking. If you move the mouse or drag
  your finger on the trackpad while double-
  clicking, you may move the item instead
  of double-clicking it.

To drag

1. Point to the item you want to drag.

2. Press the mouse button or trackpad
   button down.

3. While holding the button down, move the
   pointer. The item you are dragging moves
   (**Figure 6**).

Using a Two-Button Mouse

New Macintosh desktop computers come with Apple's Mighty Mouse (**Figure 7**), a two-button mouse that includes a scroll ball. This mouse—and similar devices offered by Logitech, Microsoft, and others—offers additional functionality:

◆ Right-clicking displays contextual menus for items you point to.

◆ Scrolling scrolls window or list contents.

✔ Tips

■ I tell you more about contextual menus on page 17 and about scrolling on page 31.

■ You can customize the button settings for a Mighty Mouse in the Mouse preferences pane, which I discuss on page 550.

■ The functionality of the scroll ball or wheel can vary by application. For example, in some applications rolling the scroll bar or wheel zooms a view in or out. Consult your application documentation to learn more about special functionality.

To right-click

1. Point to the item you want to right-click.

2. Press (and release) the right mouse button once.

✔ Tip

■ Throughout this book, when you need to right-click something, I will use the phrase *right-click*. As discussed on the previous page, *click* refers to normal clicking with the left mouse button.

To scroll

1. Point to the item you want to scroll.

2. Roll the mouse scroll ball or scroll wheel in the direction you want to scroll.

Figure 7
Apple's Mighty Mouse, which comes with new Mac desktop computers, is a two-button mouse with a scroll ball.

Figure 8 Starting in 2008, MacBook and MacBook Pro computers were shipped with buttonless trackpads.

Trackpad

Using a Multi-Touch Trackpad

In late 2008, Apple began releasing MacBook and MacBook Pro laptop computers with a "Multi-Touch" buttonless trackpad (**Figure 8**). At least that's how it seems. In reality, the entire trackpad surface is a big button. This type of trackpad offers additional options for working with Mac OS.

✔ Tips

■ You can see a video demonstration of a Multi-Touch trackpad, as well as illustrations of its use, on Apple's support site, support.apple.com/kb/HT3211.

■ Some of the techniques on Multi-Touch trackpads also work on Mac laptop models with older trackpads. Check the Trackpad preferences pane for your computer to see what's available. I tell you more on page 551.

To click or right-click

◆ To click, use one finger to tap anywhere on the trackpad.

◆ To right-click, use two fingers to tap anywhere on the trackpad.

✔ Tip

■ By default, the tap to click option is turned off. You can turn it on in the Trackpad preferences pane, which I discuss on page 551.

To scroll

Drag two fingers across the trackpad in the direction you want to scroll.

✔ Tip

■ I tell you more about scrolling a window's contents on page 31.

USING A MULTI-TOUCH TRACKPAD

Menus

The Finder—and most other Mac OS programs—offers menus full of options. There are four types of menus in Mac OS X:

◆ A pull-down menu appears on the menu bar at the top of the screen (**Figure 9**).

◆ A submenu appears when a menu option with a right-pointing triangle is selected (**Figure 10**).

◆ A pop-up menu appears within a window or dialog (**Figure 11**).

◆ A contextual menu appears when you hold down [Control] while clicking an item or right-click an item (**Figure 12**).

✔ Tips

■ Menus and the menu bar are slightly translucent, making it possible to see the desktop picture or open windows beneath them. To keep the screenshots cleaner looking for this book, most screenshots were created with a white desktop pattern.

■ A menu option followed by an ellipsis (...) (**Figures 9**, **10**, and **12**) display a dialog. Dialogs are discussed on page 205.

■ A menu option that is dimmed or gray (**Figures 9** and **10**) cannot be chosen. Command availability varies based on what is selected.

■ A menu option preceded by a check mark (**Figure 9**) is enabled, or "turned on."

■ A menu option followed by a series of keyboard characters (**Figures 9** and **10**) has a keyboard shortcut. I discuss keyboard shortcuts on page 19.

■ Contextual menus (**Figure 12**) only display options that apply to the item you are pointing to.

Figure 9 The menu bar offers pull-down menus.

Figure 10 A submenu appears when you select a menu option with a right-pointing triangle beside it.

Figure 11 To display a pop-up menu, click it.

Figure 12 A contextual menu appears when you hold down [Control] while clicking or if you right-click on certain items.

MENUS

Figure 13 Point to the menu name.

Figure 14 Click to display the menu.

Figure 15 Click (or drag) to choose the menu option you want.

Figure 16 Point to an item.

Users

Figure 17 A contextual menu appears when you click.

Figure 18 Click (or drag) to choose the option you want.

To use a menu

1. Point to the name of the menu (**Figure 13**).

2. Click. The menu opens, displaying its options (**Figure 14**).

3. Point to the menu option you want (**Figure 15**).

4. Click to choose the option. The menu disappears.

✔ Tips

■ Mac OS X's menus are "sticky menus"—a menu opens and stays open when you click its name.

■ To close a menu without choosing an option, click outside the menu.

■ This book uses the following notation to indicate menu commands: *Menu Name > Submenu Name* (if necessary) *> Command Name*. For example, the instructions for choosing the Applications command from the Recent Folders submenu under the Go menu (**Figure 10**) would be: "choose Go > Recent Folders > Applications."

To use a contextual menu

1. Point to the item on which you want to act (**Figure 16**).

2. Hold down Control and click or, if you have a two-button mouse, right-click.

   A contextual menu appears (**Figure 17**).

3. Click the menu option you want (**Figure 18**).

✔ Tip

■ Contextual menus are similar to the Action pop-up menu, which I tell you about on page 33.

USING MENUS

The Keyboard

The keyboard offers another way to communicate with your computer. In addition to typing text and numbers, you can use it to choose menu commands.

There are three types of keys on a Mac OS keyboard:

◆ **Character keys**, such as letters, numbers, and symbols, are for typing information. Some character keys have special functions, as listed in **Table 1**.

◆ **Modifier keys** alter the meaning of a character key being pressed or the meaning of a mouse or trackpad action. Modifier keys are listed in **Table 2**.

◆ **Function keys** perform specific functions in Mac OS or an application. Dedicated function keys, which always do the same thing, are listed in **Table 3**. Function keys labeled ⟨F1⟩ through ⟨F15⟩ (or higher) on the keyboard can be assigned specific functions by applications.

✔ Tips

■ ⟨⌘⟩ is called the *Command* key—not the Apple key.

■ On some keyboards, the *Control* key is labeled ⟨Control⟩ while on others it is labeled ⟨Ctrl⟩. Throughout this book, I'll use ⟨Control⟩ to refer to the Control key, no matter how it might be labeled on your computer's keyboard.

■ The ⟨Del⟩ key does not appear on all keyboards.

■ Contextual menus are discussed on the previous pages.

Table 1

Special Character Keys	
Key	**Function**
⟨Enter⟩	Enters information or "clicks" a default button.
⟨Return⟩	Begins a new paragraph or line or "clicks" a default button.
⟨Tab⟩	Advances to the next tab stop or the next item in a sequence.
⟨Delete⟩	Deletes a selection or the character to the left of the insertion point.
⟨Del⟩	Deletes a selection or the character to the right of the insertion point.
⟨Esc⟩	"Clicks" a Cancel button or ends the operation that is currently in progress.

Table 2

Modifier Keys	
Key	**Function**
⟨Shift⟩	Produces uppercase characters or symbols. Also works with the mouse to extend selections and to restrain movement in graphic applications.
⟨Option⟩	Produces special symbols.
⟨⌘⟩	Accesses menu commands via keyboard shortcuts.
⟨Control⟩	Modifies the functions of other keys and displays contextual menus.

Table 3

Dedicated Function Keys	
Key	**Function**
⟨Help⟩	Displays onscreen help.
⟨Home⟩	Scrolls to the beginning.
⟨End⟩	Scrolls to the end.
⟨Page Up⟩	Scrolls up one page.
⟨Page Down⟩	Scrolls down one page.
⟨←⟩⟨→⟩⟨↑⟩⟨↓⟩	Moves the insertion point or changes the selection.

To use a keyboard shortcut

1. Hold down the modifier key(s) in the sequence. This is usually ⌃⌘, but can be Option, Control, or Shift or a combination of any of these.

2. Press the letter, number, or symbol key in the sequence.

   For example, to choose the Open command, which can be found under the File menu (**Figure 15**), hold down ⌃⌘ and press ⊙.

✔ Tips

- You can learn keyboard shortcuts by observing the key sequences that appear to the right of some menu commands (**Figures 9** and **10**).

- Some commands include more than one modifier key. You must hold all modifier keys down while pressing the letter, number, or symbol key for the keyboard shortcut.

- You can find a list of Finder keyboard shortcuts in **Appendix A**.

- Some applications refer to keyboard shortcuts as keyboard equivalents or shortcut keys.

- You can add or modify keyboard shortcuts for the Finder and other applications in the Keyboard preferences pane, which I discuss on page 546.

Icons

Mac OS uses icons to graphically represent files and other items on the desktop, in the Dock, or within Finder windows:

◆ **Applications** (**Figure 19**) are programs you use to get work done. **Chapters 10** through **14** discuss working with applications.

◆ **Documents** (**Figure 20**) are the files created by applications. **Chapters 10** and **11** cover working with documents.

◆ **Folders** (**Figure 21**) are used to organize files. **Chapter 3** discusses using folders.

◆ **Volumes** (**Figure 22**), including hard disks, CDs, DVDs, iPods, and network disks, are used to store data. **Chapter 6** covers working with volumes.

◆ The **Trash** (**Figure 23**), which is in the Dock, is for discarding items you no longer want and for ejecting removable media. Using the Trash is covered on page 57.

✔ Tips

■ Icons can appear a number of different ways, depending on the view and view options chosen for a window. Windows are discussed on page 26 and window views are discussed in **Chapter 4**.

■ Snow Leopard introduces enhanced icon view, which enables you to scroll through the pages of a document in icon view. I explain how to use this new feature on page 25.

TextEdit   Preview   iPhoto

Figure 19 Application icons.

Letter to John   Flying Facts.pdf   butterfly.jpg

Figure 20 Document icons. In Mac OS X 10.6, they can display previews of the document's first page.

Applications   System   Letters

Figure 21 Folder icons.

Macintosh HD   mlanger   SmartDisk

Figure 22 Three different volume icons: hard disk, iDisk, and an external hard disk.

Figure 23 The three faces of the Trash icon in the Dock: empty, full, and while dragging removable media.

Figure 24 To select an icon, click it.

Figure 25 Hold down ⌘ while clicking other icons to add them to a multiple icon selection.

To select an icon

Click the icon that you want to select. A gray box appears around the icon and its name becomes highlighted (**Figure 24**).

✔ Tip

- You can also select an icon in an active window by pressing the keyboard key for the first letter of the icon's name or by pressing ⎋Tab, ⇧Shift⎋Tab, ←, →, ↑, or ↓ until the icon is selected.

To deselect an icon

Click anywhere in the window or on the desktop other than on the selected icon.

✔ Tips

- If you select one icon and then click another icon, the originally selected icon is deselected and the icon you clicked becomes selected instead.

- Windows are discussed on page 26.

To select multiple icons by clicking

1. Click the first icon that you want to select.

2. Hold down ⌘ and click another icon that you want to select (**Figure 25**).

3. Repeat step 2 until all icons that you want to select have been selected.

✔ Tip

- Icons that are part of a multiple selection must be in the same window.

SELECTING & DESELECTING ICONS

To select multiple icons by dragging

1. Position the pointer slightly above and to the left of the first icon in the group that you want to select (**Figure 26**).

2. Press the button, and drag diagonally across the icons you want to select. A shaded box appears to indicate the selection area, and the items within it become selected (**Figure 27**).

3. When all the icons that you want to select are included in the selection area, release the button (**Figure 28**).

✔ Tip

■ To select multiple icons by dragging, the icons must be adjacent.

To select all icons in a window

Choose Edit > Select All (**Figure 29**), or press ⌘ A.

All icons in the active window are selected.

✔ Tip

■ Activating windows is covered on page 28.

To deselect one icon in a multiple selection

Hold down ⌘ while clicking the icon that you want to deselect. That icon is deselected while the others remain selected.

Figure 26 Position the pointer above and to the left of the first icon that you want to select.

Figure 27 Drag to draw a shaded selection box around the icons that you want to select.

Figure 28 Release the button to complete the selection.

Figure 29
Choose Select
All from the Edit
menu to select
all items.

Figure 30 Point to the icon you want to move.

Figure 31 Drag the icon to the new location.

Figure 32 Release the button to complete the move.

To move an icon

1. Position the pointer on the icon that you want to move (**Figure 30**).

2. Press the button and drag the icon to the new location. As you drag, a shadowy image of the icon moves with the pointer (**Figure 31**).

3. Release the button when the icon is in the desired position (**Figure 32**).

✔ Tips

■ You cannot drag to reposition icons within windows set to list, column, or Cover Flow view. Window views are discussed in **Chapter 4**.

■ You move icons to rearrange them in a window or on the desktop or to copy or move the items they represent to another folder or disk. Copying and moving items is discussed in **Chapter 3**.

■ You can also move multiple icons at once. First, select the icons. Then position the pointer on one of the selected icons and follow steps 2 and 3 above. All selected icons move together.

■ To force an icon to snap to a window's invisible grid, hold down ⌃⌘ while dragging it. The grid, which I tell you more about starting on page 63, ensures consistent spacing between icons, so your window looks neat.

MOVING ICONS

To open an icon

1. Select the icon you want to open (**Figure 33**).

2. Choose File > Open (**Figure 34**), or press ⌘ O.

Or

Double-click the icon that you want to open.

✔ Tips

■ Only one click is necessary when opening an item in a Finder window's sidebar or the Dock. The sidebar and Dock are covered in detail on page 34 and page 37 respectively.

■ What happens when you open an icon depends on the type of icon you open. For example:

▲ Opening a disk or folder icon displays the contents of the disk or folder in the same Finder window (**Figure 35**). Windows are discussed next.

▲ Opening an application icon launches the application so that you can work with it. Working with applications is covered in **Chapters 10** through **14**.

▲ Opening a document icon launches the application that created that document and displays the document so you can view or edit it. Working with documents is covered in **Chapter 10**.

▲ Opening the Trash displays items that will be deleted when you empty the Trash. Using and emptying the Trash is discussed on page 57.

■ To open a folder or disk in a new Finder window, hold down ⌘ while opening it.

■ The File menu's Open With submenu, which is discussed on page 188, enables you to open a document with a specific application.

Figure 33 Select the icon.

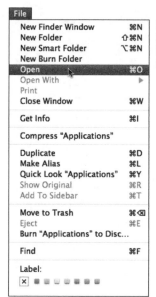

Figure 34 Choose Open from the File menu.

Figure 35 Here's the window from **Figure 37** with the Application folder's contents displayed.

Figure 36
When you point to a preview icon for a multi-page PDF file, page scrolling buttons appear.

RobbieOrderForm.pdf

Figure 37
When you point to a preview icon for a QuickTime movie, a play button appears.

Greetings from Quincy.mov

Figure 38
Clicking the right button for a document displays the next page of that document.

RobbieOrderForm.pdf

Figure 39
Clicking the play button plays the movie.

Greetings from Quincy.mov

To use enhanced icon view

1. Point to the icon for a multi-page document. A pair of arrows in circles appears (**Figure 36**).

   or

   Point to the icon for a QuickTime movie. An arrow in a circle appears (**Figure 37**).

2. To scroll through the pages of the document in its icon, click the right arrow. The icon changes to display the next page (**Figure 38**). You can use the arrows to scroll forward or backward through the pages of the document.

   or

   To play the movie in its icon, click the arrow. The movie plays (**Figure 39**). You can click again to stop movie play.

✔ Tips

- This feature works for compatible multiple-page documents, such as PDF files, or QuickTime movies that are displayed in icon, column, or Cover Flow view as previews.

- Viewing the contents of a document in enhanced icon view works best when the icon size is large or you are viewing the icon in Cover Flow. I explain how to change icon size in icon view on page 74 and tell you more about Cover Flow on page 71.

USING ENHANCED ICON VIEW

Windows

Mac OS makes extensive use of windows for displaying icons and other information in the Finder and documents in other applications. **Figures 40** and **41** show two different views of a Finder window.

Each window includes a variety of controls you can use to manipulate it:

◆ The **close button** closes the window.

◆ The **minimize button** collapses the window to an icon in the Dock.

◆ The **zoom button** toggles the window's size between full size and a custom size.

◆ The **toolbar** displays buttons and controls for working with Finder windows.

◆ The **title bar** displays the window's icon and name.

◆ The **search field** enables you to search for files using Spotlight.

◆ The **toolbar control** toggles the display of the toolbar.

◆ The **sidebar**, which is customizable, shows commonly accessed volumes and folders, as well as predefined searches.

◆ The **status bar** provides information about items in a window and space available on disk.

◆ The **resize control** enables you to set a custom size for the window.

◆ **Scroll bars** scroll the contents of the window.

◆ **Column headings** (in list view only) display the names of the columns and let you quickly sort by a column. (The selected column heading is the column by which the list is sorted.)

Close button / Minimize button / Zoom button / Toolbar / Title bar / Search field / Toolbar control

Sidebar   Status bar   Scroll bar   Size control

Figure 40 A Finder window in icon view.

Close button / Minimize button / Zoom button / Toolbar / Title bar / Column heading / Search field / Toolbar control

Sidebar   Status bar   Scroll bars   Size control

Figure 41 The same Finder window in list view.

✔ Tips

■ By default, when you open a folder or disk icon, its contents appear in the active window. As discussed on page 146, you can use Finder Preferences to tell Mac OS X to open folders in new windows.

■ I cover the Finder's three window views and the status bar in **Chapter 4**, the toolbar on page 32, and the search field on page 85.

WINDOWS

Figure 42
Choose New
Finder Window
from the File
menu.

Figure 43 The active window appears atop all other windows. The buttons on the left end of the active window's title bar appear in color.

Figure 44 Choose Close Window from the File menu...

Figure 45 ...or hold down Option and choose Close All from the File menu.

To open a new Finder window

Choose File > New Finder Window (**Figure 42**), or press ⌃⌘N. A new Home folder window for your account appears (**Figure 43**).

✔ Tip

■ The Home folder is discussed in **Chapter 3**.

To open a folder or disk in a new Finder window

Hold down ⌃⌘ while opening a folder or disk icon. A new window containing the contents of the folder or disk appears.

✔ Tip

■ Opening folders and disks is explained earlier in this chapter.

To close a window

Click the window's close button (**Figures 40** and **41**).

Or

Choose File > Close Window (**Figure 44**), or press ⌃⌘W.

To close all open windows

Hold down Option while clicking the active window's close button (**Figures 40** and **41**).

Or

Hold down Option while choosing File > Close All (**Figure 45**), or press Option ⌃⌘W.

✔ Tip

■ The Close Window/Close All commands (**Figures 44** and **45**) are examples of dynamic menu items—pressing a modifier key (in this case, Option) changes the menu command from Close Window (**Figure 44**) to Close All (**Figure 45**).

To activate a window

Click anywhere in or on the window.

Or

Choose the name of the window you want to activate from the Window menu (**Figure 46**).

✔ Tips

■ Make sure the window you want to work with is active before using commands that work on the active window—such as Close Window, Select All, and View menu commands.

■ You can distinguish between active and inactive windows by the appearance of their title bars; the buttons on the left end of an active window's title bar are in color (**Figure 43**). In addition, a check mark appears beside the active window's name in the Window menu (**Figure 47**).

■ When two or more windows overlap, the active window will always be on top of the stack (**Figure 43**).

■ You can use the Cycle Through Windows command (**Figure 47**) or its handy shortcut, ⌘ ` , to activate each open window, in sequence.

To bring all Finder windows to the top

Choose Window > Bring All to Front (**Figure 47**). All open Finder windows that are not minimized are moved in front of any windows opened by other applications.

✔ Tip

■ Finder windows can be intermingled with other applications' windows. The Bring All to Front command gathers the windows together in the top layers. This command is useful when working with many windows from several different applications.

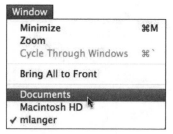

Figure 46 Choose the name of the window you want to activate from the Window menu.

Figure 47 A check mark appears beside the active window's name.

Figure 48 Position the pointer on the title bar.

Figure 49 As you drag, the window moves.

Figure 50 Position the pointer on the resize control.

Figure 51
As you
drag, the
window's
size and
shape
changes.

To move a window

1. Position the pointer on the window's title bar (**Figure 48**) or bottom border.

2. Press the button and drag the window to a new location. As you drag, the window moves along with the pointer (**Figure 49**).

3. When the outline of the window is in the desired position, release the button.

To resize a window

1. Position the pointer on the resize control in the lower-right corner of the window (**Figure 50**).

2. Press the button and drag. As you drag, the resize control moves with the pointer, changing the size and shape of the window (**Figure 51**).

3. When the window is the desired size, release the button.

✔ Tips

■ The larger a window is, the more you can see inside it.

■ By resizing and repositioning windows, you can see inside more than one window at a time. This comes in handy when moving or copying the icons for files and folders from one window to another. Moving and copying files and folders is covered in **Chapter 3**.

MOVING & RESIZING WINDOWS

To minimize a window

Use one of the following techniques:

◆ Click the window's minimize button (**Figure 40** and **41**).

◆ Choose Window > Minimize (**Figure 47**), or press ⌃ ⌘ M.

◆ Double-click the window's title bar.

The window shrinks into an icon and slips into the Dock at the bottom of the screen (**Figure 52**).

✔ Tip

■ To minimize all windows, hold down Option and choose Windows > Minimize All, or press Option ⌃ ⌘ M.

To redisplay a minimized window

Use one of the following techniques:

◆ Click the window's icon in the Dock (**Figure 52**).

◆ Choose the window's name from the Window menu (**Figure 53**).

To zoom a window

Click the window's zoom button (**Figures 40** and **41**).

Each time you click the zoom button, the window's size toggles between two sizes:

◆ **Standard state** size is the smallest possible size that would accommodate the window's contents and still fit on your screen (**Figure 1**).

◆ **User state** size, which is the size you specify with the size control (**Figure 51**).

Figure 52 A minimized window shrinks down into an icon in the Dock.

Window	
Minimize	⌘M
Zoom	
Cycle Through Windows	⌘ `
Bring All to Front	
◆ Applications	
✓ Macintosh HD	
mlanger	

Figure 53 A diamond beside a window name indicates that the window has been minimized.

Figure 54
Scroll bar
components.

Scroller   *Horizontal*   *Horizontal*
scroll track   *scroll arrows*

—Scroller

—Vertical scroll track

Vertical —scroll arrows

Figure 55 In this example, it isn't necessary to scroll from side to side so there's no horizontal scroll bar.

To scroll a window's contents

Click one of the scroll bar arrows (**Figure 54**) as follows:

◆ To scroll the window's contents up, click the down arrow on the vertical scroll bar.

◆ To scroll the window's contents down, click the up arrow on the vertical scroll bar.

◆ To scroll the window's contents to the left, click the right arrow on the horizontal scroll bar.

◆ To scroll the window's contents to the right, click the left arrow on the horizontal scroll bar.

✔ Tips

■ If you have trouble remembering which scroll arrow to click, think of it this way:

▲ Click down to see down.

▲ Click up to see up.

▲ Click right to see right.

▲ Click left to see left.

■ You can also scroll a window's contents by either clicking in the scroll track on either side of the scroller or by dragging the scroller to a new position on the scroll bar. Both of these techniques enable you to scroll a window's contents more quickly.

■ Scroll bars only appear when necessary— when part of a window's contents are hidden. In **Figure 55**, for example, it isn't necessary to scroll from side to side so the horizontal scroll bar does not appear. In **Figure 35**, all of the window's contents are displayed so no scroll bars appear.

■ The scrollers in Mac OS X are *proportional*—this means that the more of a window's contents you see, the more space the scroller will take up in its scroll bar.

The Toolbar

The toolbar (**Figure 56**) offers navigation tools and view buttons within Finder windows:

◆ The **Back** button displays the previous window's contents.

◆ The **Forward** button displays the window that was showing before you clicked the Back button.

◆ **View buttons** enable you to change the window's view.

◆ **Quick Look** enables you to see the contents of a file without opening it.

◆ The **Action pop-up menu** (**Figure 57**) offers commands for working with an open window or selected object(s) within the window.

◆ The **Search field** enables you to quickly search for a file.

✔ Tips

■ The toolbar can be customized to show the items you use most; page 151 explains how.

■ Does the Action pop-up menu in **Figure 57** look familiar? It should! It's very similar to the contextual menu shown in **Figure 12**.

■ File management and navigation are covered in **Chapter 3**, window views are covered in **Chapter 4**, using the Search box is covered in **Chapter 5**, and Quick Look is covered in **Chapter 7**.

■ If the window is not wide enough to show all toolbar buttons, a double arrow appears on the right side of the toolbar (**Figure 58**). Click the arrow to display a menu of missing buttons (**Figure 59**), and select the button you want.

Back & Forward buttons   View buttons   Quick Look button   Action pop-up menu   Search field

Figure 56 The toolbar.

Figure 57 The Action pop-up menu offers commands for working with selected items in a window.

Figure 58 When the window is narrow, some toolbar items may be hidden.

Figure 59 Click the double arrow to display a menu of hidden items.

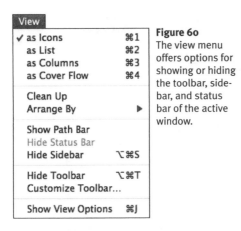

Figure 60
The view menu offers options for showing or hiding the toolbar, side-bar, and status bar of the active window.

Toolbar control button

Figure 61 The Toolbar control button can hide the toolbar...

Figure 62 ...or display it.

To hide or display the toolbar

Choose View > Hide Toolbar (**Figure 60**), View > Show Toolbar, or press Option ⌘ T.

Or

Click the toolbar control button (**Figure 61**).

One of two things happens:

◆ If the toolbar is displayed, it disappears (**Figure 61**).

◆ If the toolbar is not displayed, it appears (**Figure 62**).

✔ Tips

■ Options on the View menu (**Figure 60**) vary depending whether the toolbar is displayed or hidden.

■ As shown in **Figure 61**, hiding the toolbar also hides the sidebar (which is discussed on the next page). If the status bar is set to display in all windows, it moves right beneath the title bar. This makes the window smaller. I discuss the status bar on page 36.

To use a toolbar button

Click the button once.

To use the Action pop-up menu

1. If necessary, select the items you want to work with.

2. Click the Action pop-up menu to display a menu of commands (**Figure 57**).

3. Choose the command you want to use.

WORKING WITH THE TOOLBAR

The Sidebar

The sidebar appears on the left side of Finder windows (**Figure 63**). It offers quick access to the items you use most.

The sidebar has four sections:

◆ **Devices** displays icons for volumes that are accessible by your computer, such as your hard disk, iDisk, and CD and DVD discs.

◆ **Shared** lists volumes available over your local area network.

◆ **Places** displays the desktop, your Home folder, and several commonly accessed folders within your Home folder.

◆ **Search For** lists smart folders for popular searches, as well as searches you have created and saved to the sidebar.

✔ Tips

■ Although the sidebar normally appears whenever the toolbar is displayed, Mac OS X 10.6 adds the ability to hide it even if the toolbar is displayed (**Figure 64**).

■ You can customize the sidebar to add or remove items or change its width. I explain how on page 153.

■ I tell you about your Home folder on page 44 and about mounted volumes on page 99.

■ When a window is resized, the size of the sidebar may also change. If the sidebar is too short to display its contents, a vertical scroll bar appears within it (**Figure 62**).

Figure 63 The sidebar appears on the left side of a Finder window.

Figure 64 You can hide the sidebar while showing the toolbar.

THE SIDEBAR

Disclosure triangles

Figure 65
Clicking the disclosure triangles can show or hide items within a sidebar's category headings. In this example, the Devices and Shared items are hidden and the Places and Search For items are displayed.

To hide or display the sidebar

Choose View > Hide Sidebar (**Figure 60**), View > Show Sidebar, or press [Option] ⌃ ⌘ [S].

One of two things happens:

◆ If the sidebar is displayed, it disappears (**Figure 64**).

◆ If the sidebar is not displayed, it appears (**Figure 63**).

✔ Tips

■ Options on the View menu (**Figure 60**) vary depending whether the sidebar is displayed or hidden.

■ The toolbar must be displayed to show the sidebar. I explain how to hide or display the toolbar on page 33.

To use the sidebar

Click the icon for the item you want.

One of two things happens:

◆ If the item is a volume or folder, the window's contents change to display the contents of the item you clicked (**Figure 63**).

◆ If the item is an application or document, the item opens in its own window.

To show or hide sidebar items

Click the disclosure triangle to the left of a sidebar category heading (**Figure 65**):

◆ If the triangle points down, items in that category are displayed.

◆ If the triangle posts right, items in that category heading are hidden.

USING THE SIDEBAR

The Status Bar

The status bar is an area of a window with information about the window's contents. It can appear two different places:

◆ If the toolbar is displayed, the status bar appears at the bottom of the window (**Figure 66**).

◆ If the toolbar is hidden, the status bar appears just beneath the window's title bar (**Figure 61**).

What displays in the status bar depends on what is selected in the window:

◆ If nothing is selected, the status bar indicates how many items are in the window and how much disk space is available on that volume (**Figure 63**).

◆ If one or more items are selected, the status bar indicates how many items are selected and how much disk space is available on that volume (**Figure 66**).

◆ If the window is on a volume that cannot be written to, such as a CD, the status bar displays a write-protected icon (**Figure 67**).

◆ The status bar also includes a slider you can use to change the size of icons in the window (**Figure 66**). I tell you more about resizing window icons on page 74.

To hide or display the status bar

Choose View > Hide Status Bar or View > Show Status Bar.

One of two things happens:

◆ If the sidebar is displayed, it disappears (**Figure 68**).

◆ If the sidebar is not displayed, it appears (**Figures 63**, **66**, and **67**).

Icon size slider

Figure 66 The status bar indicates how many items in a window are selected.

Figure 67 The status bar displays a write-protected icon if the window's contents cannot be changed.

Figure 68
A window looks pretty barren without a toolbar, sidebar, or status bar.

✔ Tip

■ If the toolbar is displayed, the status bar cannot be hidden. The Hide Status Bar command on the View menu will appear in gray (**Figure 60**). I explain how to hide or display the toolbar on page 33.

THE STATUS BAR

The Dock

The Dock (**Figure 69**) offers easy access to often-used applications and documents, as well as minimized windows.

Figure 69 The Dock displays often-used applications, documents, folders, and the Trash.

Figure 70 Point to an icon to see what it represents.

Figure 71 An icon bounces as its application launches.

Figure 72 You can use a contextual menu on a Dock item, too.

✔ Tips

■ You can use a contextual menu for items on the Dock. Right-click on the Dock icon to display the menu (**Figure 72**) and choose the option you want.

■ Using applications and opening documents is discussed in **Chapter 10**; minimizing and displaying windows is discussed earlier in this chapter.

✔ Tip

■ The Dock can be customized; page 155 explains how.

To identify items in the Dock

Point to the item. The name of the item appears above the Dock (**Figure 70**).

To identify items in the Dock that are running

Look at the Dock. A tiny blue bubble appears beneath each item that is running, such as the Finder in **Figures 69**, **70**, and **71**.

To open an item in the Dock

Click the icon for the item you want to open. One of five things happens:

◆ If the icon is for an application that is running, the application becomes the active application.

◆ If the icon is for an application that is not running, it launches. Its icon in the Dock bounces (**Figure 71**) so you know something is happening.

◆ If the icon is for a minimized window (**Figure 52**), the window is displayed.

◆ If the icon is for an unopened document, the document opens in the application that created it.

◆ If the icon is for a folder, the folder's contents appear using the Stacks feature. I explain how to use Stacks on page 168.

THE DOCK

Sleeping, Restarting, & Shutting Down

The Apple menu (**Figure 73**) offers several options that change the work state of your computer:

◆ **Sleep** puts the computer into a state where it uses very little power. The screen goes blank and the hard disk may stop spinning.

◆ **Restart** instructs the computer to shut down and immediately start back up.

◆ **Shut Down** closes all open documents and programs, clears memory, and cuts power to the computer.

◆ **Log Out** *User Name* closes all open documents and programs and clears memory. Your computer remains running until you or someone else logs in.

I discuss all of these commands on the following pages.

Figure 73 The Apple menu includes four commands that let you change the work state of your computer.

✔ Tips

■ Holding down the Control key while pressing the keyboard's Media Eject key displays a dialog with buttons for the Restart, Sleep, and Shut Down commands (**Figure 74**).

■ Do not restart or shut down a computer by simply flicking off the power switch. Doing so prevents the computer from properly closing files, which may result in file corruption and related problems.

■ Mac OS X includes a screen saver, which automatically starts when your computer is inactive for a while. Don't confuse the screen saver with System or display sleep—it's different. You can customize screen saver settings with the Desktop & Screen Saver preferences pane, which is covered in on page 164.

Figure 74 This dialog appears when you hold down Control while pressing the Media Eject key.

SLEEPING, RESTARTING, & SHUTTING DOWN

To put your computer to sleep

Choose Apple > Sleep (**Figure 73**).

✔ Tips

- When you put your computer to sleep, everything in memory is preserved. When you wake the computer, you can quickly continue working where you left off.

- Sleep mode is an effective way to conserve the battery life of a laptop without turning it off.

- By default, Mac OS X automatically puts a computer to sleep when it is inactive for a while. You can change the time setting in the Energy Saver preferences pane, which I discuss on page 539.

To wake a sleeping computer

Press any keyboard key. You may have to wait several seconds for the computer to fully wake.

✔ Tips

- It's much quicker to wake a sleeping computer than to start a computer that has been shut down.

- On some computer models, pressing Caps Lock or certain other keys may not wake the computer. When in doubt, press a letter key—they always work.

PUTTING THE COMPUTER TO SLEEP

To restart your computer

1. Choose Apple > Restart (**Figure 73**).

2. In the dialog that appears (**Figure 75**), click Restart or press [Return] or [Enter].

   or

   Do nothing. Your computer will automatically restart in one minute.

✔ Tip

■ Restarting the computer clears memory and reloads all system files.

To shut down your computer

1. Choose Apple > Shut Down (**Figure 73**).

2. In the dialog that appears (**Figure 76**), click Shut Down or press [Return] or [Enter].

   or

   Do nothing. Your computer will automatically shut down in one minute.

Figure 75 This dialog appears when you choose the Restart command from the Apple menu.

Figure 76 This dialog appears when you choose the Shut Down command from the Apple menu.

Figure 77 A dialog like this one confirms that you really do want to log out.

Logging Out & In

If your computer is shared by multiple users, you may find it more convenient to log out when you're finished working. The Log Out command under the Apple menu (**Figure 73**) closes all applications and documents and closes your account on the computer. The computer remains running, making it quick and easy for the next person to log in and get right to work.

✔ Tips

■ If you are your computer's only user, you'll probably never use the Log Out command. (I hardly ever do.)

■ Mac OS X's fast user switching feature makes it quicker and easier to switch from one user account to another.

■ I tell you how to set up multiple user accounts on Mac OS X and use the fast user switching feature in **Chapter 21**.

To log out

1. Choose Apple > Log Out *User Name* (**Figure 73**), or press ⟨Shift⟩⌃ ⌘⟨Q⟩.

2. A confirmation dialog like the one in **Figure 77** appears. Click Log Out or press ⟨Return⟩ or ⟨Enter⟩.

   or

   Do nothing. Your computer will automatically log you out in one minute.

   Your computer closes all applications and documents, then displays the Login Screen.

To log in

1. If the Login Screen displays icons for user accounts, click the icon for your account.

2. Enter your password in the Password box that appears.

3. Click Log In.

Or

1. If the Login Screen displays only Name and Password boxes, enter your full or short account name in the Name box and your password in the Password box.

2. Click Log In.

Your Mac OS desktop appears, looking the same as it did when you logged out or shut down your computer.

✔ Tips

■ The appearance of the Login Screen varies depending on how the Accounts preference pane has been configured by the system administrator. (Unfortunately, Mac OS X does not allow me to take screen shots of these screens, so I can't show them to you.) Account login options are discussed on page 506.

■ Your user name and short name are created when you use the Mac OS Setup Assistant to configure Mac OS X, as discussed in **Chapter 1**. You can use either name to log in.

File Management

File Management

In Mac OS, you use the Finder to organize and manage your files. You can:

◆ Rename items.

◆ Create folders to store related items.

◆ Move items stored on disk to organize them so they're easy to find and back up.

◆ Copy items to other disks to back them up or share them with others.

◆ Delete items you no longer need.

✔ Tip

■ If you're brand new to Mac OS, be sure to read the information in **Chapter 2** before working with this chapter. That chapter contains information and instructions about techniques that are used throughout this chapter.

Mac OS X Disk Organization

Like most other computer operating systems, Mac OS X uses a hierarchical filing system (HFS) to organize and store files, including system files, applications, and documents.

The top level of the filing system is the computer level, which roughly corresponds to the Devices section of the Sidebar (**Figure 1**). This level shows the computer's internal hard disk, any other disks the computer is connected to (including iDisk, if you are a MobileMe member), the Network icon, and connected servers.

Figure 1 The top level of your computer shows all mounted disks and a Network icon.

The next level down is the computer's hard disk level. You can view this level by clicking the name of your hard disk in the Sidebar (**Figure 1**) or on the desktop. While the contents of your hard disk may differ from what's shown in **Figure 2**, some elements should be the same:

Figure 2 A typical hard disk window might look like this.

◆ Applications contains Mac OS X applications.

◆ System and Library contain the Mac OS X system files.

◆ Users (**Figure 3**) contains individual folders for each of the computer's users, as well as a Shared folder.

By default, a Mac OS X hard disk is organized for multiple users. Each user has his or her own "Home" folder, which is stored in the Users folder (**Figure 3**). You can view the items inside your Home folder by opening the house icon with your name on it on the sidebar or inside the Users folder (**Figure 3**). Your Home folder is preconfigured with folders for all kinds of items you may want to store on disk (**Figure 4**).

Figure 3 The Users folder contains a Home folder for each user, as well as a Shared folder.

Figure 4 Your Home folder is preconfigured with folders for storing a variety of item types.

✔ Tips

■ Unless you are an administrator, you cannot access the files in any other user's Home folder except those in the user's Public and Sites folders.

■ If you place an item in the Shared folder inside the Users folder (**Figure 3**), it can be opened by anyone who uses the computer.

■ I discuss applications in **Chapter 10**, sharing computers in **Chapter 21**, and networking in **Chapter 20**.

MAC OS X DISK ORGANIZATION

Pathnames

A *path*, or *pathname*, is a kind of address for a file on disk. It includes the name of the disk on which the file resides, the names of the folders the file is stored within, and the name of the file itself. For example, the pathname for a file named *SWCircle.pdf* in the Documents folder of the mlanger folder (**Figure 5**) would be: Macintosh HD/Users/mlanger/Documents/SWCircle.pdf.

When entering a pathname from a specific folder, you don't have to enter the entire pathname. Instead, enter the path as it relates to the current folder. For example, the path to the above-mentioned file from the mlanger folder would be: Documents/Letter.rtf.

To indicate a specific user folder, use the tilde (~) character followed by the name of the user account. So the path to the mlanger folder (**Figure 4**) would be: ~mlanger. (You can omit the user name if you want to open your own user folder.)

To indicate the top level of your computer, use a slash (/) character. So the path to MacBook Pro (**Figure 1**) would be: /.

When used as part of a longer pathname, the slash character indicates the *root level* of your hard disk. So /Applications/Utilities would indicate the Utilities folder inside the Applications folder on your hard disk.

Mac OS X offers two easy ways to learn the complete path to a specific file on your hard disk: the path bar (**Figure 5**), which can be displayed at the bottom of any Finder window, and a pop-up path menu on a window's title bar (**Figure 6**).

Figure 5 The path bar can be displayed at the bottom of any Finder window.

Figure 6 You can also display a pop-up menu that shows all of a window's enclosing folders and disks.

✔ Tip

■ Don't worry if all this sounds confusing to you. Fortunately, you don't really need to know it to use Mac OS X. It's just a good idea to be familiar with the concept of pathnames in case you run across it while working with your computer.

Figure 7
The View menu includes a command to show (or hide) the path bar.

Figure 8 You can display the path menu for a document within an application.

To show or hide the path bar

Choose View > Show Path Bar (**Figure 7**) or View > Hide Path Bar.

One of two things happens:

◆ If the path bar is not displayed, it appears (**Figure 5**). The path bar indicates the complete path from your computer to a selected file in the window.

◆ If the path bar is displayed, it disappears (**Figures 1, 2, 3**, and **4**).

✔ Tip

■ Options on the View menu (**Figure 7**) vary depending whether the path bar is displayed or hidden.

To display the path menu

Hold down the Control or ⌘ key and click the icon in a window's title bar. A pop-up menu like the one in **Figure 6** appears. It indicates the enclosing folders, disk, and computer for the window.

✔ Tips

■ This technique works in the Finder as well as within most Mac OS applications that enable you to work with documents. **Figure 8** shows an example in a PDF file window opened with the Preview application.

■ You can use the path menu to open an enclosing disk or folder. Simply select its name from the menu.

The Go Menu

The Go menu (**Figure 9**) offers a quick way to open specific locations on your computer:

Figure 9
The Go menu.

◆ **Back** (⌘ ⌘ [ )) displays the contents of the folder or disk you were looking in before you viewed the current folder or disk. This command is only active if the current window has displayed the contents of more than one folder or disk.

◆ **Forward** (⌘ ⌘])) displays the contents of the window you were viewing before you clicked the Back button. This command is only available if a window is active and if the Back button has been clicked.

◆ **Enclosing Folder** (⌘ ⌘ ↑)) opens the parent folder for the active window. This command is only available if a window is active and if the window was used to display the contents of a folder.

◆ **Computer** (Shift ⌘ ⌘ C)) opens the top level window for your computer (**Figure 1**).

Figure 10
The iDisk submenu on the Go menu.

◆ **Home** (Shift ⌘ ⌘ H)) opens your Home folder (**Figure 4**).

◆ **Desktop** (Shift ⌘ ⌘ D)) opens your Desktop folder.

◆ **Network** (Shift ⌘ ⌘ K)) opens the Network window.

◆ **iDisk** displays a submenu of options for accessing iDisk accounts and folders on Apple's MobileMe service via the Internet (**Figure 10**).

Figure 11
The Recent Folders submenu lists recently opened folders.

◆ **Applications** (Shift ⌘ ⌘ A)) opens the Applications folder.

◆ **Documents** (Option Shift ⌘ ⌘ D)) opens the Documents folder.

◆ **Utilities** (Shift ⌘ ⌘ U)) opens the Utilities folder inside the Applications folder.

Figure 12 Use the Go to Folder dialog to enter the pathname of the folder you want to open.

Figure 13 An error message appears in the Go to Folder window if you enter an invalid pathname.

Figure 14 If a window is active when you use the Go to Folder command, the dialog appears as a sheet attached to the window.

✔ Tips

■ If a window is open when you use the Go to Folder command, the Go to Folder dialog will appear as a *dialog sheet* attached to the window (**Figure 14**). The pathname you enter must be from that window's folder location on your hard disk.

◆ **Recent Folders** displays a submenu of recently opened folders (**Figure 11**).

◆ **Go to Folder** (Shift ⌃ ⌘ G) lets you open any folder your computer has access to.

◆ **Connect to Server** (⌃ ⌘ K) enables you to open a server accessible via a network.

✔ Tip

■ I discuss iDisk in **Chapter 19** and connecting to network servers in **Chapter 20**.

To open a Go menu item

Choose the item's name from the Go menu (**Figure 9**) or one of its submenus (**Figures 10** and **11**).

To go to a folder

1. Choose Go > Go to Folder (**Figure 9**), or press Shift ⌃ ⌘ G.

2. In the Go to Folder dialog that appears (**Figure 12**), enter the pathname for the folder you want to open.

3. Click Go.

   If you entered a valid pathname, the folder opens in a Finder window.

   or

   If you did not enter a valid pathname, an error message appears in the Go to Folder dialog (**Figure 13**). Repeat steps 2 and 3 to try again, or click Cancel to dismiss the dialog.

■ Mac OS X attempts to complete a path as you type it. Try it for yourself! Type part of a valid pathname and wait a moment. Mac OS X will complete the path with a valid pathname. (Whether it's the one you want is another story.)

Icon Names

Mac OS X is very flexible when it comes to names for files, folders, and disks.

◆ A file or folder name can be up to 255 characters long. A disk name can be up to 27 characters long.

◆ A name can contain any character except a colon (:).

This makes it easy to give your files, folders, and disks names that make sense to you.

✔ Tips

■ Normally, you name documents when you save them. Saving documents is covered on page 197.

■ A lengthy file name may appear truncated when displayed in windows and lists.

■ No two items in the same folder can have the same name.

■ Because slash characters (/) are used in pathnames, it's not a good idea to use them in names. In fact, some programs (such as Microsoft Word) won't allow you to include a slash in a file name.

■ Working with and naming disks is covered in **Chapter 6**.

To rename an icon

1. Click the icon to select it (**Figure 15**).

2. Point to the name of the icon, and click. After a brief pause, a box appears around the name and the name becomes selected (**Figure 16**).

3. Type the new name. The text you type automatically overwrites the selected text (**Figure 17**).

4. Press [Return] or [Enter], or click anywhere else. The icon is renamed (**Figure 18**).

Figure 15
Start by selecting the icon.

Figure 16
When you click, an edit box appears around the file name.

Figure 17
Type a new name for the icon.

Figure 18
When you press [Return], the name changes.

✔ Tips

■ Not all icons can be renamed. If the edit box does not appear around an icon name (as shown in **Figure 17**), that icon cannot be renamed.

■ You can also rename an icon in the Info window; I explain how on page 139.

Folders

Mac OS uses folders to organize files and other folders on disk. You can create a folder, give it a name that makes sense to you, and move files and other folders into it. It's a lot like organizing paper files and folders in a file cabinet.

Mac OS X supports three different kinds of folders:

◆ A standard **folder** is for manually storing files on disk. You create the folder, and then move or copy items into it. Throughout this book, I'll use the term *folder* to refer to this kind of folder.

◆ A **smart folder** works with Spotlight, Mac OS X's integrated searching feature, to automatically organize files and folders that meet specific search criteria. I explain how to work with Smart folders on page 89.

◆ A **burn folder** is for organizing items you want to save or "burn" onto a CD. I explain how to create and use burn folders on page 101.

✔ Tips

■ A folder can contain any number of files and other folders.

■ It's a good idea to use folders to organize the files on your hard disk. Imagine a file cabinet without file folders—that's how your hard disk would appear if you never used folders to keep your files tidy.

■ As discussed earlier in this chapter, your Home folder includes folders set up for organizing files by type. You'll find that these folders often appear as default file locations when saving specific types of files from within software programs. Saving files from within applications is covered on page 197.

To create a folder

1. Choose File > New Folder (**Figure 19**), or press [Shift][⌘][N]. A new untitled folder (**Figure 20**) appears in the active window.

2. While the edit box appears around the new folder's name (**Figure 20**), type a name for it (**Figure 21**) and press [Return].

✔ Tips

■ You can rename a folder the same way you rename any other icon. Renaming icons is discussed on page 50.

■ Working with windows is discussed in Chapter 4.

Figure 19
Choose New Folder from the File menu.

Figure 20
A new folder appears.

Figure 21
Enter a name for the folder while the edit box appears around it.

Moving & Copying Items

In addition to moving icons around within a window or on the desktop (as discussed on page 23), you can move or copy items to other locations on the same disk or to other disks by dragging them:

◆ When you drag an item to a location on the same disk, the item is moved to that location.

◆ When you drag an item to a location on another disk, the item is copied to that location.

◆ When you hold down Option while dragging an item to a location on the same disk, the item is copied to that location.

The next few pages provide instructions for all of these techniques, as well as instructions for duplicating items.

✔ Tips

■ You can move or copy more than one item at a time. Begin by selecting all of the items that you want to move or copy, and then drag any one of them to the destination. All items will be moved or copied.

■ You can continue working with the Finder or any other application—even start more copy jobs—while a copy job is in progress.

■ You can also copy Finder items using the Copy and Paste commands under the Finder's Edit menu. I explain how to use Copy and Paste on page 222.

MOVING & COPYING ITEMS

To move an item to another location on the same disk

1. Drag the icon for the item that you want to move as follows:

   ▲ To move the item into a specific folder on the disk, drag the icon onto the icon for the folder. The destination folder icon becomes selected when the pointer moves over it (**Figure 22**).

   ▲ To move the item into a specific window on the disk, drag the icon into the window. A border appears around the inside of the destination window (**Figure 23**).

2. Release the button. The item moves.

✔ Tip

■ If the destination location is on another disk, the item you drag will be copied rather than moved. To move (rather than copy) an item to another disk, hold down ⌘ while dragging it to the disk.

Figure 22 Drag the icon onto the icon for the folder you want to move to...

Figure 23 ...or drag the icon into the window you want to move it to.

Figure 24 Drag the icon to the destination disk's icon...

Figure 25 ...or to a folder icon in a window on the destination disk, ...

Figure 26 ...or to an open window on the destination disk.

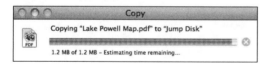

Figure 27 A window like this indicates copy progress.

Figure 28 If a file with the same name already exists in the destination, Mac OS tells you.

To copy an item to another disk

1. Drag the icon for the item that you want to copy as follows:

   ▲ To copy the item to the top (or *root*) level of a disk, drag the icon to the icon for the destination disk (**Figure 24**).

   ▲ To copy the item into a folder on the disk, drag the icon to the icon for the folder on the destination disk (**Figure 25**).

   ▲ To copy the item into a specific window on the disk, drag the icon into the window (**Figure 26**).

   When the item you are dragging moves on top of the destination location, a plus sign in a green circle appears beneath the pointer. If the destination is an icon, the icon becomes selected.

2. Release the button. A Copy window like the one in **Figure 27** appears. When it disappears, the copy is complete.

✔ Tips

- You cannot copy items to a disk that is write protected or to a folder for which you don't have write privileges. When you try, the green plus sign changes to a circle with a line through it. I tell you about write-protected disks later in this chapter.

- If a file with the same file name already exists in the destination location, an error message appears in the Copy window (**Figure 28**). Click Stop to dismiss the window without making the copy, or click Replace to replace the existing file with the one you are copying.

- Because copying small files happens so quickly in Mac OS X, you probably won't see the Copy window (**Figure 27**) very often. It doesn't have time to appear!

COPYING ITEMS TO OTHER DISKS

To copy an item to another location on the same disk

1. Hold down Option while dragging the icon for the item that you want to copy onto a folder icon (**Figure 29**) or into a window (**Figure 30**).

   When the pointer on the item you are dragging moves on top of the destination location, a plus sign in a green circle appears beneath it. If the destination is an icon, the icon becomes highlighted.

2. Release the button. A Copy window like the one in **Figure 27** appears. When it disappears, the copy is complete.

✔ Tips

- When copying an item to a new location on the same disk, you must hold down Option. If you don't, the item will be moved rather than copied.

- If a file with the same file name already exists in the destination location, an error message appears in the Copy window (**Figure 28**). Click Stop to dismiss the window without making the copy, or click Replace to replace the existing file with the one you are copying.

To duplicate an item

1. Select the item that you want to duplicate.

2. Choose File > Duplicate (**Figure 31**), or press ⌘ D.

Or

Hold down Option while dragging the item that you want to duplicate to a different location in the same window.

A copy of the item you duplicated appears in the same location as the original. The word *copy* is appended to the file name (**Figure 32**).

Figure 29 Hold down Option while dragging the item onto a folder...

Figure 30 ...or into a window on the same disk.

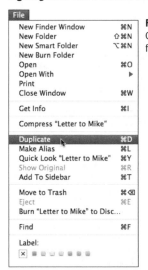

Figure 31 Choose Duplicate from the File menu.

Figure 32 A duplicate appears with the original.

Figure 33 To move an item to the Trash, drag it there...

Figure 34
...or select the item and choose Move to Trash from the File menu.

Figure 35
When an item has been moved to the Trash, the Trash icon looks full.

The Trash & Deleting Items

The Trash is a special place on your hard disk where you place items you want to delete. Items in the Trash remain there until you empty the Trash, which removes them from your disk. The Trash appears as an icon in the Dock.

To move an item to the Trash

1. Drag the icon for the item you want to delete to the Trash icon in the Dock.

2. When the pointer moves over the Trash icon, the Trash icon becomes selected (**Figure 33**). Release the button.

Or

1. Select the item that you want to delete.

2. Choose File > Move to Trash (**Figure 34**), or press ⌘ ⌫ .

✔ Tips

- The Trash icon's appearance indicates its status:
  - ▲ If the Trash is empty, the Trash icon looks like an empty wire basket.
  - ▲ If the Trash is not empty, the Trash icon looks like a wire basket with crumpled papers in it (**Figure 35**).

- You can delete more than one item at a time. Begin by selecting all the items you want to delete, and then drag any one of them to the Trash. All items will be moved to the Trash.

- Moving a disk icon to the Trash does not delete or erase it. Instead, it *unmounts* it. Working with disks is covered in **Chapter 6**.

- You cannot drag an item to the Trash if the item is locked. I tell you about locking and unlocking items on page 141.

To move an item out of the Trash

1. Click the Trash icon in the Dock to open the Trash window (**Figure 36**).

2. Drag the item from the Trash window to the Desktop or to another window on your hard disk.

   The item is moved from the Trash to the window you dragged it to.

Or

1. Click the Trash icon in the Dock to open the Trash window (**Figure 36**).

2. Select the item you want to remove from the Trash.

3. Choose File > Put Back (**Figure 37**), or press ⌃⌘Del.

   The item is moved back to where it was before you moved it to the Trash.

Or

Choose Edit > Undo Move of "*Item Name*" (**Figure 38**), or press ⌃⌘Z. The item is moved back to where it was before you moved it to the Trash.

✔ Tip

■ The Undo command (**Figure 38**) will only take an item out of the Trash if the last thing you did was put it in the Trash.

Figure 36 Opening the Trash displays the Trash window and its contents.

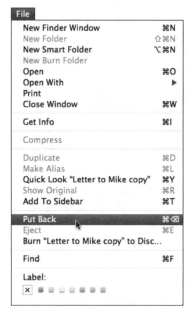

Figure 37 You can use the Put Back command to take selected items out of the Trash and put them back where they was before you trashed them.

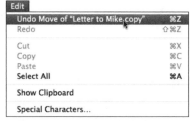

Figure 38 If the last thing you did was to put an item in the Trash, you can use the Undo command to take it back out.

MOVING ITEMS FROM & EMPTYING THE TRASH

Figure 39
The Finder menu includes two commands for emptying the Trash.

Figure 40 The Trash warning dialog asks you to confirm that you really do want to delete the items in the Trash.

Figure 41
If you point to the Trash and hold the mouse button down, a menu appears with an Empty Trash command on it.

To empty the Trash

1. Choose Finder > Empty Trash (**Figure 39**), or press Shift ⌘ Delete.

2. A Trash warning dialog like the one in **Figure 40** appears. Click Empty Trash to delete all items that are in the Trash.

Or

1. Click the Trash icon in the Dock to open the Trash window (**Figure 36**).

2. Click the Empty button.

3. A Trash warning dialog like the one in **Figure 40** appears. Click Empty Trash to delete all items that are in the Trash.

Or

1. Point to the Trash icon, press the button, and hold it down until a menu appears (**Figure 41**).

2. Choose Empty Trash.

3. A Trash warning dialog like the one in **Figure 40** appears. Click Empty Trash to delete all items that are in the Trash.

✔ Tips

- If you hold down the Option key while choosing the Empty Trash command (**Figure 39**) or press Option Shift ⌘ Delete, the Trash is emptied without displaying the warning dialog (**Figure 40**).

- You can disable the Trash warning dialog (**Figure 40**) in the Finder Preferences window. I explain how on page 146.

To permanently remove items in the Trash from your disk

1. Choose Finder > Secure Empty Trash (**Figure 39**).

2. A Trash warning dialog like the one in **Figure 42** appears. Click Secure Empty Trash to permanently remove all items that are in the Trash.

✔ Tips

■ The Secure Empty Trash command makes it impossible to use special data recovery software to unerase deleted files.

■ You may want to use the Secure Empty Trash command to erase personal files on a shared computer or a computer you plan to give away or sell.

■ Deleting files from disk with the Secure Empty Trash command may take longer than using the Empty Trash command, especially when deleting large files.

■ If you hold down the Option key while choosing the Secure Empty Trash command (**Figure 39**), the Trash is securely emptied without displaying the warning dialog (**Figure 42**).

■ You can disable the Trash warning dialog (**Figure 40**) in the Finder Preferences window. I explain how on page 146.

Figure 42 Using the Secure Empty Trash command displays a warning dialog like this.

Window
Views

Figure 1 Here's a window in icon view, ...

Figure 2 ...list view, ...

Figure 3 ...column view, ...

Figure 4 ...and Cover Flow.

Window Views

A Finder window's contents can be displayed using four different views:

◆ **Icons** displays the window's contents as small or large icons (**Figure 1**).

◆ **List** displays the window's contents as a sorted list (**Figure 2**).

◆ **Columns** displays the window's contents with a multiple-column format that shows the currently selected disk or folder and the items within it (**Figure 3**).

◆ **Cover Flow** (**Figure 4**) displays a folder's contents as preview images.

You can switch from one view to another with the click of a button, making it easy to use any view you like for any window you're viewing.

In this chapter, I tell you more about how to work with Mac OS X's window views, as well as how to customize each view.

To set a window's view

1. If necessary, activate the window for which you want to change the view.

2. Choose the view option you want from the View menu (**Figure 5**), or press the corresponding shortcut key.

   or

   Click the toolbar's view button for the view you want (**Figure 6**).

   The view of the window changes.

✔ Tips

- Commands on the View menu (**Figure 5**) work on the active window only.

- A check mark appears on the View menu beside the name of the view applied to the active window (**Figure 5**).

- If the toolbar is not showing for a window, click the Show/Hide toolbar button in the upper-right corner of the window, choose View > Show Toolbar, or press Option ⌃ ⌘ T.

- If the view buttons do not appear on the toolbar, hold down ⌃ ⌘ and click the Show/Hide toolbar button repeatedly until they do appear.

- You can set the view for each window individually.

Figure 5 The Finder's View menu.

Figure 6 Use the View buttons in the toolbar to switch from one view to another.

Figure 7 Start with a Messy window like this one...

Figure 8 ...and use the Clean Up command to put the icons in place.

Figure 9 The Arrange By submenu offers several options for neatly arranging icons.

Working with Icon View

Icon view (**Figure 1**) displays a window's contents as icons. Unlike some other views, a window in icon view displays the contents of only one disk or folder at a time.

As discussed on page 23, icons can be moved around in a window to reposition them. An invisible grid makes it easy to keep icons neat within the window. You can also use commands under the View menu (**Figure 5**) to neatly arrange icons.

I tell you more about working with icon view on the following pages.

✔ Tip

■ **Chapter 2** explains the basics of working with icons in the Finder.

To neatly arrange icons

1. Activate the window that you want to clean up (**Figure 7**).

2. Choose View > Clean Up (**Figure 5**). The icons are arranged in the window's invisible grid (**Figure 8**).

   or

   Choose one of the commands from the Arrange By submenu under the View menu (**Figure 9**) or press its corresponding shortcut key:

   ▲ **Name** (Ctrl ⌃ ⌘ 1) arranges the icons alphabetically by name (**Figure 10**).

   ▲ **Date Modified** (Ctrl ⌃ ⌘ 2) arranges the icons chronologically by the date they were last modified, with the most recently modified item last.

Continued on next page...

Continued from previous page.

▲ **Date Created** (Ctrl ⌘ 3) arranges the icons by the date they were created, with the most recently created item last.

▲ **Size** (Ctrl ⌘ 4) arranges the icons in size order, with the largest item last. (Folders have a size of 0 for this option.)

▲ **Kind** (Ctrl ⌘ 5) arranges the icons alphabetically by the kind of file.

▲ **Label** (Ctrl ⌘ 6) arranges the icons by color-coded label (if applied).

The icons are arranged in the window's invisible grid in the order you specified (**Figure 10**).

✔ Tips

■ A window's invisible grid ensures consistent spacing between icons.

■ You can manually position an icon in the window's invisible grid by holding down ⌘ while dragging it within the window.

■ Holding down the Option key changes the Clean Up command to the Clean Up Selection command (**Figure 11**). You can use this command to arrange just the selected icons in a window.

■ Holding down the Option key changes the Arrange By submenu to the Keep Arranged By submenu (**Figure 11**). Choosing one of the commands forces the window's icons to stay arranged by the criteria you choose, making it impossible for that window to get messy.

■ I tell you how to apply and customize labels on page 130.

Figure 10 Here's the messy window from **Figure 8** after arranging by name.

Figure 11
Holding down the Option key changes the Arrange By submenu to a Keep Arranged By submenu.

Figure 12 Click a column heading to sort by that column.

Figure 13 Click the same column heading to reverse that column's sort order.

Working with List View

List view (**Figure 2**) displays a window's contents in an ordered list. Items cannot be moved around so there's no need for a Clean Up command or Arrange By options.

Windows displayed in list view also have a feature not found in other views: They can display the contents of folders within the window as an outline. This makes it possible to see and select the contents of more than one folder at a time.

To sort a window's contents

Click the column heading for the column you want to sort by. The list is sorted by that column (**Figure 12**).

✔ Tips

- You can identify the column by which a list is sorted by its colored column heading (**Figures 2, 12,** and **13**).

- You can reverse a window's sort order by clicking the sort column's heading a second time (**Figure 13**).

- You can determine the sort direction by looking at the arrow in the sort column. When it points up, the items are sorted in ascending order (**Figure 13**); when it points down, the items are sorted in descending order (**Figure 12**).

- To properly sort by size, you must turn on the Calculate all Sizes option for the window. I explain how on page 76.

- You can specify which columns should appear in a window by setting view options. I explain how to do that later in this chapter, too.

To display or hide a folder's contents in outline list view

◆ To display a folder's contents, use one of the following techniques:

▲ Click the right-pointing triangle beside the folder (**Figure 14**).

▲ Click the folder once to select it, and press ⌥ ⌘ →.

The items within that folder are listed below it, slightly indented (**Figure 15**).

◆ To hide a folder's contents, use one of the following techniques:

▲ Click the down-pointing triangle beside the folder (**Figure 16**).

▲ Click the folder once to select it, and press ⌥ ⌘ ←.

The outline collapses to hide the items in the folder (**Figure 14**).

✔ Tip

■ As shown in **Figure 16**, you can use this technique to display multiple levels of folders in the same window.

Figure 14 Right-pointing triangles indicate collapsed outlines.

Click a right-pointing triangle to expand the outline.

Figure 15 Folder contents can be displayed as an outline...

Figure 16 ...that can show several levels.

Figure 17 Position the pointer in front of the first icon you want to select.

Figure 18 Drag over the other icons you want to select.

Figure 19 Select the first icon.

Figure 20 Hold down (Shift) and click the last icon.

Figure 21 Click to select the first icon.

Figure 22 Hold down (⌘ ⌘) and click another icon.

To select multiple contiguous icons in list view

1. Position the pointer in front of the first icon you want to select (**Figure 17**).

2. Hold the button down and drag over the other icons you want to select (**Figure 18**).

Or

1. Click to select the first icon you want to select (**Figure 19**).

2. Hold down (Shift) and click the last icon in the group you want to select (**Figure 20**).

To select multiple noncontiguous icons in list view

1. Click to select the first icon you want to select (**Figure 21**).

2. Hold down (⌘ ⌘) and click the next icon you want to select (**Figure 22**).

3. Repeat step 2 until all icons have been selected (**Figure 23**).

To deselect icons

Click anywhere in the window other than on an icon's line of information.

Figure 23 Continue holding down (⌘ ⌘) and clicking icons until you've finished selecting the icons you want.

To change a column's width

1. Position the pointer on the line between the heading for the column whose width you want to change and the column to its right.

2. Press the button down. The pointer turns into a vertical bar with two arrows (**Figure 24**).

3. Drag as follows:
   ▲ To make the column narrower, drag to the left (**Figure 25**).
   ▲ To make the column wider, drag to the right.

4. When the column is displayed at the desired width, release the button.

✔ Tip

■ If you make a column too narrow to display all of its contents, information may be truncated or condensed.

To change a column's position

1. Position the pointer on the heading for the column you want to move.

2. Press the button down and drag:
   ▲ To move the column to the left, drag to the left (**Figure 26**).
   ▲ To move the column to the right, drag to the right.

   As you drag, the other columns shift to make room for the column you're dragging.

3. When the column is in the desired position, release the button. The column changes its position (**Figure 27**).

✔ Tip

■ You cannot change the position of the Name column.

Figure 24 Position the pointer on the column border.

Figure 25 When you press the button down and drag, the column's width changes.

Figure 26 Drag a column heading...

Figure 27 ...to change the column's position.

Figure 28 Selecting a folder in column view displays the contents of that folder in the column to the right.

Figure 29 Selecting a document in column view can display a preview and additional information for the document in the column to the right. As shown here, pointing to a preview icon may display arrows you can click to scroll through preview pages of the document.

Figure 30 You can scroll forward or backward through the file hierarchy by using the horizontal scroll bar.

Working with Column View

Column view (**Figure 3**) displays the contents of a window in multiple columns. Clicking a folder in one column displays the contents of that folder in the column to its right. Clicking a document or application in a column displays a preview or information about the item in the column to its right.

To display a folder's contents

Click the name of the folder you want to view the contents of.

The contents of the folder appear in the column to the right of the one you clicked in (**Figure 28**).

To display a document preview

Click the icon for the document you want to preview.

If a preview for the document is available, it appears in the column to the right of the one you clicked in, along with additional information about the file (**Figure 29**).

Or

If a preview is not available, the icon for the item appears in the column to the right of the one you clicked.

To move through the folder hierarchy

To scroll through the folder hierarchy, use the horizontal scroll bar at the bottom of the window (**Figure 30**):

◆ Click the left scroll button to scroll backward and view parent folders.

◆ Click the right scroll button to scroll forward and view child folders.

To change column width

1. Position the pointer on the bottom of the divider between two columns (**Figure 31**).

2. Drag as follows:

   ▲ Drag to the right to make the column wider (**Figure 32**).

   ▲ Drag to the left to make the column narrower.

Figure 31 To resize a column, start by positioning your pointer on the divider...

To view more columns

Drag the resize handle in the bottom-right corner of the window to the right to make the window wider. The wider a window is, the more columns are displayed (**Figure 33**).

✔ Tips

■ I tell you more about resizing windows on page 29.

■ You can further increase the number of columns displayed by making each column narrower as discussed above.

Figure 32 Then drag to make the column wider or narrower, as shown here.

Figure 33 You can view more columns by making the window larger.

Click a preview or icon

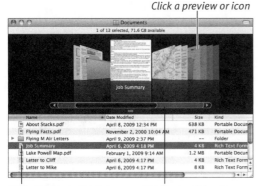

Click an item in the list
pane to view its preview.

Use the scroll bar to
scroll through previews.

Figure 34 Cover Flow displays both previews and a list of items in a folder.

Figure 35 When you position the pointer on the resize handle, it turns into a hand.

Figure 36 You can drag the handle up to reduce the size of the Cover Flow pane.

Working with Cover Flow

Cover Flow (**Figure 4**) displays each item in a folder as a preview of its first page. You can use this feature to scroll through files and find one you're looking for, even if you don't know its name.

To flip through documents in Cover Flow

Use one of the following techniques in a Cover Flow view window (**Figure 34**):

◆ Click the left or right scroll button in the scroll bar at the bottom of the Cover Flow pane.

◆ Drag the scroller in the scroll bar at the bottom of the cover flow pane.

◆ Click the icon or preview for an item in the Cover Flow pane.

◆ Press the ⬆ or ⬇ key for the previous or next item.

To change the size of the Cover Flow pane

1. Position the pointer on the resize box beneath the scroll bar in the Cover Flow pane. The pointer turns into a hand (**Figure 35**).

2. Drag as follows:
   ▲ Drag up to make the Cover Flow pane smaller (**Figure 36**).
   ▲ Drag down to make the Cover Flow pane larger.

✔ Tip

■ The smaller the Cover Flow pane is, the smaller the previews within it are.

Customizing Window & Desktop Views

You can customize views a number of ways:

◆ Change the settings for the default view for icon, list, column, and Cover Flow views.

◆ Change the settings for an individual window's view.

◆ Change the view for the desktop.

The view options window offers a number of options for the active window:

◆ Icon view settings (**Figure 37**) include icon size, grid spacing, label text size and position, display options, arrangement, and background.

◆ List view settings include icon size, text size, columns, date format, and item size calculation.

◆ Column view settings include text size, icon appearance, and preview column.

◆ Cover Flow view options include icon size, text size, columns, date format, and item size calculation.

◆ Desktop view settings include icon size, label text size and position, display options, and arrangement.

You can also display the status bar with disk information and the path bar with information about a file's location on disk in any Finder window.

✔ Tip

■ Mac OS X remembers a window's view settings and uses them whenever you display the window.

Figure 37
Default view options for icon view.

To open view options

1. Open the window you want to set view options for.

2. If necessary, switch to the view you want to customize.

3. Choose View > Show view options (**Figure 5**), or press ⌃ ⌘ J.

   The view options window for that view appears (**Figures 37, 47, 48, 51,** and **53**).

✔ Tips

- You can also open the view options window for the desktop. Just make sure no window is active before choosing the command.

- The options in the view options window will change if you make a different window active. The view options window always displays options and settings for the currently active window.

To set icon view options

1. Open the view options window (**Figure 37**) for the icon view window you want to customize (**Figure 38**).

2. To set the window so it always opens in icon view, turn on the Always open in icon view check box.

3. To change the size of icons in the window (**Figures 38** and **39**), drag the Icon size slider to the left or right.

4. To change the amount of horizontal space between each icon, drag the Grid spacing slider to the left or right (**Figures 38** and **39**).

5. Choose a type size from the Text size pop-up menu. Your options range from 10 to 16 points. The font size for item names changes accordingly (**Figure 39**).

6. Select a Label position option button to specify where icon labels should appear: Bottom (**Figure 39**) or Right (**Figure 40**).

7. Toggle check boxes to specify how icons should appear:

   ▲ **Show item info** displays information about the item beneath its name (**Figure 40**).

   ▲ **Show icon preview** displays a document's preview, if available, in place of its standard icon.

8. Choose an option from the Arrange by pop-up menu (**Figure 41**). **None** does not arrange the icons at all. **Snap to Grid** forces icons to snap to the window's invisible grid, thus ensuring consistent spacing between icons. The remaining options keep icons automatically arranged in the order you choose.

Icon size slider

Figure 38 Here's a typical icon view window with default options applied.

Figure 39 In this example, I've reduced the icon size and grid spacing and increased the font size.

Figure 40 In this example, labels are on the right and item info is displayed.

Figure 41 Use this menu to set automatic arrangement options.

SETTING ICON VIEW OPTIONS

Figures 42 & 43
When you choose Color in the Background area (above) you can use a standard Colors dialog to choose a color for a window's background.

Figure 44
When you choose Picture in the Background area...

Figure 45 ...you can use the Select a Picture dialog...

Figure 46 ...to set a background picture for a window.

9. Select a Background option:
   - ▲ **White** makes the background white.
   - ▲ **Color** enables you to select a background color for the window. If you select this option, click the color well that appears beside it (**Figure 43**), use the Colors panel (**Figure 44**) to select a color, and click OK.
   - ▲ **Picture** enables you to set a background picture for the window. If you select this option, click the Select button that appears beside it (**Figure 45**), use the Select a Picture dialog to locate and select a background picture (**Figure 46**), and click Select.

10. To make the settings the default settings for all icon view windows, click the Use as Defaults button at the bottom of the view options window (**Figure 38**).

11. When you're finished setting options, click the view option window's close button to dismiss it.

    A background picture fills the window's background behind the icons (**Figure 47**).

✔ Tips

- ■ Another way to resize the icons in a window is to drag the Icon size slider left or right (**Figure 38**).

- ■ I explain how to select a color with the Colors panel on page 161.

- ■ Working with dialogs is discussed on page 205.

SETTING ICON VIEW OPTIONS

To set list view or Cover Flow options

1. Open the view options window (**Figure 47**) for the list view window you want to customize (**Figure 49**).

   or

   Open the view options window (**Figure 48**) for the Cover Flow window you want to customize.

2. To set the window so it always opens in list view, turn on the Always open in list view check box.

   or

   To set the window so it always opens in Cover Flow, turn on the Always open in Cover Flow check box.

3. Select an Icon size option by clicking the radio button beneath the size you want. **Figure 49** shows an example with the large icon size.

4. Choose a type size from the Text size pop-up menu. Your options range from 10 to 16 points. **Figure 50** shows an example with 16-point type.

5. Select the columns you want to appear in list view by turning Show columns check boxes on or off:

   ▲ **Date Modified** is the date and time an item was last changed.

   ▲ **Date Created** is the date and time an item was first created.

   ▲ **Last Opened** is the date and time an item was last opened.

   ▲ **Size** is the amount of disk space the item occupies.

   ▲ **Kind** is the type of item. I tell you about types of items on page 20.

   ▲ **Version** is the item's version number.

Figure 47
Here are the default view options settings for a list view window...

Figure 48
...and here are the default view options settings for a Cover View window.

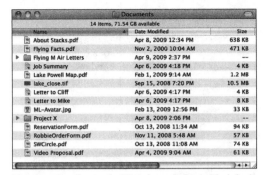

Figure 49 Here's a typical list view window with default settings applied.

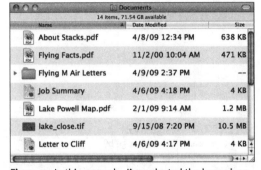

Figure 50 In this example, I've selected the larger icon and font size, enabled size calculation, and am displaying the modification date instead of the creation date. (And no, my eyes aren't that bad. Yet.)

▲ **Comments** is the information you entered in the Spotlight Comments field of the Info window. I tell you about the Info window on page 139.

▲ **Label** is the label assigned to the item.

6. Toggle check boxes to set other options:

   ▲ **Use relative dates** displays the date in relative terms (that is, using the words *today* and *yesterday*).

   ▲ **Calculate all sizes** displays the disk space occupied by items and the contents of folders in the list.

   ▲ **Show icon preview** shows a document preview for the icon if a preview is available.

7. To make the settings the default settings for all list view windows, click the Use as Defaults button at the bottom of the view options window (**Figure 47**).

   or

   To make the settings the default settings for all Cover Flow windows, click the Use as Defaults button at the bottom of the view options window (**Figure 48**).

8. When you're finished setting options, click the view option window's close button to dismiss it.

✔ Tip

■ Turning on the Calculate all sizes check box (**Figures 47** and **48**) in step 6 makes it possible to sort all of a list's contents by size, including folders. Sorting window contents is covered on page 65.

To set column view options

1. Open the view options window (**Figure 51**) for the column view window you want to customize.

2. To set the window so it always opens in column view, turn on the Always open in column view check box.

3. Choose a type size from the Text size pop-up menu. Your options range from 10 to 16 points.

4. Toggle check boxes to set other options:

   ▲ **Show icons** displays icons with item names.

   ▲ **Show icon preview** displays an item's preview as its icon.

   ▲ **Show preview column** displays an item preview in the rightmost column when the item is selected.

5. Choose an option from the Arrange by pop-up menu (**Figure 52**) to specify the sort order for each column.

6. When you're finished setting options, click the view option window's close button to dismiss it.

Figure 51
The default view options settings for a column view window.

Figure 52
The Arrange by pop-up menu.

Figure 53
The view options window for the desktop.

To set desktop view options

1. Click anywhere on the desktop to activate it.

2. Display the view options window (**Figure 53**).

3. To change the size of icons on the desktop, drag the Icon size slider.

4. To change the amount of horizontal space between each icon, drag the Grid spacing slider to the left or right.

5. Choose a type size from the Text size pop-up menu. Your options range from 10 to 16 points.

6. Select a Label position option button to specify where icon labels should appear: Bottom or Right.

7. Toggle check boxes to specify how icons should appear:

    ▲ **Show item info** displays information about the item beneath its name.

    ▲ **Show icon preview** displays a document's preview, if available, in place of its standard icon.

8. Choose an option from the Arrange by pop-up menu (**Figure 41**). **None** does not arrange the icons at all. **Snap to grid** forces icons to snap to the window's invisible grid, thus ensuring consistent spacing between icons. The remaining options keep icons automatically arranged in the order you choose.

✔ Tips

■ As you can see, these options are nearly identical to those for an icon view window (**Figure 37**).

■ You can set the desktop color or picture in the Desktop & Screen Saver preferences pane, which I cover on page 162.

Searching for Files

Searching for Files

Mac OS X offers a number of search features you can use to find files or folders:

◆ Predefined searches listed in the sidebar make it quick and easy to conduct a search.

◆ Spotlight enables you to perform a search quickly, no matter what application is active. Search results appear in a Spotlight menu or in a search results window.

◆ A Finder window's Search field enables you to initiate a search based on file name or content from a Finder window. Search results appear within the window, sorted by file type.

◆ The Finder's Find command takes Finder searching a step further by offering additional search options, including the ability to find files based on kind, dates, labels, and size.

◆ Smart folders make it possible to save your search queries. Repeating a query is as easy as opening a smart folder icon.

Once you have a list of found files, opening a file is as easy as double-clicking it.

This chapter takes a closer look at the search features in Mac OS X.

Predefined Sidebar Searches

The Finder sidebar includes a Search For section that lists a number of predefined searches. Selecting one of these searches in a Finder window's sidebar displays the results of the search within the window (**Figures 1** and 2).

✔ Tip

- As I explain on page 89, when you save a Spotlight search as a smart folder, you have the option of adding it to the sidebar with other predefined searches.

To use a sidebar search

1. Open a Finder window.

2. If necessary, display the toolbar and sidebar.

3. If necessary, click the disclosure triangle beside the Search For section heading in the sidebar.

4. Click the name of the search you want to conduct. Search results appear in that window (**Figures 1** and 2).

✔ Tip

- I discuss displaying and hiding the toolbar and sidebar in **Chapter 2**.

Figure 1 Clicking the Past Week search displays all the items that have been modified in the past week.

Figure 2 The All Movies search displays all movie files.

Figure 3 Clicking the Spotlight icon in the menu bar displays Spotlight's search field.

Figure 4 As you enter a word or phrase in the search field, Spotlight displays results in a menu.

Figure 5 Choosing Show All from a Spotlight's menu of found items displays the items in a search results window.

Searching with the Spotlight Menu

The Spotlight menu makes Finder searching available in the menu bar, no matter which application is active.

✔ Tips

- The types of items found and the order in which they appear in search results depends on settings in the Spotlight preferences pane. I tell you more about setting Spotlight preferences on page 94.

- Spotlight also works within certain Mac OS X applications, such as System Preferences, as well as in standard Open and Save Location dialogs. System Preferences is covered in **Chapter 23** and the Open and Save Location dialogs are covered in **Chapter 10**.

To find items with Spotlight

1. Click the Spotlight icon on the far right end of the menu bar.

   or

   Press ⎵ ⌘ Spacebar.

   The Spotlight search field appears in a menu (**Figure 3**).

2. Enter a search word or phrase in the search field. Spotlight immediately begins displaying matches for what you enter in a menu beneath the search field (**Figure 4**).

To display all found items

Choose Show All from the Spotlight menu of search results (**Figure 4**).

A Searching window full of search results appears (**Figure 5**).

To open a found item

Click the item in the Spotlight menu of search results (**Figure 4**).

Or

In the Searching window of found items (**Figure 5**), double-click the item you want to open.

To perform a new search

Follow the instructions in the section titled "To find items with Spotlight" on the previous page. You may have to overwrite an existing search word or phrase with the new one.

Or

In the list of found items, enter a new search word or phrase in the search box at the top-right corner of the window.

✔ Tip

■ To quickly clear the contents of the search box, click the X button on the right side of the search box.

Search field

Figure 6 The Search field appears in the toolbar of a Finder window.

Figure 7 As you enter a search word, Mac OS X immediately begins displaying search results.

Figure 8 When you finish typing the word, the final search results appear. In this example, I searched for the word *white* and found six documents that contain that word.

The Search Field

The Finder's Search field appears in the top-right corner of a Finder window's toolbar (**Figure 6**). You can use it to initiate a search based on item name or contents. Simply enter a word or phrase in the field, and Mac OS X displays a list of matches in the same window.

✔ Tip

- A window's toolbar must be displayed to use the Search field. I explain how to display or hide the toolbar in **Chapter 2**.

To find files with the Search field

1. Click in the Search field of a Finder window to position the blinking insertion point there (**Figure 6**).

2. Enter the word or phrase you want to search for.

   As soon as you begin typing, the window turns into a Searching window. Mac OS begins displaying results (**Figure 7**). When you finished typing, the search results for what you typed appear (**Figure 8**).

✔ Tips

- You can specify a search location by clicking one of the location buttons above the search results in the Searching window (**Figure 8**). I tell you more about search locations on the next page.

- Remember, the search feature searches by name or contents. If you're not sure of a file's name, search for some text you expect to find in the document. **Figure 8** shows an example.

The Find Command

Mac OS X's Find command also works with the Search field, but it automatically offers additional search options (**Figure 9**):

◆ **Search** options appear as buttons near the top of the window. Click a button to set one of two kinds of options:

▲ **Disk Location buttons** enable you to choose the location to search. **This Mac**, which always appears, searches your entire computer, as well as any shared volumes you are currently connected to. "*Location name*" is either your home folder or the folder that was selected or active when you chose the Find command.

▲ **Search Location buttons** enable you to indicate whether you want to search for the search word or phrase in file **Contents** or just the **File Name**.

◆ **Criteria filters** appear in rows above the search results area. You can set options with these filters to narrow down the search results. Use an Attributes pop-up menu (**Figure 10**) to choose a search attribute and set up a filter:

▲ **Kind** is the type of items to search. Choose an option from the pop-up menu (**Figure 11**).

▲ **Last opened date** is the date the item was last opened. You can use a pop-up menu (**Figure 12**) to set criteria options and set a date or date range.

▲ **Last modified date** is the date the item was last changed. The options are the same as Last opened date.

▲ **Created date** is the date the item was created. The options are the same as Last opened date.

Criteria filters   *Search options*

Figure 9 Choosing the Find command displays a new Searching window with additional options.

Figure 10 You can use the attributes pop-up menu to choose types of criteria to set.

Figure 11
When you choose the Kind attribute, you can select from various types of items.

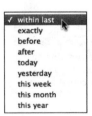

Figure 12
Use this pop-up menu to set the various date-related search criteria.

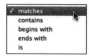

Figure 13
Use this pop-up menu to specify how a file name should match the criteria you enter.

Figure 14 This dialog enables you to customize the Attributes pop-up menu shown in **Figure 10**.

▲ **Name** is the item's name. This tells Spotlight not to search the contents of an item to match text. If you choose this option, you can use a pop-up menu (**Figure 13**) and enter text to set criteria.

▲ **Contents** is the contents of the item. This tells Spotlight not to search the name of the item to match text. You can enter the search criteria in a text box.

▲ **Other** displays a dialog (**Figure 14**) that you can use to add additional search attributes to the pop-up menu (**Figure 10**). This makes it possible to search by virtually any kind of information associated with a Finder item. Turn on the check box beside each attribute you want to add.

✔ Tips

■ You can display criteria filters when using the Search field as discussed on the previous page. Click the Add (**+**) button near the top of the New Search window (**Figure 8**) to add a filter row.

■ If you choose Other from the attribute pop-up menu (**Figure 10**), you can use the dialog (**Figure 14**) to turn off check boxes for search attributes you never use, thus fully customizing the menu.

THE FIND COMMAND

To find files with the Find command

1. If necessary, activate the Finder.

2. To search a specific location on your computer, open a Finder window for that location.

3. Choose File > Find (**Figure 15**), or press ⌃ ⌘ F .

   A Searching window like the one in **Figure 9** appears.

4. Enter a search word or phrase in the Search field.

5. Click a location button to choose one of the search locations.

6. Set up criteria filters by choosing an option from the Attribute pop-up menu (**Figure 10**) and setting related criteria options.

   Search results appear in the Searching window (**Figure 16**).

✔ Tips

■ You can perform any combination of steps 4 through 6. Each step you perform adds criteria that narrows the search results.

■ The search results must match *all* search criteria specified in steps 4 through 6.

■ To add additional criteria filters, click the Add (+) button at the right end of a criteria row (**Figure 17**).

■ To remove a criteria filter, click the Remove (−) button at the right end of its row.

■ Clicking the Save button near the top of the New Search window creates a smart folder. I tell you about smart folders next.

Figure 15 The File menu.

Figure 16 In this example, I've entered a search word in the Search box, selected a search location, and set the Kind of file to PDF.

Figure 17 In this example, I've set up two search criteria filters: Kind and Last opened date.

Figure 18 A New Smart Folder window.

Figure 19 This search example displays all Applications I've used in the past seven days.

Figure 20 The Save As dialog can appear collapsed, like this...

Figure 21 ...or expanded, like this.

Smart Folders

The smart folders feature takes the Find command one step further. It enables you to save search criteria as a special folder. Opening the folder automatically performs a search and displays matching items. The smart folder's contents always contain items that match search criteria, even if the files and folders on your computer change.

To create a smart folder

1. To create a smart folder that searches a specific location on your computer, open a Finder window for that location.

2. Choose File > New Smart Folder (**Figure 15**), or press Option⌘N. A New Smart Folder window, which looks a lot like a Searching window, appears (**Figure 18**).

3. Follow steps 4 through 6 on the previous page to set up search criteria for the smart folder. (You'll have to click the + button in the search location row to add search filters.) The search results appear in the window (**Figure 19**).

4. Click the Save button near the top of the New Smart Folder window.

5. Set options in the dialog that appears (**Figure 20** or **21**):

   ▲ **Save As** is the name of the smart folder. Give it a name that describes what the folder will contain.

   ▲ **Where** is the location in which the smart folder will be saved. You can use the Where menu to choose a location or click the disclosure triangle beside the Save As box to expand the dialog (**Figure 21**) and choose any location on disk.

Continued on next page...

CREATING SMART FOLDERS

Continued from previous page.

▲ **Add To Sidebar** instructs Mac OS X to add an alias of the folder to the Sidebar (**Figure 22**).

6. Click Save. The name you gave the smart folder appears in the window's title bar (**Figure 22**), and the smart folder is saved for future use.

✔ Tips

■ You can create a smart folder by clicking the Save button in *any* search results window. It's not necessary to use the New Smart Folder command.

■ I explain how to use a standard Save As dialog on page 197.

To open a smart folder

If the smart folder has been added to the Sidebar, click the name of the smart folder in the Sidebar (**Figure 22**).

Or

If the smart folder has not been added to the Sidebar, open the icon for the smart folder (**Figure 23**).

The contents of the smart folder appear in a window like the one in **Figure 22**.

✔ Tip

■ The Saved Searches folder, which is the default location for smart folder files, is in the Library folder in your Home folder (**Figure 23**).

Figure 22 Here's a smart folder saved to the sidebar.

Figure 23 Smart folders are files that can be opened to display search results. The default location for smart folders is in the Saved Searches folder in your Library folder.

Figure 24 To display search criteria in a search results window, choose Show Search Criteria from the window's Action pop-up menu.

Figure 25 Search criteria reappears at the top of the window.

To edit a smart folder

1. Open the smart folder you want to edit (**Figure 22**).

2. Choose Show Search Criteria from the Action pop-up menu in the window's toolbar (**Figure 24**). The search criteria you used to create the smart folder appears at the top of the window (**Figure 25**).

3. Make changes as desired to search criteria. The search results in the window change accordingly.

4. Click the Save button. The changes are saved to the smart folder's definition.

To delete a smart folder

Drag the smart folder's icon (**Figure 23**) to the Trash.

✔ Tips

- I tell you more about deleting items and using the Trash on page 57.

- Deleting a smart folder does not delete the contents of the smart folder. It simply deletes the search criteria that displays those contents. The original items remain on disk.

- Deleting a smart folder does not remove it from the sidebar. If you click the sidebar item for a smart folder that you deleted, it will not work. You can remove the item from the sidebar by dragging it off. I tell you more about customizing the sidebar on page 153.

Working with Search Results

Whether you search for items with a pre-defined sidebar search, the Spotlight menu, a Finder window's search field, the Find command, or smart folders, you will eventually wind up with a window full of found items. **Figures 1**, **2**, **5**, **8**, **16**, **17**, and **22** show examples.

In Mac OS X 10.6, search result windows work almost exactly like any other Finder window. That means you can:

◆ Use toolbar buttons to change the window view or use Quick Look.

◆ Set view options (**Figure 26**).

◆ Use options on the window's Action pop-up menu to work with window contents and set sort order (**Figure 27**).

◆ Use available Finder menu commands on any selected item in the window.

◆ Open an item by simply double-clicking it.

Here are a few other things you can do with these windows.

✔ Tip

■ Consult **Chapters 2**, **3**, and **4** for more information about using the Finder and working with windows:

Figure 26
You can set view options for a search results window.

Figure 27 You can use the Action pop-up menu to set sort options for a search results window's contents.

Figure 28 When you select an icon, the path to its location on disk appears at the bottom of the search results window.

Figure 29 Choose Open Enclosing Folder to open the folder in which a selected item in a search results window is stored on disk.

To see where an item resides on disk

In the search results window, select the item. Its location on disk appears at the bottom of the window (**Figure 28**).

To open an item's parent folder

1. In the search results window, select the item for which you want to open the enclosing folder (**Figure 28**).

2. In the directory path at the bottom of the window, double-click the folder listed to the left of the item name (**Figure 28**).

   or

   Choose File > Open Enclosing Folder (**Figure 29**), or press ⌘⇧R.

   The folder in which the item resides opens (**Figure 30**).

Figure 30 Double-clicking a folder in the path opens that folder.

WORKING WITH SEARCH RESULTS WINDOWS

Spotlight Preferences

You can set options for the way Spotlight works and the results it shows in search results windows. You do this in the two panels of the Spotlight preferences pane (**Figures** 31 and **34**).

To open the Spotlight preferences pane

1. Choose Apple > System Preferences or click the System Preferences icon in the Dock.

2. In the System Preferences window that appears, click the Spotlight icon. The Search Results (**Figure** 31) or Privacy (**Figure** 34) panel of the Spotlight preferences pane appears.

To set Spotlight keyboard shortcuts

1. Display either panel of the Spotlight preferences pane (**Figure** 31 or **34**).

2. Toggle the check boxes to enable or disable the two shortcuts:

   ▲ **Spotlight menu keyboard shortcut** displays the Spotlight menu (**Figure** 3).

   ▲ **Spotlight window keyboard shortcut** displays the Searching window for the results of a Spotlight Search (**Figure** 5).

3. To set a shortcut key, select an option from the drop-down list or select the list and press the keys you want to assign.

Figure 31 The Search Results panel of the Spotlight preferences pane.

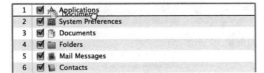

Figure 32 Drag a category to a different place in the list.

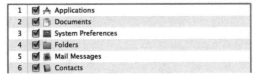

Figure 33 When you release the mouse button, the category moves.

To set Spotlight Search Results menu preferences

1. Open the Spotlight preferences pane.

2. If necessary, click the Search Results button to display its options (**Figure 31**).

3. To specify which categories of items should appear in search results, click to toggle check boxes. Categories with a check will appear in search results; categories without a check will not appear in search results.

4. To change the order in which categories should appear in search results, drag a category to a new position in the list (**Figure 32**). When you release the button, the category moves (**Figure 33**). You can repeat this step to change the order of the list.

5. When you are finished making changes, close the Spotlight preferences pane.

✔ Tip

■ The changes you make in the Spotlight Search Results panel affect the Spotlight search menu (**Figure 4**) only—not the other search features of Mac OS X.

SETTING SEARCH RESULTS PREFERENCES

To exclude locations from search

1. Open the Spotlight Preferences window.

2. If necessary, click the Privacy button to display its options (**Figure 34**).

3. Click the + button beneath the list. Then use the dialog that appears (**Figure 35**) to locate and select the folder or disk you want to exclude from searches. Click Choose to add it to the list (**Figure 36**).

   or

   Drag a folder or disk from a Finder window into the list area (**Figure 37**). The item is added to the list (**Figure 36**).

4. Repeat step 3 for each item you want to exclude from searches.

5. When you are finished making changes, close the Spotlight preferences pane.

✔ Tips

■ To remove an item from the list (**Figure 36**), select the item and click the − button at the bottom of the list. The item is removed and will be included in future searches.

■ The Privacy panel settings affect all Mac OS X search features—not just the Spotlight menu.

Figure 34 The Privacy panel of the Spotlight preferences pane.

Figure 35 Use this dialog to locate and select a folder or disk to exclude from searching.

Figure 37 You can also add a folder or disk by dragging it to the list.

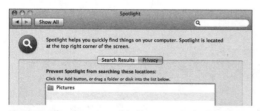

Figure 36 The item you added appears in the list and will not be searched.

Storage Media

Storage Devices & Media

A Macintosh computer can read data from, or write data to, a wide range of storage devices and media, including:

- ◆ **Hard disks**—high capacity magnetic media.

- ◆ **CD** and **DVD** discs—high capacity, removable optical media.

- ◆ **SD cards**—small, relatively high capacity media cards supported by many digital cameras. MacBook Pro computers released after June 2009 include an SD card reader slot.

- ◆ **Flash or "thumb" drives**—small, relatively high capacity USB devices that are commonly used to move files from one computer to another.

- ◆ **RAID devices**—extremely high capacity magnetic storage devices, normally used in business environments for servers or backup.

- ◆ Other legacy magnetic media, including floppy disks, or diskettes, and Zip disks.

To use storage media, it must be:

- ◆ **Mounted**—inserted, attached, or otherwise accessible to your computer.

- ◆ **Formatted or initialized**—specially prepared for use with your computer.

Continued on next page...

Continued from previous page.

This chapter covers storage devices and media. It also explains how to use Disk Utility to prepare and verify disks and how to use Time Machine to back up your important files and retrieve them if they're accidentally deleted.

✔ Tips

- Don't confuse storage media with memory. The term *memory* usually refers to the amount of RAM, or *random access memory,* in your computer, not disk space. RAM is temporary high-speed data storage space used by applications and erased when you shut down.

- At a minimum, all new Macintosh computers include a hard disk; all except the MacBook Air also include a CD/DVD drive.

- Storage devices can be:

  - ▲ **Internal** devices are inside your computer and cannot be easily removed. For example, all Mac models come with an internal hard disk. Most Macs also come with internal CD or DVD drives; the device itself (the drive) is internal even though the media (the disc) is removable.

  - ▲ **External** devices are attached to your computer by a cable. Most modern Mac models support FireWire and USB connections for external storage devices.

- Disk storage media capacity is specified in terms of bytes, kilobytes, megabytes, gigabytes, and terabytes (**Table 1**). Although terms for larger capacities do exist, these are the only ones you really need to know—at least these days.

Table 1

Terminology for Storage Media Capacity		
Term	Abbreviation	Size
byte	byte	1 character
kilobyte	KB	1,024 bytes
megabyte	MB	1,024 KB
gigabyte	GB	1,024 MB
terabyte	TB	1,024 GB

Figure 1 A write-protected icon appears in the status bar of CD or DVD discs and other write-protected media.

- If a disk is *write-protected* or *locked,* files cannot be saved or copied to it. A pencil with a line through it appears in the status bar of write-protected or locked disks (**Figure 1**). I tell you more about the status bar on page 36.

Figure 2 Here's a desktop and computer folder window with an internal hard disk, external hard disk, DVD disc, mounted network accessible folder, and iDisk.

Go	
Back	⌘[
Forward	⌘]
Enclosing Folder	⌘↑
🖥 Computer	⇧⌘C
🏠 Home	⇧⌘H
🖼 Desktop	⇧⌘D
◉ Network	⇧⌘K
🗂 iDisk	▶
🅰 Applications	⇧⌘A
🗋 Documents	⇧⌘O
✖ Utilities	⇧⌘U
Recent Folders	▶
Go to Folder...	⇧⌘G
Connect to Server...	⌘K

Figure 3
You can use the Go menu to open the top-level computer folder or connect to a server.

Mounting Disks

Mounting a disk makes it available for your computer to use. When a disk is mounted, your computer "sees" it and can access the information it contains.

✔ Tips

■ You must mount a disk to use it.

■ To learn how to mount disks that are not specifically covered in this book, consult the documentation that came with the disk drive.

■ Mounted disks appear in the top-level window for your computer (**Figure 2**). To display this window, choose Go > Computer (**Figure 3**) or press ⟨Shift⟩⟨⌘⟩⟨C⟩, as discussed on page 49.

■ Mounted disks may also appear on the desktop, as shown in **Figure 2**, depending on how Finder preferences are set for the display of items on the desktop. I explain how to set Finder preferences on page 146.

■ You mount a network volume by using the Connect to Server command under the Go menu (**Figure 3**) or by browsing the network and opening the disk you want to mount. I explain how to access network volumes on page 481.

To mount a CD or DVD disc

Insert the CD or DVD disc into the CD/DVD drive slot.

Or

1. Follow the manufacturer's instructions to open the CD or DVD disc tray or eject the CD or DVD caddy.

2. Place the CD or DVD disc in the tray or caddy, label side up.

3. Push the tray or caddy into the drive.

After a moment, the disc icon appears in the top-level computer window. **Figure 2** shows a mounted DVD (Mac OS X Install DVD).

✔ Tip

■ Do not insert a mini CD or DVD disk into a slot-loading CD or DVD drive. Most Mac CD and DVD slot-loading drives do not support mini discs; inserting one can damage the drive mechanism.

To mount an external hard disk

1. If necessary, connect the hard drive's power cord and plug it into a power outlet.

2. Connect the drive's FireWire or USB cable to the drive and your computer.

3. If necessary, turn on the drive's power switch.

After a moment, the drive's hard disk icon should appear in the top-level computer window. **Figure 2** shows a mounted external hard disk (Red Drive).

✔ Tips

■ Some external hard disk drives can draw their power from your computer via USB or FireWire cable. These drives do not require a power cord and do not have a power switch; you can skip steps 1 and 3.

Figure 4 When you connect a new hard disk, your Mac may offer to enable Time Machine.

■ When you connect an external hard drive for the first time, a dialog may ask if you want to use the disk with Time Machine (**Figure 4**). If you don't, click Ignore. I tell you about Time Machine on page 122.

MOUNTING DISKS

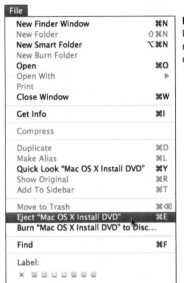

Figure 5
Use the File menu's Eject command.

Ejecting Discs

When you eject a disc, the disc is physically removed from the disc drive and its icon disappears from the top-level computer window.

✔ Tip

- When the disc's icon disappears from the top-level computer window, it is said to be *unmounted*.

To eject a disc

1. Click the disc's icon once to select it.

2. Choose File > Eject "*Disc Name*" (**Figure 5**), or press ⌘ ⌘ E.

Or

Click the eject button to the right of the disc name in the sidebar (**Figure 6**).

Or

1. Drag the disc's icon to the Trash. As you drag, the Trash icon turns into a rectangle with a triangle on top and the word *Eject* appears above it (**Figure 7**).

2. When the pointer moves over the Trash icon, release the button.

Or

Press and hold the Media Eject key on the keyboard until the disc slides out.

✔ Tip

- Not all keyboards include a Media Eject key. Check the documentation that came with your computer for more information.

Figure 6
An eject button appears on the sidebar beside each device that can be unmounted.

Figure 7
When you drag a disc icon to the Trash, the Trash icon changes and the word *Eject* appears above it.

EJECTING DISCS

Burning CDs & DVDs

If your Macintosh includes a Combo drive or SuperDrive, you can write, or burn, files onto blank optical media. This is a great way to archive important files that you don't need on your computer's hard disk and to share files with other computer users.

The type of drive your computer has determines the type of media it can write to:

◆ A *combo drive* can write to CD-R and CD-RW discs.

◆ A *SuperDrive* may be able to write to CD-R, CD-RW, DVD-R, DVD-W, DVD-RW, DVD+R, and DVD+RW discs.

The Finder offers three ways to burn a CD or DVD:

◆ Select a disc or folder and use the Burn command to burn its contents to a CD or DVD.

◆ Create a burn folder, fill the folder with the files you want to include on the CD or DVD, and use the Burn Disc command to burn the disc.

◆ Insert a blank CD or DVD, name it, and then drag the icons for the files you want to include on it onto its icon on the desktop. Then use the Burn Disc command to burn the CD or DVD.

On the following pages, I explain how to use all three techniques.

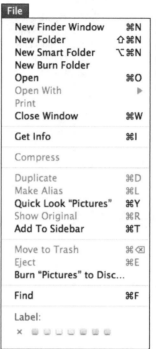

Figure 8
The File menu includes commands for creating burn folders and burning discs.

✔ Tips

■ Not all SuperDrives can write to DVD+RW discs. You can use System Profiler to see what formats your optical drive supports. I tell you more about System Profiler on page 589.

■ You can also burn CDs or DVDs from within iTunes, iDVD, or other third-party utilities, such as Roxio Toast. iTunes is discussed on page 270.

Figure 9 The Burn Disc dialog instructs you to insert a disk with enough capacity for the folder or disc you want to copy to a CD or DVD.

Figure 10 You can use a dialog like this to enter a name for the new disc and set a burn speed.

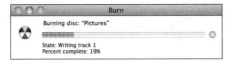

Figure 11 A progress bar indicates the new disc is being prepared.

Figure 12 The new disc appears in the Computer window.

To burn an existing folder or disc to CD or DVD

1. Select the folder or disc you want to copy to a CD or DVD.

2. Choose File > Burn "*Folder or disc name*" to Disc (**Figure 8**).

3. A Burn Disc dialog appears (**Figure 9**). Insert a CD or DVD in your computer. You may need to press the Media Eject button to open the media tray and then press it again to slide the tray and disc back into the computer.

4. A dialog like the one in **Figure 10** appears next. Set options as desired:
   - ▲ **Disc Name** is the name you want to give the disc.
   - ▲ **Burn Speed** is the speed your computer will use to burn the disc.

5. Click Burn.

   A Burn status dialog appears as the disc is burned (**Figure 11**). When the dialog disappears, an icon for the CD or DVD appears on the desktop and in the Sidebar (**Figure 12**). The disc is ready to read.

To burn a CD or DVD from a burn folder

1. Choose File > New Burn Folder (**Figure 8**). A burnable folder icon named Burn Folder appears in the active window (**Figure 13**).

2. While the folder name is selected, enter a new name for the folder and press Return. The folder's name changes (**Figure 14**).

3. Drag the files you want to include on the new CD or DVD to the burnable folder. You can create regular folders inside the burnable folder to organize the files you add to it. **Figure 15** shows an example of the contents of a burn folder that includes both files and folders.

4. When you are finished adding files, click the Burn button near the top of the burn folder's window (**Figure 15**) or select the burn folder icon and choose File > Burn "*Folder name*" to Disc (**Figure 8**).

5. A Burn Disc dialog appears (**Figure 9**). Insert a CD or DVD in your computer. You may need to press the Media Eject button to open the media tray and then press it again to slide the tray and disc back into the computer.

6. A dialog like the one in **Figure 10** appears next. Set options as desired:
   - ▲ **Disc Name** is the name you want to give the disc.
   - ▲ **Burn Speed** is the speed your computer will use to burn the disc.

7. Click Burn.

   A Burn status dialog appears as the disc is burned (**Figure 11**). When the dialog disappears, an icon for the CD or DVD appears on the desktop and in the Sidebar (**Figure 12**). The disc is ready to read.

Figure 13 An icon for the burn folder appears in the active window.

Figure 14
The name you give the folder is the name that will be given to the CD.

Figure 15 The contents of a burn folder can include folders and aliases to files and folders.

✔ Tips

- You can only create a burn folder in a window you have write permissions for.

- When you drag files to a burn folder, Mac OS creates aliases to the original files. When it burns the disc, however, it copies the original files rather than the aliases to the disc. I tell you more about aliases on page 132.

- When you're finished using a burn folder you can delete it or keep it:
  - ▲ If you delete the burn folder none of the original files are lost because the burn folder contains only aliases for original files.
  - ▲ If you keep a burn folder, you can create new discs from it again and again in the future. Because the burn folder contains aliases rather than original files, the latest versions of the files will always be burned onto the disc.

- You can use the burn folder feature to create a backup folder for periodically backing up important files to CD or DVD. Just create a burn folder and fill it with the files you want to back up. Burn a disc each time you want to back up the files. Be sure to retain the burn folder each time you burn a disc.

USING BURN FOLDERS

To burn files directly to a blank CD or DVD

1. Insert a blank CD or DVD into your computer.

2. A dialog like the one in **Figure 16** appears. Make sure Open Finder is chosen from the Action pop-up menu (**Figure 17**) and click OK.

   An Untitled CD or Untitled DVD icon appears on the desktop and in the Side-bar (**Figure 18**).

3. If desired, rename the icon. The name that appears on the icon is the name that will be burned onto the disc.

4. Drag the files you want to include on the disc to the disc icon. You can create regular folders inside the disc to organize the files you add to it. **Figure 19** shows an example of a recordable CD that includes both files and folders.

5. Click the Burn button beside the disc's icon in the Sidebar or near the top of the disc's window (**Figure 19**) or choose File > Burn "*Disc name*" to Disc (**Figure 8**).

6. A dialog like the one in **Figure 20** appears next. Set options as desired:

   ▲ **Disc Name** is the name you want to give the disc.

   ▲ **Burn Speed** is the speed your computer will use to burn the disc.

   ▲ **Save Burn Folder To** enables you to specify a name for a burn folder that will be created and saved to your computer.

7. Click Burn.

   A Burn status dialog appears as the disc is burned (**Figure 11**). When the dialog disappears, the disc is ready to read.

Figure 16 A dialog like this appears when you insert a blank CD or DVD without being prompted to.

Figure 17 The Action pop-up menu enables you to choose an application to use to burn the CD or DVD.

Figure 18 The disk appears in the sidebar as a sort of burn folder.

Figure 19 Here's an example of the contents of a recordable CD might look like when ready to burn.

Figure 20 A dialog like this offers the usual options, along with the ability to save the disc contents as a burn folder.

Newly burned CD

Burn folder

Figure 21 In this example, I've burned a CD using the settings shown in **Figure 20**. Mac OS created a burn folder on the desktop and added it to the sidebar.

✔ Tips

- The dialog shown in **Figure 16** is what appears if you have not changed CD & DVD Preferences. I explain these preferences starting on the next page.

- If you choose a different application from the Action pop-up menu (**Figure 17**) in step 2, Mac OS will open that application so you can use it to burn the disc. The remaining steps do not apply.

- If you turn on the check box for Save Burn Folder To, the burn folder is saved to your desktop and a link to it appears in the sidebar (**Figure 21**). You can move the burn folder anywhere you like to save it on your computer. You can also remove it from the sidebar as discussed on page 154.

CDs & DVDs Preferences

The CDs & DVDs preferences pane lets you specify what should happen when you insert a CD or DVD. The options that appear vary depending on your computer's CD and DVD capabilities. **Figure 23** shows how this preferences pane appears for a MacBook Pro with a SuperDrive, which is capable of reading and writing both CDs and DVDs.

To specify what should happen when you insert a CD or DVD

1. Choose Apple > System Preferences (**Figure 22**) to open the System Preferences pane.

2. Click the CDs & DVDs icon to display the CDs & DVDs preferences pane (**Figure 23**).

3. Choose an option from the pop-up menu beside each event that you want to set. The menus are basically the same; **Figures 24** and **25** show examples for a blank CD and a music CD. Your options are:

   ▲ **Ask what to do** displays a dialog like the one in **Figure 16**, which enables you to tell your computer what to do when you insert that type of disc.

   ▲ **Open** *application name* always opens the specified application when you insert that type of disc.

   ▲ **Open other application** displays a dialog like the one in **Figure 26**. Use it to select the application that should open when you insert that type of disc.

   ▲ **Run script** displays a dialog like the one in **Figure 26**. Use it to select an AppleScript applet that should open when you insert that type of disc. (I discuss AppleScript briefly in **Chapter 25**.)

   ▲ **Ignore** tells your computer not to do anything when you insert that type of disc.

Figure 22
Choose System Preferences from the Apple menu.

Figure 23 The CDs & DVDs preferences pane.

Figure 24
The pop-up menu for inserting a blank CD...

Figure 25
...and the one for inserting a music CD.

Figure 26 Use this dialog to select an application or script to run when you insert a disc.

Figure 27 Disk Utility can be found in the Utilities folder.

Disk Utility

Disk Utility, which can be found in the Utilities folder (**Figure 27**), is a utility for working with disks. Specifically, it can:

◆ Provide general information about a disk or volume.

◆ Verify and repair a disk or volume.

◆ Erase a selected disk or volume, including a rewritable CD or DVD.

◆ Divide a disk into several volumes or partitions.

◆ Set up a RAID disk.

◆ Create a blank disk image or a disk image from a file or a disk.

◆ Mount a disk image as a disk.

◆ Burn a disk image to CD or DVD.

◆ Restore a disk from a backup image.

In this part of the chapter, I explain how to use Disk Utility's most commonly used features.

✔ Tips

■ A *disk* is a storage device. A *volume* is a part of a disk formatted for storing files.

■ A *disk image* is a single file that contains everything on a disk. You can mount a disk image on your desktop just like any other disk.

■ I tell you about mounting disks on page 99.

■ Disk images are often used to distribute software on the Internet. They often include a *.dmg* filename extension.

■ Disk Utility's RAID and Restore panes are not covered in this book. To learn more about these features, enter a search phrase of *RAID* or *restore* in Mac Help and follow links that appear for specific instructions.

To open Disk Utility

Open the Disk Utility icon in the Utilities folder in your Applications folder (**Figure 27**). Disk Utility's main window appears (**Figure 28**).

To get information about a disk or volume

1. On the left side of the Disk Utility window, select the disk or volume you want information about. Some information about the item appears at the bottom of the window (**Figure 28**).

2. Click the Info button on the toolbar, choose File > Get Info (**Figure 29**), or press ⌘I. A window with additional information appears (**Figure 30**).

To verify or repair a disk or volume or its permissions

1. In the Disk Utility window, click the First Aid button.

2. Select the disk or volume you want to verify or repair (**Figure 28**).

3. Click the button for the action you want to perform:

   ▲ **Verify Disk Permissions** verifies file permissions on a Mac OS X startup volume.

   ▲ **Repair Disk Permissions** repairs file permissions on a Mac OS X startup volume.

   ▲ **Verify Disk** verifies the directory structure and file integrity of a disk or volume.

   ▲ **Repair Disk** repairs damage to the directory structure of any disk or volume other than the startup disk, as long as it is not write-protected.

Figure 28 Select the disk or volume you want to work with in Disk Utility's main window. The list includes physical disks and their volumes as well as disk image files you have created and saved on disk.

Figure 29 Disk Utility's File menu.

Figure 30 This window provides additional information about a selected disk or volume.

Figure 31 If you tell Disk Utility to verify your startup disk, a dialog like this may appear.

Figure 32 At the end of the verification (or repair) process, Disk Utility's First Aid feature reports results. In this example, Disk Utility found a bunch of errors in the permissions on my startup disk.

4. If you are verifying the startup disk, a dialog like the one in Figure 31 may appear. Click Verify Disk to continue.

5. Wait while your computer checks and/or repairs the selected disk or volume and its permissions. When it's done, it reports its results on the right side of the window (**Figure 32**).

✔ Tips

■ Permissions determine how users can access files. If permissions are incorrectly set for a file, it may not be accessible by the users who should be able to use it. If permissions are really messed up, your computer might not work correctly.

■ The startup disk is verified and, if necessary, repaired when you start your computer.

■ To repair your startup disk or volume, start your computer from the Mac OS X install disc. When the Installer launches, choose Installer > Disk Utility to run Disk Utility.

■ To select more than one disk or volume in step 2, hold down ⌘ while clicking each item.

■ Disk Utility's First Aid feature cannot repair all disk problems. For severely damaged disks, you may need to acquire third-party utilities, such as Alsoft's DiskWarrior or Micromat's TechTool Deluxe.

VERIFYING OR REPAIRING DISKS

To erase a disk or volume

1. In the Disk Utility window, click the Erase button.

2. Select the disk or volume you want to erase (**Figure 33**).

3. Set options for the volume:

   ▲ **Format** is the format applied to the volume. Depending on what you are erasing, your options include Mac OS Extended (Journaled), Mac OS Extended, Mac OS Extended (Case-sensitive, Journaled), Mac OS Extended (Case-sensitive), and MS-DOS (FAT).

   ▲ **Name** is the name of the volume.

4. To specify how disk space occupied by deleted files should be erased, click the Erase Free Space button. (This option is only available if you have selected a volume to erase.) Then select an option in the Erase Free Space Options dialog (**Figure 34**) and click OK.

5. To increase security and prevent the disk from being unerased, click the Security Options button. Then select an option in the Secure Erase Options dialog (**Figure 35**) and click OK.

6. Click Erase.

7. A dialog sheet like the one in **Figure 36** appears. Click Erase.

8. Wait while your computer erases the disk or volume. A progress dialog appears as it works. When it's finished, an icon for the erased disk or volume reappears on the desktop.

Erasing Disks or Volumes

Figure 33 Select the disk or volume you want to erase.

Figures 34 & 35 These dialogs offer more secure options for erasing a disk.

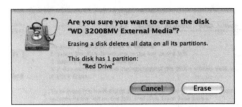

Figure 36 Click the Erase button to erase the disk.

✖ Caution!

- Erasing a disk or volume permanently removes all data. Do not erase a disk if you think you will need any of the data it contains.

✔ Tips

- You cannot erase the startup disk. (And that's a good thing.) If you want to erase your computer's startup disk, you must start your computer with another disk.

- When you erase a disk, you replace all volumes on the disk with one blank volume. When you erase a volume, you replace that volume with a blank volume.

- If you're not sure what volume format to choose in step 3, choose Mac OS Extended (Journaled). If you wanted one of the other formats, you'd know it.

- In steps 4 and 5, the explanations that appear beneath each option (**Figures 34** and **35**) should be enough information to help you decide which option is right for you.

- Using the security options in steps 4 and 5 can considerably lengthen the amount of time it takes to erase the disk.

- After erasing a disk or volume, a dialog like the one in **Figure 4** may appear, asking if you want to use that volume to back up with Time Machine. I tell you about Time Machine on page 122.

- If you're concerned about unauthorized persons recovering data from files you erase, be sure to check out the Secure Empty Trash command, which is covered on page 60.

ERASING DISKS OR VOLUMES

To partition a disk

1. In the Disk Utility window, click the Partition tab.

2. Select the disk you want to partition (**Figure 37**).

3. Choose an option from the Volume Scheme pop-up menu (**Figure 38**). The area beneath the pop-up menu changes (**Figure 39**).

4. In the Volume Scheme area, select a volume. Then set options in the Volume Information area as desired:

   ▲ **Name** is the name of the volume.

   ▲ **Format** is the format applied to the volume. Depending on what you are erasing, your options include Mac OS Extended (Journaled), Mac OS Extended, Mac OS Extended (Case-sensitive, Journaled), Mac OS Extended (Case-sensitive), and Free Space.

   ▲ **Size** is the amount of disk space allocated to that partition.

5. Repeat step 4 for each partition.

6. Click Apply.

7. A warning dialog like the one in **Figure 40** appears. Click Partition.

8. Wait while your computer erases the disk and creates the new partitions. When it's finished, icons for each formatted partition appear on the desktop.

Figure 37 Use Disk Utility's Partition pane to set up partitions on a disk.

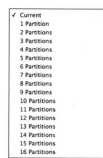

Figure 38
The Volume Scheme pop-up menu.

Figure 39 When the volume scheme is set for multiple volumes, you can set options for each one.

PARTITIONING DISKS

Figure 40 If you're sure you want to change the volume scheme, click Partition.

Figure 41
Another way to change the size of the partitions is to drag the divider between two partitions.

✖ Caution!

■ As warned in **Figure 40**, creating new volumes will erase all existing volumes, thus erasing data.

✔ Tips

■ You can also change the partition size in step 4 by dragging the divider between partitions in the Volume Scheme area (**Figure 41**).

■ If you select Free Space as the format for any partition in step 4, that partition cannot be used to store files.

■ If you're not sure what volume format to choose in step 5, choose Mac OS Extended (Journaled). If you wanted one of the other formats, you'd know it.

■ If you are partitioning removable media that may be used as a startup disk for a Macintosh or a Windows PC, before step 6, click the Options button in the Partition pane. Select the appropriate option in the dialog that appears (**Figure 42**) and click OK.

Figure 42 When partitioning removable media, you may need to set the partition scheme.

To create a blank disk image file

1. On the left side of the Disk Utility window, click beneath the list of disks and volumes so that none of them are selected.

2. Click the New Image button in Disk Utility's toolbar.

3. In the top half of the dialog that appears (**Figure 43**) enter a name and specify a disk location in which to save the disk image file.

4. Set options in the bottom part of the dialog:

   ▲ **Name** is the name of the volume within the Disk Image file. This is the name that will appear on the disk's icon on the desktop when the disk image is mounted.

   ▲ **Size** is the size of the volume. Choose an option from the pop-up menu (**Figure 44**). If you choose Custom, use a dialog sheet (**Figure 45**) to set the size.

   ▲ **Format** enables you to select the format of the volume: Mac OS Extended (Journaled), Mac OS Extended, Mac OS Extended (Case-sensitive), Mac OS Extended (Case-sensitive, Journaled), Mac OS Standard, MS-DOS (FAT).

   ▲ **Encryption** offers file encryption options for the disk image file. Choose an option from the menu. The selections are none, 128-bit AES encryption, and 256-bit AES encryption.

Figure 43 Use this dialog to set options for a new disk image file.

Figure 44 The Volume Size pop-up menu enables you to select from a number of common disk sizes...

Figure 45 ...or choose Custom and use this dialog to enter a custom size.

```
Hard disk
CD/DVD
No partition map
✓ Single partition – Apple Partition Map
Single partition – Master Boot Record Partition Map
Single partition – GUID Partition Map
Single partition – CD/DVD
Single partition – CD/DVD with ISO data
```

Figure 46 You can choose from among several partition schemes.

▲ **Partitions (Figure 46)** enables you to set a partition map for the disk image file.

▲ **Image Format** refers to the type of disk image. In most cases, you'll want to select read/write disk image.

5. Click Create. Disk Utility creates a disk image file to your specifications and mounts it on the desktop.

✔ Tips

■ The size of a disk image file is determined by the size specified in step 4.

■ If you're not sure what to choose for one of the options in step 4, leave them set to the default values.

■ Once you have created and mounted a blank disk image, you can copy items to it as if it were a regular disk. The items you copy to the disk are automatically copied into the disk image file. Copying files is discussed in **Chapter 3**.

To create a disk image file from a folder

1. In Disk Utility, choose File > New > Disk Image from Folder (**Figure 47**) or press [Shift] [⌘] [N].

2. Use the Select Folder to Image dialog that appears (**Figure 48**) to locate and select the folder you want to create a disk image of. Then click Image.

3. In the top half of the New Image from Folder dialog that appears (**Figure 49**), enter a name and choose a disk location for the image file.

4. In the bottom half of the dialog, set options as desired:

   ▲ **Image Format** refers to the type of disk image.

   ▲ **Encryption** offers file encryption options for the disk image file. Choose an option from the menu. The selections are none, 128-bit AES encryption, and 256-bit AES encryption.

5. Click Save. Disk Utility creates a disk image file containing the contents of the folder and mounts it on the desktop.

✔ Tips

■ The size of a disk image file is determined by the amount of data in the folder and the Image Format option you chose in step 4.

■ If you choose read/write from the Image Format pop-up menu (**Figure 50**), you can add files to the mounted disk image disk. Otherwise, you cannot.

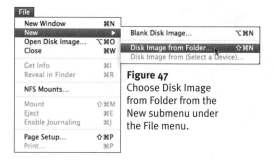

Figure 47
Choose Disk Image from Folder from the New submenu under the File menu.

Figure 48 Start by selecting the folder you want to create a disk image for.

Figure 49 Use the New Image from Folder dialog to set options for the image file.

Figure 50 The Image Format pop-up menu offers several options for the type of disk image file.

CREATING DISK IMAGES FROM FOLDERS

Figure 51
Choose Disk Image from "*Disk or Volume Name*" from the New submenu under the File menu.

Figure 52 Use this dialog to set options for a new disk image from another disk or volume.

To create a disk image file from another disk or volume

1. On the left side of the Disk Utility window, select the disk or volume you want to create an image of.

2. Choose File > New > Disk Image from "*Disk or Volume Name*" (**Figure 51**).

3. In the top half of the dialog that appears (**Figure 52**), enter a name and choose a disk location for the image file.

4. In the bottom half of the dialog, set options as desired:
   - ▲ **Image Format (Figure 50)** refers to the type of disk image.
   - ▲ **Encryption** offers file encryption options for the disk image file. Choose an option from the menu. The selections are none, 128-bit AES encryption, and 256-bit AES encryption.

5. Click Save. Disk Utility creates a disk image file containing the contents of the disk and mounts it on the desktop.

✔ Tips

- The size of a disk image file is determined by the amount of data in the original disk and the Image Format option you chose in step 4.

- If you choose read/write from the Image Format pop-up menu (**Figure 50**), you can add files to the mounted disk image disk. Otherwise, you cannot.

- You cannot save a disk image file on the same disk you are creating an image of. For example, if you wanted to back up your hard disk to an image file, you must save that image to another disk.

CREATING DISK IMAGES FROM DISKS

To mount a disk image

Double-click the disk image file's icon in the Finder (**Figure 53**).

Or

1. On the left side of the Disk Utility window, select the name of the disk image you want to mount in the list on the left side of the main window (**Figure 54**).

2. Click the Open button in the toolbar.

Or

1. In Disk Utility, choose File > Open Disk Image (**Figure 29**).

2. Use the Select Image to Attach dialog that appears (**Figure 55**) to locate, select, and open the disk image file.

   The disk image file's disk icon appears on the desktop and, if Disk Utility is open, in the list of disks and volumes (**Figure 56**).

✔ Tip

■ To mount an unmounted disk or partition, select it in the list on the left side of Disk Utility's main window and click the Mount button in the toolbar.

To unmount a disk image, disk, or partition

In the Finder, drag the mounted disk icon to the Trash.

Or

1. In the Disk Utility main window, select the icon for the disk you want to unmount (**Figure 57**).

2. Click the Unmount button in the toolbar.

   Although the icon disappears from the desktop, all of its contents remain in the disk image file.

Figure 53
A disk image file's icon.

SnapzProX2.dmg

Figure 54
Select the name of the disk image file you want to mount.

Figure 55 Use the Select Image to Attach dialog to locate, select, and open a disk image file.

Figure 56
The disk image's disk icon appears in the list of disks and volumes.

✔ Tip

■ To eject removable media, you can select it on the right side of the window and click the Eject button in the toolbar (**Figure 55**).

Figure 57 Select the volume you want to unmount.

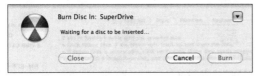

Figure 58 When a dialog like this appears, insert a disc and click Burn.

Figure 59 A dialog like this confirms the disk image has been burned to disc.

Figure 60 You can set additional options before burning a disk image to disc.

To burn a disc from a disk image

1. In the Disk Utility window, select the disk image you want to burn to CD or DVD (**Figure 56**).

2. Click the Burn button in the toolbar.

3. A dialog like the one in **Figure 58** appears. Insert a writable CD or DVD disc in your drive as instructed and click Burn.

4. Wait while Disk Utility writes to the disc. A progress dialog appears as it works.

5. When the disc finished, Disk Utility ejects the disc and displays a dialog like the one in **Figure 59**. Click OK.

✔ Tips

- You must have a Combo Drive, Super-Drive, or compatible disc writer to burn CD or DVD discs.

- If a disk image file you want to burn to disc does not appear in the Disk Utility window, mount it as instructed on the previous page, then follow these instructions.

- If you click the triangle button in the Burn Disc dialog (**Figure 58**), the dialog expands to offer additional options (**Figure 60**).

BURNING DISKS

Time Machine

Time Machine is an application (**Figure 61**) that makes it possible to protect your computer's contents from loss due to accidental deletion or disk damage. It does this by keeping an up-to-date copy of everything on your Mac. But unlike other backup software, Time Machine also remembers your system configuration on any given day, making it possible to go back in time (so to speak) to recover any of your files.

Time Machine is preconfigured to keep the following backups:

◆ Hourly backups for the past 24 hours.

◆ Daily backups for the past month.

◆ Weekly backups for all previous months until your backup disk is full.

In this part of the chapter, I explain how to set up and use Time Machine.

✔ Tips

■ Time Machine requires a connection to an external hard disk or mounted network volume to work.

■ You can use any mounted writable volume as a Time Machine backup disk, including Time Capsule or a disk available via a network connection. I tell you more about mounting network volumes and using Time Capsule in **Chapter 20**.

■ To minimize the amount of disk space needed for backups and prevent you from backing up files you may not need backed up, you can configure Time Machine to exclude certain folders from its automatic backups.

■ You configure Time Machine with the Time Machine preferences pane. You access its back up data with the Time Machine application.

Figure 61 You can find Time Machine in the Applications folder.

Figure 62 When you first open Time Machine preferences it displays a button for selecting the backup disk.

Figure 63 All volumes that can be used for Time Machine backups are displayed in the dialog.

Figure 64 The disk you selected appears in the Time Machine window and Time Machine is turned on.

To enable Time Machine

1. Connect an external hard disk to your Macintosh as discussed earlier in this chapter.

   or

   Mount an external hard disk or network volume as discussed in **Chapter 20**.

2. If a dialog like the one in **Figure 4** appears, click Use as Backup Disk and skip ahead to step 6.

3. Choose Apple > System Preferences (**Figure 22**) and click the Time Machine icon in the System Preferences window that appears.

4. In the Time Machine preferences pane that appears (**Figure 62**), click the Set Backup Disk button.

5. A window listing available disks and mounted volumes appears (**Figure 61**). Select the disk you want to use as your Time Machine backup disk and click Use for Backup. The name of the backup disk appears in the Time Machine window (**Figure 62**):

6. If necessary, click in the slider control beside On to move the slider to the On position (**Figure 62**).

7. Choose System Preferences > Quit System Preferences to close the Time Machine preferences pane.

To set Time Machine options

1. Choose Apple > System Preferences (**Figure 22**) and click the Time Machine icon in the System Preferences window that appears.

2. In the Time Machine window (**Figure 63**), click the Options button to display a list of items that should not be included in the backup (**Figure 65**), as well as one or more option check boxes.

3. To exclude an item from backup, click the + button and use the dialog that appears to locate and select the disk or folder you want to exclude from the backup (**Figure 65**). Then click Exclude. The item is added to the list of items that will not be backed up (**Figure 66**). Repeat this process for each item you want to exclude from the backup.

4. To back up a laptop even when it's running on battery power, turn on the Back up while on battery power check box.

5. To see a warning when old backup items are deleted, turn on the Notify after old backups are deleted check box.

6. Click Done.

7. Choose System Preferences > Quit System Preferences to close the Time Machine preferences pane.

✔ Tip

- If you change your mind and want to start backing up an item you have previously excluded, follow steps 1 and 2 to display the list of excluded items, select the item you want to start backing up, and click the − button at the bottom of the list. The item is removed from the list and will be backed up from that point forward.

Figure 65 This dialog lists the disks and folders that should not be included in the backup.

Figure 66 Use a standard Open dialog to locate and select the items you want to exclude from the backup.

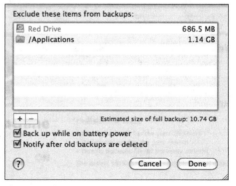

Figure 67 The item you selected is added to the list.

SETTING TIME MACHINE OPTIONS

Figure 68 Once Time Machine is enabled, you can see backup status in the Time Machine preferences pane.

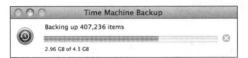

Figure 69 When Time Machine creates a backup, a window like this appears.

Figure 70 Backup progress also appears in the Time Machine preferences pane.

Figure 71 If you have the Time Machine menu enabled, you can see the last backup date and time at the top of the menu and choose commands to work with Time Machine.

To check Time Machine backup status

Choose Apple > System Preferences (**Figure 23**) and click the Time Machine icon in the System Preferences window that appears. Backup information appears in the Time Machine preferences pane (**Figure 67**).

Or

If a backup is in progress, a Time Machine Backup progress window appears (**Figure 68**), even if the Time Machine preferences pane is closed.

Or

If you have the Show Time Machine status in the menu bar check box turned on in the Time Machine preferences window (**Figure 69**), you can display a Time Machine menu with status information (**Figure 71**)

✔ Tips

- If a backup is in progress when you open the Time Machine preferences pane, a progress bar appears beside Backing Up (**Figure 70**).

- You can click the X button beside the progress bar (**Figures 69** and **70**) to stop a backup.

- If the backup disk is not available when Time Machine needs to create a backup, it simply postpones the backup until the disk is available.

- The first backup takes the longest. After that, backups occur very quickly since only the changes to the original backup are recorded.

To restore a backed up file or folder

1. Open the window for the disk or folder you want to restore.

2. Click the Time Machine icon in the Dock. The window's size reduces slightly and the desktop slides away. The Time Machine interface appears (**Figure 72**).

3. Navigate to the version of the window that displays the contents you want to restore. You can do this in a number of ways:

   ▲ Click the backward or forward arrows in the lower-right corner of the screen to scroll through various versions of the window.

   ▲ Click along the timeline on the right side of the screen (**Figure 73**) to go to a specific backup.

   ▲ Click the title bar of the window version you want to see.

4. Select the item you want to restore (**Figure 74**).

5. Click Restore. Time Machine displays a cool little animation as it copies the files back to the folder and displays them in the Finder (**Figure 75**).

✔ Tip

■ You can also use Time Machine in conjunction with Spotlight. Perform a search for the missing item, then launch Time Machine and browse backward through search results until it appears. I tell you more about searching with Spotlight in **Chapter 5**.

Figure 72 When you launch Time Machine, it begins by displaying the current window as it looks now.

Figure 73 You can use the timeline on the right side of the screen to go to a specific backup.

Figure 74 When you find the item you're looking for, select it.

Figure 75 When you click restore, the file is copied to its original location.

Advanced Finder Techniques

7

Advanced Finder Techniques

In addition to the basic Finder and file management techniques covered in **Chapters 2** through **4**, Mac OS X offers more advanced techniques you can use to work with files:

- ◆ Use spring-loaded folders to access folders while copying or moving items.

- ◆ Apply color-coded labels to Finder items.

- ◆ Use aliases to make frequently used files easier to access without moving them.

- ◆ Quickly reopen recently used items.

- ◆ Use the Quick Look feature to view the contents of a file or folder without opening it.

- ◆ Use the Info window to learn more about an item or set options for it.

- ◆ Compress files and folders to save space on disk or minimize data transfer time.

- ◆ Undo actions you performed while working with the Finder.

✔ Tip

- ■ If you're brand new to Mac OS, be sure to read the information in **Chapters 2** through **4** before working with this chapter. Those chapters contain information and instructions about techniques that are used throughout this chapter.

Spring-Loaded Folders

The spring-loaded folders feature lets you move or copy items into folders deep within the file structure of a disk—without manually opening a single folder. Instead, you simply drag icons onto folders (**Figures 1** and **3**) and wait as they're automatically opened (**Figures 2** and **4**). When you drop the icon into the window you want, all windows except the source and destination windows automatically close (**Figure 5**).

✔ Tips

- The spring-loaded folders feature is sometimes referred to as *spring-open folders*.

- Using the spring-loaded folders feature requires a steady hand, good mouse or trackpad skills, and knowledge of the location of folders on your disk.

- To use the spring-loaded folders feature, it must be enabled in the Finder preferences. Although this feature is normally turned on by default, if it's not, you can learn how to enable it on page 146.

- To use the spring-loaded folders feature to move or copy more than one item at a time, select the items first, and then drag any one of them.

- You can use spring-loaded folder techniques to work with folder icons (or stacks) on the Dock. So, for example, you can drag a PDF file icon from a Finder window onto the Applications stack to open it and drop the file icon onto a compatible application. This capability is new in Mac OS X 10.6.

Figure 1 Drag an icon onto a folder and wait...

Figure 2 ...until the folder opens.

Figure 3 Continue to drag the icon onto a folder in that window and wait...

Figure 4 ...until that folder opens.

Figure 5 When you're finished, only the source window (which is active) and destination window remain open.

To move an item using spring-loaded folders

1. Drag the item you want to move onto the folder to which you want to move it (**Figure 1**), but do not release the button. After a moment, the folder blinks and opens (**Figure 2**).

2. Without releasing the button, repeat step 1. The destination folder becomes selected (**Figure 3**), then blinks and opens (**Figure 4**). Do this until you reach the final destination.

3. Release the button to place the item into the destination window. All windows other than the source and destination windows close; the source window remains active (**Figure 5**).

✔ Tips

- In steps 1 and 2, to open a folder immediately, press Spacebar while dragging an item onto it.

- To close a folder's window so you can open a different folder in the same window, drag the item away from the open window. The window closes so you can drag the item onto a different folder and open it.

To copy an item using spring-loaded folders

Hold down Option while following the above steps.

✔ Tip

- If the destination folder is on another disk, it is not necessary to hold down Option to copy items; they're automatically copied.

Labels

Mac OS X's Labels feature enables you to assign color-coded labels to Finder icons. You can then sort list view windows by label or search for items based on the assigned label.

With a little imagination, labels can be a useful file management tool. For example, when I write a book and it goes through the editing process, I use labels to indicate each chapter's status. Yellow means it's a first draft, orange means it's a second draft, and green means it's final. This color-coding makes it possible for me to see a project's status just by looking inside a folder containing its files. (Imagine how good I feel when all of a book's chapter folders are green!)

✔ Tips

- You can only sort a window by labels if the Label column is displayed in that window. I explain how to customize a list view window on page 76.

- You can change the name associated with a label or its color. I tell you how on page 148.

Figure 6 Select the icon you want to apply a label to.

Figure 7 Choose a label color from the bottom of the File menu.

Figure 8 The color you chose is applied to the icon's name. (I know it doesn't look red here, but it is.)

Figure 9 In list view, the label color is applied to the entire line for the item.

Figure 10 Choosing the X under Label removes the label from selected icons.

To assign a label to an item

1. In a Finder window, select the icon(s) you want to apply a label to (**Figure 6**).

2. From the File menu, choose the color of the label you want to apply (**Figure 7**).

   The name of the icon is enclosed in an oval in the color you choose (**Figure 8**).

✔ Tips

- In list view, an item's entire line turns the color you chose (**Figure 9**).

- You can also assign a label to an item in the Info window for the item. I tell you more about the Info window on page 139.

To remove a label from an item

1. In a Finder window, select the icon you want to remove a label from.

2. From the File menu, choose the X beneath Label (**Figure 10**).

   The label is removed.

ASSIGNING & REMOVING LABELS

Aliases

An *alias* (**Figure 11**) is a pointer to an item. You can make an alias of an item and place it anywhere on your computer. Then, when you need to open the item, just open its alias.

✔ Tips

- It's important to remember that an alias is not a copy of the item—it's a pointer. If you delete the original item, the alias will not open (**Figure 12**).

- By putting aliases of frequently used items together where you can quickly access them—such as on your desktop— you make the items more accessible without actually moving them.

- The sidebar, Dock, and recent items features work with aliases. The sidebar and Dock are discussed on page 34, page 37, and page 155 ; recent items are discussed on page 135.

- You can name an alias anything you like, as long as you follow the file naming guidelines discussed on page 50. An alias's name does not need to include the word *alias*.

- The icon for an alias looks very much like the icon for the original item but includes a tiny arrow in the bottom-left corner (**Figure 11**).

- You can move, copy, rename, open, and delete an alias just like any other file.

iTunes　　　**iTunes alias**

Figure 11 The icon for an alias looks like the original item's icon but includes a tiny arrow.

The alias "iTunes alias" can't be opened because the original item can't be found.

Delete Alias　　Fix Alias...　　OK

Figure 12 If the original for an alias cannot be found, a dialog like this appears when you attempt to open it.

Figure 13
Select the item
you want to make
an alias for.

File	
New Finder Window	⌘N
New Folder	⇧⌘N
New Smart Folder	⌥⌘N
New Burn Folder	
Open	⌘O
Open With	▶
Print	
Close Window	⌘W
Get Info	⌘I
Compress "iTunes"	
Duplicate	⌘D
Make Alias	⌘L
Quick Look "iTunes"	⌘Y
Show Original	⌘R
Add To Sidebar	⌘T
Move to Trash	⌘⌫
Eject	⌘E
Burn "iTunes" to Disc...	
Find	⌘F
Label:	
⊠ ● ● ● ● ● ● ●	

Figure 14
Choose Make
Alias from the
File menu.

Figure 15 The alias
appears with the
original.

File	
New Finder Window	⌘N
New Folder	⇧⌘N
New Smart Folder	⌥⌘N
New Burn Folder	
Open	⌘O
Open With	▶
Print	
Close Window	⌘W
Get Info	⌘I
Compress "iTunes alias"	
Duplicate	⌘D
Make Alias	⌘L
Quick Look "iTunes alias"	⌘Y
Show Original	⌘R
Add To Sidebar	⌘T
Move to Trash	⌘⌫
Eject	⌘E
Burn "iTunes alias" to Disc...	
Find	⌘F
Label:	
⊠ ● ● ● ● ● ● ●	

Figure 16
To find an alias's
original, choose
Show Original from
the File menu.

To create an alias

1. Select the item you want to make an alias for (**Figure 13**).

2. Choose File > Make Alias (**Figure 13**), or press ⌘⌘L.

    The alias appears right beneath the original item (**Figure 15**).

Or

Hold down ⌘⌘Option and drag the item for which you want to make an alias to a new location. The alias appears in the destination location.

✔ Tip

■ An alias's name is selected right after it is created (**Figure 15**). If desired, you can immediately type a new name to replace the default name.

To find an alias's original file

1. Select the alias's icon.

2. Choose File > Show Original (**Figure 16**), or press ⌘⌘R.

    A window for the folder in which the original resides opens with the original item selected.

To fix a broken alias

1. Select the alias's icon.

2. Choose File > Show Original (**Figure 16**), or press ⌃ ⌘ R.

   or

   Open the alias icon.

   A dialog like the one in **Figure 12** appears if the original cannot be found.

3. Click Fix Alias.

4. Use the Select New Original dialog that appears (**Figure 17**) to locate and select the item that you want to use as the original for the alias.

5. Click Choose. The item you selected is assigned to the alias.

✔ Tips

- The Select New Original dialog is similar to a standard Open dialog, which is covered on page 194.

- If you would prefer to delete a broken alias instead of fixing it, click Delete Alias in the dialog that appears when you try to open it (**Figure 12**).

- If an alias is not broken but you want to reassign it to a new original anyway, you can click the Select New Original button in its Info window (**Figure 18**). I tell you more about the Info window later in this chapter.

Figure 17 Use this dialog to select a new original item for an alias.

Figure 18 The Info window for an alias includes a Select New Original button to change the original for an alias.

Figure 19
Mac OS tracks recently used applications, documents, servers, ...

Figure 20
...and folders.

Recent Items

Mac OS automatically tracks the things you open. It creates submenus of the most recently opened items in four categories—applications, documents, servers, and folders—making it quick to open them again.

✔ Tip

■ You can specify how many recent items Mac OS X tracks in the Recent Items submenu (**Figure 19**) by setting options in the Appearance preferences pane. I explain how on page 158.

To open recent items

To open a recently used application, document, or server, choose its name from the Recent Items submenu under the Apple menu (**Figure 19**).

Or

To open a recently used folder, choose its name from the Recent Folders submenu under the Go menu (**Figure 20**).

✔ Tips

■ Recent Items works with aliases, which are discussed on page 132.

■ Working with applications and documents is discussed in **Chapter 10**; working with servers is discussed in **Chapter 20**.

To clear the Recent Items or Recent Folders submenu

Choose Apple > Recent Items > Clear Menu (**Figure 19**) or choose Go > Recent Folders > Clear Menu (**Figure 20**).

✔ Tip

■ Clearing the Recent Items or Recent Folders submenu does not delete any items.

Quick Look

Mac OS X's Quick Look feature makes it possible to see what's in a folder or file without actually opening it. Instead, Quick Look shows a preview of the item within a resizable Quick Look window (**Figures 22** through **24**).

To view a file with Quick Look

1. In a Finder window, select the item you want to view with Quick Look.

2. Click the Quick Look icon on the toolbar.

   or

   Choose File > Quick Look "*Item Name*" (**Figure 21**), or press ⌃⌘Y.

   The Quick Look window appears as a charcoal gray, translucent window that displays the item's icon (**Figure 22**) or contents (**Figures 23** and **24**).

✔ Tips

- If you use Quick Look to view a multiple-page document, you can use a scroll bar to view any document page.

- If iPhoto is installed, you can click the Add to iPhoto button in the Quick Look window for an image file to add the image to your iPhoto library.

Figure 21
The Quick Look command displays a selected file or folder using the new Quick Look feature.

File	
New Finder Window	⌘N
New Folder	⇧⌘N
New Smart Folder	⌥⌘N
New Burn Folder	
Open	⌘O
Open With	▶
Print	
Close Window	⌘W
Get Info	⌘I
Compress "Documents"	
Duplicate	⌘D
Make Alias	⌘L
Quick Look "Documents"	⌘Y
Show Original	⌘R
Add To Sidebar	⌘T
Move to Trash	⌘⌫
Eject	⌘E
Burn "Documents" to Disc…	
Find	⌘F
Label:	

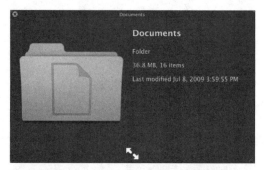

Figure 22 The Quick Look window for a folder.

Figure 23 The Quick Look window for an image file.

Figure 24 The Quick Look window for a document—in this case, a PDF.

Figure 25 In full screen view, Quick Look's preview fills your entire screen.

Close
Exit Full Screen

To browse the Finder with Quick Look

1. Open a Finder window for the folder you want to browse.

2. Click the Quick Look icon on the toolbar.

   or

   Choose File > Quick Look "*Item Name*" (**Figure 21**) or press ⌃ ⌘ Y.

   The Quick Look window appears.

3. Use standard Finder browsing techniques to select the items you want to browse. Each time a new item is selected, the Quick Look window changes to display its icon or contents (**Figures 22** through **24**).

✔ Tip

■ I tell you more about navigating folders and selecting icons in **Chapters 2** and **3**.

To switch to full screen view

Click the Full Screen button at the bottom of a Quick Look window. The screen turns black and fills with the Quick View window (**Figure 25**).

✔ Tips

■ A button bar appears in full screen view (**Figure 25**) so you have the same options you would have in the Quick Look window.

■ If the button bar disappears, move the pointer to display it again.

■ To leave full screen view, click the Exit Full Screen button (**Figure 25**) or press Esc.

To close the Quick Look window

Use one of the following techniques:

◆ Click the Quick Look window's close button (**Figures 22** through **24**).

◆ Choose File > Close Quick Look (**Figure 26**).

◆ Press ⌃ ⌘ Y.

◆ In full-screen view, click the close button in the Quick Look window's button bar (**Figure 25**).

File	
New Finder Window	⌘N
New Folder	⇧⌘N
New Smart Folder	⌥⌘N
New Burn Folder	
Open	⌘O
Open With	▶
Print	
Close Window	⌘W
Get Info	⌘I
Compress "Padres Butte.JPG"	
Duplicate	⌘D
Make Alias	⌘L
Close Quick Look	⌘Y
Show Original	⌘R
Add To Sidebar	⌘T
Move to Trash	⌘⌫
Eject	⌘E
Burn "Padres Butte.JPG" to Disc...	
Find	⌘F
Label:	

Figure 26 When the Quick Look window is open, the Close Quick Look command appears on the File menu.

Figures 27, 28, 29, & 30 The Info window for a hard disk (top-left), folder (top-right), application (bottom-left), and document (bottom-right).

The Info Window

You can learn more about an item by opening its Info window (**Figures 18** and **27** through **30**). Depending on the type of icon (disk, folder, application, document, alias, and so on), the General information in the Info window will provide some or all of the following:

◆ **Kind** or type of item.

◆ **Size** of item or contents (folders and files only).

◆ **Where** item is on disk.

◆ **Created** date and time.

◆ **Modified** date and time.

◆ **Format** of item (disks only).

◆ **Capacity** of item (disks only).

◆ **Available** space on item (disks only).

◆ **Used** space on item (disks only).

◆ **Version** number or copyright date or both (applications only).

◆ **Original** location on disk (aliases only).

◆ **Color label** assigned to the item.

◆ **Stationery Pad** check box (documents only) to convert the file into a stationery format file, which is like a document template.

◆ **Locked** check box to prevent the file from being deleted or overwritten (folders and files only).

Continued on next page...

THE INFO WINDOW

Continued from previous page.

In addition to the General category of information, the Info window offers additional categories (**Figure 31**), depending on the type of item. You can click the disclosure triangle beside a category heading to display or hide the details for the category. Some categories you might find in an Info window include:

◆ **Spotlight Comments** enable you to enter searchable comments or keywords for an item.

◆ **More Info** provides additional information about the file, including when the content was created and modified and when the item was last opened.

◆ **Name & Extension** displays an edit box you can use to modify the file name and its file name extension. A check box enables you to hide the extension in Finder windows.

◆ **Open with** enables you to choose the application that should open the item—and change the default application for all items of that type. This category is available for documents only.

◆ **Preview** displays a preview for the item if one is available. Otherwise, it simply displays the item's icon.

◆ **Languages** (not shown in **Figure 31**) is a list of the languages built in to the application. This category is available for applications only.

◆ **Sharing & Permissions** enables you to set file sharing permissions for the item.

✔ Tip

■ I tell you about using labels earlier in this chapter, searching for files with Spotlight in **Chapter 5**, and file permissions in **Chapter 20**.

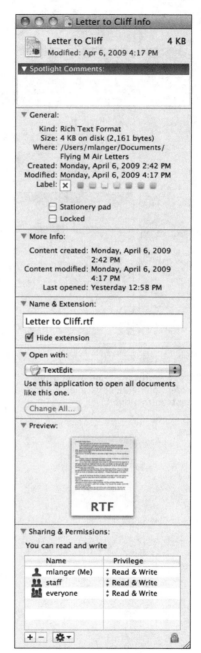

Figure 31 Here are all the categories of information in the Info window for a typical document.

THE INFO WINDOW

Figure 32
Choose Get
Info from the
File menu.

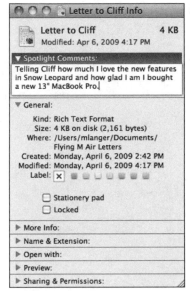

Figure 33 Enter comments for an item
in the Spotlight Comments section.

To open the Info window

1. Select the item for which you want to
   open the Info window (**Figure 13**).

2. Choose File > Get Info (**Figure 32**), or
   press ⌃ ⌘ I .

   The Info window for that item appears
   (**Figure 29**).

To enter Spotlight comments in the Info window

1. Open the Info window for the item you
   want to enter comments for (**Figure 30**).

2. If necessary, click the disclosure triangle
   beside Spotlight Comments near the top
   of the window. The window expands to
   show the Spotlight Comments box.

3. Type your comments into the Spotlight
   Comments box (**Figure 33**). They are
   automatically saved.

✔ Tip

■ As discussed on page 76, you can set a
   window's list view to display comments
   entered in the Info window.

To lock an application or document

1. Open the Info window for the item
   you want to lock (**Figures 18** and **27**
   through **30**).

2. Turn on the Locked check box.

✔ Tip

■ Locked items cannot be deleted or overwritten. They can, however, be moved.

USING THE INFO WINDOW

Compressing Files & Folders

Mac OS X's file compression feature enables you to create compressed copies of items sometimes called *archived files* or *archives*. Compressed files take up less space on disk than regular files. You may find them useful for backing up files or for sending files to others over a network or via e-mail.

✔ Tips

- In previous versions of Mac OS X, the compression feature was known as the archive feature.

- The compression feature uses ZIP format compression, which was originally developed as a DOS and Windows PC format. As a result, document archives created with this feature are fully compatible with DOS and Windows PCs.

Figure 34 To compress an item, begin by selecting its icon.

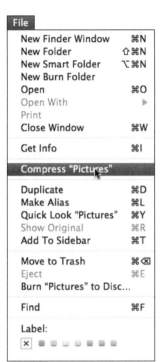

Figure 35
Choose the Compress command from the File menu.

Figure 36 A copy progress dialog like this one appears when you compress an item.

Figure 37
The compressed file appears with the original.

Pictures.zip

To compress a file or folder

1. Select the item you want to compress (**Figure 34**).

2. Choose File > Compress "*Item Name*" (**Figure 35**).

3. Wait while your computer creates the archive. While it works, a Copy status dialog appears (**Figure 36**). When the dialog disappears, the archive file appears in the same location as the original as a .zip file (**Figure 37**).

✔ Tips

- In previous versions of Mac OS X, you compressed files with the Create Archive command on the File menu. This is the same command with a different name.

- You can compress multiple items at once. Select the items, then choose File > Compress *n* Items (where *n* is the number of selected items). When the archive appears, it will be named Archive.zip.

To open a compressed file

Double-click the compressed file. The file's contents are uncompressed and appear in the same window as the compressed file.

COMPRESSING FILES & FOLDERS

Undoing Finder Actions

The Mac OS X Finder includes limited support for the Undo command, which can reverse the most recently completed action. Say, for example, that you move a file from one folder to another folder. If you immediately change your mind, you can choose Edit > Undo Move (**Figure 38**) to put the file back where it was.

Figure 38
The Undo command enables you to undo the last action you performed.

✔ Tips

■ Don't depend on the Undo command. Unfortunately, it isn't available for all actions (**Figure 39**).

■ The exact wording of the Undo command varies depending on the action and the item it was performed on. In **Figure 38**, for example, the command is Undo Move of "Letter to John" because the last action was to move a document icon named Letter to John.

■ The Undo command is also available (and generally more reliable) in most Mac OS applications. You'll usually find it at the top of the Edit menu.

Figure 39
In this example, I can redo the last thing I undid but I can't undo anything.

To undo an action

Immediately after performing an action, choose Edit > Undo "*action description*" (**Figure 38**), or press ⌘⌥Z. The action is reversed.

To redo an action

Immediately after undoing an action, choose Edit > Redo "*action description*" (**Figure 39**). The action is redone—as if you never used the Undo command.

✔ Tip

■ Think of the Redo command as the Undo-Undo command since it undoes the Undo command.

Customizing the Finder

8

Customizing the Finder

One of the great things about Mac OS is its user interface flexibility. Although the Mac OS X Finder looks the same on every computer when first installed, it is highly customizable, making it possible for every Mac user to set up his or her computer so it looks and works just right.

This chapter covers the following ways to customize the Finder:

◆ **Finder preferences** enable you to set general Finder options, as well as text for labels, sidebar contents, and advanced options.

◆ **Toolbar customization** enables you to specify what icons appear in Finder window toolbars and what order they appear in.

◆ **Sidebar customization** enables you to add, remove, and shuffle Finder window sidebar contents.

◆ **Dock customization** enables you to add, remove, and shuffle Dock contents and to set options that control the way the Dock looks and works.

◆ **Appearance preferences** enable you to set system colors, scroll bar functionality, recent items, and font smoothing.

◆ **Desktop & Screen Saver preferences** enable you to specify a desktop image and choose a screen saver.

✔ Tip

■ You can find other options and techniques for customizing the way your computer works in **Chapter 23** and elsewhere throughout this book.

Finder Preferences

Finder preferences enables you to customize several aspects of the desktop and Finder. The Finder's preferences window is organized into four different panes of options:

◆ **General** (**Figure 2**) lets you set basic options for the desktop and Finder windows.

◆ **Labels** (**Figure 9**) enables you to set label names for the Finder's label feature.

◆ **Sidebar** (**Figure 14**) lets you set options for the sidebar.

◆ **Advanced** (**Figure 15**) enables you to set options for the display of file extensions and the Trash warning.

To open Finder Preferences

Choose Finder > Preferences (**Figure 1**) or press ⌘,. The Finder Preferences window opens, displaying the last pane of options you accessed.

To set General Finder Preferences

1. In the Finder Preferences window, click the General button to display General options (**Figure 2**).

2. Toggle check boxes to specify what items should appear on the desktop:

   ▲ **Hard disks** displays icons for internal hard disks.

   ▲ **External Disks** displays icons for external hard disks and thumb drives.

   ▲ **CDs, DVDs, and iPods** displays icons for removable media, including CDs and DVDs, as well as iPods.

   ▲ **Connected servers** displays icons for mounted server volumes.

Figure 1
Choose Preferences from the Finder menu.

Figure 2 The default settings for General Finder preferences.

Figure 3
Use this pop-up menu to specify what should appear in a new Finder window.

Figures 4, 5, 6, & 7 A new Finder window can display the top-level computer window, your hard disk contents, your Home folder contents, or your Documents folder contents.

Figure 8
Use a dialog like this to display a specific folder when you open a new Finder window.

3. Choose an option from the New Finder windows open pop-up menu (**Figure 3**) to determine what should appear in a new Finder window (the window that appears when you choose File > New Finder Window or press ⌘N):

   ▲ *Computer name* displays the icons for the computer and all mounted volumes (**Figure 4**).

   ▲ *Hard Disk name* displays the root level of your hard disk (**Figure 5**).

   ▲ **iDisk** displays the top level of your iDisk. (This option only appears if you are a MobileMe subscriber and use iDisk.)

   ▲ *Your account name* displays the contents of your Home folder (**Figure 6**).

   ▲ **Desktop** displays the contents of your Desktop folder.

   ▲ **Documents** displays the contents of your Documents folder (**Figure 7**).

   ▲ **Other** displays a dialog that you can use to select a different folder to display (**Figure 8**).

4. Toggle check boxes to set other options:

   ▲ **Always open folders in a new window** opens a new window to display the contents of the folder you open. This makes Mac OS X work more like Mac OS 9.2 and earlier.

   ▲ **Spring-loaded folders and windows** enables the spring-loaded folders feature. You can use the slider to set the delay time for this feature.

✔ Tip

■ I discuss views in **Chapter 4**, disks and mounting disks in **Chapter 6**, spring-loaded folders in **Chapter 7**, and iDisk in **Chapter 19**.

To customize labels

1. In the Finder Preferences window, click the Labels button to display Labels options (**Figure 9**).

2. To change the name of a label, select the text for the label you want to change (**Figure 10**) and enter new text (**Figure 11**).

3. Repeat step 2 for each label you want to change.

✔ Tip

■ The names of labels appear on the File menu when you point to a label (**Figure 12**) and in a list view window when the Label column is displayed (**Figure 13**). I explain how to display specific columns in list view on page 76.

Figure 9 The default settings in the Labels window of Finder preferences.

Figure 10 To change a label, select it...

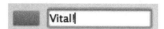

Figure 11 ...and then enter new label text.

Figure 12 The new label appears on the File menu when you point to its color.

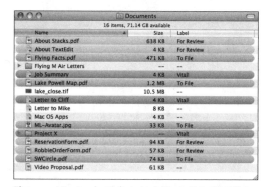

Figure 13 Here's what labels look like in list view. Three different customized labels have been applied and the Label column is displayed.

CUSTOMIZING LABELS

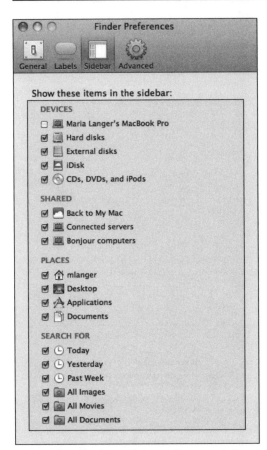

Figure 14 Options in the Sidebar preferences window of Finder preferences.

To set Sidebar preferences

1. In the Finder Preferences window, click the Sidebar button to display Sidebar options (**Figure 14**).

2. Toggle check boxes to specify what items should appear in the sidebar.

✔ Tip

■ I tell you more about customizing the sidebar on page 153.

To set Advanced preferences

1. In the Finder Preferences window, click the Advanced button to display Advanced options (**Figure 15**).

2. Toggle check boxes to set options:

   ▲ **Show all file extensions** tells the Finder to display file extensions in Finder windows (**Figure 16**). This option, in effect, turns off the Hide extension check box in the Name & Extension area of the Info window (**Figure 17**) for all files on a go-forward basis.

Continued on next page...

Figure 15 The default settings for Advanced Finder preferences.

Figure 16 You can set up the Finder so it always displays file extensions as part of an item's name.

SETTING SIDEBAR & ADVANCED PREFERENCES

Continued from previous page.

▲ **Show warning before changing an extension** displays a warning dialog like the one in **Figure 18** when you change a file name extension.

▲ **Show warning before emptying the Trash** displays a dialog like the one in **Figure 20** when you choose Finder > Empty Trash or Finder > Secure Empty Trash. Turning off this check box prevents the dialog from appearing.

▲ **Empty Trash securely** enables the secure empty Trash feature for each time you empty the Trash.

3. Choose an option from the When performing a search pop-up menu (**Figure 19**) to set how Mac OS X's search feature should work.

✔ Tips

■ As Mac OS warns (**Figure 18**), changing a file's extension may cause the file to open in another application. If that application can't read the file, it may not open at all.

■ I discuss renaming files and the Trash in **Chapter 3**, the Info window in **Chapter 7**, and the search feature in **Chapter 5**.

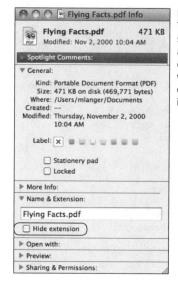

Figure 17
The Hide extension check box in a file's info window determines whether the file's extension appears in Finder windows.

Figure 18 Mac OS can warn you about the consequences of changing a file name extension.

✓ Search This Mac
  Search the Current Folder
  Use the Previous Search Scope

Figure 19 You can use this pop-up menu to set the default search scope for Mac OS X's search feature.

Figure 20 By default, this confirmation dialog appears when you empty the Trash.

Figure 21
Choose Customize Toolbar from the View menu.

Figure 22 The Customize Toolbar dialog appears over the current window.

Figure 23 To add an item, drag it from the center part of the dialog to the toolbar.

Figure 24 When you release the button, the item is added.

Customizing the Toolbar

The toolbar, which is discussed on page 32, can be customized to include buttons and icons for a variety of commands and items.

✔ Tips

■ When you customize the toolbar, your changes affect the toolbar in all windows in which the toolbar is displayed.

■ To display the toolbar, click the toolbar control button in the upper-right corner of a Finder window, choose View > Show Toolbar, or press Option ⌃ ⌘ T .

To customize the toolbar

1. With any Finder window open and the toolbar displayed, choose View > Customize Toolbar (**Figure 21**). The Customize Toolbar dialog appears (**Figure 22**).

2. Make changes to the toolbar contents as follows:

   ▲ To add an item to the toolbar, drag it from the dialog to the position you want it to occupy on the toolbar (**Figure 23**). When you release the button, the item appears on the toolbar (**Figure 24**).

   ▲ To remove an item from the toolbar, drag it off the toolbar. When you release the button, the item disappears in a puff of digital smoke (**Figure 25**).

   ▲ To rearrange the order of items on the toolbar, drag them into the desired position (**Figure 26**). When you release the button, the items are rearranged (**Figure 27**).

Continued on next page...

CUSTOMIZING THE TOOLBAR

Continued from previous page.

3. To specify how items should appear on the toolbar, choose an option from the Show pop-up menu at the bottom of the window (**Figure 28**):

   ▲ **Icon & Text** displays both the icon and the icon's name (**Figure 22**).

   ▲ **Icon Only** displays only the icon (**Figure 29**).

   ▲ **Text Only** displays only the name of the icon (**Figure 30**).

4. To display smaller size toolbar buttons, turn on the Use Small Size check box.

5. When you are finished making changes, click Done.

✔ Tips

■ You don't have to use the Customize Toolbar dialog to rearrange or remove toolbar items. Just hold down ⌃ ⌘ and drag the item you want to move to a new position or drag the item you want to remove off the toolbar.

■ The toolbar includes spacers that you can move or remove like buttons. They appear on the toolbar as light gray boxes.

To restore the toolbar to its default settings

1. With any Finder window displaying the toolbar open, choose View > Customize Toolbar (**Figure 20**). The Customize Toolbar dialog appears.

2. Drag the group of items in a box near the bottom of the window to the toolbar (**Figure 31**). When you release the button, the toolbar is reset to default (**Figure 22**).

3. Click Done.

Figure 25 To remove an item, drag it off the toolbar.

Figure 26 To move a toolbar item, drag it to a new position on the toolbar.

Figure 27 When you release the button, the item moves.

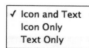

Figure 28
The Show pop-up menu's options.

Figure 29 You can also display the toolbar as icons and text...

Figure 30 ...or as just text.

Figure 31 Drag the default set of icons to the toolbar.

Figure 32 Position the pointer on the border between the sidebar and the rest of the window.

Figure 33 Drag to move the border and change the width of the sidebar.

Customizing the Sidebar

In addition to using Finder preferences to specify what standard items should appear in the sidebar (as discussed on page 149) you can customize the sidebar a number of other ways:

◆ Change the width of the sidebar to better display long item names.

◆ Add or remove folders, files, and other items in the bottom half of the sidebar.

✔ Tips

■ I tell you more about the sidebar on page 34.

■ The sidebar only appears if the toolbar is displayed. I tell you more about the toolbar on page 151 and page 32.

To change the sidebar width

1. Position the pointer on the divider between the sidebar and the rest of the Finder window. The pointer turns into a line with two arrows coming out of it (**Figure 32**).

2. Press the button down and drag. As you drag, the sidebar's width changes (**Figure 33**).

3. When the sidebar is the desired width, release the button.

✔ Tip

■ As shown in **Figure 33**, making the sidebar wider does not make the entire window wider. Instead, it just shifts the dividing point between the sidebar and the rest of the window.

To add a sidebar item

Drag the icon for the item you want to add to the sidebar. A blue line indicates where it will appear (**Figure 34**). When you release the button, the item appears on the sidebar (**Figure 35**).

✔ Tips

- In step 1, the icon you drag can be the one that appears in the item's title bar.

- Adding an item to the sidebar does not move it from where it resides on disk. Instead, it creates and adds a pointer to the original item to the sidebar.

- Be careful when adding an icon to the sidebar. If you drag the icon on top of a folder or disk icon on the sidebar, the icon will move into that folder or disk.

To remove a sidebar item

Drag the item off the sidebar (**Figure 36**) When you release the button, the item disappears in a puff of digital smoke (**Figure 37**).

✔ Tips

- Removing an item from the sidebar does not delete it from disk. Instead, it removes the pointer to the original item from the sidebar.

- If you remove all the items under a sidebar heading, the heading disappears. It reappears if you add an item that belongs under that heading.

To rearrange sidebar items

Drag the item you want to move into a new position on the sidebar. Other items on the sidebar will shift to make room for it (**Figure 38**). When you release the button, the item moves (**Figure 39**).

Figure 34
To add an item to the sidebar, drag it on.

Figure 35
The item is added in the position you dragged it.

Figures 36 & 37
Drag an item off the sidebar (left) to remove it (right).

Figures 38 & 39
Drag an item to a new position (left) to move it on the sidebar (right).

WORKING WITH SIDEBAR ITEMS

Figure 40 Drag an item from the window to the Dock.

Figure 41 The item's icon appears in the Dock.

Figure 42 Drag an icon off the Dock.

Figure 43 The icon is removed.

✔ Tips

■ You cannot remove the Finder or Trash from the Dock.

■ Removing an item from the Dock does not delete it from disk.

Customizing the Dock

The Dock, which is discussed on page 37, can be customized to include icons for items that you use often. This makes them quick and easy to open any time you need them.

✔ Tip

■ Stacks and Exposé are two other Mac OS X features that workswith the Dock. I explain how to use Stacks on page 168 and Exposé on page 172.

To add an item to the Dock

1. Open the window containing the item you want to add to the Dock.

2. Drag the item from the window to the Dock. Items on the Dock shift to make room for the new item (**Figure 40**).

3. Release the button. The icon appears (**Figure 41**).

✔ Tips

■ Dragging an item to the Dock does not remove it from its original location.

■ Add applications to the left of the Dock's divider and documents, folders, Web sites, and servers to the right of the divider.

To remove an item from the Dock

1. Drag the item from the Dock to the desktop (**Figure 43**).

2. Release the button. The item disappears in a puff of digital smoke.

■ If you remove an icon for an application that is running, the icon will not disappear from the Dock until you quit.

ADDING & REMOVING DOCK ITEMS

To set Dock preferences

1. Choose Apple > Dock > Dock Preferences (**Figure 44**) to display the Dock preferences pane (**Figure 45**).

2. Set options as desired:

   ▲ **Size** changes the size of the Dock and its icon. Drag the slider to resize.

   ▲ **Magnification** magnifies a Dock icon when you point to it (**Figure 46**). Use the slider to specify how much magnification there should be.

   ▲ **Position on screen** lets you move the Dock to the left side, bottom, or right side of the screen. When positioned on the left or right, the Dock fits vertically down the screen (**Figure 47**).

   ▲ **Minimize windows using** enables you to choose one of two special effects to use when minimizing a window to the Dock: Genie Effect or Scaling.

   ▲ **Minimize windows into application icon**, which is a new option in Snow Leopard, makes an application's minimized windows accessible from the application's icon in the Dock using Exposé.

   ▲ **Animate opening applications** bounces an application's icon in the Dock as it opens.

   ▲ **Automatically hide and show the Dock** hides the Dock until you point to where it is hiding. This is a great way to regain screen real estate normally occupied by the Dock.

Figure 44 The Dock submenu under the Apple menu includes commands for customizing the Dock, as well as access to the Dock preferences pane.

Figure 45 The Dock preference pane includes all Dock customization options.

Figure 46 When magnification is enabled, pointing to an icon enlarges it.

Fi **Figure 47**
Who says the
Dock has to be
at the bottom of
the screen? Here's
what it might look
like on the left.

✔ Tips

- In step 1, you could also choose Apple > System Preferences and then click the Dock icon in the System Preferences window that appears.

- Another way to change the size of the Dock, is to drag the divider line up or down (**Figure 48**).

- As shown in **Figure 44**, the Dock submenu under the Apple menu offers several options also found in the Dock preferences pane (**Figure 45**). You might find it quicker or easier to make changes in settings by simply selecting an option from the menu.

- I explain how to use Exposé on page 172.

Figure 48 You can resize the
Dock by dragging the divider.

Appearance Preferences

The Appearance preferences pane (**Figure 50**) enables you to set options for color, scroll bar functionality, recent items, and text smoothing. These options help customize the Finder so it looks and works the way you want it to.

To set Appearance preferences

1. Choose Apple > System Preferences (**Figure 49**) to display the System Preferences window.

2. Click the Appearance icon to display Appearance preferences (**Figure 50**)

3. Set options as desired:

   ▲ **Appearance** sets the color for buttons, menus, and windows throughout your computer and its applications. Your options are Blue and Graphite.

   ▲ **Highlight Color** sets the highlight color for text in documents, fields, and lists. Choose an option from the pop-up menu (**Figure 51**).

   ▲ **Place scroll arrows** determines whether scroll arrows in windows and scrolling lists should appear **Together** at the bottom or right end of the scroll bar (**Figure 52**) or **At top and bottom**, which places a scroll arrow at each end of the scroll bar (**Figure 53**).

   ▲ **Click in the scroll bar to** determines what happens when you click in the scroll track of a scroll bar. **Jump to the next page** scrolls to the next window or page of the document. **Jump to the spot that's clicked** scrolls to the relative location in the document. For example, if you click in the scroll track two-thirds of the way between the top and bottom, you'll scroll two-thirds of the way through the document. This is the same as dragging the scroller to that position.

Figure 49 Choose System Preferences from the Apple menu to open System Preferences.

Figure 50 The Appearance preferences pane includes options for customizing the appearance of what you see onscreen.

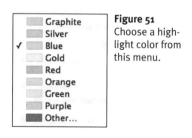

Figure 51 Choose a highlight color from this menu.

Figures 52 & 53
A window with scroll bars together (top) and with scroll bars at top and bottom (bottom).

Figure 54
The Recent Items submenu under the Apple menu.

▲ **Use smooth scrolling** scrolls the contents of a window smoothly, without jumping.

▲ **Double-click a window's title bar to minimize** minimizes a window to the Dock when you double-click its title bar.

▲ **Number of Recent Items** enables you to specify how many **Applications**, **Documents**, and **Servers** to consider "recent" when displaying recent applications, documents, and servers on the Recent Items submenu (**Figure 54**). Options range from None to 50.

▲ **Use LCD font smoothing when available** determines how Mac OS X smooths text onscreen for LCD displays, such as those on a MacBook, MacBook Pro, or iMac. This option varies depending on your computer model and display.

▲ **Turn off text smoothing for font sizes** enables you to choose a minimum font size for text smoothing. Text in the font size you set and smaller will not be smoothed. Your options range from 4 to 12.

4. When you are finished setting options, click the Appearance preferences window's close button to dismiss it.

Continued on next page...

SETTING APPEARANCE PREFERENCES

Continued from previous page.

✔ Tips

- If you choose other from the Highlight Color pop-up menu, you can use a standard Color panel (**Figure 55**) to select any color supported by your computer. I explain how to use the Color panel on the next page.

- I tell you about minimizing windows on page 30.

- You can clear the Recent Items submenu by choosing Apple > Recent Items > Clear Menu (**Figure 54**).

- Font or text smoothing uses a process called antialiasing to make text more legible onscreen. Antialiasing creates gray pixels between black ones and white ones to eliminate sharp edges. **Figure 56** shows what text looks like with text smoothing turned on and off.

Figure 55
The Colors panel offers a standard interface for choosing colors.

12-point text with text smoothing turned on.

12-point text with text smoothing turned off.

Figure 56 As these examples show, text smoothing can change the appearance of text onscreen.

Figures 57, 58, 59, & 60 The Colors panel offers several color picker interfaces. Shown here are color sliders (top-left), color palettes (top-right), image palettes (bottom-left), and crayons (bottom-right).

To use the Colors panel

1. Click the icon along the top of the Colors panel to select one of the color models.

2. How you choose a color depends on the model you selected:

   ▲ **Color Wheel (Figure 55)** displays a circle of color. Click inside the circle to choose a color. You can drag the vertical slider up or down to change the brightness.

   ▲ **Color Sliders (Figure 57)** displays several sliders you can use to change color values. Start by selecting a slider group from the pop-up menu, and then move the sliders to create a color.

   ▲ **Color Palettes (Figure 58)** displays clickable color samples. Choose a palette from the List pop-up menu, and then click the color you want.

   ▲ **Image Palettes (Figure 59)** displays colors from an image. Click a color to select it.

   ▲ **Crayons (Figure 60)** displays different colored crayons. Click a crayon to choose its color.

The color of the selected item changes immediately.

✔ Tip

■ You can use the color wells at the bottom of the Colors panel to store frequently used colors. Simply drag a color into an empty spot. Then, when you open the Colors panel, you can click a stored color to apply it.

Desktop & Screen Saver Preferences

The Desktop & Screen Saver preferences pane (**Figures 61** and **66**) enables you to set the background color or picture for the Mac OS X desktop and configure a screen saver that appears when your computer is idle.

✔ Tips

- Mac OS X's built-in screen saver doesn't really "save" anything. All it does is cover the normal screen display with graphics, providing an interesting visual when your computer is inactive.

- The Energy Saver preferences pane offers more protection for LCD displays than Screen Saver. Energy Saver is covered on page 539.

To set the desktop picture

1. Choose Apple > System Preferences (**Figure 49**) to display the System Preferences window.

2. Click the Desktop & Screen Saver icon to display Desktop & Screen Saver preferences.

3. If necessary, click the Desktop button to display its options (**Figure 61**).

4. In the list on the left side of the window, select an image collection or folder. The images in the collection appear on the right side of the window.

5. Click to select the image you want. It appears in the image well above the collection list and the desktop's background picture changes (**Figure 62**).

6. If desired, choose an option from the pop-up menu beside the image preview (**Figure 63**) to indicate how it should appear.

Figure 61 The Desktop pane of the Desktop & Screen Saver preferences pane.

Figure 62 In this example, I've selected a photo of a bay in Alaska from my Pictures folder.

SETTING THE DESKTOP PICTURE

Figure 63
Choose an option to indicate how the picture should appear onscreen.

Figure 64
Use this pop-up menu to set the picture changing frequency.

Figure 65 In this example, the Translucent menu bar check box has been turned off. The menu bar is a plain gray.

7. To change the picture periodically, turn on the Change picture check box and select a frequency option from the pop-up menu (**Figure 64**). Turning on the Random order check box beside this displays the images in random order.

8. To change the menu bar so it is opaque (**Figure 65**) rather than translucent (**Figure 62**), turn off the Translucent menu bar check box.

9. When you are finished setting options, click the Desktop & Screen Saver preferences window's close button to dismiss it.

✔ Tips

- For best results, use pictures that are the same size or larger than your screen resolution. For example, if your screen resolution is set to 1024 x 768, the image should be at least this size. You can check or change your screen resolution in the Displays preferences pane, which I discuss on page 537.

- The image collection list on the left side of the Desktop pane (**Figure 61**) includes predefined collections installed with Mac OS X, as well as access to your Pictures folder, and your iPhoto library and albums (if iPhoto is installed).

- In step 4, you can click the + button at the bottom of the collections column and use the dialog that appears (**Figure 8**) to locate and choose another folder that contains images.

- Although you can have your desktop display a virtual slide show by setting the picture changing frequency in step 5 to a low value like 5 seconds, you may find it distracting to have the background change that often. I know I would!

SETTING THE DESKTOP PICTURE

To configure the screen saver

1. Choose Apple > System Preferences (**Figure 49**) to display the System Preferences window.

2. Click the Desktop & Screen Saver icon to display Desktop & Screen Saver preferences.

3. If necessary, click the Screen Saver button to display its options (**Figure 66**).

4. In the Screen Savers list, select a screen saver module. The preview area changes accordingly.

5. To set options for the screen saver, click Options. Not all screen savers can be configured and the options that are available vary depending on the screen saver you selected in Step 4. **Figures 67 and 68** show two examples.

6. To see what the screen saver looks like on your screen, click Test. The screen goes black and the screen saver kicks in. To go back to work, move your mouse or move a finger across your trackpad.

7. To have the screen saver start automatically after a certain amount of idle time, drag the Start screen saver slider to the desired value.

8. To set "hot corners" that activate or deactivate the screen saver, click the Hot Corners button to display the Active Screen Corners dialog (**Figure 69**). Choose an option from each pop-up menu (**Figure 70**) to specify what should happen when you position the pointer in the corresponding corner. When you're finished, click OK to save your settings.

9. When you are finished setting options, click the Desktop & Screen Saver preferences window's close button to dismiss it.

Figure 66 The Screen Saver pane of the Desktop & Screen Saver preferences pane.

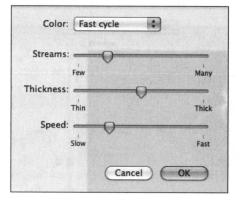

Figure 67 Configuration options for the Flurry screen saver module.

Figure 68 Configuration options for slide show screen savers.

CONFIGURING THE SCREEN SAVER

Figure 69 Use this dialog to set hot corners for activating or deactivating the screen saver. In this example it's set so that if I put my pointer in the upper-left corner of the screen, the screen saver never goes on, and if I put my pointer in the lower-right corner of the screen, the screen saver goes on immediately.

Figure 70
This pop-up menu includes Screen Saver, Exposé, and Dashboard options.

Figure 71 Use a menu at the bottom of the Screen Savers list to set up slide show screen savers with your own pictures or pictures available online.

✔ Tips

- If you're not picky about what screen saver appears, you can turn on the Use random screen saver check box after step 3 and skip the remaining steps.

- In step 4, you can click the + button at the bottom of the Screen Savers list for additional options (**Figure 71**). This makes it possible to create slide show screen savers based on a folder of pictures, a gallery on MobileMe, or an RSS feed. Or you can choose Browse Screen Savers to see screen savers available for download from Apple's Web site.

- To include a clock as part of the screen saver, turn on the Show with clock check box after step 5.

- Several of the screen saver modules are interactive. For example, pressing Ⓓ while the Word of the Day screen saver is active opens the Dictionary application to the currently displayed word. I tell you more about using Dictionary on page 289.

- As shown in **Figure 70**, you can use the Active Screen Corners dialog to set up hot corners for Exposé and Dashboard, too.

- In step 8, you can configure the hot corners any way you like. For example, you can set it up so every corner starts the screen saver.

Desktop Management

Desktop Management Tools

Mac OS X includes three desktop management tools that you might find helpful to work more efficiently and productively:

◆ **Stacks** puts expandable folders in the Dock. Clicking a folder displays its contents, making it quick and easy to open files you use often.

◆ **Exposé** helps you cope with screen clutter by arranging open windows so you can see their contents or your desktop with a press of a button. Snow Leopard adds Exposé integration to the Dock, making it even more functional.

◆ **Spaces** enables you to organize windows into groups, thus helping you to manage projects or tasks.

In this chapter, I explain how to take advantage of each of these features. I also explain how you can set preferences for them so they work the way you want them to.

Stacks

Mac OS X Stacks feature displays the contents of any folder in the Dock as a fan (**Figure 1**), grid (**Figure 2**), or list (**Figure 3**). Click the folder icon to display the stack. Then click the item in the stack to open it. This makes it easy to organize Dock items and access the applications, folders, and files you use most.

By default, Mac OS X 10.6 is preconfigured with three stacks folders (**Figure 3**):

◆ **Applications** is the computer's Applications folder—default location for installed applications.

◆ **Documents** is your Documents folder—the default location for saved documents.

◆ **Downloads** is your Downloads folder—the default location for files you download from the Internet.

You can add your own stacks to the Dock by simply adding folders.

✔ Tips

■ Whether a stack appears as a fan, grid, or list depends, in part, on settings for the stacks folder or the number of items in the folder. I explain how to set Stacks options for a folder on page 170.

■ A stack's Dock icon appears as a pile (or stack) of icons with the most recently added item on top (**Figure 4**). This helps give you an idea of the folder's contents.

■ I explain how to customize the Dock, including how to add and remove Dock items, on page 155.

Figure 1 The Stacks feature displays the contents of a folder in the Dock as a fan...

Figure 2 ...a grid, ...

Click here to see more

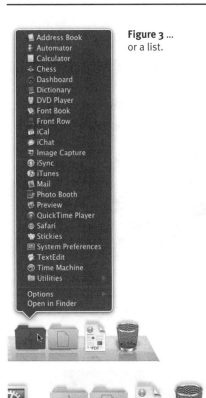

Figure 3 ... or a list.

Figure 4 Here are three stacks folders: Applications, Documents, and Downloads folders.

Figure 5 If there are many items in a grid, you can scroll down within it.

To display a stack

In the Dock, click the icon for the stack folder you want to display.

The contents of the folder appear in a fan (**Figure 1**), grid (**Figure 2**), or list (**Figure 3**).

To hide a stack

Click anywhere other than on a stack item.

Or

Click the stack folder again.

The stack collapses back into the Stack icon in the Dock.

To open an item in a stack

1. Display the stack containing the item you want to open (**Figure 1, 2, or 3**).

2. Click the item you want to open.

   The item opens.

To open a stack folder

1. In the Dock, click the folder to open to display its stack (**Figure 1, 2, or 3**).

2. Click the appropriate button:

   ▲ For a fan (**Figure 1**), click the Show in Finder or More in Finder button at the top of the fan. The wording of this command varies depending on whether all items are showing.

   ▲ For a grid, click the Open in Finder button at the bottom of the grid. You may have to scroll down in the grid (**Figure 2**) to display this button (**Figure 5**).

   ▲ For a list (**Figure 3**), click the Open in Finder button at the bottom of the list.

   The stacks folder opens in its own Finder window.

WORKING WITH STACKS

169

To navigate folders within a stack grid

1. Display the stack grid you want to navigate and, if necessary, scroll to display the folder you want to open (**Figure 5**).

2. To open a folder in the grid, click it. The grid displays the contents of the folder you clicked. **Figure 6** shows what the Applications stack might look like after clicking the Utilities folder within it.

3. To back out of a folder, click the name of the parent folder in the upper left corner of the grid stack (**Figure 6**).

✔ Tips

■ You can repeat step 2 as desired to dig deeply into the file hierarchy.

■ Stacks navigation as discussed here is brand new in Snow Leopard.

To navigate folders within a stack list

1. Display the stack list you want to navigate (**Figure 3**).

2. To open a folder in the list, point to it. The list turns into a hierarchical menu with the folder's contents displayed in a submenu (**Figure 7**).

✔ Tips

■ You can repeat step 2 as desired to open multiple submenus for deeply nested folders.

■ This is a great way to organize the files and folders you need to access using the stacks feature.

Click the name of the parent folder to view the contents of that folder again.

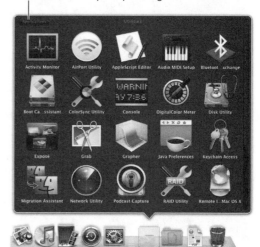

Figure 6 Clicking a folder in a grid displays the contents of that folder in the grid.

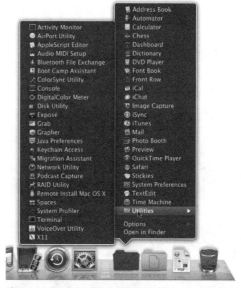

Figure 7 When viewing a stack as a list, point to the name of a folder to display its contents in a subfolder.

Figure 8
You can display a menu of options for a stack.

Figure 9
If a stack is displayed as a list, you'll need to display the Options submenu to change its options.

Figure 10 In this example, I've changed the Display as option for the Applications and Documents folder from Folder to Stack.

To customize the display of a stack folder

1. In the Dock, point to the folder you want to set options for.

2. Do one of the following to display a menu of options (**Figure 6**):

   ▲ Hold down Control and click.

   ▲ Right-click or, on a buttonless track-pad, click with two fingers.

   ▲ If the stack is set to display as a list, click to display the list and then choose Options to display the Options submenu (**Figure 9**).

3. To change the sort order of items in the stack, choose a Sort by option.

4. To set the appearance for the the stack's icon on the dock, choose a Display as option:

   ▲ **Folder** displays the stack's icon using the same icon as its source folder.

   ▲ **Stack** displays the stack's icon as a stack of icons (**Figure 10**).

5. To set the appearance for the folder's open stack, choose a View content as option:

   ▲ **Fan** always displays the stack as a fan (**Figure 1**).

   ▲ **Grid** always displays the stack as a grid (**Figure 2**).

   ▲ **List** always displays the stack as a list (**Figure 3**).

   ▲ **Automatic** displays the stack as a fan (**Figure 1**) unless there are too many items in the folder to fit—then it displays them as a grid (**Figure 2**).

CUSTOMIZING STACK APPEARANCE

Exposé

If you're like most Mac OS X users, you probably have multiple applications and windows open at the same time while you work. The result can be a cluttered screen, with many layers of windows hiding other windows and the desktop.

Exposé helps solve the problem of screen clutter by making it easy to see all open windows in all applications (**Figure 11**), all open windows in a single application (**Figure 12**), or the entire desktop (**Figure 16**) at once. Simply press one of Exposé's shortcut keys (**Table 1**) to see what you need to see.

Mac OS X 10.6 adds Exposé integration with the Dock. Now you can view all open windows in a specific application by simply clicking that application's icon in the Dock (**Figure 13**). And when windows are displayed in Exposé, they now appear in a neat grid, making them even easier to see and access.

✔ Tips

- If you're using a laptop Macintosh, such as a MacBook or MacBook Pro, you may need to hold down the Fn key while pressing the appropriate key in **Table 1** to activate Exposé.

- You can customize Exposé's shortcut keys or add additional Exposé triggers. I explain how on page 174.

- You can use Exposé while copying or moving items. Begin dragging the item you want to move or copy, use the appropriate Exposé keystroke for the view you need, and complete the drag and drop while Exposé is active.

Table 1

Standard Shortcut Keys for Exposé	
Key	Description
F9	Displays all open windows at once.
F10	Displays all open windows for the current application at once.
F11	Displays the desktop.

EXPOSÉ

Figure 11 Pressing F9 displays all open windows.

Figure 12 Pressing F10 displays all of the windows in the currently active application—in this case, Preview.

Figure 13 Clicking an icon in the Dock displays the open windows for that application, as well as a small menu of options.

Figure 14 Exposé also gives you access to a menu of options for an application.

To see all open windows at once

Press F9.

All open windows resize and arrange themselves into a grid so you can see into each one (**Figure 11**).

✔ Tip

- Another way to open Exposé is to open the Exposé icon in the Utilities folder inside your Applications folder. This is not exactly as easy as pressing a single key, but you could add the Exposé icon to the Dock, making it accessible with just a click.

To see all open windows in the active application

Press F10.

All open windows in the active application resize and arrange themselves into a grid while other windows simply disappear (**Figure 12**).

To see all open windows in a specific application

1. Press F9 or F10 to activate Exposé (**Figure 11 or 12**).

2. Click the Dock icon for the application windows you want to view. Exposé displays only the windows for that application (**Figure 13**).

✔ Tip

- As shown in **Figures 13** and **14** clicking a Dock icon while Expose is active displays a menu of options for an active application.

To activate a specific window

1. With Exposé active, point to the window you want to activate. A blue border appears around it (**Figure 15**).

2. Click the window. Exposé is released and the window comes to the front.

To see the desktop

◆ Press F11.

All open windows shift to the edges of the screen so you can see the desktop (**Figure 16**).

To switch from one Exposé view to another

Press the shortcut key for the other view.

To release Exposé

Press Esc.

Figure 15 When you point to a window while Exposé is active, a dark blue border appears around it. (It's times like these when I wish they'd let me do color books.)

Figure 16 Exposé also enables you to display just the desktop. You might find this handy if you keep a lot of icons on your desktop, like I do on my main production Mac.

Figure 17 Use the Exposé panel of the Exposé & Spaces preferences pane to set hot corners, shortcut keys, and mouse buttons for Exposé functions.

Figure 18
Use pop-up menus like this one to set up hot corners for Exposé and other Mac OS X features.

To set Exposé preferences

1. Choose Apple > System Preferences, or click the System Preferences icon in the Dock.

2. In the System Preferences window that appears, click the Exposé & Spaces icon.

3. If necessary, click the Exposé button to display Exposé configuration options (**Figure 17**).

4. To set "hot corners" to activate Exposé, choose an option from the appropriate pop-up menu in the Active Screen Corners area. Each menu is the same (**Figure 18**) and corresponds to a specific corner of the screen. The Exposé options are:

    ▲ **All Windows** uses Exposé to display all open windows (**Figure 8**). This is the same as pressing F9 with default Exposé settings.

    ▲ **Application Windows** uses Exposé to display all windows for the active application (**Figure 10**). This is the same as pressing F10 with default Exposé settings.

    ▲ **Desktop** uses Exposé to move all windows aside so you can see the Desktop (**Figure 12**). This is the same as pressing F11 with default Exposé settings.

5. To set shortcut keys and mouse buttons for Exposé functions, choose options from the pop-up menus in the Exposé area (**Figures 15** and **16**).

6. When you're finished setting options, click the Exposé & Spaces preferences pane's close button to save your settings and dismiss the window.

Continued on next page...

SETTING EXPOSÉ PREFERENCES

Continued from previous page.

✔ Tips

■ When you position the pointer in a "hot corner" of the screen, your computer performs the task you assigned to it with the corresponding Active Screen Corners pop-up menu (**Figure 18**).

■ The Active Screen Corners pop-up menus (**Figure 18**) enable you to set corners for Dashboard activation (page 312), screen saver (page 164), and display sleep (page 539).

■ Right and Left on the keyboard shortcuts pop-up menu (**Figure 19**) refer to the →| and |← keys.

■ Shift, Control, Option, and Command on the keyboard shortcuts pop-up menu (**Figure 19**) refer to the Shift, Control, Option, and ⌃⌘ keys.

■ If you hold down the Shift, Control, Option, or ⌃⌘ key while displaying the keyboard shortcuts or mouse button pop-up menu, the menu changes to reflect the key(s) being held. **Figure 21** shows an example with the Shift and Option keys held down.

■ To assign mouse buttons to Exposé functions with the mouse button pop-up menu (**Figure 19**), it's best to have a multibutton mouse. I tell you more about Mac OS-compatible mice on page 12 and how to set mouse options on page 550.

F1
F2
F3
F4
F5
F6
F7
F8
✓ F9
F10
F11
F12
F13
Right Shift
Right Control
Right Option
Right Command
Left Shift
Left Control
Left Option
Left Command
fn
-

Figure 19
Use this pop-up menu to choose a keystroke to assign to one of the Exposé functions.

Secondary Mouse Button
Mouse Button 3
✓ Mouse Button 4
-

Figure 20
If you have a multi-button mouse, you can configure its buttons for Exposé functions, too.

⌥⇧ F1
⌥⇧ F2
⌥⇧ F3
⌥⇧ F4
⌥⇧ F5
⌥⇧ F6
⌥⇧ F7
⌥⇧ F8
⌥⇧ F9
⌥⇧ F10
⌥⇧ F11
⌥⇧ F12
⌥⇧ F13
Right Shift
Right Control
Right Option
Right Command
Left Shift
Left Control
Left Option
Left Command
fn
-

Figure 21
Holding down modifier keys—such as Option and Shift in this example—enables you to choose a keyboard shortcut with the modifier keys you pressed.

Figure 22 In this example, I've created four different spaces.

Figure 23 When you switch to a space, only its windows appear.

Spaces

Mac OS X's Spaces feature enables you to organize groups of windows into multiple spaces (**Figure 22**). Then, when you work in a space, only the windows that are part of that space appear onscreen (**Figure 23**).

For example, while working on a chapter of this book, I might have a space that includes my InDesign chapter document, Photoshop (which I use to edit screenshots), and the three Finder windows that I use for the chapter's documents. I might also have another space set up with Mail, iChat, and Safari. I can then quickly switch from my work space to my communication space when I need to check e-mail or track down someone for a chat. When I want to return to work without distractions from those other applications, I can quickly switch back to my work space.

Setting up Spaces is pretty straightforward. After enabling the feature and specifying the number and layout of spaces that you want, simply switch to a space and start filling it with windows. You can also assign applications to specific spaces, ensuring that they open in the space you plan to use them in. You can have up to 16 spaces and access them several ways, including clicking, shortcut keys, or the Spaces menu.

In this part of the chapter, I explain how to set up and use the Spaces feature.

To enable & configure Spaces

1. Choose Apple > System Preferences or click the System Preferences icon in the Dock.

2. In the System Preferences window that appears, click the Exposé & Spaces icon.

3. If necessary, click the Spaces button to display Spaces configuration options (**Figure 24**).

4. Turn on the Enable Spaces check box.

5. To display a Spaces menu in the menu bar (**Figures 25** and **26**), turn on the Show Spaces in menu bar check box.

6. Set the number of spaces in the black box. To add a row or column, click the **+** button beside Rows or Columns.

7. To always switch to a space with open windows for an application you switch to, turn on the check box at the bottom of the Spaces pane. This keeps all of an application's open windows in the same space.

8. Click the Exposé & Spaces preferences pane's close button to save your settings and dismiss the window.

✔ Tips

- You can configure Mac OS to have from 2 to 16 spaces.

- To change the number of spaces, you can repeat these steps and click the **+** or **–** button beside Rows or Columns to add or remove spaces.

- The Spaces menu displays the number of the currently displayed space as its menu bar icon (**Figures 25** and **26**).

Figure 24 The Spaces panel of the Exposé & Spaces preferences pane.

Figure 25 You can add a Spaces menu to the menu bar.

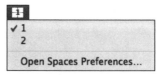

Figure 26 The Spaces menu makes it easy to switch from one space to another.

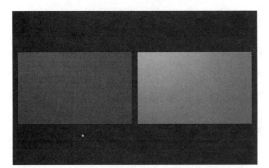

Figure 27 In this very simple example, I've created two spaces and I haven't added any windows to either one.

Figure 28 Adding windows to a space is as simple as opening the windows you want to add.

To switch from one space to another

1. Press F8 (or Fn F8 on a laptop, such as a MacBook or MacBook Pro) or click the Spaces icon in the Dock.

   The screen goes black and rectangles representing each space appear (**Figures 22** and **27**).

2. Click the space you want to view.

Or

If the Spaces menu is enabled (**Figure 25**), choose the space you want from the menu (**Figure 26**).

Or

Press Control ← or Control → to cycle through all spaces, one at a time.

Or

Press Control with the number key corresponding to the space you want to view. For example, Control 2 displays space No. 2.

To add windows to a space

1. Switch to the space you want to add windows to.

2. Open the windows you want to add. Those windows become part of that space (**Figure 28**).

✔ Tip

■ If a window belongs to an application that is associated with a specific space, that window will only open in that space. For example, if you set Preview to open in space No. 2, when you open a Preview document, it appears in space No. 2, no matter which space was open when you opened the document. I explain how to associate applications with spaces next.

SWITCHING SPACES, ADDING WINDOWS

To associate an application with a specific space

1. Follow steps 1 through 3 under "To enable & configure Spaces" on page 178 to open the Spaces preferences panel (**Figure 24**).

   or

   Choose Open Spaces Preferences from the Spaces menu (**Figure 26**).

2. Under Application Assignments, click + to display a menu like the one in **Figure 29**.

3. Choose an open application's name to add it to the Application Assignments list (**Figure 31**).

   or

   Choose Other to display dialog like the one in **Figure 30**. Use the dialog to locate and select the application you want to assign to a specific space. Then click Add to add it to the Application Assignments list (**Figure 31**).

4. In the Space column of the application's line in the Application Assignments list, use the pop-up menu (**Figure 32**) to choose the space you want to assign the application to.

5. Repeat steps 2 through 4 for each application you want to add.

✔ Tips

■ In step 4, the Every Space option (**Figure 32**) allows the application to display in any space.

■ When you associate an application with a specific space, that application and its document windows will only open in that space. If you want an application to open in any space, choose Every Space in step 4 or simply do not add the application to the Application Assignments list.

Figure 29
When you click the + button, a menu of open applications appears.

Figure 30 Use this dialog to add an application to the Application Assignments list.

Figure 31 The item you added appears in the list.

Figure 32 Choose a space assignment from the pop-up menu in the Space column.

F1 F2 F3 F4 F5 F6 F7 ✓ F8 F9 F10 F11 F12 F13 -	**Figure 33** Use this pop-up menu to choose a shortcut key for invoking the Spaces feature.

✓ Secondary Mouse Button Mouse Button 3 Mouse Button 4 -	**Figure 34** If you have a multi- button mouse, you can choose a button to invoke Spaces.

✓ ^ Arrow Keys ⌘ Arrow Keys ⌥ Arrow Keys -	**Figure 35** You can also set a shortcut key to cycle through all spaces...

✓ ^ Number Keys ⌘ Number Keys ⌥ Number Keys -	**Figure 36** ...and to go directly to a specific space.

To set Spaces shortcuts

1. Follow steps 1 through 3 under "To enable & configure Spaces" on page 178 to open the Spaces preferences panel (**Figure 24**).

   or

   Choose Open Spaces Preferences from the Spaces menu (**Figure 26**).

2. Choose options from the pop-up menus at the bottom of the Spaces panel (**Figure 24**):

   ▲ **To activate Spaces** enables you to choose a shortcut key (**Figure 33**) and mouse button (**Figure 34**) to display the spaces panes (**Figures 22** and **27**).

   ▲ **To switch between spaces** enables you to choose a shortcut key combination (**Figure 35**) to cycle through all spaces.

   ▲ **To switch directly to a space** enables you to choose a shortcut key combination (**Figure 36**) to switch directly to a specific space.

✔ Tip

■ If you hold down the Shift, Control, Option, or ⌘ key while displaying any of the pop-up menus, the menu changes to reflect the key(s) being held, thus offering additional shortcut key options.

Application Basics

Applications

Applications, which are also known as *programs*, are software packages you use to get work done. Here are some examples:

- ◆ **Word processors**, such as TextEdit, iWork's Pages, and Microsoft Office's Word, are used to write letters, reports, and other text-based documents.

- ◆ **Spreadsheets**, such as iWork's Numbers and Microsoft Office's Excel, have built-in calculation features that are useful for creating number-based documents such as worksheets and charts.

- ◆ **Databases**, such as FileMaker Pro, are used to organize information, such as the names and addresses of customers or the artists and titles in a music collection.

- ◆ **Personal information management** programs, such as Address Book and iCal, help you keep track of contacts and appointments.

- ◆ **Presentation** programs, such as iWork's Keynote and Microsoft Office's Power-Point, are used to create presentations and animations.

- ◆ **Graphics** programs, such as Adobe Photoshop, are used to work with images.

- ◆ **Utility** software, such as Disk Utility and Activity Monitor, performs tasks to manage computer files or operations or keep your computer in good working order.

✔ Tips

- ■ Your Macintosh comes with some application software, most of which is discussed throughout this book.

- ■ Make sure the software you buy is Mac OS-compatible.

Multitasking & the Dock

Mac OS uses a form of *multitasking*, which makes it possible for more than one application to be open at the same time. Only one application, however, can be active. You must make an application active to work with it. Other open applications continue running in the background.

Mac OS X uses *preemptive multitasking*, a type of multitasking in which the operating system can interrupt a currently running task to run another task, as needed.

✔ Tips

■ Mac OS X also features *protected memory*, a memory management system in which each program is prevented from modifying or corrupting the memory partition of another program. This means that if one application freezes up, your computer won't freeze up. You can continue using the other applications that are running.

■ One application that is always open is Finder, which I cover in detail in **Chapters 2** through **4**.

■ The active application is the one whose name appears at the top of the application menu—the menu to the right of the Apple menu—on the menu bar (**Figure 3**). The application menu is covered on page 190.

To learn which applications are running

Look at the Dock. A tiny blue bubble appears beneath each application that is running (**Figure 1**).

Figure 1 A tiny blue bubble appears beneath each open application. Click an icon to make its application active.

Figure 2 When you hold down ⌃ ⌘ and press [Tab], icons for each open application appear onscreen.

Figure 3 The name of the active application appears at the top of the application menu.

To switch from one open application to another

In the Dock (**Figure 1**), click the icon for the application you want to activate.

Or

1. Hold down ⌃ ⌘ and press [Tab], [←], or [→]. A large icon for each open application appears onscreen (**Figure 2**).

2. While holding down ⌃ ⌘, press [Tab], [←], or [→] repeatedly to cycle though the icons until the one you want to activate is selected. Release the keys.

   or

   Click the icon for the application you want to activate (**Figure 2**).

The windows for the application you selected come to the front and the application name appears on the Application menu (**Figure 3**).

✔ Tips

- Another way to activate an application is to click any of its windows. This brings the window to the foreground onscreen and makes the application active.

- You can also use Exposé to activate an application's windows. I explain how to use Exposé on page 172.

SWITCHING APPLICATIONS

185

Using Applications & Creating Documents

You use an application by opening, or *launching*, it. It loads into the computer's memory. Its menu bar replaces the Finder's menu bar and offers commands that can be used only with that application. It may also display a document window and tools specific to that program.

Most applications create *documents*—files written in a format understood by the application. When you save documents, they remain on disk so you can open, edit, print, or just view them at a later date.

For example, you may use iWork's Pages application to write a letter. When you save the letter, it becomes a Pages document file that includes all the text and formatting you put into the letter, written in a format that Pages can understand.

Your computer keeps track of applications and documents. It automatically associates documents with the applications that created them. That's how your computer is able to open a document with the correct application when you open the document from the Finder.

✔ Tips

- You can launch an application by opening a document that it created.

- A document created by an application that is not installed on your computer is sometimes referred to as an *orphan document* since no parent application is available. An orphan document usually has a generic document icon (**Figure 4**).

function.xls

Figure 4
An orphan document often has a generic document icon. This example shows a Microsoft Excel document copied to a computer that does not have Excel installed.

TextEdit

Figure 5
Select the icon for the application you want to open.

File	
New Finder Window	⌘N
New Folder	⇧⌘N
New Smart Folder	⌥⌘N
New Burn Folder	
Open	⌘O
Open With	▶
Print	
Close Window	⌘W
Get Info	⌘I
Compress "TextEdit"	
Duplicate	⌘D
Make Alias	⌘L
Quick Look "TextEdit"	⌘Y
Show Original	⌘R
Add To Sidebar	⌘T
Move to Trash	⌘⌫
Eject	⌘E
Burn "TextEdit" to Disc...	
Find	⌘F
Label:	
☒ ▪ ▪ ◡ ◡ ▪ ◡ ▪	

Figure 6
Choose Open from the Finder's File menu.

Figure 7 When you launch TextEdit by opening its application icon, it displays an empty document window.

Figure 8
Select the icon for the document you want to open.

Figure 9 When you launch TextEdit by opening one of its documents, it displays the document.

To launch an application

Double-click the application's icon.

Or

1. Select the application's icon (**Figure 5**).

2. Choose File > Open (**Figure 6**), or press ⌃ ⌘ O.

Or

If an icon for the application is in the sidebar or the Dock, click that icon once.

The application opens (**Figure 7**).

To open a document & launch the application that created it at the same time

Double-click the icon for the document that you want to open.

Or

1. Select the icon for the document that you want to open (**Figure 8**).

2. Choose File > Open (**Figure 6**), or press ⌃ ⌘ O.

Or

If an icon for the document is in the sidebar or the Dock, click that icon once.

If the application that created the document is not already running, it launches. The document appears in an active window (**Figure 9**).

LAUNCHING APPS & OPENING DOCS

To open a document with drag & drop

1. Drag the icon for the document that you want to open onto the icon for the application with which you want to open it.

2. When the application icon becomes selected (**Figure 10**), release the button. The application launches and displays the document (**Figure 9**).

✔ Tips

- Drag and drop is a good way to open a document with an application other than the one that created it.

- Not all applications can read all documents. Dragging a document icon onto the icon for an application that can't open it either won't launch the application, will open the document but display only gibberish, or will display an error message.

- In step 1, the application icon can be in a Finder window (or the desktop), in the sidebar, or on the Dock.

To open a document with the Open With command

1. Select the icon for the document that you want to open (**Figure 8**).

2. Choose File > Open With to display the Open With Submenu (**Figure 11**) and choose the application you want to use to open the file. The application you chose opens and displays the document.

✔ Tip

- The Open With submenu (**Figure 11**) will only list applications that are installed on your computer and are capable of opening the selected document.

Figure 10 Drag the icon for the document you want to open onto the icon for the application you want to open it with.

Figure 11 The Open With submenu lists installed applications that can open a selected document. The options that appear depend on what type of document is selected and what applications are installed on your computer.

Standard Application Menus

Apple's Human Interface Guidelines provide basic recommendations to software developers to ensure consistency from one application to another. Nowhere is this more obvious than in the standard menus that appear in most applications: the application, File, Edit, Window, and Help menus. You'll see these menus with the same kinds of commands over and over in most of the applications you use. This consistency makes it easier to learn Mac OS applications.

The next few pages provide a closer look at the standard menus you'll find in most applications.

✔ Tips

- The Finder, which is covered in **Chapters 2 through 4**, has standard menus similar to the ones discussed here.

- The Finder rules regarding the ellipsis character (**...**) and keyboard shortcuts displayed on menus also apply to applications. **Chapter 2** explains these rules.

The Application Menu

The application menu takes the name of the currently active application—for example, the TextEdit application menu (**Figure 12**) or the iTunes application menu (**Figure 13**). It includes commands for working with the entire application.

To learn about an application

1. From the application menu, choose About *application name* (**Figures 12** and **13**).

2. A window with version and other information appears (**Figure 14**). Read the information it contains.

3. When you're finished reading about the application, click the window's close button.

To set application preferences

1. From the application menu, choose Preferences (**Figures 12** and **13**).

2. The application's Preferences window (**Figure 15**) or dialog appears. Set options as desired.

3. Click the window's close button.

   or

   Click the dialog's OK or Save button.

✔ Tip

■ Preference options vary greatly from one application to another. To learn more about an application's preferences, check its documentation or onscreen help.

Figures 12 & 13
The TextEdit application menu (left) and the iTunes application menu (right).

Figure 14 The about window for TextEdit provides its version number and other information.

Figure 15 TextEdit's Preferences window offers two panes of options you can set to customize the way TextEdit looks and works.

To hide an application

From the application menu, choose Hide *application name* (**Figures 12** and **13**) or press ⌃ ⌘ H. All of the application's windows, as well as its menu bar, are hidden from view.

✔ Tip

- You cannot hide the active application if it is the only application that is open (the Finder) or if all the other open applications are already hidden.

To hide all applications except the active one

From the application menu, choose Hide Others (**Figures 12** and **13**) or press Option ⌃ ⌘ H.

To hide the active application and display another application

Hold down Option while switching to another application.

To display a hidden application

Click the application's icon (or any of its minimized document icons) in the Dock (**Figure 1**).

To unhide all applications

From the application menu, choose Show All (**Figures 12** and **13**).

To quit an application

1. From the application menu, choose Quit *application name* (**Figures 12** and **13**), or press ⌃ ⌘Q.

2. If unsaved documents are open, a dialog appears, asking whether you want to save changes to documents. The appearance of this dialog varies depending on the application that displays it. **Figure 16** shows an example from TextEdit when a single unsaved document is open. Click the appropriate button to save the document(s) or quit without saving (Don't Save).

   The application closes all windows, saves preference files (if applicable), and quits.

✔ Tips

- Closing all of an application's open windows is not the same as quitting. An application normally remains running until you quit it.

- I tell you more about saving documents later on page 197.

- If an application is unresponsive and you cannot access its menus or commands, you can use the Force Quit command to make it stop running. I explain how on page 208.

Figure 16 This dialog appears when you close a TextEdit document that contains unsaved changes.

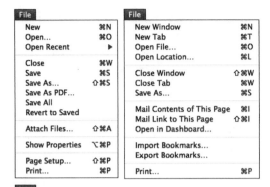

Figures 17, 18, & 19
The file menu in TextEdit (top left), Address Book (bottom left), and Safari (above).

Figure 20 Safari's New Window command opens a new Web browser window that displays the default Home page.

The File Menu

The File menu (**Figures 17, 18**, and **19**) includes commands for working with files or documents. This section discusses the commands most often found under the File menu: New, Open, Close, and Save.

✔ Tip

■ The Page Setup and Print commands are also found on the File menu. These commands are discussed in detail in **Chapter 17**.

To create a new document or window

Choose File > New (**Figure 17**).

Or

Choose File > New Window (**Figure 19**).

Or

Press ⌃ ⌘ N.

A new untitled document (**Figure 7**) or window (**Figure 20**) appears.

✔ Tip

■ As shown in **Figures 17, 18**, and **19**, the exact wording of the command for creating a new document or window varies depending on the application and what the command does. This command, however, is usually the first one on the File menu.

CREATING NEW DOCUMENTS & WINDOWS

To open a file

1. Choose File > Open (**Figure 17**) or press
   ⌃ ⌘ O to display the Open dialog
   (**Figure 21**).

2. Use any combination of the following
   techniques to locate the document you
   want to open:

   ▲ Use the pop-up menu at the top of
   the dialog (**Figure 22**) to backtrack
   from the currently displayed location
   to one of its enclosing folders or to a
   recently accessed folder.

   ▲ Click one of the items in the sidebar
   list on the left side of the dialog to
   view the contents of that item.

   ▲ Press ⇧ ⌃ ⌘ H to view the contents
   of your Home folder.

   ▲ Click one of the items in either list to
   view its contents in the list on the
   right side of the window. (The list
   containing the item you clicked shifts
   to the left if necessary.)

   ▲ Use the scroll bar at the bottom of
   the two lists to shift lists. Shifting lists
   to the right enables you to see your
   path from the item selected in the
   sidebar list.

3. When the name of the file you want to
   open appears in the list on the right side
   of the window, use one of the following
   techniques to open it:

   ▲ Select the file name and then click
   Open or press (Return) or (Enter).

   ▲ Double-click the file name.

Figure 21 TextEdit's Open dialog includes all of the elements found in a standard Open dialog.

Figure 22
The pop-up menu at the top of the Open dialog enables you to backtrack from the currently displayed location to the folders in which it resides or a recently accessed folder.

Figure 23 TextEdit's Open Recent submenu makes it easy to reopen a recently opened document.

Figure 24 When you select a file in the Open dialog, the file's icon or a preview and other information for the file appears. This example shows Preview's Open dialog with a JPEG format file selected. The image in the right side of the dialog is a preview of the file.

Figure 25 The Spotlight feature works within the Open dialog, too. In this example, I've searched for the word *letter* on my entire computer. Selecting one of the search results displays the path to the file at the bottom of the file list.

✔ Tips

- The exact wording of the Open command varies depending on the application and what you want to open. For example, the Open command on Safari's File menu (**Figure 19**) is Open File.

- The Open Recent command, which is available on the File menu of some applications (**Figure 17**), displays a submenu of recently opened items (**Figure 23**). Choose the item you want to open it again.

- As illustrated in **Figures 21** and **24**, the Open dialog has many standard elements that appear in all Open dialogs.

- In step 3, you can only select the files that the application can open; other files will either not appear in the list or will appear in gray. Some applications, such as Microsoft Word, include a pop-up menu that enables you to specify the types of files that appear in the Open dialog.

- In step 3, selecting a file's name in the Open dialog displays its icon or a preview and other information for the file on the right side of the dialog (**Figure 24**).

- Spotlight is also available in the Open dialog. Simply enter a part of the file's title or contents in the Search field within the Open dialog and a list of files that match appears in the dialog (**Figure 25**). Select a file and click Open to open it. I tell you more about Spotlight in **Chapter 5**.

- The sidebar is covered on page 36, file paths are discussed on page 46, and iDisk is covered on page 438.

To close a window

1. Choose File > Close (**Figures 17** and **18**),
   File > Close Window (**Figure 19**), or press
   ⌃ ⌘W.

   or

   Click the window's close button.

2. If the window contains a document with
   changes that have not been saved, a
   dialog sheet similar to the one in **Figure
   16** appears.

   ▲ Click Don't Save to close the window
   without saving the document.

   ▲ Click Cancel or press Esc to keep the
   window open.

   ▲ Click Save or press Return or Enter to
   save the document.

✔ Tip

■ The exact appearance of the dialog sheet
  that appears when you close a document
  with unsaved changes varies depending
  on the application. All versions of the
  dialog should offer the same three
  options, although they may be worded
  differently. **Figure 16** shows the dialog
  that appears in TextEdit.

CLOSING WINDOWS

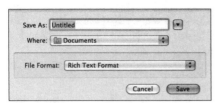

Figure 26 The Save dialog sheet can be collapsed to offer fewer options...

Figure 27 ...or expanded to offer more options.

Figure 28 Use the New Folder dialog to enter a name for a new folder.

To save a document for the first time

1. Choose File > Save (**Figure 17**) or press ⌃⌘S to display the Save dialog (**Figure 26 or 27**).

2. Use the pop-up menu (**Figure 22**) to select a location in which to save the document.

   or

   If necessary, click the triangle beside the Save As field (**Figure 26**) to expand the dialog (**Figure 27**). Then use any combination of the following techniques to select a location in which to save the document:

   ▲ Use the pop-up menu near the top of the dialog (**Figure 22**) to backtrack from the currently displayed location to one of its enclosing folders or a recently accessed folder.

   ▲ Click one of the items in the sidebar list on the left side of the dialog to view the contents of that item.

   ▲ Press Shift⌃⌘H to view the contents of your Home folder.

   ▲ Click one of the items in either list to view its contents on the right side of the dialog. (The list containing the item you clicked shifts to the left if necessary.)

   ▲ Use the scroll bar at the bottom of the two lists to shift lists. Shifting lists to the right enables you to see your path from the item selected in the sidebar.

   ▲ Click the New Folder button to create a new folder inside the currently selected folder. Enter a name for the folder in the New Folder dialog that appears (**Figure 28**), and click Create.

Continued on next page...

SAVING DOCUMENTS

Continued from previous page.

3. When the name of the folder in which you want to save the document appears on the Where pop-up menu, enter a name for the document in the Save As box and click Save.

The document is saved in the location you specified. The name of the file appears in the document window's title bar (**Figure 29**).

✔ Tips

- Not all applications enable you to save documents. Disk Utility, for example, does not include a Save command on its File menu.

- The Save dialog (**Figures 26** and **27**) is also known as the Save Location dialog because it enables you to select a location in which to save a file.

- In step 1, you can also use the Save As command. The first time you save a document, the Save and Save As commands do the same thing: display the Save dialog.

- Some applications automatically append a period and a three-character extension to a file's name when you save it. Extensions are used by Mac OS X and Windows applications to identify the file type. You can toggle the display of file name extensions in Advanced Finder preferences, which I discuss on page 149.

- The sidebar is covered on page 36, file paths are discussed on page 46, and iDisk is covered on page 438.

Figure 29 The name of the newly saved file appears in the window's title bar.

Bullet in close button

Faded document icon

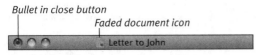

Figure 30 A bullet in the close button of a document window indicates that the document has unsaved changes.

To save changes to a document

Choose File > Save (**Figure 17**), or press ⌃ ⌘ S.

The document is saved in the same location with the same name, thus overwriting the existing version of the document with the new version.

✔ Tip

■ Mac OS X includes three ways to indicate whether a window contains unsaved changes:

▲ A bullet character appears in the close button on the title bar of the window for a document with unsaved changes (**Figure 30**).

▲ The document icon appears faded on the title bar of the window for a document with unsaved changes (**Figure 30**).

▲ In some applications, a bullet character appears in the Window menu beside the name of the window for a document with unsaved changes (**Figure 34**). The Window menu is discussed on page 202.

SAVING DOCUMENT CHANGES

To save a document with a new name or in a new location

1. Choose File > Save As (**Figures 17** and **19**) to display the Save dialog sheet (**Figure 26** or **27**).

2. Follow steps 2 and 3 in the section titled "To save a document for the first time" to select a location, enter a name, and save the document.

✔ Tips

■ Saving a document with a new name or in a new location creates a copy of the existing document. The open document is the copy, not the original. Any further changes you make and save for the open document are saved to the copy rather than the original.

■ If you use the Save dialog to save a document with the same name as a document in the selected location, a confirmation dialog like the one in **Figure 31** appears. You have two options:

▲ Click Cancel or press (Esc) to return to the Save dialog and either change the document's name or the save location.

▲ Click Replace or press (Return) or (Enter) to replace the document on disk with the current document.

Figure 31 A dialog like this appears when you try to save a file with the same name as another file in a folder. This is what the dialog looks like in TextEdit.

Edit	
Undo Typing	⌘Z
Redo Typing	⇧⌘Z
Cut	⌘X
Copy	⌘C
Paste	⌘V
Paste and Match Style	⌥⇧⌘V
Delete	
Complete	⌥⎋
Select All	⌘A
Insert	▶
Add Link...	⌘K
Find	▶
Spelling and Grammar	▶
Substitutions	▶
Transformations	▶
Speech	▶
Special Characters...	⌥⌘T

Edit	
Undo Add to Group	⌘Z
Redo	⇧⌘Z
Cut	⌘X
Copy	⌘C
Paste	⌘V
Delete Card	
Remove From Group	
Select All	⌘A
Find	▶
Spotlight: "John Aabbott"	
Rename Group	
Edit Smart Group	
Edit Card	⌘L
Edit Distribution List...	
Special Characters...	⌥⌘T

Figures 32 & 33
The Edit menus for TextEdit (top) and Address Book (bottom).

The Edit Menu

The Edit menu (**Figures 32** and **33**) includes commands for modifying the contents of a document. Here's a quick list of the commands you're likely to find, along with their standard keyboard equivalents:

◆ **Undo** (⌃⌘Z) reverses the last editing action you made.

◆ **Redo** (Shift ⌃⌘Z) reverses the last undo.

◆ **Cut** (⌃⌘X) removes a selection from the document and puts a copy of it in the Clipboard.

◆ **Copy** (⌃⌘C) puts a copy of a selection in the Clipboard.

◆ **Paste** (⌃⌘V) inserts the contents of the Clipboard into the document at the insertion point or replaces selected text in the document with the contents of the Clipboard.

◆ **Clear** or **Delete** removes a selection from the document. This is the same as pressing (Delete) when document contents are selected.

◆ **Select All** (⌃⌘A) selects all text or objects in the document.

✔ Tips

■ Not all Edit menu commands are available in all applications at all times.

■ Edit menu commands usually work with selected text or graphic objects in a document.

■ Most Edit menu commands are discussed in greater detail in **Chapter 11**, which covers TextEdit.

The Window Menu

The Window menu (**Figures 34** and **35**) includes commands for working with open document windows as well as a list of the open windows.

✔ Tips

- The windows within applications have the same basic parts and controls as Finder windows, which are discussed in detail on page 26.

- A bullet character beside the name of a window in the Window menu (**Figure 34**) indicates that the window contains a document with unsaved changes.

To zoom a window

Choose Window > Zoom (**Figures 34** and **35**).

The window toggles between its full size and a custom size you create with the window's size control.

✔ Tip

- I explain how to resize a window with the size control on page 29.

To minimize a window

Choose Window > Minimize (**Figures 34** and **35**), or press ⌃ ⌘ M.

Or

Click the Minimize button on the window's title bar.

The window shrinks down to the size of an icon and slips into the Dock (**Figure 36**).

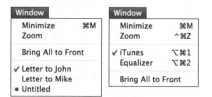

Figures 34 & 35 The Window menus for TextEdit (left) and iTunes (right).

Figure 36 The icon for a minimized window appears in the Dock. If you look closely, you can see a tiny icon for the application in which it is open.

ZOOMING & MINIMIZING WINDOWS

To display a minimized window

With the application active, choose the window's name from the Window menu (**Figures 34** and **35**).

Or

Click the window's icon in the Dock (**Figure 36**).

The window expands out of the Dock and appears onscreen.

To bring all of an application's windows to the front

Choose Window > Bring All to Front (**Figures 34** and **35**).

All of the application's open windows are displayed on top of open windows for other applications.

✔ Tip

■ Mac OS X allows an application's windows to be mingled in layers with other applications' windows.

To activate a window

Choose the window's name from the Window menu (**Figures 34** and **35**).

DISPLAYING WINDOWS

The Help Menu

The Help menu (**Figures 37** and **38**) includes commands for viewing onscreen help information specific to the application. Choosing the primary Help command opens the application's Help window with information and links (**Figure 39**).

Figures 37 & 38 The Help menu for TextEdit (top) and Preview (bottom).

✔ Tips

■ The first option on an application's Help menu is a Spotlight search field. I explain how to use Spotlight in **Chapter 5**.

■ Onscreen help is covered in **Chapter 25**.

■ Although the Help menu may only have one command for a simple application (**Figures 37** and **38**), it can have multiple commands to access different kinds of help for more complex applications.

Figure 39 Choosing an application's primary help command displays its help feature.

Figure 40 The Spelling dialog in TextEdit is an example of a modeless dialog—you can interact with the document while the dialog is displayed.

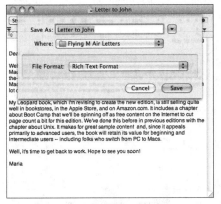

Figure 41 A standard Save Location dialog sheet is an example of a document modal dialog—you must address and dismiss it before you can continue working with the document it is attached to.

Figure 42 An application modal dialog like this one requires your attention before you can continue working with the application.

Dialogs

Mac OS applications use dialogs to tell you things and get information from you. Think of them as the way your computer has a conversation—or dialog—with you.

Mac OS X has three main types of dialogs:

◆ *Modeless* dialogs enable you to work with the dialog while interacting with document windows. These dialogs usually have their own window controls to close and move them (**Figure 40**).

◆ *Document modal* dialogs usually appear as dialog sheets attached to a document window (**Figure 41**). You must address and dismiss these dialogs before you can continue working with the window, although you can switch to another window or application while the dialog is displayed.

◆ *Application modal* dialogs appear as movable dialogs (**Figure 42**). These dialogs must be addressed and dismissed before you can continue working with the application, although you can switch to another application while the dialog is displayed.

✔ Tips

■ You don't need to remember *modeless* vs. *modal* terminology to work with Mac OS X. Just understand how the dialogs differ and what the differences mean.

■ Some dialogs are very similar from one application to another. This chapter covers some of these standard dialogs, including Open (**Figure 21**), Save Location (**Figures 25**, **26**, and **41**), Save Changes (**Figures 16** and **42**), and Replace Confirmation (**Figure 31**). Two more standard dialogs—Page Setup and Print— are covered in **Chapter 17**.

To use dialog parts

◆ Click a *pane button* to view a *pane* full of related options (**Figure 43**).

◆ Use *scroll bars* to view the contents of *scrolling lists* (**Figure 44**). Click a list item once to select it or to enter it in a combination box (**Figure 44**).

◆ Enter text or numbers into *entry fields* (**Figure 45**), including those that are part of *combination boxes* (**Figure 44**).

◆ Click a *pop-up menu* (**Figures 44** and **45**) to display its options. Click a menu option to choose it.

◆ Click a *check box* (**Figure 46**) to toggle it on or off. (A check box is turned on when a check mark or X appears inside it.)

◆ Click a *radio button* (**Figure 46**) to choose its option. (A radio button is chosen when a bullet appears inside it.)

◆ Drag a slider control (**Figures 44** and **46**) to change a setting.

◆ Consult a preview area (**Figure 43**) to see the effects of your changes.

◆ Click a push button (**Figures 43** and **45**) to activate it.

Pane　　　Pane buttons　　　Preview area

Figure 43 The Screen Saver pane of Desktop & Screen Saver preferences.　Push buttons

Scrolling lists　　　Scroll bar　Combination box

Figure 44 The Font panel.　　　Slider control

Pop-up menu　Entry fields

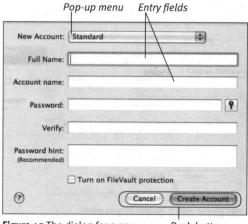

Figure 45 The dialog for a new user account to your Mac.　Push buttons

Check box   Slider control   Radio button

Figure 46 Dock preferences.

✔ Tips

- An entry field with a colored border around it is the active field (**Figure 45**). Typing automatically enters text in this field. You can advance from one entry field to the next by pressing Tab.

- If an entry field has a pair of arrows or triangles beside it you can click the triangles to increase or decrease a value already in the field.

- The default push button is the one that pulsates. You can always select a default button by pressing Enter and often by pressing Return.

- You can usually select a Cancel button (**Figure 45**) by pressing Esc.

- You can select as many check boxes (**Figure 46**) in a group as you like.

- One and only one radio button in a group can be selected (**Figure 46**). If you try to select a second radio button, the first button becomes deselected.

- If you click the Cancel button in a dialog (**Figure 45**), any options you set are lost.

- To select multiple items in a scrolling list, hold down ⌘ while clicking each one. Be aware that not all dialogs support multiple selections in scrolling lists.

- There are other standard controls in Mac OS X dialogs. These are the ones you'll encounter most often.

Force Quitting Applications

Occasionally, an application may freeze, lock up, or otherwise become unresponsive. When this happens, you can no longer work with that application or its documents.

The Force Quit command (**Figure 47**) enables you to force an unresponsive application to quit. Then you can either restart it or continue working with other applications.

✖ Warning!

- When you use the Force Quit command to quit an application, any unsaved changes in that application's open documents may be lost. Use the Force Quit command only as a last resort, when the Quit command cannot be used.

✔ Tips

- Mac OS X's protected memory, which is discussed on page 184, makes it possible for applications to continue running properly on your computer when one application locks up.

- If more than one application experiences problems during a work session, you might find it helpful to restart your computer. This clears out RAM and forces your computer to reload all applications and documents into memory.

To force quit an application

1. Choose Apple > Force Quit (**Figure 47**), or press Option ⌘ Esc.

2. In the Force Quit Applications window that appears (**Figure 48**), select the application you want to force to quit.

3. Click Force Quit.

4. A confirmation dialog like the one in **Figure 49** appears. Click Force Quit. The application immediately quits.

Figure 47
Choose Force Quit from the Apple menu.

Figure 48 Select the application you want to force to quit.

Figure 49 Use this dialog to confirm that you really do want to force quit the application.

✔ Tip

- If you selected Finder in step 2, the button to click in step 3 is labeled Relaunch.

Using
TextEdit

Figure 1
The TextEdit application icon.

TextEdit

Figure 2
A TextEdit document's icon.

Letter

TextEdit

TextEdit (**Figure 1**) is a text editing application that comes with Mac OS. As its name implies, TextEdit lets you create, open, edit, and print text documents (**Figure 2**), including the "Read Me" files that come with many applications.

This chapter explains how to use TextEdit to create, edit, format, open, and save documents.

✔ Tips

- TextEdit can open and save Microsoft Word 2007 and earlier format files. This makes it possible to work with and create Microsoft Word documents, even if you don't have Microsoft Word.

- Although TextEdit offers many of the features found in a word processing application, it falls far short of the feature list of word processors such as Microsoft Word and the word processing components of iWork's Pages.

- If you're new to computers, don't skip this chapter. It not only explains how to use TextEdit but provides instructions for basic text editing skills—such as text entry and the Copy, Cut, and Paste commands —that you'll use in all Mac OS applications.

Launching & Quitting TextEdit

Like any other application, you must launch TextEdit before you can use it. This loads it into your computer's memory so your computer can work with it.

To launch TextEdit

Double-click the TextEdit application icon in the Applications folder window (**Figure 3**).

Or

1. Select the TextEdit application icon in the Applications folder window (**Figure 3**).

2. Choose File > Open, or press ⌘O.

   TextEdit launches. An untitled document window appears (**Figure 4**).

✔ Tip

- As illustrated in **Figure 4**, the TextEdit document window has the same standard window parts found in Finder windows. I tell you how to use Finder windows in **Chapter 2**; TextEdit and other application windows work the same way.

Figure 3 You can find TextEdit in the Applications folder.

Figure 4 A TextEdit document window has the same basic parts as a Finder window.

LAUNCHING TEXTEDIT

Figure 5
Choose Quit
TextEdit from
the TextEdit
menu.

Figure 6 A dialog sheet like this appears when you quit
TextEdit with an unsaved document open.

Figure 7 A dialog like this appears when you quit Text-
Edit with multiple unsaved documents open.

To quit TextEdit

1. Choose TextEdit > Quit TextEdit (**Figure 5**), or press ⌃ ⌘ Q.

2. If a single unsaved document is open, a dialog sheet like the one in **Figure 6** appears, attached to the document window.

   ▲ Click **Don't Save** to quit without saving the document.

   ▲ Click **Cancel** or press Esc to return to the application without quitting.

   ▲ Click **Save** or press Return or Enter to save the document.

   or

   If multiple unsaved documents are open, a dialog like the one in **Figure 7** appears:

   ▲ Click **Discard Changes** to quit TextEdit without saving any of the documents.

   ▲ Click **Cancel** or press Esc to return to the application without quitting.

   ▲ Click **Review Changes** or press Return or Enter to view each unsaved document with a dialog like the one in **Figure 6** to decide whether you want to save it.

   TextEdit closes all windows and quits.

✔ Tip

■ You learn more about saving TextEdit documents on page 230.

Entering & Editing Text

You enter text into a TextEdit document by typing it in. Don't worry about making mistakes; you can fix them as you type or when you're finished. This section tells you how.

✔ Tip

■ The text entry and editing techniques covered in this section work exactly the same in most word processors, as well as many other Mac OS applications.

To enter text

Type the text you want to enter. It appears at the blinking insertion point (**Figure 8**).

✔ Tips

■ It is not necessary to press Return at the end of a line. When the text you type reaches the end of the line, it automatically begins a new line. This is called *word wrap* and is a feature of all word processors. By default, in TextEdit, word wrap is determined by the width of the document window.

■ The insertion point moves as you type.

■ To correct an error as you type, press Delete. This key deletes the character to the left of the insertion point.

Figure 8 The text you type appears at the blinking insertion point.

Figure 9
Position the pointer...

Figure 10
...and click to move the insertion point.

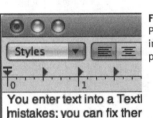

Figure 11
Position the insertion point...

Figure 12
...and type the text that you want to appear.

To move the insertion point

Press ⬅, ➡, ⬆, or ⬇ to move the insertion point left, right, up, or down one character or line at a time.

Or

1. Position the pointer, which looks like an I-beam pointer, where you want the insertion point to appear (**Figure 9**).

2. Click once. The insertion point appears at the pointer (**Figure 10**).

✔ Tips

■ Since the text you type appears at the insertion point, it's a good idea to know where the insertion point is before you start typing.

■ When moving the insertion point with the mouse or trackpad, you must click to complete the move. If you simply point with the I-beam pointer, the insertion point will stay right where it is (**Figure 9**).

To insert text

1. Position the insertion point where you want the text to appear (**Figure 11**).

2. Type the text that you want to insert. The text is inserted at the insertion point (**Figure 12**).

✔ Tip

■ Word wrap changes automatically to accommodate inserted text.

To select text by dragging

Drag the I-beam pointer over the text you want to select (**Figure 13**).

To select text with Shift-click

1. Position the insertion point at the beginning of the text you want to select (**Figure 14**).

2. Hold down (Shift) and click at the end of the text you want to select. All text between the insertion point's original position and where you clicked becomes selected (**Figure 15**).

✔ Tip

■ This is a good way to select large blocks of text. After positioning the insertion point as instructed in step 1, use the scroll bar to scroll to the end of the text you want to select. Then Shift-click as instructed in step 2 to make the selection.

To select a single word

Double-click the word (**Figure 16**).

✔ Tip

■ In some applications, such as Microsoft Word, double-clicking a word also selects the space after the word.

To select all document contents

Choose Edit > Select All (**Figure 17**), or press ⌘ A.

✔ Tip

■ TextEdit and other applications offer other selection techniques. The techniques on this page work in every application.

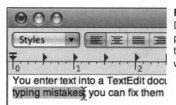
Figure 13
Drag the I-beam pointer over the text that you want to select.

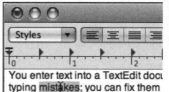
Figure 14 Position the insertion point at the beginning of the text you want to select.

Figure 15 Hold down (Shift) and click at the end of the text you want to select.

Figure 16
Double-click the word that you want to select.

Figure 17
The Edit menu.

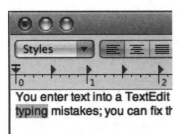

Figure 18 Select the text that you want to delete.

Figure 19 When you press Delete, the selected text disappears.

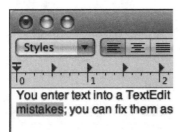

Figure 20 Select the text that you want to replace.

Figure 21 The text you type replaces the selected text.

To delete text

1. Select the text that you want to delete (**Figure 18**).

2. Press Delete or Del. The selected text disappears (**Figure 19**).

✔ Tips

- You can delete a character to the left of the insertion point by pressing Delete. You can delete a character to the right of the insertion point by pressing Del.

- Not all keyboards include the Del key. For example, the Del key cannot be found on a MacBook Pro keyboard. This key exists on the Apple keyboard introduced with iMacs in Summer 2007, but it is labeled with the word *delete* followed by a symbol like this: ⌦.

To replace text

1. Select the text that you want to replace (**Figure 20**).

2. Type the new text. The selected text is replaced by what you type (**Figure 21**).

Basic Text Formatting

TextEdit also offers formatting features that you can use to change the appearance of text.

◆ **Font formatting** enables you to change the appearance of text characters. This includes the font typeface and family, character style, character size, and character color.

◆ **Text formatting** enables you to change the appearance of entire paragraphs of text. This includes alignment, line spacing, and ruler settings such as tabs and indentation.

✔ Tips

■ This chapter introduces the most commonly used formatting options in TextEdit. You can further explore these and other options on your own.

■ Some text formatting options are on the ruler. If the ruler is not showing, you can display it by choosing Format > Text > Show Ruler or by pressing ⌃ ⌘ R.

To apply font formatting

1. Select the text you want to apply font formatting to (**Figure 22**).

2. Use any combination of the following techniques to apply font formatting:

   ▲ Choose Format > Font > Show Fonts (**Figure 23**), or press ⌃ ⌘ T, to display the Fonts panel (**Figure 24**). Set options in the Font panel as desired. You can immediately see the results of your changes in the document window behind the Fonts panel (**Figure 25**); make changes if you don't like what you see. You can also select different text and format it without closing the Fonts panel window.

Figure 22 Select the text you want to format.

Figure 23 The Font submenu under the Format menu.

Figure 24 The Fonts panel.

Figure 25 The changes you make in the Fonts panel are immediately applied to the selected text.

Figure 26
A check mark appears beside the name of each style applied to selected text.

Figure 27
You can use the Styles pop-up menu to apply certain font styles to selected text.

Table 1

Shortcut Keys for TextEdit Font Formatting	
Keystroke	**Formatting Applied**
⌃ ⌘ B	Bold
⌃ ⌘ I	Italic
⌃ ⌘ U	Underline
⌃ ⌘ +	Bigger
⌃ ⌘ −	Smaller

▲ Choose options from the Format menu's Font submenu (**Figure 23**) to apply formatting. You can choose any combination of options. A check mark appears beside the type of formatting applied to selected text (**Figure 26**).

▲ Choose an option from the Styles pop-up menu on the ruler (**Figure 27**). The Default option removes formatting applied with the Styles pop-up menu.

▲ Press the shortcut key for the type of formatting you want to apply. Consult **Table 1** for a list.

✔ Tips

■ Generally speaking, a font is a style of typeface.

■ You can apply more than one style to text (**Figure 26**).

■ A check mark appears on the Font submenu beside each style applied to a selection.

■ To remove an applied style, choose it from the Font submenu again.

■ Some styles are automatically applied when you select a specific typeface for a font family in the Font panel (**Figure 25**). Similarly, if you select a typeface in the Font panel, certain style options become unavailable for characters with that typeface applied. For example, if you apply Futura Medium Italic font, as shown in **Figure 25**, the Bold option on the Font submenu cannot be applied to that text.

■ I tell you more about fonts and explain how to use the Fonts panel in **Chapter 16**.

To apply text formatting

1. Select the paragraph(s) you want to format.

2. Use any combination of the following techniques to apply font formatting:

   ▲ Choose an option from the Format menu's Text submenu (**Figure 28**) to apply formatting.

   ▲ Click one of the alignment buttons on the ruler (**Figure 29**).

   ▲ Choose an option from the Line and paragraph spacing pop-up menu on the ruler (**Figure 30**).

   ▲ Choose an option from the Lists bullets and numbering pop-up menu on the ruler (**Figure 31**).

   ▲ Press the shortcut key for the type of formatting you want to apply. Consult **Table 2** for a list.

✔ Tip

■ Alignment and spacing options affect all lines in a paragraph.

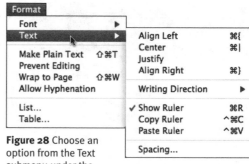

Figure 28 Choose an option from the Text submenu under the Format menu.

Figure 29 You can use buttons and pop-up menus on the ruler to set alignment, line spacing, bullet and numbering formats, and tabs.

Figure 30 Use the Line and paragraph spacing pop-up menu to set line spacing for selected paragraphs.

Figure 31 Use the List bullets and numbering pop-up menu to set bullet or numbered list formatting for the selected paragraphs.

Table 2

Shortcut Keys for TextEdit Text Formatting	
Keystroke	**Formatting Applied**
⌃ ⌘ {	Align Left
⌃ ⌘ |	Center
⌃ ⌘ }	Align Right

APPLYING TEXT FORMATTING

Figure 32 Drag the tab off the ruler. (The pointer disappears as you do this, so it isn't easy to illustrate.)

Figure 33 Drag one of the tab icons from the top half of the ruler into position on the ruler. Although the pointer disappears as you drag, a tiny box with the tab location in it appears as you drag.

Figure 34 Start by setting tabs and positioning the insertion point at the beginning of the line.

Figure 35 If desired, enter text at the beginning of the line.

Figure 36 Press ⟨Tab⟩ and enter text at the first tab stop.

Figure 37 The first line of a table created with tabs.

Figure 38 A complete table. Note how the text lines up with each type of tab stop.

To set tab stops

Add and remove tab stops from the bottom half of the ruler as follows:

◆ To remove a tab stop, drag it from the ruler into the document window (**Figure 32**). When you release the button, the tab is removed.

◆ To add a tab stop, drag one of the tab icons on the ruler—left, center, right, or decimal—into position on the ruler (**Figure 33**). When you release the button, the tab is placed.

✔ Tips

■ A tab stop is the position the insertion point moves to when you press ⟨Tab⟩.

■ Tab settings affect entire paragraphs. When you press ⟨Return⟩ to begin a new paragraph, the tab stops you set for the current paragraph are carried forward.

To use tab stops

1. Add and remove tab stops as instructed above.

2. Position the insertion point at the beginning of the paragraph for which tab stops are set (**Figure 34**).

3. If desired, enter text at the beginning of the line (**Figure 35**).

4. Press ⟨Tab⟩.

5. Enter text at the tab stop (**Figure 36**).

6. Repeat steps 4 and 5 until you have entered text as desired at all tab stops. **Figure 37** shows an example.

7. Press ⟨Return⟩.

8. Repeat steps 2 through 7 for each paragraph you want to use the tab stops for. **Figure 38** shows a completed table using tab stops.

To set indentation

1. Select the paragraph(s) for which you want to set indentation (**Figure 39**).

2. Drag one of the icons on the end of the ruler (**Figure 40**) to the left or right:

   ▲ To set the first line indentation for a paragraph, drag the horizontal rectangle icon.

   ▲ To set the left indent, drag the downward-facing triangle on the left end of the ruler.

   ▲ To set the right indent, drag the downward-facing triangle on the right end of the ruler.

As you drag, a yellow box with a measurement inside it indicates the exact position of the indent. When you release a marker, the text shifts accordingly (**Figure 41**).

✔ Tip

■ TextEdit Help refers to the left and right indents as margins. Technically speaking, this is incorrect terminology, since margins normally refer to the area between the printable area and edge of the paper.

Figure 39 Select the paragraphs you want to format.

Figure 40 The indent markers on TextEdit's ruler.

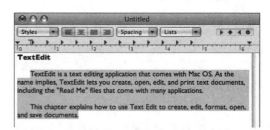

Figure 41 In this example, the first line indent marker was shifted to the right, thus indenting just the first line of each paragraph.

SETTING INDENTATION

Edit	
Undo Center	⌘Z
Redo Underline	⇧⌘Z
Cut	⌘X
Copy	⌘C
Paste	⌘V
Paste and Match Style	⌥⇧⌘V
Delete	
Complete	⌥⌥
Select All	⌘A
Insert	▶
Add Link...	⌘K
Find	▶
Spelling and Grammar	▶
Substitutions	▶
Transformations	▶
Speech	▶
Special Characters...	⌥⌘T

Figure 42 The Edit menu with Undo and Redo commands displayed. If one of these commands were not available, it would be gray.

Undoing & Redoing Actions

The Undo command enables you to reverse your last action, thus offering an easy way to fix errors immediately after you make them. The Redo command, which is available only when your last action was to use the Undo command, reverses the undo action.

✔ Tips

- The Undo and Redo commands are available in most applications and can be found at the top of the Edit menu.

- TextEdit supports multiple levels of undo (and redo). That means you can undo (or redo) several actions, in the reverse order that they were performed (or undone).

- The exact wording of the Undo (and Redo) command depends on what was last done (or undone). For example, if the last thing you did was to center selected text, the Undo command will be Undo Center (**Figure 42**).

To undo the last action

Choose Edit > Undo (**Figure 42**), or press ⌘ ⌘ Z. The last thing you did is undone.

✔ Tip

- To undo multiple actions, choose Edit > Undo repeatedly.

To redo an action

After using the Undo command, choose Edit > Redo (**Figure 42**), or press Shift ⌘ ⌘ Z. The last thing you undid is redone.

✔ Tip

- To redo multiple actions, choose Edit > Redo repeatedly.

Copy, Cut, & Paste

The Copy, Cut, and Paste commands enable you to duplicate or move document contents. Text that is copied or cut is placed on the Clipboard. You can then paste it into a document.

✔ Tips

- Almost all Mac OS-compatible applications include the Copy, Cut, and Paste commands on the Edit menu. These commands work very much the same in all applications.

- The Copy, Cut, and Paste commands work between applications because the Clipboard is shared by all Mac OS applications. So, for example, you can copy text from a TextEdit document and then paste it into a Microsoft Word document.

- The Copy, Cut, and Paste commands also work with images and other content.

To copy text

1. Select the text that you want to copy (**Figure 43**).

2. Choose Edit > Copy (**Figure 44**), or press ⌃ ⌘ C.

   The text is copied to the Clipboard so it can be pasted elsewhere. The original remains in the document.

To cut text

1. Select the text that you want to cut (**Figure 43**).

2. Choose Edit > Cut (**Figure 44**), or press ⌃ ⌘ X.

   The text is copied to the Clipboard so it can be pasted elsewhere. The original is removed from the document.

Figure 43 Select the text you want to copy or cut.

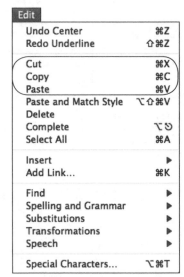

Figure 44 The Copy, Cut, and Paste commands are all on the Edit menu.

Figure 45 Position the insertion point where you want the contents of the Clipboard to appear.

Figure 46 The contents of the Clipboard are pasted into the document.

To paste Clipboard contents

1. Position the insertion point where you want the Clipboard contents to appear (**Figure 45**).

2. Choose Edit > Paste (**Figure 44**), or press ⌃ ⌘ V.

   The Clipboard's contents are pasted into the document (**Figure 46**).

✔ Tips

- The Clipboard contains only the last item that was copied or cut. Using the Paste command, therefore, pastes in the most recently cut or copied selection.

- Right after using the Paste command, what's in the Clipboard? Answer: The same thing that was in it right before using the Paste command. Using the paste command pastes a *copy* of what's on the Clipboard. That content remains on the Clipboard to use again and again until you use the Copy or Cut command again to replace it with new content.

COPYING, CUTTING, & PASTING TEXT

Find & Replace

TextEdit's find and replace features enable you to quickly locate or replace occurrences of text strings in your document.

✔ Tip

■ Most word processing and page layout applications include find and replace features. Although these features are somewhat limited in TextEdit, full-featured applications such as Microsoft Word and Adobe InDesign enable you to search for text, formatting, and other document elements as well as plain text.

To find text

1. Choose Edit > Find > Find (**Figure 47**), or press ⌘F. The Find dialog appears (**Figure 48**).

2. Enter the text that you want to find in the Find field.

3. To find text from the insertion point forward (rather than the entire document), turn off the Wrap Around check box.

4. To perform a case-sensitive search, turn off the Ignore Case check box.

5. To indicate how TextEdit should match the Find text, select the appropriate option from the pop-up menu (**Figure 49**).

6. Click Next, or press Return or Enter. If the text you entered in the Find field is found, it is highlighted in the document.

✔ Tip

■ To find subsequent or previous occurrences of the Find field entry, choose Edit > Find > Find Next or Edit > Find > Find Previous (**Figure 47**) or press ⌘G or Shift ⌘G.

Figure 47
You'll find commands for finding and replacing text on the Find submenu under the Edit menu.

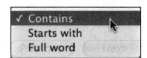

Figure 48 The Find dialog.

Figure 49 Use this pop-up menu to indicate how TextEdit should match the Find text.

Figure 50 You can set up the Find dialog to find and replace text.

To replace text

1. Choose Edit > Find > Find (**Figure 47**), or press ⌃⌘F. The Find dialog appears (**Figure 48**).

2. Enter the text that you want to replace in the Find field.

3. Enter the replacement text in the Replace with field (**Figure 50**).

4. To replace text from the insertion point forward (rather than the entire document), turn off the Wrap Around check box.

5. To perform a case-sensitive search, turn off the Ignore Case check box.

6. To indicate how TextEdit should match the Find text, select the appropriate option from the pop-up menu (**Figure 49**).

7. Click the buttons at the bottom of the Find dialog to find and replace text:

   ▲ **Replace All** replaces all occurrences of the Find word with the Replace word.

   ▲ **Replace** replaces the currently selected occurrence of the Find word with the Replace word.

   ▲ **Replace & Find** replaces the currently selected occurrence of the Find word with the Replace word and then selects the next occurrence of the Find word.

   ▲ **Previous** selects the previous occurrence of the Find word.

   ▲ **Next** selects the next occurrence of the Find word.

8. When you're finished replacing text, click the Find dialog's close button to dismiss it.

✖ Warning!

■ Use the Replace All button with care! It will not give you an opportunity to preview and approve any of the replacements it makes.

Checking Spelling & Grammar

TextEdit includes a spelling checker and a grammar checker. These two features can be used either manually, to check a document that is fully or partially completed, or automatically, to check a document as you create it. Together, they can help you identify problems in your documents so you can correct them before sharing them with others.

✔ Tip

■ Don't depend solely on the spelling and grammar checkers in TextEdit (or any other application, for that matter) to make your documents perfect. Spelling checkers will not identify misspelled words that correctly spell other words— for example, *then* and *them*. Grammar checkers cannot identify all grammatical errors—and sometimes they inaccurately identify errors that aren't errors at all. These tools are no substitute for a good, old-fashioned proofreading!

Figure 51
Use commands on the Spelling and Grammar submenu to check spelling and grammar in your document.

Figure 52 Use the Spelling and Grammar dialog to resolve possible spelling errors.

Figure 53
Be sure to choose the right language from the pop-up menu at the bottom of the Spelling and Grammar dialog.

To manually check spelling

1. Choose Edit > Spelling and Grammar > Show Spelling and Grammar (**Figure 51**), or press Shift ⌃ ⌘ :, to display the Spelling and Grammar dialog and start the spelling check.

   TextEdit selects and underlines the first possible misspelled word it finds. The word appears in a field in the Spelling and Grammar dialog and any suggested corrections appear in a list (**Figure 52**).

2. You have several options:
   ▲ To replace the word with a listed word, select the replacement word and click Change.
   ▲ To enter a new spelling for the word, enter it in the box where the incorrect spelling appears and click Change.
   ▲ To ignore the word, click Ignore.
   ▲ To skip the word and continue checking, click Find Next.
   ▲ To add the word to TextEdit's dictionary, click Learn. TextEdit will never stop at that word again in any document.

3. Repeat step 2 for each word that TextEdit identifies as a possible misspelling.

4. When you're finished checking spelling, click the Spelling and Grammar dialog's close button to dismiss it.

✔ Tip

■ To ensure that TextEdit uses the correct spelling dictionary, choose the language your document is written in from the pop-up menu at the bottom of the Spelling and Grammar dialog (**Figure 53**).

To manually check grammar with spelling

1. Choose Edit > Spelling and Grammar > Check Grammar With Spelling (**Figure** 51) to enable the grammar checker. A check mark appears beside the command on the menu (**Figure 54**) and in the Spelling and Grammar dialog (**Figure** 55) when this feature is enabled.

2. Follow steps 1 through 2 on the previous page to start the spelling and grammar checker and resolve any spelling problems that TextEdit finds.

3. If TextEdit finds a grammar problem, it selects and underlines the problem. The selected text appears in a field in the Spelling and Grammar dialog and any suggested corrections appear in a list. A description of the problem also appears in the dialog. You can see all this in **Figure** 55. You have several options:

   ▲ To replace the text with listed text, select the replacement text and click Change.

   ▲ To use different text, enter it in the box where the incorrect text appears and click Change.

   ▲ To ignore the problem text, click Ignore.

   ▲ To skip the problem text and continue checking, click Find Next.

   ▲ To tell TextEdit never to bother you again about this kind of problem, click Learn.

4. Repeat steps 2 and 3 for each problem that TextEdit identifies.

5. When you're finished checking spelling and grammar, click the Spelling and Grammar dialog's close button to dismiss it.

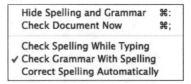

Figure 54 When grammar checking is enabled, a check mark appears beside the Check Grammar With Spelling command on the Grammar and Spelling submenu.

Figure 55 The Grammar checker works a lot like the spelling checker, but it watches out for potential grammar problems.

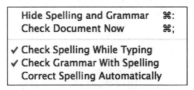

Figure 56 Here's what the Spelling and Grammar submenu looks like with both Check Spelling While Typing and Check Grammar With Spelling enabled.

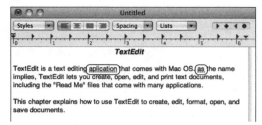

Figure 57 TextEdit identifies potential errors with dashed underlines.

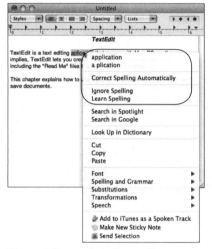

Figure 58 The contextual menu for a potential spelling problem.

Figure 59 The contextual menu for a potential grammar problem.

To check spelling & grammar as you type

1. If necessary, choose Edit > Spelling and Grammar > Check Spelling While Typing (**Figure 51**). A check mark appears beside this menu command to indicate that it is enabled (**Figure 56**).

2. To check grammar as you type, if necessary, choose Edit > Spelling and Grammar > Check Grammar with Spelling to enable grammar checking (**Figure 56**).

   As you enter text in the document, TextEdit checks its spelling (and grammar, if enabled). It places a dashed red underline under each word that isn't in its dictionary and a green dashed underline under each word or phrase that could be a grammar error (**Figure 57**).

3. Manually correct a potential problem with standard text editing techniques covered near the beginning of this chapter.

   or

   Right-click the problem and choose a correction or other option from the contextual menu that appears (**Figure 58** or **59**). The problem word or phrase is resolved as you specified.

✔ Tips

- The Check Spelling While Typing option in TextEdit may automatically be enabled. To disable it, choose Edit > Spelling and Grammar > Check Spelling While Typing (**Figure 56**).

- The Correct Spelling automatically option (**Figure 58**), which is new in TextEdit, automatically replaces an unknown word with the first listed possible replacement word. Use this new feature with care! TextEdit doesn't always get it right!

Saving & Opening Files

When you're finished working with a TextEdit document, you may want to save it. You can then open it another time to review, edit, or print it or send it to someone else who might want to work with it.

To save a document for the first time

1. Choose File > Save (**Figure 60**), or press ⌘ S.

   or

   Choose File > Save As (**Figure 60**), or press Shift ⌘ S.

   The Save As dialog appears (**Figure 61**).

2. Enter a name and select a location for the file.

3. If desired, choose an option from the File Format pop-up menu (**Figure 62**):

4. Click Save, or press Return or Enter.

   The document is saved with the name you entered in the location you specified. The name of the document and a document icon appear on the document's title bar (**Figure 63**).

✔ Tips

- I explain how to use the Save As dialog on page 197.

- There's only one difference between the File menu's Save and Save As commands (**Figure 60**):

  ▲ The Save command opens the Save As dialog only if the document has never been saved.

  ▲ The Save As command *always* opens the Save As dialog.

Figure 60
The File menu includes commands for working with files.

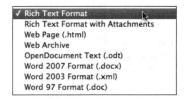

Figure 61 Use the Save As dialog to enter a name and select a location for saving a file.

Figure 62 The File Format pop-up menu enables you to save documents in eight different formats.

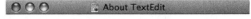

Figure 63 The name of a saved document appears in its title bar, along with a document icon.

SAVING DOCUMENTS

Figure 64
Choose Make Plain Text from the Format menu.

Figure 65 When you save a Plain Text document, TextEdit offers other formatting options. If you're not sure what to choose here, leave it set to the default setting.

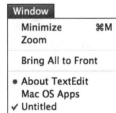

Figure 66 A bullet in the document window's close button...

Figure 67
...or beside its name in the Window menu indicates that the document has unsaved changes.

- By default, TextEdit creates *Rich Text Format (RTF)* files and appends the *.rtf* extension to the files it saves. This extension does not appear unless the Show all file extensions option is enabled in Advanced Finder Preferences, which I discuss on page 149.

- To save a TextEdit document as a plain text document (with a *.txt* extension), choose Format > Make Plain Text (**Figure 64**) or press Shift ⌃ ⌘ T and click OK in the confirmation dialog that may appear. Then follow the steps on the previous page to save the document. As shown in **Figure 65**, the pop-up menu in the Save As dialog offers several Plain Text Encoding options. Keep in mind that if you save a document as a plain text document, any formatting applied to document text will be lost.

- Generally speaking, plain text documents are more compatible than RTF or Word documents and RTF documents are more compatible than Word documents.

To save changes to an existing document

Choose File > Save (**Figure 60**), or press ⌃ ⌘ S. The document is saved. No dialog appears.

✔ Tips

- TextEdit identifies a document with changes that have not been saved by displaying a bullet in the document window's close button (**Figure 66**) and to the left of the document's name in the Window menu (**Figure 67**).

- It's a good idea to save changes to a document frequently as you work with it. This helps prevent loss of data in the event of an application or system crash or power outage.

SAVING DOCUMENTS

231

To save an existing document with a new name or in a new location

1. Choose File > Save As (**Figure 60**).

2. Use the Save As dialog that appears (**Figure 61**) to enter a different name or select a different location (or both) for the file.

3. Click Save, or press ⌷Return⌷ or ⌷Enter⌷.

   A copy of the document is saved with the name you entered in the location you specified. The new document name appears in the document's title bar. The original document remains untouched.

✔ Tip

- You can use the Save As command to create a new document based on an existing document—without overwriting the original document with your changes.

To open a document

1. Choose File > Open (**Figure 60**), or press ⌘ O.

2. Use the Open dialog that appears (**Figure 68**) to locate and select the document that you want to open.

3. Click Open, or press ⌷Return⌷ or ⌷Enter⌷.

✔ Tip

- I explain how to use the Open dialog on page 194.

Figure 68 Use the Open dialog to locate and open a file.

To close a document

1. Choose File > Close (**Figure 60**), or press ⌘ W.

2. If the document contains unsaved changes, a Close dialog like the one in (**Figure 6**) appears.

   ▲ Click Don't Save to close the document without saving it.

   ▲ Click Cancel or press ⌷Esc⌷ to return to the document without closing it.

   ▲ Click Save or press ⌷Return⌷ or ⌷Enter⌷ to save the document.

   The document closes.

Information Management

Figure 1 The Applications folder includes three applications for managing and synchronizing personal information.

Personal Information Management Software

Mac OS X includes three applications (**Figure 1**) to help you keep track of and synchronize personal information:

- ◆ **Address Book** is contact management software. You can use it to record the names and contact information for family members, friends, and business associates.

- ◆ **iCal** is event calendar software. You can use it to record upcoming events as well as to-do list items.

- ◆ **iSync** is synchronization software that enables you to synchronize Address Book and iCal information to compatible Bluetooth or USB mobile phone or Palm OS devices.

In this chapter, I explain how you can get started using these three applications to organize and synchronize your contact and calendar data.

Figure 2 By default, Address Book and iCal are added to the Dock.

✔ Tip

- ■ Icons for Address Book and iCal are automatically added to the Dock (**Figure 2**) as part of a Mac OS X installation.

Address Book

Address Book enables you to keep track of the names, addresses, phone numbers, e-mail addresses, and Web URLs of people you know. The information you store in Address Book's database can be used by Mail to send e-mail messages, iChat to send instant messages, and iCal to invite people to events.

In this chapter, I provide enough information to get you started using Address Book for your contact management needs.

✔ Tip

■ You must have an Internet connection to send e-mail or use iChat. I cover Mail and iChat in **Chapter 19**.

To launch Address Book

Open the Address Book icon in the Applications folder (**Figure 1**).

Or

Click the Address Book icon in the Dock (**Figure 2**).

Address Book's main window appears (**Figure 3**).

✔ Tip

■ If the Address Book window looks more like what's shown in **Figure 4**, you can click the View Card and Columns button in its upper-left corner to expand the view to show all three columns (**Figure 3**).

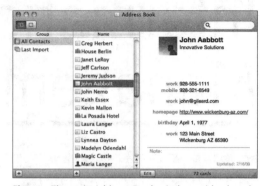

Figure 3 The main Address Book window, with a bunch of records already created.

View Card and Columns
View Card Only

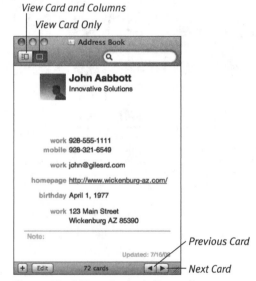

Previous Card
Next Card

Figure 4 The Address Book window can be collapsed to display just one record's card.

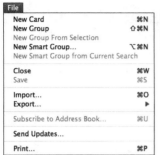

Figure 5
Address Book's
File menu.

Figure 6 When you use the New Card command, Address Book creates an unnamed card record and selects the first field for entry.

Figure 7 Each active field prompts you for entry.

To add a new card

1. Click the Create a new card button (**+**) beneath the Name column in the main Address Book window (**Figure 3**).

   or

   Choose File > New Card (**Figure 5**), or press ⌘ ⌘ N.

   A No Name record is created in the Name column and a blank address card appears beside it, with the First field active (**Figure 6**).

2. Enter information about the contact into appropriate fields. When a field is active, text appears within it to prompt you for information (**Figure 7**). Press Tab or click a field to move from field to field.

3. To change the label that appears beside a field, click the tiny triangles beside it (**Figure 8**) to display a menu (**Figure 9**), and then choose the label you prefer.

Continued on next page...

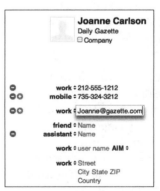

Figure 8
Once you have entered some contact information, buttons and menu icons appear beside field names.

Figure 9
Click the triangles beside a field to display a menu of applicable field labels.

ADDING CONTACT CARDS

Continued from previous page.

4. To add more fields, click the green plus sign button beside a similar field (**Figure 8**). For example, to add another phone number field, click the plus sign beside a phone number. Then enter information and choose a field label as discussed in steps 2 and 3.

5. To remove a field, click the red minus sign button beside it.

6. When you are finished entering information, click the Edit button to view the completed card (**Figure 10**).

✔ Tips

■ You can enter information into any combination of fields; if you do not have information for a specific field, skip it and it will not appear in the completed card.

■ To list the entry by company name, rather than the person's name, as shown in **Figure 11**, turn on the Company check box beneath the Company field (**Figure 7**) when entering contact information. A contact that does not include a person's name is automatically listed by the company name.

■ By default, Address Book automatically formats telephone numbers. It doesn't matter how you enter a phone number; Address Book will change it to this format. You can change or turn off automatic phone number formatting in the Phone preferences pane (**Figure 12**); choose Address Book > Preferences and click the Phone button to display it.

■ In step 3, if you choose Custom from the pop-up menu, use the Adding custom label dialog that appears (**Figure 13**) to enter a custom label and click OK.

Figure 10 The Completed contact record appears in the column on the right side of the window.

Figure 11 You can choose to list a contact by its company name rather than the person's name.

Figure 12 Address Book's Phone preferences pane lets you set up phone number formatting options.

Figure 13
You can use this dialog to create a custom label for a record's card.

ADDING CONTACT CARDS

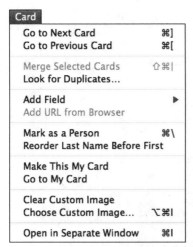

Figure 14 The card menu includes commands for working with contact cards.

To delete a contact record

1. In the Name column of the Address Book window, select the contact you want to delete.

2. Press (Delete).

3. In the confirmation dialog that appears, click Delete or press (Return). The contact disappears.

To edit a contact card

1. In the Name column of the Address Book window, select the contact you want to edit.

2. Click the Edit button.

3. Make changes as desired in the record's address card.

4. When you are finished making changes, click Edit again to save your changes and view the modified card.

✔ Tip

■ The Card menu (**Figure 14**) includes commands you can use to modify the currently selected card. For example, if you choose Card > Add Field, you can edit the template to add (or remove) fields you want.

To add an image to a contact card

1. In the Name column of the Address Book window, select the contact that you want to add a picture or logo to.

2. If necessary, click the Edit button to go into editing mode.

3. Drag the icon for the file containing the photo or logo you want to add from a Finder window to the image well in the address card window (**Figure 15**).

4. When you release the button, the image appears in a dialog like the one in **Figure 16**.

5. Drag the slider at the bottom of the dialog to resize the image. You can then drag the image around in the black frame to determine the resized image's edges. **Figure 17** shows an example.

6. Click Set. The image appears in the contact card (**Figure 18**).

✔ Tips

- Another way to add an image to a card is to choose Card > Choose Custom Image (**Figure 14**) to display a dialog like the one in **Figure 16**. Then either drag the image into that dialog or click the Choose button to use another dialog to locate and select the image you want to use.

- If your computer has an iSight or other compatible camera, you can use buttons near the bottom of the dialog to take a photo and apply affects. I tell you more about taking photos with your Mac on page 295.

- To remove a photo or logo from a contact record, select the contact and choose Card > Clear Custom Image (**Figure 14**) or simply click the image while the record is in editing mode and press [Delete].

ADDING IMAGES TO CARDS

Figure 15 To add a picture for a record, drag its icon to the image well.

Figure 16
The image appears in a dialog like this one. (That's my husband, Mike, and Jack the Dog.)

Figure 17
Use controls in the window to resize and reframe the image. (Jack the Dog has his own contact card.)

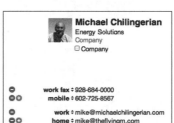

Figure 18
The picture is added to the contact's card.

Figure 19 Drag a vCard file's icon into the Address Book window's Name column.

Figure 20 The vCard information is added to your Address Book as a contact.

Figure 21 Drag the name of a contact from the Name column of the Address Book window to a Finder window.

Figure 22
A saved vCard file's icon looks like this.

Maria Langer.vcf

To import a vCard

1. Drag the icon for the vCard from a Finder window to the Name column in the Address Book window (**Figure 19**).

   or

   Double-click the icon for a vCard file.

2. A dialog appears, asking if you're sure you want to add the card. Click Add.

   An Address Book contact card is created based on the vCard contents (**Figure 20**).

✔ Tips

- vCard, or virtual address card, files are commonly used to share contact information electronically.

- When you import a vCard, Address Book creates (or modifies) a Last Import group. I tell you about groups on the next page.

To save information as a vCard

Drag the name of a contact from the Name column of the Address Book window to a Finder window (**Figure 21**).

The vCard file's icon (**Figure 22**) appears where you dragged it.

✔ Tips

- You can save multiple vCards at once. Simply hold down ⌘ while clicking contact names to select multiple contacts and then drag any of them to a Finder window as discussed above.

- You can send your vCard via e-mail to anyone you like. This makes it easy for people to add your contact information to their contact database.

- The vCard format is recognized by most Mac OS and Windows contact management software.

WORKING WITH VCARDS

To organize contact cards into groups

1. Click the Create a new group button (+) under the Group column of the Address Book window (**Figure 3**).

   or

   Choose File > New Group (**Figure 5**), or press [Shift][⌥][⌘][N].

2. A new entry appears in the Group column. Its name, *untitled group*, is selected (**Figure 23**). Enter a new name for the group and press [Return] to save it (**Figure 24**).

3. Repeat steps 1 and 2 to add as many groups as you need to organize your contacts.

4. Click to select All Contacts in the Group column.

5. Drag a contact name from the Name column onto the name of the group you want to associate it with in the Group column. When an outline appears around the group name (**Figure 25**), release the button to add the contact to that group.

6. Repeat step 5 to organize contact cards as desired.

✔ Tips

■ To see which contact cards are in a group, click the name of the group in the Group column. The Name column changes to display only those contacts in the selected group (**Figure 26**).

■ A contact can be included in more than one group.

Figures 23 & 24
A new group appears in the Group list with its name selected (left). Type a new name and press [Return] to give it a name (right).

Figure 25
To add a contact to a group, drag its name to the group name.

Figure 26
To see what contacts are in a group, select the name of the group.

ORGANIZING CONTACTS INTO GROUPS

Figure 27 This dialog confirms that you want to delete a record from a group...

Figure 28 ...and this dialog confirms that you want to delete a group.

To remove a contact from a group

1. In the Group column, select the group you want to remove the contact from (**Figure 26**).

2. In the Name column, select the contact you want to remove.

3. Press ⌈Delete⌋.

4. Click the appropriate button in the confirmation dialog that appears (**Figure 27**):

   ▲ **Cancel** does not delete the contact.

   ▲ **Delete** deletes the contact from the Address Book database.

   ▲ **Remove from Group** removes the contact from the group. The contact remains in the Address Book database.

✔ Tip

- If you delete a contact from the All Contacts group, you will remove the contact from the Address Book database.

To remove a group

1. In the Group column, select the group you want to remove (**Figure 26**).

2. Press ⌈Delete⌋.

3. In the confirmation dialog that appears (**Figure 28**), click Delete. The group is removed but all contacts within it remain in the Address Book database.

✔ Tip

- You cannot remove the All Contacts group.

REMOVING CONTACTS & GROUPS

To create a smart group

1. Choose File > New Smart Group (**Figure** 5). A dialog like the one in **Figure 29** appears.

2. Enter a name for the group in the Smart Group Name box.

3. Use options in the middle of the dialog to set criteria for matching contacts. **Figure 30** shows an example.

4. To add more matching criteria, click the **+** button at the far right end of the line of criteria you already set. The dialog expands to offer an additional line and a pop-up menu for matching options (**Figure 31**). Set options as desired.

5. Repeat step 4 as necessary to add more matching criteria.

6. Click OK.

   The smart group is created and populated with contacts that match the criteria you specified (**Figure 32**).

✔ Tips

- You can delete a smart group the same way you delete a regular group. I explain how on the previous page.

- You cannot manually remove a contact from a smart group. The only way a contact can be removed from a smart group is if it no longer matches the criteria you specified when you set up the smart group.

- To edit a smart group's matching criteria, select the group and choose Edit > Edit Smart Group (**Figure 33**). Then use the dialog that appears (**Figure 32**) to modify settings and click OK.

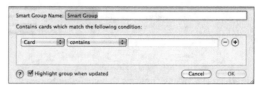

Figure 29 Use this dialog to set options for a new smart group.

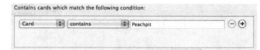

Figure 30 You can use pop-up menus and a text box to set matching criteria.

Figure 31 Clicking a + button expands the dialog so you can set up additional matching criteria.

Figure 32 In this example, the smart group matched all contacts in my Address Book data file who work or write for Peachpit Press.

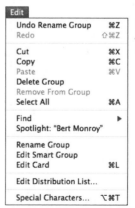

Figure 33 Address Book's Edit menu.

Figure 34 Enter all or part of a contact name in the search box to find that contact.

To search for a contact card

1. In the Group column, select the name of the group in which you expect to find the contact.

2. Enter all or part of the contact name in the Search box at the top of the Address Book window (**Figure 34**).

   The names of contacts that match what you typed appear in the Name column (**Figure 34**).

✔ Tips

- In step 1, if you're not sure which group a contact is in, select All Contacts.

- Search results begin appearing in the Name column as soon as you begin entering search characters in the Search box (**Figure 34**). The more you enter, the fewer results are displayed.

- If no contact cards match your search criteria, the Name column will be empty.

- You can search by any text that might appear in a contact's record. For example, if you're trying to find a person who works at a certain company but can't remember the person's name, you can enter the company name to display a list of all contacts at that company.

- To create a smart group from search results, choose File > New Smart Group from Current Search (**Figure 5**).

SEARCHING FOR CONTACTS

To print Address Book records

1. In the Group column, select the group containing the records you want to print.

2. To print information for only some records in the group, hold down ⌃ ⌘ and click in the Name column to select each record you want to print.

3. Choose File > Print (**Figure** 5), or press ⌃ ⌘ P. A Print dialog like the one in **Figure** 35 appears.

4. Choose the name of the printer you want to use from the Printer pop-up menu.

5. Choose an option from the Style pop-up menu:

   ▲ **Mailing Labels (Figure 36)** prints mailing labels on a variety of widely available label sheets.

   ▲ **Envelopes (Figure 35)** prints envelopes on common envelope sizes.

   ▲ **Lists (Figure 37)** prints contact lists that include the database fields you specify.

   ▲ **Pocket Address Book (Figure 38)** prints pocket-sized address books.

6. Set options in the dialog as desired:

   ▲ For mailing labels, click the Layout button (**Figure 36**) and set label layout options. Then click the Label button and set options for label content, sort order, color, and font.

   ▲ For envelopes, click the Layout button (**Figure 35**) and set envelope layout options. Then click the Label button and set options for envelope content, print order, color, and font. Finally, click the Orientation button and select an envelope print orientation.

Figure 35 The Envelopes Layout options in the Print dialog.

Figure 36 The Mailing Labels Layout options in the Print dialog.

Figure 37 The Lists options in the Print dialog.

Figure 38 The Pocket Address Book options in the Print dialog.

▲ For lists (**Figure 37**), set Paper Size, Orientation, and Font Size options. Then turn on check boxes in the Attributes area to specify what information you want to print for each record.

▲ For pocket address books (**Figure 38**), set Orientation, Flip Style, and Font options. Then turn on check boxes in the Attributes area to specify what information you want to print for each record.

7. Click Print. Address Book sends the information to your printer, and it prints.

✔ Tips

■ After step 3, if the Print dialog that appears is a lot smaller than the one in **Figure 35**, click the disclosure triangle next to the Printer pop-up menu to expand it.

■ I discuss printing in greater detail in **Chapter 17**.

iCal

iCal is a personal calendar application that enables you to keep track of appointments and other events. With iCal, you can:

◆ Create multiple color-coded calendars for different categories of events—for example, home, business, or school. You can view your calendars individually or together.

◆ View calendars by day, week, or month.

◆ Share calendars on the Web with family, friends, and business associates.

◆ Send e-mail invitations for events to people in your Mac OS X Address Book.

◆ Get notification of upcoming events on screen or by e-mail.

◆ Create and manage a priorities-based to-do list.

This part of the chapter provides basic instructions for setting up and using iCal.

To launch iCal

Open the iCal icon in the Applications folder (**Figure 1**).

Or

Click the iCal icon in the Dock (**Figure 2**).

iCal's main window appears (**Figure 39**).

Calendar list
Mini-month calendar

Figure 39 iCal's main window, showing a week at a glance view.

Figure 40 Day view shows one day at a time.

Figure 41 Month view shows a month at a time.

Figure 42
The mini calendar is full of clickable buttons.

Figure 43
iCal's View menu.

To change the calendar view

Click one of the view buttons at the top of the calendar window (**Figure 39**).

◆ **Day** shows a day at a glance (**Figure 40**).

◆ **Week** shows a week at a glance (**Figure 39**).

◆ **Month** shows a month at a glance (**Figure 41**).

To view a specific day, week, or month

1. Follow the instructions in the previous section to change the view.

2. Click the Next or Previous button above the mini calendar (**Figure 42**) until the date's month appears as a mini calendar. For example, to view June 30, 2010, you'd click the Next or Previous button until June 2010 appeared.

3. In the mini calendar, click the day, week, or month you want to view. It appears in the main calendar window.

Or

1. Choose View > Go to Date (**Figure 43**), or press (Shift)(⎇)(⌘)(T).

2. Enter the date you want to go to in the tiny dialog sheet that appears (**Figure 44**).

3. Click Show.

✔ Tips

■ If the mini calendar is not displayed, you can click the View or hide mini calendar button in the lower-left corner of the iCal window to display it.

■ To view today's date, click the Today button in the upper-left corner of the iCal window, choose View > Go to Today (**Figure 43**), or press (⎇)(⌘)(T).

Figure 44 Enter the date you want to view in this dialog.

To add an event by dragging

1. In the Calendar list on the upper-left corner of the calendar window, click the name of the calendar you want to add the event to.

2. Display the day you want to add the event to.

3. In Day or Week view, drag from the event's start time to end time (**Figure 45**). When you release the button, a box for the event appears in the calendar window with its default name (*New Event*) selected (**Figure 46**).

4. Enter a new name for the event, and press Return.

5. Continue following instructions in the section titled "To set event details" on page 249.

✔ Tip

- Another way to create an event is to double-click anywhere in the date box. This is almost the same as using the New Event command discussed next; it creates a new event with default settings.

To add an event with the New Event command

1. In any calendar view window, select the day you want to add the event to.

2. Choose File > New Event (**Figure 47**), or press ⌘N. A box for the event appears in the calendar window with its default name (*New Event*) selected.

3. Enter a new name for the event, and press Return.

4. Continue following instructions in the section titled "To set event details" on page 249.

Figure 45 Drag from the event's start time to end time.

Figure 46 When you release the button, the event box appears with its default name selected.

Figure 47 iCal's File menu.

Figure 48 When you double-click an event, its details appear in a pop-up dialog.

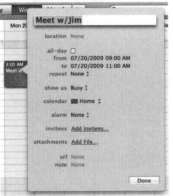

Figure 49
Click the Edit button in an event's details dialog to display editable details for the event.

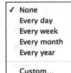

Figure 50 When you turn on the all-day check box, the times disappear.

Figure 51
Use this pop-up menu to choose a repeating option.

Figure 52
This dialog enables you to set custom repeating options for an event.

repeat Every week :
end On date : 07/21/2010

Figure 53 Here's an example of a repeating event with an ending date in the future.

To set event details

1. In the calendar window, double-click the event you want to set details for.

   Information about the event appears in a pop-up dialog (**Figure 48**).

2. Click the Edit button to display editable details about the event.

3. To modify the event name, click the existing name to display an edit box (**Figure 49**) and edit the contents.

4. To specify a location for the event, click to the right of location and type what you want to appear.

5. To set the beginning and ending dates for the event, click numbers in the date fields and type new values.

6. To indicate that the event lasts all day (or multiple days), turn on the all-day check box. The time fields disappear (**Figure 50**).

   or

   To specify starting and ending times for the event, make sure the all-day check box is turned off and then enter the starting and ending times in the two time areas (**Figure 49**).

7. To set the event to repeat on a regular basis, choose an option from the repeat pop-up menu (**Figure 51**). If none of the standard options apply, you can choose Custom and use the dialog that appears (**Figure 52**) to set a custom repeating schedule. Then, if necessary, set an ending option in the end field that appears (**Figure 53**).

Continued on next page...

Continued from previous page.

8. To specify how the event time should appear on a shared calendar, choose an option from the show as pop-up menu. Your options are Free or Busy.

9. To specify a calendar to add the event to, choose a calendar from the calendar pop-up menu. The menu lists all calendars you have created.

10. To be reminded about the event, choose an option from the alarm pop-up menu (**Figure 54**). Then set other alarm options as necessary (**Figure 55**). You can repeat this process with a new alarm pop-up menu that appears to set multiple alarms.

11. To identify one or more people involved with the event, click the Add Invitees link to display an edit box. Enter contact names in the box. As you type, iCal attempts to match names to those in your Address Book database with an e-mail address recorded (**Figure 56**).

12. To attach a file to the event, click the Add File link. Use the standard Open dialog that appears (**Figure 57**) to locate and select the file you want to attach. Click Open. The file is added to the event details dialog (**Figure 58**).

13. To associate a Web page with the event, click to the right of url and type a URL in the box that appears.

14. To add notes about the event, click to the right of note and type what you want to appear (**Figure 59**).

15. When you're finished entering event details (**Figure 60**), click Done. The details are saved with the event; some details appear in the main calendar window (**Figure 61**).

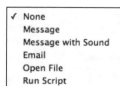

Figure 54
If you choose an option from the alarm pop-up menu, …

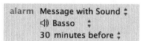

Figure 55
…you can set up a reminder for the event.

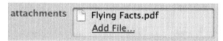

Figure 56 As you enter a name in the invitees field, iCal attempts to match it to an Address Book contact with an e-mail address.

Figure 57 Use a standard Open dialog to select a file to attach to an event.

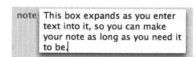

Figure 58 The attachment name appears in the dialog with a link to add another file.

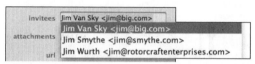

Figure 59 You can enter a note about the event in the note field.

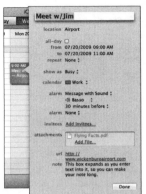

Figure 60
In this example, the event has plenty of details.

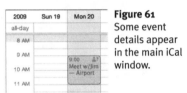

Figure 61
Some event details appear in the main iCal window.

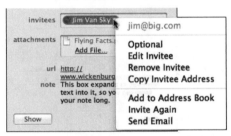

Figure 62 Clicking an invitee name may display a menu of options like this one.

Figure 63
You may see a Send button if the event includes invitees.

Figure 64 If you change a recurring event, you'll see this dialog.

✔ Tips

- You can follow these steps to add details for a new event or make changes to an existing event.

- The all-day event check box is handy for entering information about vacations and other events that span multiple days.

- In steps 4 and 5, the ending time or date must be after the starting time or date. It may be necessary to change AM to PM before entering the second time.

- A quick way to change an event's time is to drag its top or bottom border in Day or Week view of the main calendar window. This automatically changes the time information in the event details dialog.

- A quick way to change an event's date is to drag its event box from one date to another in the main calendar window. This automatically changes the date information in the event details dialog.

- You can click an invitee's name to access a menu of options for that invitee and the invitee field (**Figure 62**).

- If an event has invitees who have not yet been invited to the event, the Done button appears as a Send button at the bottom of the event details dialog (**Figure 63**). Clicking Send sends e-mail invitations to invitees.

- You can enter multiple invitees for an event by separating each name with a comma.

- If you set an event to repeat, any time you change that event's details, a dialog like the one in **Figure 64** appears. Click the appropriate button for the change.

To view event details

In any view of the main calendar window, double-click the event. Details appear in a pop-up dialog (**Figures 48** and **65**).

To delete an event

1. In the calendar window, select the event you want to delete.

2. Press Delete. The event disappears.

✔ Tips

- When you delete an event with an attachment, a confirmation dialog appears to warn you that it cannot be undone. Click Continue to delete the event anyway.

- When you delete a recurring event, a dialog like the one in **Figure 66** appears. You have three options:

  ▲ **Cancel** doesn't delete the event at all.

  ▲ **Delete All Future Events** deletes the selected event as well as all those occurrences after it.

  ▲ **Delete Only This Event** deletes just the selected event.

To add a to-do item

1. Choose File > New To Do (**Figure 47**), or press ⌃ ⌘ K. If the To Do Items list was not already showing, it appears. An untitled to-do item appears in the list with its default name (*New To Do*) selected (**Figure 67**).

2. Enter a name for the to-do item, and press Return.

Figure 65 Double-click an event to display its details.

Figure 66 When you delete a recurring event, you can indicate whether you want to delete one or all future occurrences.

Figure 67 The To Do Item list pane with a brand new to-do item.

Figure 68 Double-clicking a to-do item displays a pop-up dialog of editable details.

✓	None
	Low
	Medium
	High

Figure 69 Choose a priority from the pop-up menu.

due date ☑ 07/17/2009
alarm None ⬍

Figure 70 You can set a due date for a to-do item.

Figure 71 Here's a to-do item with a bunch of details.

To set to-do item details

1. If necessary, click the View or Hide To Dos button in the lower-right corner of the window or press ⌥⌘T to display the To Do Items list.

2. In the To Do Items list, double-click the item you want to modify.

   Details about the item appear in an editable pop-up dialog (**Figure 68**).

3. To modify the item name, click the existing name to display an edit box (**Figure 68**) and edit the contents.

4. To mark the item as completed, turn on the completed check box.

5. To set a priority for the item, choose an option from the priority pop-up menu (**Figure 69**).

6. To set a due date for the item, turn on the due date check box and enter a date in the field beside it (**Figure 70**). You can then use the alarm pop-up menu (**Figure 54**) and associated options (**Figure 55**) to set a reminder for the item.

7. To specify a calendar to add the item to, choose a calendar from the calendar pop-up menu. The menu lists all calendars you have created.

8. To associate a Web page with the item, click to the right of url and type a URL in the box that appears.

9. To add notes about the item, click to the right of note and type what you want to appear (**Figure 59**).

10. When you're finished entering information (**Figure 71**), click Done.

Continued on next page...

SETTING TO DO ITEM DETAILS

Continued from previous page.

✔ Tips

- You can mark a To Do item as complete by clicking its check box in the To Do Items list (**Figure 72**).

- The stack of lines on the button to the left of a To Do item's name in the To Do items list (**Figure 72**) indicates its priority: the more lines, the more important the item is. You can click this button to change the priority.

To sort the To Do Items list

Choose a sort order from the column heading menu at the top of the To Do Items list (**Figure 73**).

To delete a to-do item

1. If necessary, click the View or Hide To Do Items button in the lower-right corner of the window or press Option ⌅ ⌘ T to display the To Do Items list.

2. In the To Do Items list, select the item you want to delete.

3. Press Delete. The item disappears.

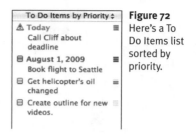

Figure 72
Here's a To Do Items list sorted by priority.

Figure 73 Change the priority by selecting a new option from the pop-up menu.

Figure 74 The To Do Item list column heading is a menu that you can use to set sort order and other display options for the To Do Item list.

SORTING & DELETING TO DO ITEMS

Figure 75 A new calendar appears in the Calendars list.

Figure 76
Toggle check boxes in the Calendars list to determine which calendars' items appear in iCal.

Figure 77 A confirmation dialog like this appears when you delete a calendar that includes events or to-do items.

To add a calendar

1. Choose File > New Calendar (**Figure 47**), press [Option] [⌃] [⌘] [N], or click the Add a new calendar (**+**) button in the lower-left corner of the main iCal window. An untitled calendar appears in the Calendars list with its default name (*Untitled*) selected (**Figure 75**).

2. Enter a name for the Calendar, and press [Return] (**Figure 76**).

✔ Tips

- To rename a calendar, click its name to display a box around it (**Figure 75**). Type a new name, and press [Return].

- To display events from only certain calendars, in the Calendars list (**Figure 76**), turn off the check boxes for the calendars you don't want to view.

- You can use the New Calendar Group command on the File menu (**Figure 47**) to add calendar groups. You can then organize your calendars by dragging them into groups.

To delete a calendar

1. In the Calendars list, select the calendar you want to delete.

2. Choose Edit > Delete or press [⌃] [⌘] [Delete].

3. If a confirmation dialog like the one in **Figure 77** appears, click Delete. The calendar and all of its events are removed.

WORKING WITH CALENDARS

To publish a calendar

1. In the Calendars list (**Figure 76**), select the calendar you want to publish.

2. Choose Calendar > Publish (**Figure 78**).

3. A dialog like the one in **Figure 79** appears. Set options as desired:

   ▲ **Publish calendar as** is the name of the calendar as it will be published.

   ▲ **Publish on** enables you to specify whether the calendar should be published on your MobileMe account or on a private server. If you choose a Private Server, the dialog expands to offer more options (**Figure 80**).

   ▲ **Base URL** is the Web address for accessing your calendar. This option only appears if you are publishing to a private server.

   ▲ **Login** and **Password** is your login information for the server you are publishing on. These options only appears if you are publishing to a private server.

   ▲ **Publish changes automatically** updates the calendar online whenever you make changes to it in iCal.

   ▲ **Publish titles and notes** includes event or item names and notes in the published calendar.

   ▲ **Publish To Do items** includes to-do items in the published calendar.

   ▲ **Publish alarms** includes event or item alarms in the published calendar.

   ▲ **Publish attachments** includes file attachments as clickable links in the published calendar.

4. Click Publish.

Figure 78
The Calendar menu looks like this when no calendars have been published or subscribed to.

Figure 79 Use this dialog to set options for publishing a calendar on MobileMe...

Figure 80 ...and this dialog to set options for publishing a calendar on a private calendar server.

Figure 81 A dialog like this appears when your calendar has been published to the Web.

Figure 82 iCal can generate an e-mail message with information for accessing the calendar online.

Figure 83
When you select a published calendar, additional commands become available.

Figure 84
A broadcast icon appears beside the names of calendars you are publishing on the Web.

5. Wait while your computer connects to the Internet and uploads the calendar. When the upload is complete, a dialog like the one in **Figure 81** appears. You have three options:

▲ **Visit Page** launches your Web browser, connects to the Internet, and displays the calendar page.

▲ **Send Mail** launches your default e-mail application and creates a message with the calendar's access information (**Figure 82**). You can address the message and send it to people you want to inform about the calendar.

▲ **OK** simply dismisses the dialog.

✔ Tips

■ You must have a connection to the Internet to publish a calendar.

■ You must have a MobileMe account to publish a calendar on MobileMe. I tell you more about MobileMe on page 433.

■ In step 3, if you choose not to automatically update the calendar, you can do so manually. Select the calendar in the Calendars list and choose Calendar > Refresh (**Figure 83**) or press ⌘R.

■ To create a new e-mail message with information about accessing a calendar (**Figure 82**), select the calendar in the Calendars list and choose Calendar > Send Publish Email (**Figure 83**).

■ In the Calendars list, a broadcast icon appears beside the name of a calendar that has been published (**Figure 84**).

PUBLISHING CALENDARS

To unpublish a calendar

1. In the Calendars list, select the calendar you want to remove from the Web.

2. Choose Calendar > Unpublish (**Figure 83**).

3. In the confirmation dialog that appears (**Figure 85**), click Unpublish.

To subscribe to a calendar

1. Choose Calendar > Subscribe (**Figure 78** or **83**).

2. A dialog like the one in **Figure 86** appears. Enter the URL for the calendar you want to subscribe to and click Subscribe.

3. After a moment, iCal displays a dialog like the one in **Figure 87**. Set options as desired:

   ▲ **Name** is the name of the calendar as it should appear in your Calendar list.

   ▲ **Description** is a description of the calendar.

   ▲ **Subscribed to** is the URL of the calendar on the Web.

   ▲ **Remove** enables you to toggle check boxes to remove or disable alarms, attachments, and to-do items for the calendar.

   ▲ **Last updated**, which cannot be changed, indicates the last time the calendar was refreshed.

   ▲ **Auto-refresh** enables you to set a frequency for iCal to refresh the calendar automatically. Choose an option based on how often you expect the calendar to change. Choosing No disables automatic refreshing.

4. Click OK.

   The calendar's events appear in the calendar window under Subscriptions (**Figure 88**).

Figure 85 Confirm that you really do want to unpublish a calendar.

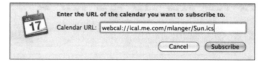

Figure 86 Enter a URL for the calendar you want to subscribe to in this dialog.

Figure 87 Use this dialog to set options for the calendar you are subscribing to.

Figure 88 The calendar appears in the Subscriptions list and its events appear in the main iCal window.

Figure 89 The info dialog for a calendar that is not published.

Figure 90 The info dialog for a calendar that you have published.

✔ Tips

■ You cannot add, modify, or delete events on a calendar that you subscribe to.

■ To update the contents of a calendar you have subscribed to, select the name of the calendar in the Calendars list and choose Calendar > Refresh (**Figure 83**) or press ⌃ ⌘ R.

■ To unsubscribe from a calendar, delete it from the Subscriptions list. I explain how to delete calendars on page 255.

■ To find more calendars you can subscribe to, choose Calendar > Find Shared Calendars (**Figure 83**). You can find everything from Apple Store events to professional sports game dates.

To modify calendar settings

1. In the Calendar or Subscriptions list, select the calendar you want to modify settings for.

2. Choose File > Get Info (**Figure 47**), or press ⌃ ⌘ I.

   A dialog like the one in **Figure 87**, **89**, or **90** appears, depending on whether the calendar is subscribed to, unpublished, or published.

3. Set options as desired:

   ▲ **Name** is the name of the calendar as it appears in iCal.

   ▲ **Description** is a description of the calendar.

   ▲ **Ignore alarms** tells iCal to ignore any alarms associated with the calendar.

   ▲ **Published to** is the location the calendar is published to.

Continued on next page...

Continued from previous page.

▲ **Publish** enables you to toggle check boxes to publish titles and notes, alarms, attachments, and to-do items with the calendar.

▲ **Subscribed to** is the URL of the calendar on the Web.

▲ **Remove** enables you to toggle check boxes to remove or disable alarms, attachments, and to-do items for the calendar.

▲ **Last updated**, which cannot be changed, indicates the last time the calendar was refreshed.

▲ **Auto-refresh** enables you to set a frequency for iCal to refresh the calendar automatically. Choose an option based on how often you expect the calendar to change. Choosing No disables automatic refreshing.

4. Click OK.

✔ Tips

■ To publish an unpublished calendar, you can click the Publish button in its info window (**Figure 89**). Consult the section titled "To publish a calendar" on page 256 for more information.

■ To change the location of a published calendar, click the Change Location button in its info window (**Figure 90**). Consult the section titled "To publish a calendar" on page 256 for more information.

Figure 91 iSync's window before it has been configured to sync with devices.

iSync

iSync is synchronization software that keeps your iCal calendar information and Address Book contact information up to date on your Bluetooth or USB mobile phone, smart phone, or PDA.

This part of the chapter provides instructions for using iSync to synchronize information between your computer and a mobile phone.

✔ Tips

- Although the information here does not include specific instructions for using iSync with every device it supports, it should be enough to get you started using iSync with your compatible device.

- To use iSync with a Bluetooth-enabled device, your computer must have Bluetooth installed or supported through the use of an adapter. You can learn more about Bluetooth on page 463.

- For a complete list of devices that work with iSync, use your Web browser to visit http://support.apple.com/kb/HT2824.

To launch iSync

Open the iSync icon in your Applications folder (**Figure 1**). iSync's main window appears (**Figure 91**).

iSync

To add a device

1. Choose Devices > Add Device (**Figure 92**), or press ⌃⌘N. The Add Device window appears and iSync begins looking for devices. When it is finished, it displays icons for all devices it found (**Figure 93**).

2. Double-click the icon for the device you want to add. An icon for the device appears in the iSync window and the window expands to show device synchronization options (**Figure 94**).

✔ Tips

- The device you are trying to add must be accessible to your Macintosh to appear in the Add Device window (**Figure 93**). If a device does not appear, make sure it is properly connected (or paired and within range, in the case of a Bluetooth-enabled device) and turned on. Then follow steps 1 and 2 above again.

- To add a Palm OS device, make sure Palm Desktop 4.2.1 or later is installed on your Macintosh. (You can get the latest version of Palm Desktop for Mac OS at www.palm.com.) Then, in iSync, choose Devices > Enable Palm OS Syncing and follow the instructions that appear to complete the setup. The Palm device should appear in the iSync window (**Figure 94**).

- I explain how to pair Bluetooth devices on page 466.

Figure 92 The Devices menu before any devices have been added.

Figure 93 A list of devices accessible to your Macintosh appears in the Add Device window.

Figure 94 This example shows the synchronization options for a Palm Treo 700p smart phone.

To configure a synchronization

1. If necessary, in the iSync window, click the device's icon to show configuration options (**Figure 94**).

2. Turn on check boxes and choose other options to set synchronization preferences. Here are some of the options you might find for a Palm device (**Figure 94**); the options you see for your device may differ:

   ▲ **For first sync** enables you to choose what iSync should do for the first synchronization. **Merge data on computer and device** combines the data in both locations. **Erase data on device then sync** erases whatever data is on the device, and then copies data from your computer to the device.

   ▲ **Force slow synchronization** slows down the synchronization, which could help prevent syncing errors.

   ▲ **Contacts** synchronizes Address Book contacts to the contacts database in the device. With this option turned on, you can select All contacts or a specific group name from the Synchronize pop-up menu to determine which contacts should be synchronized.

   ▲ **Calendars** synchronizes iCal calendars to the calendar database in the device. With this option turned on, if you have multiple calendars, you can select the Selected option and toggle check marks to indicate which calendars should be synchronized. You can also specify which calendar events created on the device should be copied and whether old events should be ignored.

   ▲ **Set** displays a dialog you can use to select the time zone for the device.

CONFIGURING A SYNCHRONIZATION

To perform a synchronization

Click the Sync Devices button in the iSync window (**Figure 94**). As shown in **Figure 95**, a progress bar appears in the iSync window to indicate that a sync is in progress. In addition, the Sync Now button turns into a Cancel Sync button.

When the progress bar disappears from the iSync window, the synchronization is complete.

✔ Tip

■ If you are synchronizing a Palm device, a dialog like the one in **Figure 96** may appear. If so, follow the instructions in the dialog to initiate the sync.

Figure 95 iSync displays a progress bar as it synchronizes.

Figure 96 If you have a Palm device, additional instructions may appear in a dialog like this one.

Front Row

Figure 1 Front Row with a DVD inserted.

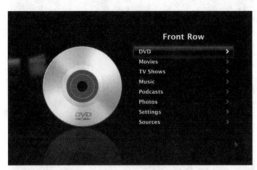

Figure 2 The Applications folder includes the Front Row application and other applications for accessing Front Row content.

Front Row

Front Row (**Figure 1**) is an application for accessing multimedia content on your Macintosh—specifically, content played with DVD Player and managed with iTunes (**Figure 2**) and iPhoto.

With Front Row, you can use an Apple Remote to control your computer via an infrared connection. Sit across the room, point the control at your Mac, and navigate through Front Row's menus to display and play DVDs, movies, television shows, music, podcasts, and photo slide shows.

But even if your computer doesn't have an Apple Remote, you can still use Mac OS X's Front Row application. Use keyboard keys to navigate through content—if you have a wireless keyboard, it's almost as good as having the remote!

In this part of the chapter, I explain how to work with Front Row to access and display content. Then I tell you how you can use DVD Player without the Front Row application and manage content with iTunes.

To use an Apple Remote

1. Point the Apple Remote at the infrared port on your computer.

2. Press the Menu button. The screen goes dark and Front Row appears (**Figure 1**).

3. Navigate using the following techniques:

   ▲ To move the selection bar up and down in the list of options (**Figure 3** and **6**), press the + and − buttons.

   ▲ To view an option's submenu (**Figures 4, 5, 7,** and **8**), press the >>| button.

   ▲ To return to the previous menu level, press the Menu button.

   ▲ To select an item, press the >|| button.

   ▲ To stop playing an item, press the >|| button or the Menu button.

✔ Tips

■ Your Apple Remote may need to be paired with your computer before use. Consult the manual that came with the computer and remote to prepare it for use before following these instructions.

■ When playing audio content, you can use the + and − buttons to raise or lower the volume.

Figure 3 Move up and down through the main menu's list of options.

Figure 4 Select an item to view subitems...

Figure 5 ...and more subitems.

Figure 6 Move up and down through the main menu's list of options.

Figure 7 Select an item to view subitems...

Figure 8 ...or more subitems.

To use the Front Row application

1. Open the Front Row icon in the Applications folder (**Figure 2**).

   The screen goes dark and Front Row appears (**Figure 1**).

2. Navigate using the following techniques:

   ▲ To move the selection bar up and down in the list of options (**Figure 3** and **6**), press ⬆ and ⬇.

   ▲ To view an option's submenu (**Figures 4, 5, 7,** and **8**)), press Return.

   ▲ To return to the previous menu level, press Esc.

   ▲ To select an item, press Return.

   ▲ To stop playing an item, press Esc.

✔ Tip

■ When playing audio content, you can press ⬆ and ⬇ to raise or lower the volume.

DVD Player

DVD Player enables you to play DVD-Video on your Macintosh.

✔ Tip

- To play a DVD using Front Row, start Front Row using one of the methods on the previous two pages and then insert the DVD disk. You can then use your Apple Remote or Keyboard to access the DVD.

To launch DVD Player

Insert a DVD-Video disc into your computer. DVD Player should launch and do one of two things:

◆ Display a black Viewer window with a floating Controller palette (**Figure 9**).

◆ Immediately begin DVD play (**Figure 10**).

If DVD Player does not launch at all, then:

Open the DVD Player icon in the Applications folder (**Figure 2**).

✔ Tip

- If a Drive Region Code dialog appears the first time you play a DVD-Video, click the Set Drive Region button to set DVD Player's region to match that of the disc you inserted. Then click OK to dismiss the confirmation dialog that appears.

Figure 9 DVD Player either starts with a blank viewer window and Controller palette...

Figure 10 ...or begins playing the DVD-Video. (This is a DVD I created with iDVD to promote my company's multiday helicopter excursions. Not bad, if I do say so myself.)

DVD menu controls — Title/Chapter Indicator — Go to DVD Menu / Go to Title Menu / Eject Disc

Rewind | Stop | Playback volume
Play/ Pause | Fast Forward

Figure 11 DVD Player's Controller.

Figure 12 A Controller, expanded to show additional control buttons. Point to a button to learn its name.

Controls	
Pause	Space bar
Stop	⌘.
Slow Motion	⌥⇧→
Scan Forward	⇧⌘→
Scan Backwards	⇧⌘←
Scan Rate	▶
Slow Motion Rate	▶
Volume Up	⌘↑
Volume Down	⌘↓
Mute	⌥⌘↓
Timer	▶
New Bookmark...	⌘=
New Video Clip...	⌘−
Use Current Frame as Jacket Picture	
Close Control Drawer	⌘]
Eject DVD	⌘E

Figure 13 The Controls menu includes commands for controlling DVD play.

View	
Half Size	⌘0
Actual Size	⌘1
Double Size	⌘2
Fit to Screen	⌘3
Enter Full Screen	⌘F
Deinterlace	▶
Viewer Above Other Apps	

Figure 14 Use the View menu to set the size of the Viewer window.

To display the Controller

Move the mouse or drag your finger across the trackpad while the DVD is playing.

Or

Choose Window > Show Controller (the menu appears, if necessary, when you point to it), or press Control ⌘ C.

The Controller appears (**Figure 11**).

✔ Tip

■ To display additional DVD controls on the Controller, double-click the pair of tiny lines on the right (**Figure 11**) of the Controller. **Figure 12** shows the Controller expanded to show these controls.

To control DVD play

Click buttons on the Controller (**Figure 11** or 12).

Or

Choose a command from the Controls menu (**Figure 13**).

✔ Tip

■ The Pause command on the Controls menu (**Figure 13**) changes into a Play command when a DVD is not playing.

To resize the Viewer window

Choose an option from the View window (**Figure 14**) or press the corresponding shortcut key.

CONTROLLING DVD PLAY

269

iTunes

iTunes (**Figure 15**) is a computer-based "jukebox" that enables you to do several things:

- Play MP3 and AAC format audio files.

- Record music from audio CDs on your Macintosh as AAC and MP3 files.

- Buy music, audio books, television shows, and movies from the iTunes Store.

Figure 15 The main iTunes window after importing a few songs iTunes found on my hard disk.

- Subscribe to and listen to podcasts.

- Create custom CDs of your favorite music.

- Save AAC and MP3 files to an iPod and save MP3 files to other MP3 players.

- Listen to Internet-based radio stations.

- Sync content with your iPod or iPhone.

The next few pages explain how you can use iTunes to record and play music, copy content to an iPod, and burn audio CDs.

✔ Tip

- MP3 and AAC are standard formats for audio files. iTunes 8 can read and save to MP3, AIFF, WAV, MPEG-4, AAC and Apple Lossless file formats.

Figure 16 Start the setup process with a Welcome message.

Figure 17 Set options for Internet audio playback.

Figure 18 Tell iTunes to search for and import music files it finds on disk.

To set up iTunes

1. Double-click the iTunes icon in the Applications folder (**Figure 2**) or in the Dock.

2. If a license agreement window appears, click Agree.

3. The iTunes Setup Assistant window appears (**Figure 16**). Read the welcome message, and click Next.

4. In the Internet Audio screen (**Figure 17**), choose an option and click Next:

   ▲ **Yes, use iTunes for Internet audio content** tells your computer to set Web browser helper settings to use iTunes for all Internet audio playback.

   ▲ **No, do not modify my Internet settings** does not change your Web browser's helper settings.

5. In the Find Music Files screen (**Figure 18**), select an option and click Next:

   ▲ **Yes, find MP3 and AAC files in my Home folder** tells iTunes to search your hard disk for music files and add them to your library.

   ▲ **No, I'll add them myself later** tells iTunes not to look for music files.

6. Read the information in the Download Album Artwork screen and click Done.

   iTunes completes its configuration and displays the iTunes main window (**Figure 15**).

To view & listen to content by source

1. Click one of the items in the source list on the left side of the iTunes window (**Figure 19**) to display the contents of the source:

   ▲ **Library** is a list of all the content you have stored in your iTunes library. Categories within this area can include Music (**Figure 15**), Movies, TV Shows, Podcasts, Audiobooks, Applications, Radio (**Figure 20**), and Ringtones.

   ▲ **Store** displays iTunes store related items, including the iTunes Store (**Figure 21**) and Downloads, while you download content.

   ▲ **Devices** displays iTunes-compatible devices connected to your computer, including iPods and inserted CDs (**Figure 27**).

   ▲ **Shared** displays content available via network from a shared library.

   ▲ **Playlists** displays the iTunes DJ and Genius features, which automatically choose songs to play from your iTunes music library or playlist, as well as any smart or regular playlists you may have created.

2. To play content, double-click it or select it and click the Play button at the top of the window (**Figure 22**).

Figure 19
The source list includes several different music sources.

Figure 20 The Radio source list offers access to streaming audio on the Internet.

Figure 21 The iTunes Store is a great place to shop for music, movies, television shows, games, and iPhone applications.

Play   Volume

Figure 22 The play controls when content is not playing.

Backward Stop Forward

Figure 23 The play controls when content is playing.

New Playlist   Repeat
       Shuffle   Artwork

Figure 24 Use buttons at the bottom of the source list to work with the list and control music play.

Figure 25 You may have to authorize your computer to play protected music purchased from the iTunes store.

✔ Tips

- You must have access to the Internet to use the Radio and Store sources.

- When you play music, iTunes automatically plays all music in the list.

- You can use buttons at the top of the iTunes window (**Figures 22** and **23**) to control play.

- You can use buttons at the bottom of the source list (**Figure 24**) to work with the list and change the way music is played.

- To listen to protected songs purchased from the iTunes Store or accessible via shared library, you may have to authorize your computer. If so, a dialog like the one in **Figure 25** will appear; enter the account name and password for the owner of the music and click Authorize. You only need to do this once on your computer to listen to protected music. You can authorize up to five computers to play the protected songs you purchase.

- The View buttons at the top of the iTunes window enable you to display items in a list (**Figure 26**), as a grid (**Figure 15**), or with Cover Flow (**Figure 27**).

Figure 26 In addition to grid view, you can also view items in list view...

Figure 27 ...or Cover Flow view.

VIEWING & LISTENING TO CONTENT BY SOURCE

To add songs from an audio CD to the Library

1. Insert an audio CD in your CD drive. If your computer has access to the Internet, it goes online to get CD song information. Then the CD's name appears in the source list and a list of its tracks appears in the song list. A dialog offers to import the songs (**Figure 28**).

2. Click Yes in the dialog.

   or

   If the dialog does not appear, turn on the check box beside each song you want to add to the Library and click the Import CD button at the bottom of the window.

   iTunes begins importing the first song. The status area provides progress information (**Figure 29**). The song may play while it is imported.

Figure 28 When you insert a CD, iTunes fetches track info from the Internet and offers to import tracks.

Figure 29 You can see import progress at the top of the iTunes window.

✔ Tips

- Please observe copyright law and only import music you own into iTunes.

- Copying songs from a CD to a computer or MP3 player is often referred to as *ripping* songs.

- You can set import format by setting iTunes preferences. Choose iTunes > Preferences, click the General button, and then click the Import Settings button (**Figure 30**) to get started.

- When iTunes is finished importing songs, it plays a sound. In most cases, iTunes will finish importing songs from a CD long before it finishes playing them.

- When you are finished importing songs from a CD, you can click the eject button beside the CD name in the source list (**Figure 20**) to eject the disc.

Figure 30 The default Import Settings for iTunes.

ADDING SONGS FROM A CD

Figure 31 Importing an audio file on disk is as easy as dragging it into the iTunes window.

Figure 32 Exporting a song as an audio file is as easy as dragging it from the iTunes window to the Finder.

Figure 33
The icon for an exported audio file appears where the song was dragged.

To import music files on disk to the Library

Drag the icon for the music file from the Desktop or a Finder window to the iTunes window (**Figure 31**).

After a moment, the song appears in the Library window.

✔ Tips

■ You can use this technique to add a bunch of music files at once. Simply select their icons and drag any one of them into the window. I explain how to select multiple icons in the Finder on page 21.

■ You could also import music with the Add to Library command on the iTunes File menu. Personally, I think the drag-and-drop technique is quicker and easier.

To export songs from the iTunes Library as audio files

Drag the name of the song you want to export from the iTunes Library window to the desktop or a Finder window (**Figure 32**).

After a moment, an audio file icon for the exported song appears in the Finder (**Figure 33**).

✔ Tips

■ You can use this technique to export a bunch of audio files at once. Simply hold down ⌘ while clicking each song you want to select. Then drag any one of them into the Finder window.

■ Audio export format is also determined by Import Settings in iTunes preferences (**Figure 30**).

IMPORTING & EXPORTING MUSIC

To create a playlist

1. Click the New Playlist button (**Figure 24**), choose File > New Playlist, or press ⌃ ⌘ N.

2. A new untitled playlist appears in the Playlist area of the source list (**Figure 34**). Type a name for the playlist, and press Return (**Figure 36**).

To add songs to a playlist

1. If necessary, select the source of the music you want to add to the playlist.

2. Drag a song you want to include from the Song list pane to the playlist name in the source list (**Figure 36**).

3. Repeat step 2 for each song you want to add to the playlist.

4. When you're finished adding songs, click the playlist name. The songs appear in the list.

✔ Tips

- In step 2, you can select and drag multiple songs. Hold down ⌃ ⌘ while selecting songs to select more than one, and then drag any one of them.

- You can use the same technique to manually copy songs to an iPod or MP3 player that is not synced to iTunes. I tell you more about syncing to an iPod on page 279.

To remove a song from a playlist

1. Select the song you want to remove.

2. Press Delete. The song is removed from the playlist.

✔ Tip

- Removing a song from a playlist does not remove it from the iTunes Library.

Figure 34
Clicking the New Playlist button creates a new, untitled playlist.

Figure 35
To give the playlist a name, simply type it in and press Return.

Figure 36 To add songs to a playlist, drag them from the Song list to the playlist name.

Figure 37 The Smart Playlist dialog starts off like this.

Figure 38 Here's an example of smart playlist settings with multiple criteria.

Figure 39
Use this pop-up menu to specify how you want to limit the selection.

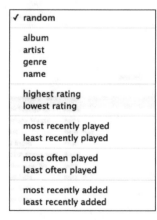

Figure 40
Use this pop-up menu to specify how iTunes should select songs when you limit the selection.

To create a smart playlist

1. Choose File > New Smart Playlist or press (Option) ⌃ ⌘ N to display the Smart Playlist dialog (**Figure 37**).

2. Choose an option from the first pop-up menu, which includes all data fields iTunes tracks for each item, and set criteria using options on that line.

3. To add additional matching criteria, click the + button. The dialog expands to offer an additional line for criteria. Set criteria as desired in this line. You can repeat this step as necessary to set all criteria. **Figure 38** shows an example with multiple criteria set.

4. If you set up multiple criteria in step 3, choose an option from the Match pop-up menu:

   ▲ **All** matches all criteria you set. This narrows down the search and produces fewer matches. Keep in mind that if criteria is mutually exclusive (for example, "Genre contains Jazz" and "Genre contains New Age") no items will be found.

   ▲ **Any** matches any criteria. This expands the search and produces more matches.

5. To limit the size of the playlist by time, file size, or number of songs, turn on the Limit to check box, choose an option from the pop-up menu (**Figure 39**), and enter a value in the box beside it. You can also use the selected by pop-up menu in that line (**Figure 40**) to specify how songs should be chosen.

6. To match only songs that are checked in the song list, turn on the Match only checked items check box.

Continued on next page...

CREATING SMART PLAYLISTS

Continued from previous page.

7. To automatically update the playlist each time songs are added or removed from the Library, turn on the Live updating check box.

8. Click OK.

9. A new smart playlist appears in the source list with a suggested name based on what you entered. When the list is selected, you can see the songs iTunes selected (**Figure 41**).

✔ Tip

■ The types of criteria iTunes can use are divided into two categories: information you can change and information you can't change. To see (and change) information for a song, select the song in the song list and choose File > Get Info or press ⌃⌘I. **Figures 42** and **43** show examples of two panes of information for a song.

To delete a playlist

1. In the source window, select the playlist you want to delete (**Figure 41**).

2. Press Delete.

3. In the confirmation dialog that appears, click Delete. The playlist is removed.

✔ Tip

■ Deleting a playlist does not delete the songs on the playlist from your music library.

Figure 41 iTunes selected these songs, based on the criteria shown in **Figure 39**.

Figures 42 & 43 Two examples of the Info window for a song: Info (top) and Options (bottom).

Figure 44 You'll need to sign in to the iTunes store to use the Genius feature.

Figure 45 Your computer sends the iTunes store information about your music in before turning on Genius.

Figure 46 Here's the playlist Genius created based on the selected song. The Genius sidebar on the right side of the iTunes window helps you find other items on the iTunes store to round out your library.

To enable the Genius feature

1. Choose Store > Turn on Genius.

2. iTunes goes online, then displays a screen with information about the Genius feature. Click the Turn on Genius button.

3. A Sign In screen appears (**Figure 44**). Select the Apple or AOL option and then enter the appropriate ID and password. Click Continue.

4. A Genius Terms & Conditions screen appears next. Read the terms, turn on the check box at the bottom of the terms box and click Continue.

   The Turning on Genius screen displays progress information (**Figure 45**). When Genius is enabled, another screen tells you. You're done.

✔ Tips

- If you don't have an iTunes Store or AOL account in step 3, you can create an iTunes Store account. Select the Create a new iTunes Store Account option, choose your location, and click Continue. Then follow the instructions to create your account.

- For Genius to work properly it's a good idea to update it periodically. Choose Store > Update Genius and follow any onscreen instructions that appear.

To create a Genius playlist

1. Select or play any song in your library.

2. Click the Start Genius button in the lower-right corner of the iTunes window.

   iTunes displays the Genius playlist, with a list of 25 songs it thinks are a good match for the one you selected (**Figure 46**).

3. Play the playlist like any other playlist.

To set iPod options

1. Use the cable that came with your iPod to connect it to your Macintosh. If iTunes is not already running, it launches, and the iPod appears in the source list (**Figure 19**).

2. Select the iPod in the source list. iPod options appear in the main iTunes window (**Figure 47**).

3. Set options in each tab of the window:

   ▲ **Summary (Figure 47)** displays basic information about your iPod, enables you to check for updates or restore its settings, and set options for using your iPod with iTunes and your Mac.

   ▲ **Music (Figure 48)**, **Movies**, **TV Shows**, **Podcasts**, and **Games** enables you to set up your iPod to automatically sync content with iTunes when connected.

   ▲ **Photos** enables you to set up your iPod to automatically sync content with iPhoto (if installed) or a folder on your hard disk.

   ▲ **Contacts (Figure 49)** enables you to set up your iPod to automatically sync content with Address Book and iCal.

4. Click Apply to save your settings. If you changed any syncing options, your iPod automatically syncs in accordance with your changes.

✔ Tips

- The settings here are for my Video iPod. The settings for your iPod may differ.

- The amount of content you copy to your iPod is limited by the amount of space available on it.

- I tell you about Address Book and iCal in **Chapter 12**. A discussion of iPhoto, which is not part of Mac OS X, is beyond the scope of this book.

Figure 47 When you select the iPod in a source list, iPod options appear in the main iTunes window.

Figure 48 You can set music syncing options in the Music tab.

Figure 49 You can set Address Book and iCal syncing options in the Contacts tab.

SETTING IPOD OPTIONS

Figure 50 Use this dialog to set disc-burning options.

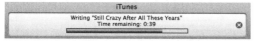

Figure 51 You can see the burn progress in the iTunes window status area.

Figure 52 This dialog appears if you try to put too many songs on an audio CD.

Figure 53 Protected songs cannot be burned to CD.

✔ Tips

■ Your computer must have a compatible CD-R drive or SuperDrive to burn audio CDs or data to CD or DVD.

■ If you are creating an audio CD and the playlist you have selected won't fit on a single disc, iTunes displays a dialog like the one in **Figure 52**. If you click Audio CDs, iTunes prompts you to insert a blank CD each time it needs one.

To burn iTunes content to disc

1. Create a playlist that contains the content you want to include on the disc.

2. Select the playlist (**Figure 41**).

3. Click the Burn Disc button at the bottom of the iTunes window.

4. A Burn Settings dialog like the one in **Figure 50** appears. Set options as desired:

   ▲ **Preferred Speed** is the burn speed. Options vary depending on your CD/DVD writer.

   ▲ **Disc Format** enables you to choose from three formats: **Audio CD**, which will play in any CD player, **MP3 CD** which will play in any CD player that supports MP3 CDs, including your computer, and **Data CD or DVD**, which stores the files as data.

5. Click Burn.

6. Insert a blank disc.

7. Wait while iTunes prepares and burns the disc. A progress indicator appears at the top of the iTunes window (**Figure 51**) as it works.

   When iTunes is finished, it makes a sound and the disc icon appears on your desktop.

■ A dialog like the one in **Figure 53** appears if you try to burn an audio or MP3 CD containing protected audio files. Click the disclosure triangle to see a list of the songs that can't be burned to disc; you must remove those songs from your playlist before burning it to disc.

■ Do not cancel the disc burning process after it has begun. Doing so can render the disc unusable.

BURNING iTUNES CONTENT TO DISC

To share content with other network users

1. Choose iTunes > Preferences.

2. Click the Sharing button to display Sharing preferences (**Figure 54**).

3. To play content shared by other network users, turn on the Look for shared libraries check box. This displays any shared libraries in the source list (**Figure 19**) on your computer, so you can listen to it.

4. To share your iTunes content with other network users, turn on the Share my library on my local network check box. Then select one of the radio buttons:

   ▲ **Share entire library** shares all of your music.

   ▲ **Share selected playlists** enables you to toggle check boxes for individual playlists you want to share.

5. To require other network users to enter a password to listen to your music, turn on the Require password check box and enter a password in the box beside it.

6. Click OK.

7. A dialog like the one in **Figure 55** may appear. Click OK.

✔ Tips

■ Once sharing is enabled, the Status area in the Sharing preferences dialog reports whether your music is being accessed by other users on the network (**Figure 54**).

■ I tell you more about Mac OS X's networking features in **Chapter 16**.

Figure 54 Sharing preferences enable you to share iTunes content.

Figure 55 This dialog appears when you enable sharing. (Apple's lawyers obviously had a hand in this one.)

Mac OS X Applications

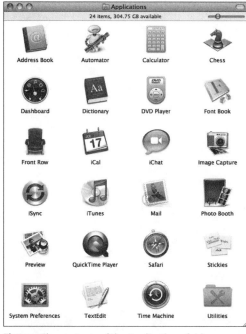

Figure 1 The contents of the Applications folder.

Mac OS Applications

Mac OS X includes a variety of software applications that you can use to perform tasks on your computer.

This chapter provides instructions for getting started with the following Apple programs in the Applications folder (**Figure 1**):

◆ **Calculator**, which enables you to perform calculations and conversions.

◆ **Chess**, which is a computerized version of the game of chess.

◆ **Dictionary**, which provides word definitions and synonyms and access to other reference materials.

◆ **Image Capture**, which enables you to download image files from a digital camera or import images from a scanner and save them on disk.

◆ **Photo Booth**, which enables you to use your computer's built-in camera to take photos and apply special effects to them.

◆ **Preview**, which enables you to view images and PDF files.

◆ **QuickTime Player**, which enables you to view and record QuickTime movies and audio.

◆ **Stickies**, which enables you to place colorful notes on your computer screen.

Continued on next page...

Continued from previous page.

✔ Tips

■ The Mac OS X 10.6 installer places icons for some Mac OS X applications in the Dock (**Figure 2**).

■ Mac OS X includes a number of other applications that are discussed elsewhere in this book:

▲ Address Book, iCal, and iSync, in **Chapter 12**.

▲ Automator, in **Chapter 24**.

▲ Dashboard, in **Chapter 15**.

▲ DVD Player, Front Row, and iTunes, in **Chapter 13**.

▲ Font Book, in **Chapter 16**.

▲ iChat, Mail, and Safari, in **Chapter 19**.

▲ System Preferences, in **Chapter 23**.

▲ TextEdit, in **Chapter 11**.

▲ Time Machine, in **Chapter 6**.

■ Most applications in the Utilities folder are covered in **Chapter 24**.

Figure 2 The Dock is preconfigured to include a number of Mac OS X applications. Your Dock may include even more applications if your Mac came with iLife or iWork preinstalled or you have installed additional software on your computer.

Figure 3
The Calculator looks and works like a $5 pocket calculator.

Figure 4
Calculator's Window menu.

Figure 5
The Paper Tape window makes it easy to keep track of your entries.

Figure 6
The File menu includes commands for working with the paper tape.

Calculator

Calculator (**Figure 3**) displays a simple calculator that can perform addition, subtraction, multiplication, and division, as well as complex mathematical calculations and conversions.

To launch Calculator

Open the Calculator icon in the Applications folder window (**Figure 1**).

The Calculator window appears (**Figure 3**).

To perform basic calculations

Use your mouse or trackpad to click buttons for numbers and operators.

Or

Press keyboard keys corresponding to numbers and operators.

The numbers you enter and the results of your calculations appear at the top of the Calculator window (**Figure 3**).

To keep track of your entries

Choose Window > Show Paper Tape (**Figure 4**) or press ⌃⌘T. The Paper Tape window appears. It displays your entries as you make them (**Figure 5**).

✔ Tips

- To hide the Paper Tape window, choose Window > Hide Paper Tape, press ⌃⌘T. or click the Paper Tape window's close button.

- To start with a fresh tape, click the Clear button.

- You can use commands under the File menu (**Figure 6**) to save or print the paper tape.

To perform scientific calculations

1. Choose View > Scientific (**Figure 7**) or press ⌃⌘2. The window expands to show a variety of functions used for scientific calculations (**Figure 8**).

2. Click buttons for the functions, values, and operators to perform your calculations.

✔ Tip

■ To hide scientific functions, choose View > Basic (**Figure 7**) or press ⌃⌘1.

To use programmer functions

1. Choose View > Programmer (**Figure 7**) or press ⌃⌘3. The window expands to show a variety of programming-related functions (**Figure 9**).

2. Click buttons for the functions, values, and operators to perform your calculations.

✔ Tip

■ To hide programmer functions, choose View > Basic (**Figure 7**) or press ⌃⌘1.

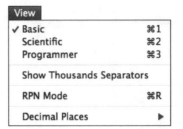

Figure 7 Calculator's View menu offers several options.

Figure 8 Choosing Scientific from the View menu expands the Calculator to display scientific functions.

Figure 9 Choosing Programmer from the View menu displays programming-related functions.

Figure 10
The Calculator also supports Reverse Polish Notation (RPN).

Figure 11
Start by entering the value you want to convert in the Calculator window.

Figure 12
Choose a type of conversion from the Convert menu.

Figure 13
Set conversion options in a dialog like this.

Figure 14
The converted value appears in the Calculator window.

To use Reverse Polish Notation

1. Choose View > RPN (**Figure 7**). The entry area expands and the letters RPN appear in the calculator's window (**Figure 10**).

2. Click buttons for the functions, values, and operators to perform your calculations.

✔ Tips

- Reverse Polish Notation, or RPN, is an alternative format for entering calculations. It is commonly used on Hewlett-Packard brand calculators.

- If you don't know what RPN is, you probably don't need to use it.

To perform conversions

1. Enter the value you want to convert (**Figure 11**).

2. Choose the conversion you want from the Convert menu (**Figure 12**).

3. In the dialog that appears, set options for the conversion you want to perform. **Figure 13** shows an example that converts speed from miles per hour to knots.

4. Click Convert. The original value you entered is converted and appears at the top of the Calculator window (**Figure 14**).

✔ Tip

- The Convert menu's Recent Conversions submenu makes it easy to repeat conversions you have done recently.

USING THE CALCULATOR

287

Chess

Chess is a computerized version of the classic strategy game of chess. Your pieces are white and you go first; the computer's pieces are black.

To launch Chess

Open the Chess icon in the Applications folder window (**Figure 1**).

The Chess window appears (**Figure 15**).

To move a chess piece

Drag the piece onto any valid square on the playing board.

✔ Tips

■ The computer moves automatically after each of your moves.

■ If you attempt to make an invalid move, an alert sounds and the piece returns to where it was.

■ If Speakable Items is enabled, you can use spoken commands to move chess pieces. I tell you about Speakable Items in **Chapter 23**.

To start a new game

1. Choose Game > New (**Figure 16**) or press ⌘N. A dialog sheet like the one in **Figure 17** appears.

2. Choose an option from the Players pop-up menu (**Figure 18**).

3. If desired, choose an option from the Variant pop-up menu (**Figure 19**).

4. Click Start.

Figure 15 The Chess window displays a colorful, three-dimensional chess board.

Figure 16 Chess's Game menu.

Figure 17 A dialog sheet like this one appears when you choose New from the File menu.

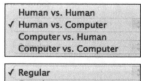

Figures 18 & 19 The Players (top) and Variant (bottom) pop-up menus enable you to set options for a new game.

PLAYING CHESS

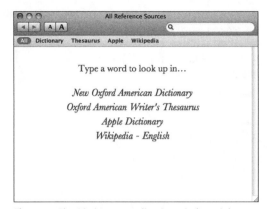

Figure 20 The Dictionary application window, right after launching Dictionary.

Dictionary

Dictionary is like a reference library, with all the features of a dictionary and thesaurus, without all that paper. Simply type a word or phrase into the search box at the top of Dictionary's window. Dictionary comes up with a list of matches. Double-click the one that interests you to get definitions, pronunciations, and synonyms. You'll never have an excuse to use the wrong word again!

To launch Dictionary

Open the Dictionary icon in the Applications folder window (**Figure 1**).

The Dictionary window appears (**Figure 20**).

To look up a word or phrase

1. Near the top of the Dictionary window, click the button for the reference you want to search:

    ▲ **All** searches all references.

    ▲ **Dictionary** searches the *New Oxford American Dictionary*. Use this option to look up pronunciations and definitions.

    ▲ **Thesaurus** searches the *Oxford American Writer's Thesaurus*. Use this option to look up synonyms.

    ▲ **Apple** searches the *Apple Dictionary*. Use this option to look up Apple-related terms.

    ▲ **Wikipedia** searches the Wikipedia online encyclopedia. Use this option to look up more detailed information than what you'd find in a dictionary.

Continued on next page...

USING DICTIONARY

Continued from previous page.

2. Enter the word or phrase you want to look up in the search box at the top of the Dictionary window. As you type, Dictionary begins displaying a list of matches (**Figure 21**).

3. Double-click the word or phrase that interests you. The window displays information for that entry from the reference you selected in step 1 (**Figures 22, 23, and 24**).

✔ Tips

- To change the size of font characters in the Dictionary window, click one of the font size buttons in the window's toolbar.

- To print an entry, choose File > Print. I tell you more about printing in **Chapter 17**.

- You can click a word in an entry to look up that word, too.

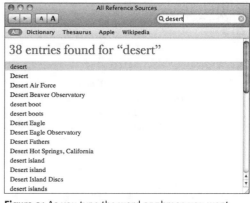

Figure 21 As you type the word or phrase you want to look up, a list of matches appears in Dictionary's window.

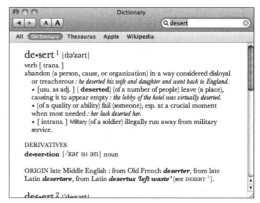

Figure 22 The definition of a word appears in the Dictionary window.

Figure 23 Synonyms for a word in the Thesaurus window.

Figure 24 An encyclopedia entry for a word in the Wikipedia window.

USING DICTIONARY

Image Capture

Image Capture is an application that performs three functions:

◆ Import image files from a digital camera to your computer's hard disk.

◆ Operate your scanner to scan and save images.

◆ Share images from a camera on a Web site or in a slide show.

In this part of the chapter, I explain how to import images from a digital camera and scan a document with Image Capture.

✔ Tips

■ Some digital cameras and scanners require that driver software be installed on Mac OS X before the camera or scanner can be used. Consult the documentation that came with your scanner or camera or check the device manufacturer's Web site for Mac OS X compatibility and driver information.

■ Not all digital cameras or scanners are compatible with Image Capture. Generally speaking, if Image Capture does not "see" your camera or scanner when it is connected and turned on, the camera or scanner is probably not compatible with Image Capture and Image Capture cannot be used.

■ If you have Apple's iLife suite of products, you can also import images from a digital camera using iPhoto, which offers additional features for managing photos saved to disk.

To download images from a digital camera

1. Attach your digital camera to your computer's USB or FireWire port, using the applicable cable.

2. Turn the camera on and, if necessary, set it to review mode. The main Image Capture window should appear.

3. If necessary, select your camera in the Devices list (**Figure 25**).

4. Use the Import To pop-up menu at the bottom of the window (**Figure 26**) to select the location you want to import images to. There are four groups of options:

    ◆ Folders that are commonly used for storing downloaded items or images.

    ◆ Applications that can open images.

    ◆ Tasks you can use to automate the creation of a Web page or PDF file of the imported images.

    ◆ Other enables you to choose a disk location or application for saving or opening the images.

    For this example, I chose the default option, which is the Pictures folder in your Home folder.

5. To import all images on the camera, click the Import All button.

    or

    To import some of the images on the camera, select the images you want to import and click the Import button.

    A note at the bottom of the window indicates import progress (**Figure 27**). When it disappears, the import is complete.

6. If necessary, eject or unmount the camera's desktop icon before disconnecting it.

Figure 25 Image capture displays a list of images on your camera in its main window.

Figure 26
Use this pop-up menu to specify where you want to import images to.

Importing "DSC_4462.JPG" 4 of 50 selected

Figure 27 A note at the bottom of the window indicates import progress.

Figure 28 You can set options for a connected device in the lower-left corner of the Image Capture window.

✔ Tips

■ If Image Capture doesn't launch automatically after step 2, you can open it by double-clicking its icon in the Applications folder window (**Figure 1**).

■ If iPhoto is installed on your computer, it may launch instead of Image Capture when you connect a digital camera. If so, you must manually launch Image Capture by double-clicking its application icon (**Figure 1**) to open and use it.

■ In step 4, to select multiple images, hold down the ⌘ key while clicking each one.

■ I explain how to eject a volume on page 101.

■ You can also use Image Capture to work with a card reader containing image files. You can see an SD card inserted in a MacBook Pro's card slot in **Figure 25**. This offers an easy alternative to connecting your camera with a cable.

■ You can also use the thumbnail window (**Figure 26**) to delete images on the camera. Select the images you want to delete, click the Delete button, and click Delete in the confirmation dialog that appears.

■ You can set options in the bottom-left corner of the Image Capture window (**Figure 28**) for the connected camera:

  ▲ **Connecting this camera opens** enables you to specify an application that should open when you connect the camera.

  ▲ **Share camera** enables you to share the camera's content on your network. I tell you more about sharing volumes on page 474.

  ▲ **Delete after import** instructs Image Capture to delete images from the camera after you import them.

To scan a document

1. Make sure your scanner is properly installed, connected, and turned on.

2. Place the document you want to scan on the scan bed.

3. Open Image Capture. The scanner should appear in the Devices list. If necessary, select it (**Figure 29**).

4. Choose the location you want to scan the document to from the Scan To pop-up menu. There are three groups of options:

   ◆ Folders that are commonly used for storing scanned documents.

   ◆ Applications that can open scanned documents.

   ◆ Other enables you to choose a disk location or application for saving or opening the scanned document.

5. Click Scan.

6. Wait while the scanner scans the document. This could take a few moments and multiple scanner passes, depending on your scanner model. When it's finished, an image of the document you scanned appears in the Image Capture window (**Figure 30**) and the document is saved to the location you selected in step 4.

✔ Tip

■ Clicking the Show Details button may offer additional options for scanning a document, including resolution, type of document, and size (**Figure 31**). The options that appear vary depending on your scanner model and installed driver software.

Figure 29 Your scanner should appear in the Devices list.

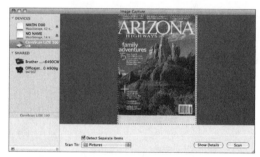

Figure 30 An image of the scanned document—in this example, a magazine cover—appears in Image Capture's window.

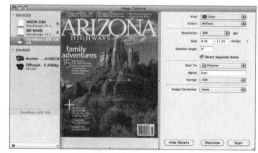

Figure 31 Clicking the Show Details button may display additional options for the scan, depending on your scanner and its driver software.

SCANNING DOCUMENTS

Figure 32 Photo Booth's window shows what an attached camera sees. (And no, special effects have not been applied to this image. This glazed look is what I usually have halfway through a revision of this book.)

Figure 33 Photo Booth counts down before snapping photos.

Figure 34 Here's an example of a still picture, four quick pictures, and a movie clip.

Photo Booth

Photo Booth is an application that enables you to take snapshots with an iSight camera or digital video camera. You can take still photos or short movies and can include special effects with the photos you take.

To launch Photo Booth

Open the Photo Booth icon in the Applications folder window (**Figure 1**).

The Photo Booth window appears (**Figure 32**).

To create a snapshot or movie

1. Click a snapshot type button:
   - ▲ **Take a still picture** takes a single still photo.
   - ▲ **Take four quick pictures** takes four still photos a second or so apart.
   - ▲ **Take a movie clip** records a movie.

2. Click the Camera button. A countdown timer appears beneath the video preview (**Figure 33**). When it reaches 0, one of three things happens:
   - ▲ For still photos, the photo is snapped and appears as a thumbnail in the bottom of the window (**Figure 34**).
   - ▲ For four quick photos, four photos are snapped, one after the other. They appear in a single frame at the bottom of the window (**Figure 34**).
   - ▲ For a movie clip, the camera begins recording. Click the stop button to stop recording movie frames. A thumbnail of the movie appears at the bottom of the window (**Figure 34**).

To include special effects or a background image in a photo

1. Click the Effects button.

2. Click the arrow buttons on either side of the Effects button to scroll through the four screens of effects (**Figures 35, 36, 37,** and **38**) until you find the one you like.

3. To apply a visual effect (**Figures 35** and **36**), click to select it.

   Or

   To apply a backdrop (**Figures 37** and **38**), click to select the backdrop you want. Then follow the instructions that appear in the window to move out of the frame until the background is detected.

4. Follow the steps on the previous page to create a snapshot.

✔ Tips

- The fourth screen of effects (**Figure 38**) is for your own backdrop images. Drag the image you want to use to one of the blank spaces to add it to those available for use.

- To turn off an effect, choose Normal in any of the effects screens.

Figures 35 & 36 The first two screens of effects apply visual effects to the image.

Figures 37 & 38 The last two screens of effects apply backdrops—including ones you can add.

Figure 39 Select the image you want to use.

Figure 40 Photo Booth copies the image to your user account.

Figure 41
Photo Booth copies the image to the Buddy Picture window in iChat.

To set an image as an account picture

1. At the bottom of the Photo Booth window, select the thumbnail for the image you want to use (**Figure 39**).

2. Click the Account Picture button.

   Photo Booth opens the Accounts preferences pane for your account and pastes in the image (**Figure 40**).

3. Click the Accounts preferences pane window's close button to dismiss it.

✔ Tip

■ I tell you more about the Accounts preferences pane on page 489.

To set an image as an iChat buddy icon

1. At the bottom of the Photo Booth window, select the thumbnail for the image you want to use (**Figure 39**).

2. Click the Buddy Picture button.

   Photo Booth opens iChat and displays its Buddy Picture window (**Figure 41**). You can use the zoom slider at the bottom of the window to change the magnification of the image.

3. When you're finished working with iChat, choose iChat > Quit iChat to dismiss it.

✔ Tip

■ I tell you more about iChat in on page 420.

USING IMAGES

To e-mail an image

1. Select the image you want to send via e-mail (**Figure 39**).

2. Click the Email button.

   Photo Booth launches Mail (or your default e-mail application) and creates a new message form with the image attached (**Figure 42**).

3. Complete the form and click Send.

4. When you're finished using Mail, choose Mail > Quit Mail to dismiss it.

✔ Tip

- I tell you more about using Mail on page 407.

To show an image on disk

1. Select the image you want to find on your hard disk.

2. Choose File > Reveal in Finder (**Figure 43**) or press ⌃⌘R.

   The Finder window for your Photo Booth folder opens (**Figure 44**).

✔ Tip

- Photo Booth stores its images in the Photo Booth folder inside your Pictures folder.

Figure 42 Photo Booth launches Mail and creates a new message with the image attached.

Figure 43 Use the Reveal in Finder command...

Figure 44 ...to quickly open the Photo Booth folder and select the image.

Figure 45 Here's an image file opened with Preview: A photo of me hard at work at my other job.

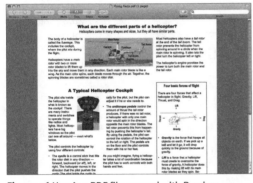

Figure 46 Here's a PDF file opened with Preview.

Preview

Preview is a program that enables you to open and view two kinds of files:

◆ Image files (**Figure 45**), including JPG, GIF, HDR, TIFF, PSD, PICT, PNG, BMP, RAW, and SGI.

◆ PDF, or Portable Document Format, files (**Figure 46**) created with Mac OS X's Print command, Adobe Acrobat software, or other software capable of creating PDFs.

Preview also includes tools you can use to edit images and annotate images and PDFs.

✔ Tips

■ When you open PostScript (PS) or EPS format files, Preview automatically converts them to PDF files for viewing.

■ I explain how to create PDF files with the Print command on page 380.

■ You can also open PDF files with Adobe Reader software. You can learn more about Adobe Reader—and download a free copy of the software—on the Adobe Systems Web site, get.adobe.com/reader.

PREVIEW

To open a file with Preview

Drag the document file's icon onto the Preview icon in the Applications folder (**Figure 47**).

Or

Double-click the file icon for a Preview-compatible document (**Figure 48**).

Preview launches and displays the file in its window (**Figures 45** and **46**).

✔ Tips

- You can also use Preview's Open command to open any compatible file on disk. I explain how to use an application's Open command on page 194.

- To open multiple files at once, select all of their icons and drag any one of them onto the Preview icon.

- You can use options on a Preview window's toolbar (**Figures 45** and **46**) or Preview's View menu (**Figure 49**) to zoom in or out, rotate the window's contents, or view a specific page.

- If a document has multiple pages or if you opened multiple image files at once, you can click the Sidebar button in the window's toolbar to display or hide a sidebar with thumbnail images of each open image (**Figure 50**) or page. Click a thumbnail to move quickly to that page or image.

Figure 47
You can open a file with Preview by dragging its icon on top of the Preview icon.

Flying Facts.pdf

Figure 48
Here's an example of the icon for a PDF file that can be opened with Preview.

Figure 49
The View menu offers options for changing the view of documents within Preview.

Figure 50 The sidebar displays thumbnails of open documents or document pages.

Figure 51 When you enter search text in the Search box, Preview quickly displays matches and highlights occurrences in the displayed page.

Figure 52 Preview's tool buttons for a PDF file.

Figure 53 The Tools menu offers commands for working with images and PDF files.

Tools	
Show Inspector	⌘I
Show Fonts	⌘T
Adjust Color...	⌥⌘C
Adjust Size...	
Move Tool	⌘1
Text Tool	⌘2
Select Tool	⌘3
Annotate	▶
Rotate Left	⌘L
Rotate Right	⌘R
Flip Horizontal	
Flip Vertical	
Crop	⌘K
Assign Profile...	

The Finder & Desktop

The *Finder* is a program that is part of Mac OS. It launches automatically when you start your computer.

The Finder provides a graphic user interface called the *desktop* (**Figure 1**) that you can use to open, copy, delete, list, organize, and perform other operations on computer files.

Figure 54 Drag to select text.

To search for text in a PDF file

1. Open the PDF file you want to search.

2. If necessary, click the Sidebar button to display the sidebar.

3. Enter a search word or phrase in the Search box at the top of the drawer.

   As you type, Preview searches the document for the text you entered. It displays the thumbnails of pages containing that text in the sidebar. It also highlights the occurrences of the search text in the page that is displayed in the main document window. You can see all this in **Figure 51**.

✔ Tips

■ To display a specific occurrence of the search text, click its page thumbnail in the sidebar. The search text is highlighted in yellow wherever it appears on that page (**Figure 51**).

■ The more text you enter in the Search box, the fewer matches Preview finds.

To select text in a PDF file

1. In Preview's toolbar, click the Text tool button (**Figure 52**), choose Tools > Text Tool (**Figure 53**), or press ⌘2.

2. Position the pointer over text in the document window. It turns into an I-beam pointer.

3. Press the button down and drag to select text (**Figure 54**).

✔ Tip

■ Once text is selected, you can use the Copy command to copy it to the clipboard and use it in another document. I tell you about the Copy and Paste commands on page 222.

SEARCHING FOR & SELECTING TEXT IN PDFS

To select part of a picture

1. In Preview's toolbar, click the Select tool button (**Figure 52**), choose Tools > Select Tool (**Figure 53**), or press ⌃ ⌘ 3.

2. Position the pointer in the upper-left corner of the area you want to select.

3. Drag down and to the right. A selection box appears over the image, along with an indicator that shows the size of the selection in pixels (**Figure 55**).

4. Release the button to complete the selection.

✔ Tips

- Once you have selected part of a picture, you can use the Copy command to copy it to the clipboard for use in another document. I tell you about the Copy and Paste commands on page 222.

- You can use the Select tool to crop an image. Simply select the part of the image you want to keep and choose Tools > Crop (**Figure 53**) or press ⌃ ⌘ K. This command is only available if part of an image has been selected.

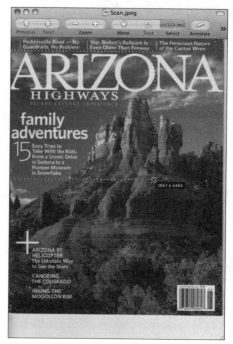

Figure 55 Drag a selection box.

Figure 56
A QuickTime movie's icon displays a thumbnail image from the movie.

EscalanteRun.mov

Figure 57 The first frame of the movie appears in a QuickTime Player window.

Figure 58
Pointing to a QuickTime movie's icon displays a play button.

EscalanteRun.mov

QuickTime Player

QuickTime is a video and audio technology developed by Apple, Inc. It is widely used for digital movies as well as streaming audio and video available via the Internet.

QuickTime Player is an application you can use to view QuickTime movies and streaming Internet content. In this latest version of QuickTime, you can also create your own audio, video, and screencast recordings and easily save them for sharing in iTunes, in your MobileMe Gallery, or on YouTube.

✔ Tips

■ Previous versions of QuickTime required an upgrade to the Pro version to edit or save QuickTime Player content.

■ To share content on MobileMe or YouTube, you must have an account on the service you want to use.

■ You can learn about QuickTime technology on Apple's QuickTime Web site, www.apple.com/quicktime/.

■ Internet access is covered in **Chapter 18**.

To launch QuickTime Player

Open the QuickTime Player icon in the Applications folder window (**Figure 1**).

Or

Open a QuickTime movie file (**Figure 56**). The movie appears in a player window (**Figure 57**).

✔ Tip

■ If you point to a QuickTime movie's document icon, a play button appears (**Figure 58**). Clicking that button plays the movie in its icon. This technique also works in the Finder's column view and the Info window for a QuickTime movie.

QUICKTIME PLAYER

To open a QuickTime movie file

Double-click the QuickTime movie file icon (**Figure 56**).

Or

Drag the icon for a QuickTime movie onto the QuickTime Player icon in the Applications folder window (**Figure 1**).

If QuickTime Player is not already running, it launches. The movie's first frame appears in a window (**Figure 57**).

✔ Tip

- You can also open a QuickTime movie by using the Open File command on QuickTime Player's File menu (**Figure 59**). The Open dialog is covered in **Chapter 10**.

To open a QuickTime movie file on the Internet

1. Open QuickTime Player.

2. Choose File > Open URL (**Figure 59**) or press ⌘U.

3. In the Open URL dialog that appears (**Figure 60**) enter the complete URL for a movie file on the Internet and click Open.

   Your computer accesses the Internet and loads the movie at the address you specified (**Figure 61**). It begins playing the movie as soon as enough of it has loaded to assure uninterrupted play.

✔ Tips

- As you've probably realized, an Internet connection is required to view movies on the Internet in QuickTime Player.

- A *URL* is a unique address for a file on the Internet. I tell you more about URLs and accessing the Internet in **Chapters 18** and **19**.

Figure 59
QuickTime Player's File menu.

Figure 60 Enter the URL for the movie you want to view.

Figure 61 The movie appears in a QuickTime window.

Volume   Fast rewind   Share
         Play / Pause   Full
         Fast forward   screen

Playhead   Timeline

Figure 62 QuickTime player's controls appear when the pointer is over the movie window.

View	
Enter Full Screen	⌘F
Actual Size	⌘1
Fit to Screen	⌘3
Fill Screen	⌘4
Panoramic	⌘5
Increase Size	⌘+
Decrease Size	⌘−
Show Closed Captioning	⌥⌘T
Languages	▶
Subtitles	▶
Show Chapters	⌘R
Loop	⌘L

Figure 63
Use the View menu to set the size of the movie.

To control movie play

You can use controls in the QuickTime Player window (**Figure 62**) to control movie play:

◆ **Volume** changes movie volume; drag the slider left or right or click the volume icon to mute/unmute.

◆ **Fast rewind** plays the movie backward quickly, with sound.

◆ **Play** starts playing the movie. When the movie is playing, the Play button turns to a **Pause** button, which pauses movie play.

◆ **Fast Forward** plays the movie forward quickly, with sound.

◆ **Share** displays a menu you can use to copy the movie to iTunes or share it on MobileMe or YouTube.

◆ **Full screen** toggles between normal and full screen view.

◆ **Timeline** tracks movie progress. By dragging the **Playhead**, you can quickly move to a specific scene in the movie.

✔ Tips

■ If the play controls are not visible, position the pointer anywhere over the movie window.

■ Each time you click the fast rewind or fast forward button, the speed is increased up to 8x normal speed. To play at normal speed, click the Play button.

■ You can drag the play controls to another location within the QuickTime Player window.

To specify movie size

Select a size option from the View menu (**Figure 63**). The size of the movie's window changes accordingly.

CONTROLLING QUICKTIME MOVIES

305

To record a movie with QuickTime Player

1. In QuickTime Player, choose File > New Movie Recording (**Figure 59**) or press [Option] [⇧ ⌘ N].

   QuickTime Player displays a Movie Recording window, using the video input from your computer's built-in iSight camera (**Figure 64**) or another compatible camera connected to your computer.

2. Click the Record button (**Figure 65**) to begin recording your movie. A timer appears in the upper-right corner of the window and the volume level bar shows how well QuickTime Player can "hear" you (**Figure 66**).

3. When you want to stop recording, click the Stop button. (If the Stop button isn't showing, move your pointer into the window to display it.) QuickTime Player saves the movie in your Movies folder (**Figure 67**). The movie remains open so you can play it.

✔ Tips

- Clicking the Options button in the Movie Recording window displays a menu like the one in **Figure 68**, which you can use to fine-tune settings for your movie.

- You can use similar techniques to record audio or to make a movie of what appears on your computer screen as you work. Just start with commands under the File menu: New Audio Recording or New Screen Recording. The controls that appears are very similar to those that appear when you record a movie.

Figure 64 The Movie Recording window displays what your iSight camera "sees."

Figure 65 Use these controls to record your movie.

Figure 66 Here's what QuickTime Player's window might look like while recording...well, if I were sitting in front of your camera, anyway.

Figure 67 The movie is automatically saved in your Movies folder.

Figure 68 An options menu like this makes it possible to change default settings for movies you record.

Figure 69 Choose an option from the Share menu on the menu bar...

Figure 70 ...or from the Share menu inside the QuickTime Player window.

To share movies

1. If necessary, open the movie you want to share.

2. Choose an option from the Share menu on the menu bar (**Figure 69**) or in the QuickTime Player window (**Figure 70**):

   ▲ **iTunes** enables you to add the movie to your iTunes library.

   ▲ **MobileMe Gallery** enables you to save the movie to your MobileMe account.

   ▲ **YouTube** enables you to save the movie to your YouTube account.

3. What happens next depends on which option you chose:

   ▲ If you chose iTunes, a dialog like the one in **Figure 71** appears. Select the size you want and click Share. The movie is exported and added to your iTunes library's Movies list.

   ▲ If you chose MobileMe Gallery, a dialog like the one in **Figure 72** appears. Enter a title and description for the movie and set other options. When you click Share, the movie is exported and uploaded to your MobileMe account.

Continued on next page...

Figure 71 This dialog offers three size options for saving a movie to iTunes.

Figure 72 Fill out a form like this to provide information to a movie you save to MobileMe.

SHARING MOVIES

Continued from previous page.

▲ If you chose YouTube, a dialog like the one in **Figure 73** appears. Fill in the form and click Sign In. A second dialog (**Figure 74**) prompts you for movie information. Fill that in and click Next. A final dialog reminds you about copyright. When you click Share, the movie is exported and uploaded to your YouTube account.

✔ Tips

■ If a security dialog appears in step 3, click Allow to allow QuickTime Player to access your keychain. I tell you more about Keychain Access on page 514.

■ Internet access is required to save movies to MobileMe or YouTube. I discuss accessing the Internet in **Chapter 18** and **19**.

■ You must have a MobileMe account to publish to MobileMe. You must have a YouTube account to publish to YouTube.

■ I discuss iTunes on page 270 and MobileMe on page 433.

Figure 73 To save a movie to YouTube, you must start by logging in to your YouTube account.

Figure 74 The title and description you provide will appear with the movie on YouTube after it is uploaded.

SHARING MOVIES

Figure 75 The default windows that appear when you first launch Stickies tell you a little about the program.

Figure 76 Stickies' File menu.

Figure 77 Here's a blank new sticky note...

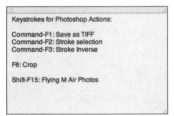

Figure 78 ...and here's the same note with a reminder typed in.

Figures 79 & 80 Use the Color (left) and Font (right) menus to change the appearance of notes.

Stickies

Stickies is an application that displays computerized "sticky notes" that you can use to place reminders on your screen.

To launch Stickies

Open the Stickies icon in the Applications folder window (**Figure 1**).

The default Stickies windows appear (**Figure 75**).

✔ Tips

- Read the text in the default Stickies windows (**Figure 75**) to learn more about Stickies.

- Sticky notes remain on the desktop until you quit Stickies.

- When you quit Stickies, all notes are automatically saved to disk and will reappear the next time you launch Stickies.

To create a sticky note

1. Choose File > New Note (**Figure 76**) or press ⌘N to display a blank new note (**Figure 77**).

2. Type the text that you want to include in the note (**Figure 78**).

✔ Tip

- You can use options under the Color and Font menus (**Figures 79** and **80**) to change the appearance of notes or note text. Common text formatting options are covered in **Chapters 11** and **16**.

USING STICKIES

To print sticky notes

1. To print a sticky note, click it to activate it and then choose File > Print (**Figure 76**) or press ⌘ ⌘ P.

2. Use the Print dialog that appears to set options for printing and click the Print button.

✔ Tip

■ **Chapter 17** covers the Print dialog and printing.

To close a sticky note

1. Click the close box for the sticky note you want to close.

   or

   Activate the sticky note you want to close and choose File > Close (**Figure 76**) or press ⌘ ⌘ W.

2. A Close dialog like the one in **Figure 81** may appear.

   ▲ **Don't Save** closes the note without saving its contents.

   ▲ **Cancel** leaves the note open.

   ▲ **Save** displays the Export dialog (**Figure 82**), which you can use to save the note as plain or formatted text in a file on disk. Enter a name, select a disk location, choose a file format, and then click Save.

✔ Tips

■ Once a sticky note has been saved, it can be opened and edited with TextEdit or any other text editing application.

■ I explain how to save files on page 230.

Figure 81 This dialog asks if you want to save note contents.

Figure 82 Use the Export dialog to save a note as plain or formatted text in a file on disk.

Dashboard

15

Dashboard & Widgets

Dashboard is a feature of Mac OS X that gives you instant access to simple applications called *widgets*. Widgets work with other applications such as iTunes, iCal, and Address Book to provide you with quick access to the most commonly used features. They also work with the Internet to get up-to-date information such as stock quotes, weather, and business listings.

Mac OS X comes with a bunch of widgets, all accessible from the widget bar that you can display at the bottom of your screen. Click a widget to display and use it.

In this chapter, I explain how to use Dashboard to display the widget bar and widgets. I also tell you how to use the widget manager to add, remove, and disable widgets. Finally, I provide a brief discussion of how you can use each of the widgets that come with Mac OS X.

✔ Tip

■ Apple is actively encouraging developers to build more widgets. If you like using widgets and want more, be sure to check out Apple's Dashboard Widgets Web page, www.apple.com/downloads/dashboard/.

Opening & Closing Dashboard

The main purpose of Dashboard is to make widgets easily accessible without interfering with your work. Apple achieves this by making Dashboard quick and easy to open and close.

To open Dashboard

Press F12 or, on a laptop, press Fn F12.

Your screen dims and the last widgets you accessed appear (**Figure 1**).

✔ Tips

- These instructions assume your Mac has default settings in the Exposé pane of the Exposé & Spaces preferences pane (**Figure 2**), which assign Dashboard to the F12 key. I explain how to change these settings on page 174.

- As shown in **Figures 2** and **3**, if you have a Mighty Mouse you can configure one of its buttons to activate Dashboard. I explain how to set mouse preferences on page 550.

To close Dashboard

Click anywhere on the screen other than on a widget.

Or

Press F12 or, on a laptop, press Fn F12.

The widgets disappear and your screen returns to normal brightness.

✔ Tip

- Closing Dashboard does not close the widgets that were open when you used it. It just hides them from view.

Figure 1 Dashboard with four widgets displayed: Calculator, Weather (but it's a *dry* heat), Calendar, and World Clock.

Figure 2 You can specify an F key and mouse button for Dashboard in the Exposé pane of the Exposé & Spaces preferences pane.

Figure 3 If you have a Mighty Mouse, you can configure one of its buttons to show and hide Dashboard.

Figure 4 The widget bar appears at the bottom of your screen.

Figure 5 Click one of the arrow buttons...

Figure 6 ...to view other installed widgets.

Working with the Widget Bar

The widget bar gives you access to all installed widgets.

To display the widget bar

With Dashboard open, click the **+** button in the lower-left corner of your screen (**Figure 3**).

Your screen's view slides up to make room for the widget bar at the bottom of your screen (**Figure 4**). Close buttons appear for each widget that is open and the Manage Widgets button appears.

To see other installed widgets

Click the arrow button on the left or right end of the widget bar (**Figure 5**).

The widget bar scrolls to show more installed widgets (**Figure 6**).

To hide the widget bar

Click the **X** button near the lower-left corner of your screen.

The widget bar disappears and your screen's view slides back down to display all of the screen's contents (**Figure 1**).

Displaying Widgets

To use a widget, you must open it. If you want a widget to appear automatically every time you open Dashboard, you can leave it open when you close Dashboard. Otherwise, you can close the widget.

To open a widget

1. Open Dashboard (**Figure 1**). If the widget you want to use is already displayed, you can skip the following steps; the widget is already open and ready to use.

2. If the widget you want to use is not already displayed or you want to open a second copy of it, open the widget bar (**Figure 4**).

3. Click the icon for the widget you want to use (**Figure 7**).

   or

   Drag the icon for the widget you want to open from the widget bar to the location you want it to appear onscreen.

   The widget you clicked appears onscreen and is ready to use (**Figure 8**).

✔ Tips

■ Why would you want to open more than one copy of a widget? Well, suppose you want to view the weather for Wickenburg, AZ and New York, NY. You simply open the Weather widget twice and configure each one for one of the cities.

■ If your computer has enough RAM and graphics capabilities, the widget will open with a cool flowing water effect. I attempted to capture this effect in a screen shot (**Figure 9**). (I like this effect so much, sometimes I open a few widgets just to watch them open.)

Figure 7 In the widget bar, click the icon for the widget you want to open.

Figure 8 The widget you opened appears among other open widgets.

Figure 9 You can call me a geek, but I love the special effects that appear when you open a widget on a powerful Mac.

Figure 10 To move a widget, simply drag it into a new position onscreen.

Figure 11 To display the close button for a widget, hold down Option and points to the widget.

To move a widget

Once a widget is displayed, you can drag its border to move it to a new position onscreen (**Figure 10**).

✔ Tip

- Arrange the widgets you keep open so you know exactly where to look onscreen when you open Dashboard to access their features.

To close a widget

1. If the widget bar is displayed, an X button should appear at the upper-left corner of the widget (**Figure 4**).

   or

   If the widget bar is not displayed, hold down the Option key and point to the widget you want to close. An X button appears at its upper-left corner (**Figure 11**).

2. Click the X button. The widget closes.

✔ Tip

- Keep in mind that many widgets lose their settings when you close them. If you plan to use a widget with custom settings often, you may want to keep it open so you don't have to reset it each time you use it.

MOVING & CLOSING WIDGETS

Installing Widgets

You can customize Dashboard by adding or removing widgets.

Additional widgets are available on Apple's Dashboard Widgets Web page, www.apple. com/downloads/dashboard/. You can also find widgets on shareware distribution Web sites and on Web sites for third-party vendors.

To install a widget

1. Copy the widget file you want to install to your computer.

2. Double-click the widget file's icon (**Figure 12**).

3. A widget installer window appears (**Figure 13**). Click Install.

   Dashboard opens. The widget appears within a "test drive" window (**Figure 14**).

4. Test the widget to make sure it works as expected.

5. To complete the installation, click Keep. The test drive window disappears, but the widget remains open.

   or

   To remove the widget without installing it, click Delete. The installation and widget disappear, but Dashboard remains open.

✔ Tips

■ If you download a widget with Safari, the Widget Installer window (**Figure 13**) may open automatically when the download is complete. Follow steps 3 through 5 to complete the installation.

■ Installing a widget moves its file to the Widgets folder inside the Library folder in your Home folder.

Figure 12
A widget file usually has an icon like this.

RadarInMotion.wdgt

Figure 13 Opening a widget icon launches the Widget Installer.

Figure 14 When you install a widget, it first appears in a "test drive" window.

Figure 15 The Widget Manager lists all of your installed widgets.

Figure 16 Red minus buttons appear beside widgets that can be deleted with the Widget Manager.

Figure 17 The Widget Manager asks you to confirm that you really do want to delete a widget.

Managing Widgets

Mac OS X includes the Widget Manager widget, which you can use to open, disable, enable, or delete widgets on your Mac.

To open the Widget Manager

1. Open Dashboard and display the widget bar (**Figure 4**).

2. Click the Widgets icon (in the first row of widgets in the widget bar) or the Manage Widgets button.

   The Widget Manager opens among your other widgets (**Figure 15**).

To manage widgets

In the Widget Manager window (**Figures 15 and 16**):

◆ To open a widget, double-click its name.

◆ To sort the widgets in the Widget Manager window, choose an option from the pop-up menu: Sort by Name or Sort by Date.

◆ Toggle the check box beside a widget name to disable or enable it. Disabled widgets do not appear on the widget bar.

◆ To delete a widget, click the red − (minus) button beside the widget. Then click OK in the confirmation screen that appears (**Figure 17**).

✔ Tip

■ You cannot use the Widget Manager to delete widgets that are installed with Mac OS X. Instead, consider disabling them. If you really *must* remove one of the Mac OS X widgets, you can delete its widget file from the Widgets folder in the Library folder of your hard disk.

MANAGING WIDGETS

Address Book

The Address Book widget works with the Address Book application to give you quick access to your contacts.

✔ Tip

■ I tell you how to use the Address Book application on page 234.

To use the Address Book widget

1. Open the Address Book widget (**Figure 18**).

2. Enter a search word or phrase in the box. As you type, the widget attempts to match your search string with your Address Book contents (**Figure 19**).

3. If necessary, click the name of the contact you want. The contact's details appear in the widget window (**Figure 20**).

✔ Tip

■ You can click data in a contact's record to perform additional tasks. For example:

   ▲ Clicking a phone number displays it in a larger size so it's easier to read from a distance.

   ▲ Clicking an e-mail address launches your default e-mail application and creates a new message form with the address in the To field.

   ▲ Clicking an address launches your Web browser and searches for the address on the Google Maps Web site.

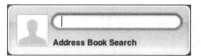

Figure 18 When you first open the Address Book widget, all it displays is a search box.

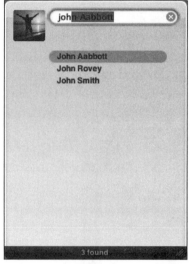

Figure 19 When you type in a search string, the widget immediately begins to find matches.

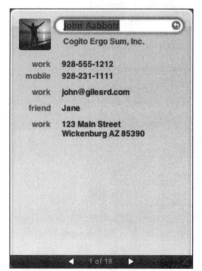

Figure 20 Clicking a contact name displays his record from your Address Book data.

Figure 21 The Business widget, when you first open it.

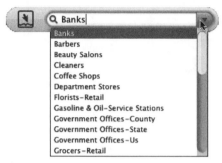

Figure 22 You can choose a business category from the drop-down list.

Figure 23 Search results appear in an expanded window.

Figure 24 You can configure the widget on its reverse side.

Business

The Business widget puts a yellow pages directory at your fingertips.

✔ Tip

- The Business widget requires an Internet connection to use.

To use the Business widget

1. Open the Business widget (**Figure 21**).

2. Enter a business name in the edit box.

   or

   Choose a category from the drop-down list (**Figure 22**).

   When you press (Return), the Business widget searches for matching businesses and displays results in an expanded window (**Figure 23**).

3. To fine-tune search options, click the i button that appears in the lower-right or -left corner of the widget when you point to it to flip the widget over (**Figure 24**). Then set options with the text box and pop-up menus and click Done.

✔ Tip

- You can click data in business listing to perform additional tasks. For example:

   ▲ Clicking a phone number displays it in a larger size so it's easier to read from a distance.

   ▲ Clicking the + symbol beside a business address adds the company's information to Address Book.

   ▲ Clicking a business name or address launches your Web browser and searches for the business on the Directory Assistance Plus Web site.

Calculator

The Calculator widget puts simple calculations at your fingertips.

To use the Calculator widget

1. Open the Calculator widget.

2. Use your keyboard to enter the formula you want to calculate.

   or

   Click the buttons on the Calculator's keypad to enter the formula you want to calculate.

   The results appear in the Calculator window (**Figure 25**).

✔ Tip

■ For more advanced calculations, be sure to check out the Calculator application, which I discuss in on page 285.

Figure 25
For simple calculations, you can't beat the handy Calculator widget.

Figure 26 Here's what the Dictionary widget looks like when you first open it.

Figure 27 You can use this pop-up menu to choose the kind of lookup you want to perform.

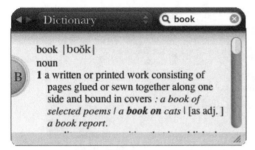

Figure 28 The information you want appears in an expanded window.

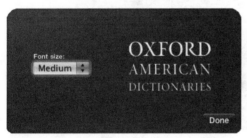

Figure 29 The back side of the Dictionary widget offers a pop-up menu to change the widget's font size.

Dictionary

The Dictionary widget offers a quick way to look up the definitions, pronunciations, and synonyms for a word. The Dictionary widget also includes Apple, Inc., terminology.

✔ Tip

■ You may also be interested in the Dictionary application, which I discuss on page 289.

To use the Dictionary widget

1. Open the Dictionary widget (**Figure 26**).

2. Choose the type of lookup you want to perform from the pop-up menu at the top of the widget (**Figure 27**).

3. Enter a word in the box on the right end of the widget's window and press Return. The window expands to show the information you want (**Figure 28**).

✔ Tips

■ To scroll back and forth through recent lookups, click the triangles in the upper-left corner of the widget.

■ You can change the type of information to display after a word has been looked up by choosing a different option from the pop-up menu at the top of the widget (**Figure 27**).

■ You can configure Dictionary to change its display type size. Click the i button that appears in the lower-left corner of the widget window when you point to it. When the widget flips over (**Figure 29**), choose a font size from the pop-up menu and click Done.

ESPN

The ESPN widget puts sports news links and scores on your Dashboard. You can configure it to show the sport that interests you most.

✔ Tip

■ The ESPN widget requires an Internet connection to use.

To use the ESPN widget

1. Open the ESPN widget.

2. Click the i button that appears in the upper-right corner of the widget when you point to it. The widget flips over.

3. Choose the sport that interests you from the drop-down list.

4. Click the Done button. The widget flips back to the front.

5. Click the button for the information you want:

   ▲ **News (Figure 31)** displays News headlines. You can click a headline to open the ESPN story in your default Web browser.

   ▲ **Scores (Figure 32)** displays the day's scores. If a game has not yet been played (or is not in progress) the game time appears.

✔ Tip

■ If you're a sports nut and follow multiple sports, you can open multiple copies of the ESPN widget and set each one up for a different sport.

Figure 30 Use the pop-up menu on the back side of the widget to choose a sport.

Figure 31 The News button displays news headlines.

Figure 32 The Scores button displays upcoming game times (as shown here) or scores for games that are either in progress or over.

Figure 33 Here's what the Flight Tracker widget looks like when you first open it.

Figure 34 Flight Tracker lists all the flights that match your search criteria.

Figure 35 When you click Track Flight, Flight Tracker displays a graphic showing the location of the flight and its status. (Looks like Flight 71 has a good tailwind today!)

Flight Tracker

Flight Tracker can provide you with information about airline flights all over the world, including arrival and departure times, en route progress, and delays.

✔ Tip

■ Flight Tracker requires an Internet connection to gather information.

To use the Flight Tracker widget

1. Open the Flight Tracker widget (**Figure 33**).

2. Use the edit boxes on the left side of the window to enter the Airline, Depart City, and Arrive City.

3. Click the Find Flights button. Flight Tracker lists all of the flights that match your criteria (**Figure 34**).

4. To check the status of an en route flight, select the flight and click the Track Flight button. Flight Tracker displays a graphic of the route with information about the plane's location and speed (**Figure 35**).

Google

The Google widget offers an easy-access search box for performing a Google search.

Figure 36 The Google widget is a search box for performing a Google search.

✔ Tip

■ The Google widget requires an Internet connection to use.

To use the Google widget

1. Open the Google widget (**Figure 36**).

2. Enter a search word or phrase in the box.

3. Press [Return]. Dashboard closes, your default Web browser opens, and the results of your Google search appear in a Web browser window.

Figure 37 The iCal widget shows you what's in your calendar for today.

iCal

The iCal widget gives you access to the events you manage with the iCal application.

✔ Tip

■ I tell you about iCal on page 246.

To use the iCal widget

1. Open the iCal widget (**Figure 37**).

2. To toggle the display to see one, two, or three panes, click the day number.

3. To view a specific month click the left and right arrows at the top of the calendar to scroll through the months.

4. To open an event in iCal, click the title of the event.

✔ Tip

■ The iCal widget shows the current day's events only.

Previous
Stop/Start Volume dial
Next Shuffle Repeat

Figure 38 The iTunes widget offers access to basic iTunes application controls while it is running.

iTunes

The iTunes widget gives you an alternate means to control iTunes playback. Once iTunes is running and playing a song, you can use the iTunes widget to stop or start play, change play volume, go to the previous or next song, or change the playlist.

✔ Tip

- ■ I explain how to use iTunes on page 270.

To use the iTunes widget

1. If iTunes isn't already running, launch it.

2. Open the iTunes widget (**Figure 38**).

3. Use widget buttons and sliders to control iTunes play:

   ▲ Click the Stop/Start button to stop or start playing the current song.

   ▲ Click the Previous button once to go to the beginning of the current song; click it twice to go to the previous song.

   ▲ Click the Next button to go to the next song.

   ▲ Drag the volume dial around to change play volume.

   ▲ Click the Shuffle button to toggle iTunes's shuffle feature.

   ▲ Click the Repeat button to toggle iTunes's repeat feature.

4. To change the playlist, click the i button that appears at the bottom of the widget when you point to it to flip over the widget. Choose a different playlist from the pop-up menu and click Done.

iTunes

Movies

The Movies widget can help you learn what's playing at nearby movie theaters.

✔ Tip

- The Movies widget requires an Internet connection to use.

To use the Movies widget

1. Open the Movies widget. It begins displaying a slide show of movie posters in a small window (**Figure 39**).

2. Click the window. It expands and gathers information from the Internet to display movie information from local theaters (**Figure 40**).

3. To find a theater playing a specific movie, click the Movies button at the top of the window, and then click the name of the movie that interests you. A list of theaters appears in the middle window. Click a theater name to display show times in the far right column (**Figure 40**).

   or

   To learn what movies are playing at a specific theater, click the Theaters button at the top of the window, and then click the name of the theater that interests you. A list of movies appears in the middle of the window. Click a movie name to display show times in the far right column (**Figure 41**).

Figure 39
The Movie widget opens with a slide show of movie posters for current movies.

Figure 40 You can browse based on movies...

Figure 41 ...or based on theaters.

Figure 42 You can view information about the theater at the bottom of the window.

✔ Tips

- Have patience while the movie information loads. If your connection to the Internet isn't very fast, it could take a minute or more for data to appear.

- The first time you use the Movies widget, you should enter your zip code on its back. Click the i button that appears in the lower left corner when you point to it to flip the widget over and set your zip code. Click done to reload movie information.

- You can click the i button for the name of a selected theater to display its address in the bottom of the window (**Figure 42**). Clicking the address opens your Web browser and displays a map of the theater's location on the Google Maps Web site.

- You can click the name of a movie to display more about it in the bottom of the window (**Figures 40** and **41**). You can click a Trailer link there to display the movie's trailer right in the widget window.

- For some theaters, you may be able to purchase tickets online from within the widget. Look for an active Buy Tickets link.

MOVIES

People

The People widget enables you to search the Directory Assistance Plus Web site for telephone listings of people. Think of it as a super-sized white pages inside your Mac.

✔ Tips

- The People widget requires an Internet connection to use.

- Like any phone book, not everyone is listed.

To use the People widget

1. Open the People widget (**Figure 43**).

2. Fill in the fields in the widget's form. You don't need the entire address; just the city, state, or zip will do.

3. Press Return. The search results appear in an expanded window (**Figure 44**).

✔ Tips

- You can customize the People widget. Click the i button that appears in the lower-right corner to flip the widget over (**Figure 45**). Use pop-up menus to set the search range and number of search results that should appear on each page.

- You can click data in a listing to perform additional tasks. For example:

  ▲ Clicking a phone number displays it in a larger size so it's easier to read from a distance.

  ▲ Clicking a name or address launches your Web browser and searches for the person or address on the Directory Assistance Plus Web site.

  ▲ Clicking the + button in to the left of an address adds that person to your Address Book.

Figure 43 Here's what the People widget looks like when you first open it.

Figure 44 The search results appear in an expanded window. (As you can see, there are a lot of John Smiths listed in Arizona.)

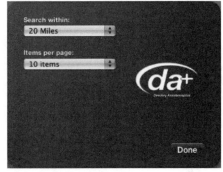

Figure 45 You can set options for the widget on its reverse side.

Figure 46 Enter the name of the resort you're interested in on the back of the widget.

Figure 47 Ski conditions appear on the front of the widget.

Ski Report

The Ski Report widget provides information of interest to skiers about ski resorts all over the world, including new snow, base depth, and trails open.

✔ Tip

- The Ski Report widget requires an Internet connection to use.

To use the Ski Report widget

1. Open the Ski Report widget.

2. Click the i button that appears in the lower-right corner when you point to it. The widget flips over (**Figure 46**).

3. Enter the name of the ski resort you're interested in and press Return.

4. When the resort name is validated, click Done. The widget flips back over with information about the ski resort's current conditions (**Figure 47**).

✔ Tip

- Want to monitor multiple ski resorts in your area? Open several copies of the widget and set up each one for a different ski resort.

SKI REPORT

Stickies

The Stickies widget enables you to create reminder notes that look a lot like the sticky notes you might already have all over your computer's display—hopefully, on the plastic part around the glass.

✔ Tip

■ Mac OS X also includes a more powerful Stickies application. I tell you about it on page 309.

To use the Stickies widget

1. Open the Stickies widget. A blank note window appears (**Figure 48**).

2. Click in the top of the window to position an insertion point and type your note (**Figure 49**).

3. To set Stickies formatting options, point to the lower-right corner of the Stickies window and click the i button that appears. The widget flips over so you can set paper color, font, and text size (**Figure 50**). Click Done to flip the widget back to the front.

✔ Tip

■ To create another sticky note, open the Stickies widget again.

Figure 48 A blank Stickies window.

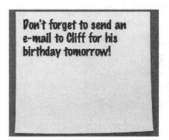

Figure 49 Type a note right into the window.

Figure 50 You can set formatting options on the back of the widget.

Figure 51
The Stocks widget with one of my favorite investments selected. (I bought at $13 and the stock has split twice since then.)

Figure 52
Use the flip side of the widget to add and remove securities from its list.

Stocks

The Stocks widget enables you to keep track of your favorite securities throughout the day.

✔ Tips

- The Stocks widget requires an Internet connection to download security price information.

- Stock quotes, which are provided by Quote.com, are delayed up to 20 minutes.

To use the Stocks widget

1. Open the Stocks widget. It displays a list of stocks preprogrammed into it (**Figure 51**).

2. To see a chart for a security, click the symbol for the security in the list (**Figure 51**).

3. To change the chart period, click one of the buttons within the chart area.

4. To customize the list of securities, click the i button that appears when you point to the bottom-right corner of the Stocks widget to flip the widget over (**Figure 52**). Then:

   ▲ To add a security to the list, enter the company name or ticker symbol in the box at the top of the window and click the + button.

   ▲ To remove a security from the list, select the security you want to remove and click the Remove button.

   ▲ To display the daily value change as a percentage rather than a dollar value, turn on the Show change as a percentage check box.

   ▲ To save your changes, click Done.

✔ Tip

- To view a Web page at finance.yahoo.com with information about a security, double-click the security's name on the front side of the Stock widget window (**Figure 51**).

Tile Game

Feel like a break? You can play the Tile Game to test your puzzle-solving skills.

To use the Tile Game widget

1. Open the Tile Game widget (**Figure 53**).

2. To shuffle the tiles, click the picture.

3. To stop shuffling the tiles, click the picture again (**Figure 54**).

4. To slide a tile into the adjacent blank space, click the tile. Repeat this process until you have unshuffled all the tiles to reform the picture.

To customize the picture

1. If the Tile Game widget is not already open, open it (**Figure 53**).

2. Close Dashboard.

3. In the Finder, locate the icon for the picture you want to use in the Tile Game and start dragging it out of the Finder window. Do not release the mouse button.

4. Open Dashboard (**Figure 55**).

5. Continue dragging the icon onto the Tile Game window.

6. Release the mouse button. The picture appears in the Tile Game widget (**Figure 56**).

Figure 53
The Tile Game widget features a Leopard.

Figure 54
Shuffle the tiles before starting to play.

Figure 55 Drag the icon for an image file from the Finder onto the Tile Game widget window.

Figure 56
When you release the mouse button, the image appears in the game.

TILE GAME

Figure 57
Use the pop-up menus to choose the languages you want to translate from and to.

Figure 58 When you type in one language in the top of the widget, the translation appears in the other language at the bottom of the widget.

Translation

The Translation widget can translate text on the fly from one language to another.

✔ Tips

- The Translation widget requires an Internet connection to work.

- Remember, the Translation widget generates a computer-based translation. Although it should make sense to a native speaker of the other language, it probably won't be perfect.

To use the Translation widget

1. Open the Translation widget.

2. Use the pop-up menus (**Figure 57**) to choose the languages you want to translate from and to.

3. Type the text you want to convert in the top half of the window. The translation appears almost immediately in the bottom half of the window (**Figure 58**).

Unit Converter

The Unit Converter widget enables you to convert from one unit of measurement to another.

✔ Tips

- You can also find a conversion feature in the Calculator application, which I discuss on page 287.

- You must have an Internet connection to convert currency units.

To use the Unit Converter widget

1. Open the Unit Converter widget.

2. Choose an option from the Convert pop-up menu (**Figure 59**).

3. Choose options from the two units pop-up menus. Make sure one unit is what you want to convert from and the other is what you want to convert to.

4. Enter a value in the box beneath the unit you want to convert from.

   The conversion appears in the other box (**Figure 60**).

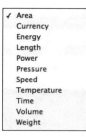

Figure 59
Use this pop-up menu to specify the type of conversion you want to do.

Figure 60 When you enter a unit on the left, the converted value appears on the right.

Figure 61 By default, the Weather widget displays weather for your time zone city.

Figure 62 Set options for the Weather widget on its flip side.

Figure 63 The weather for your location appears. In this example, the lows are also displayed for each day. (Perhaps you can understand why I no longer spend my summers in Wickenburg.)

Figure 64 Clicking the top of the widget window collapses the view to show current conditions only.

Weather

The Weather widget provides basic weather information for cities throughout the world.

✔ Tip

■ You must have an Internet connection to use the Weather widget.

To use the Weather widget

1. Open the Weather widget. By default, the weather for the city set in the Time Zone pane of the Date & Time preferences pane appears (**Figure 61**).

2. Click the i button that appears in the lower-right corner of the widget when you point to it to flip the widget over (**Figure 62**).

3. Set options as necessary:

   ▲ **City, State, or ZIP Code** is the city and state or ZIP code of the city you want weather for.

   ▲ **Degrees** is the unit of measurement: °F or °C.

   ▲ **Include lows in 6-day forecast** includes low temperatures in the forecast (**Figure 63**).

4. Click Done to save your settings and view the weather (**Figure 63**).

✔ Tips

■ Clicking the top part of the weather widget toggles it between the six day forecast (**Figures 61** and **63**) and current conditions (**Figure 64**).

■ I explain how to set your time zone and select a time zone city on page 535.

Web Clip

Web Clip is a do-it-yourself widget that makes it easy to capture information from the Web and display it in your Dashboard. Best of all, as the source information changes, so does the information in the Web Clip widget.

✔ Tip

- Due to the nature of Web Clip, it requires an Internet connection to use.

To use Web Clip

1. Open the Safari browser and use it to go to a Web page with content you want to clip.

2. Scroll down, if necessary, to display the content you want to clip. It needs to fit within the Web browser window.

3. Choose File > Open in Dashboard (**Figure 65**). The contents of the Web browser window become shaded and a white box appears with your mouse pointer. Instructions in a purple bar appear at the top of the page (**Figure 66**).

4. Move the white box over the content you want to clip.

5. If the content is formatted as a separate section in the Web page, the box will expand to surround it (**Figure 67**). Click to select it.

   or

   If the box does not automatically expand to surround your selection, click the content.

   Selection handles appear around the box (**Figure 68**).

6. If necessary, drag the selection handles so that the white box fully surrounds the content you want to clip.

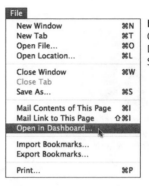

Figure 65
Choose Open in Dashboard from Safari's File menu.

Figure 66 Safari displays a selection box and some instructions over the Web page.

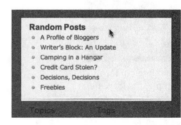

Figure 67
In some cases (like this one), the box will resize to fit over content.

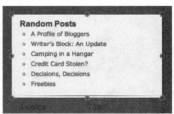

Figure 68
Selection handles appear around the box when you click.

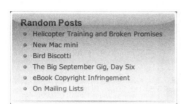

Figure 69
The Web Clip widget you created appears in Dashboard.

Figure 70 You can set the appearance of your widget by choosing a theme.

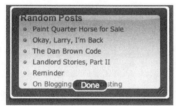

Figure 71
You can adjust the content of your widget by moving it within a frame or changing the size of the frame.

7. Click Add or press Return.

Dashboard launches and opens a new widget that contains the content you clipped (**Figure 69**).

✔ Tips

- You can create as many Web Clip widgets as you like.

- You must keep the Web Clip widget you created open on your Dashboard to save its settings. If you close it, you will have to re-create it from scratch.

To customize a Web Clip widget

1. Create the widget as discussed on these two pages.

2. Click the i button that appears in the lower-right corner of the widget when you point to it to flip the widget (**Figure 70**).

3. To determine the appearance of the widget, click to choose a theme.

4. To ensure that audio from the clip only plays when Dashboard is open, turn on the Only play audio in Dashboard button

5. Click Done to save your settings.

To modify a Web Clip widget's contents

1. Create the widget as discussed on these two pages.

2. Click the i button that appears in the lower-right corner of the widget when you point to it to flip the widget (**Figure 70**).

3. Click the Edit button. The clip flips back over with a frame around it (**Figure 71**).

4. Use your mouse pointer to drag the clip's contents or resize the frame as necessary.

5. Click Done.

WEB CLIP

World Clock

The World Clock widget enables you to check the time in any major city in the world.

Figure 72
The World Clock displays your local time when you first open it.

✔ Tip

■ For the World Clock's time to be accurate, the correct time must be set in the Date & Time preferences pane. I explain how to use the Date & Time preferences pane on page 534.

To use the World Clock widget

Figure 73
Chose a region and city from these pop-up menus.

1. Open the World Clock widget. By default, it displays your local time, as set in the Date & Time preferences pane (**Figure 72**).

2. Click the i button that appears in the lower-right corner of the widget when you point to it to flip it over (**Figure 73**).

3. Choose a region and city from the pop-up menus.

4. Click Done. The clock displays the city you chose.

✔ Tip

■ Want to see clocks for more than one city at a time? Just open another World Clock widget window.

WORLD CLOCK

Fonts

Figure 1 Font Book offers an easy-to-use interface for managing and previewing fonts.

Fonts

Fonts are typefaces that appear onscreen and in printed documents. When they're properly installed, they appear on all Font menus and in font lists.

Mac OS, which has long been a favorite operating system among design professionals who work extensively with fonts, has several tools for managing fonts and using them in documents:

◆ **Font Book** (**Figure 1**) is an application that enables you to install, preview, search, activate, and deactivate fonts with an easy-to-use interface.

◆ The **Fonts panel** (**Figure 46**) enables you to apply and manage fonts within documents.

◆ The **Character Palette** (**Figure 54**) makes it easy to insert characters—including characters in Roman and non-Roman character sets—in your documents.

In this chapter, I tell you how to use all of these Mac OS features.

FONTS

Font Formats

Mac OS X supports several types of fonts in both Mac OS and Windows specific formats:

◆ **PostScript Type 1 fonts** are used primarily for printing. These fonts must be accompanied by corresponding screen font files. PostScript font technology was developed by Adobe Systems, Inc.

◆ **TrueType font** (.ttf) and **TrueType font collections** (.ttc), can display high-quality output onscreen and in print.

◆ **Multiple Master** is a special PostScript format that enables you to create custom styles, called *instances*, by setting font weight, width, and other variables. Mac OS X supports Multiple Master instances.

◆ **System** or **Data fork suitcase format** (**.dfont**) stores all information in the data fork of the file, including resources used by Mac OS drawing routines.

◆ **OpenType font format** (**.otf**), which can contain 65,000 different *glyphs* or characters, are popular for non-Roman languages. OpenType format fonts come in two versions: PostScript-based fonts from Adobe and TrueType-based fonts from Microsoft.

✔ Tips

■ Prior to Mac OS X, Mac OS files could contain two parts, or forks: a resource fork and a data fork. This causes incompatibility problems with non-Mac OS systems, which do not support a file's resource fork. Data fork suitcase format fonts don't have resource forks, so they can work on a variety of computer platforms.

■ Mac OS 10.6 does not support Mac OS 9 bitmapped fonts.

Table 1

Font Installation Locations	
Font Use	**Font Folder**
User	HD/Users/UserName/Library/Fonts/
Computer	HD/Library/Fonts/
System	HD/System/Library/Fonts/
Application	HD/Library/Application Support/ *CompanyName*/Fonts
Network	Network/Library/Fonts/

Figure 2 User fonts are installed in the Fonts folder within the user's Library folder.

Figure 3 Computer fonts are installed in the Fonts folder within the startup disk's Library folder.

Figure 4 System fonts are installed in the Fonts folder within the System's Library folder.

Font Locations

On a typical Mac OS X system, fonts can be installed in three or more places (**Table 1**). Where a font is installed determines who can use it.

◆ **User** fonts are installed in a user's Fonts folder (**Figure 2**). Each user can install, control, and access his or her own fonts. Fonts installed in a user's Fonts folder are available only to that user.

◆ **Computer** fonts are installed in the Fonts folder for the startup disk (**Figure 3**). These fonts are accessible to all local users of the computer. Only an Admin user can modify the contents of this Fonts folder.

◆ **System** fonts are installed in the Fonts folder for the system (**Figure 4**). These fonts are installed by the Mac OS X installer and are used by the system. The contents of this Fonts folder should not be modified.

◆ **Application** fonts are sometimes copied to a developer- or application-specific Fonts folder in the Application Support folder in your hard disk's Library folder when you install an application. These fonts are only available to the applications they are installed for.

◆ **Network** fonts are installed in the Fonts folder for the network. These fonts are accessible to all local area network users. This feature is normally used on network file servers—not the average user's computer. Only a network administrator can modify the contents of this Fonts folder.

◆ **Font Book library** fonts are fonts installed by a user someplace other than one of the standard Fonts folders listed here. These fonts are only available to the user who installed them.

✔ Tips

- You can make a user font or application font available to all users or applications by moving it to the Fonts folder in your hard disk's Library folder.

- Changes to the Fonts folders can take effect immediately for some applications. For other applications, changes do not take effect until after the application is reopened.

- Admin privileges are required to add or remove computer and system fonts. If you try to change the contents of a Fonts folder that requires admin privileges, a dialog like the one in **Figure 5** will appear. Click Authenticate, enter your password in the authentication dialog that appears (**Figure 6**), and click OK.

To manually install a font

Drag all files that are part of the font into the appropriate Fonts folder (**Figure 7**).

✔ Tip

- The best way to install a font is with Font Book, which can also validate fonts and resolve conflicts in the case of duplicate fonts. I tell you about Font Book starting on the next page.

To manually uninstall a font

Drag all files that are part of the font out of the Fonts folder they were installed in (**Figure 8**).

✔ Tips

- The best way to uninstall a font is with Font Book, which I tell you about starting on the next page.

- To avoid problems with your computer, do not remove fonts from HD/System/Library/Fonts.

Figure 5 A dialog like this appears if you try to change a Fonts folder and do not have enough privileges.

Figure 6 If you have an Admin password, you can enter it in this dialog to complete the change.

Figure 7 To manually install a font, drag it into (or onto) the appropriate Fonts folder. This illustration shows a PostScript Type 1 font family with its accompanying bitmap font file being installed.

Figure 8 To manually uninstall a font, drag it out of the Fonts folder. This illustration shows the font installed in **Figure 6** being uninstalled.

Figure 9
In the Collection column of Font Book, libraries appear above the split line and collections appear beneath it.

Figure 10
The Font column displays the Fonts within a selected library or collection. You can click the disclosure arrow beside a font name to see the typefaces within it.

Font Book

Font Book (**Figure 1**) is a Mac OS X application that enables you to install, uninstall, organize, preview, search, activate, and deactivate fonts.

As shown in **Figure 9**, Font Book organizes all of your fonts into libraries and collections. Libraries, which appear above the split line in the Collection column, are groups of fonts organized by language or where they are installed. Collections, which appear below the split line, are groups of fonts organized to meet your needs. Font Book comes preconfigured with several libraries and collections, but you can add, remove, or modify others as desired.

Within each library or collection is one or more fonts (**Figure 10**), each of which may contain one or more typefaces. Each typeface is a slightly different version of the font—for example, bold, italic, or condensed.

Font Book makes it possible to turn fonts on or off. This helps keep your applications' font menus and lists neat by letting you display only those fonts that you want to display.

✔ Tips

- Font Book is integrated with the Fonts panel, which I discuss on page 356.

- With Font Book, you can create libraries of fonts that reside anywhere on your computer—not just in a Fonts folder.

FONT BOOK

To launch Font Book

Use one of the following techniques:

◆ Double-click the Font Book icon in the Applications folder (**Figure 11**).

◆ Choose Manage Fonts from the shortcut menu in the Fonts Panel (**Figure 48**).

Font Book's main window appears (**Figure 1**).

✔ Tip

■ Another way to launch Font Book is to double-click a font file's icon. Doing so displays a font preview window like the one in Figure 15.

To set Font Book preferences

1. Choose Font Book > Preferences (**Figure 12**) or press ⌘,. The Font Book Preferences window appears (**Figure 13**).

2. Set Options as desired:

    ▲ **Default Install Location** is the library in which Font Book should copy installed fonts if no library is specified.

    ▲ **Validate fonts before installing** checks fonts for problems before installing them. This prevents the installation of corrupted or duplicate fonts.

    ▲ **Automatic font activation** automatically enables any disabled fonts on your system when you open a document that uses those fonts. If you enable this option, you can also turn on the **Ask me before activating** check box to have Font Book tell you when it is activating a font.

    ▲ **Alert me if system fonts change** displays an alert if any of the fonts used by Mac OS X to display onscreen text change.

3. Click the close button to save your settings.

Figure 11 You can find Font Book in the Applications folder.

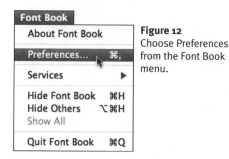

Figure 12 Choose Preferences from the Font Book menu.

Figure 13 The Font Book Preferences window.

Figure 14 Here's a handful of font files in a folder.

Figure 15 A preview of the font's primary characters appears in a window like this.

Figure 16 The newly installed font appears selected in Font Book.

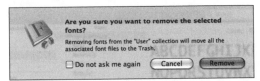

Figure 17 A confirmation dialog like this appears when you uninstall a font.

To install a font

1. Insert the disc containing the font files you want to install or copy the font files to your hard disk.

2. Double-click one of the Font files (**Figure 14**). A font preview window like the one in **Figure 15** appears.

3. Click the Install Font button.

   The font files are copied to the default font location set in Font Book Preferences (**Figure 13**). The name of the Font appears selected in the main Font Book window (**Figure 16**).

✔ Tip

■ You can also install a font by dragging the font's file icon(s) onto a library or collection name in the main Font Book window or by using the Add Fonts command, which I discuss on page 348.

To uninstall a font

1. Select the name of the font in the Font column of the main Font Book window (**Figure 16**).

2. Press [Delete].

3. A dialog like the one in **Figure 17** appears. Click Remove.

   The font's files are moved to the Trash. Emptying the Trash removes them from your computer.

✔ Tip

■ If you turn on the check box in the confirmation dialog that appears when you delete a font (**Figure 17**), you will never be warned again when you delete a font.

To view fonts by library or collection

In the Collection column of the main Font Book window, select the name of the library or collection you want to view.

The fonts in that library appear in the Font column (**Figure 18**).

✔ Tips

- **Figure 18** shows the default libraries and collections in Mac OS X. I explain how to add libraries and collections later in this section.

- A font can be in more than one library or collection.

- As the name suggests, the All Fonts library includes all installed fonts.

- You can copy a font from one collection to another by dragging it from the Font list to the name of another collection (**Figure 19**).

Figure 18 Selecting a collection displays a list of the fonts within it.

Figure 19
You can copy a font from one collection to another by dragging it.

Figure 20 As shown here, you can select a specific typeface within a font to see its characters.

Figure 21
You can choose a font size from the Size drop-down list.

Figure 22
The Preview menu offers options for previewing font characters.

To preview font or typeface characters

1. In the Collection list of the main Font Book window, select All Fonts or the name of a library or collection that the font is part of (**Figure 18**).

2. In the Font list, select the name of the font you want to preview. The characters for the regular typeface of the font appear on the right side of the window (**Figure 18**).

3. To see a specific typeface for the font, click the disclosure triangle to the left of the font name to display all typefaces. Then click the name of the typeface you want to see. Its characters appear on the right side of the window (**Figure 20**).

✔ Tips

- To change the size of characters in the preview part of the window, enter a value in the Size box, choose a value from the Size drop-down list (**Figure 21**), or drag the slider on the far right side of the window. The currently displayed size appears at the bottom-right of the window (**Figure 20**).

- To change the text that appears in the preview part of the window, choose one of the first three options on the Preview menu (**Figure 22**):

  ▲ **Sample** (⌘1) displays the characters shown throughout this chapter.

  ▲ **Repertoire** (⌘2) displays all characters in ASCII order (**Figure 23**).

  ▲ **Custom** (⌘3) enables you to specify your own sample text (**Figure 24**).

Figure 23 Here's another font in Repertoire preview...

Figure 24 ...and yet another one with custom preview text.

To add a library

1. Choose File > New Library (**Figure 25**), or press ⌥ ⌘ N. An untitled library appears in the Collection list with its name selected (**Figure 26**).

2. Enter a new name for the collection and press Return (**Figure 27**).

✔ Tip

- As shown in **Figures 26** and **27**, libraries appear above the split line in the Collection list.

To add fonts to a library

1. In the Collection list, select the library you want to add fonts to (**Figure 27**).

2. Choose File > Add Fonts (**Figure 25**) or press ⌘ O.

3. Use the Open dialog that appears (**Figure 28**) to locate and select the folder containing the font(s) you want to add.

4. Click Open.

   Font Book adds the fonts in that folder to the library (**Figure 29**).

✔ Tips

- Adding fonts to a library you created does not copy or move the font from the folder you added it from. This makes it possible to use fonts stored in any folder on disk—even folders accessible via network.

- I tell you more about using the Open dialog on page 194.

Figure 25 Font Book's File menu.

Figure 26 An untitled library is added to the Collection list.

Figure 27 Enter a name for the library and press Return.

Figure 28 Use a dialog like this to locate and select a folder containing the fonts you want to add.

Figure 29 The fonts in the folder you selected are added to the library.

Figure 30
An untitled collection appears in the Collection list with its name selected.

Figure 31
When you name the collection, it appears in alphabetical order in the Collection list.

To add a collection

1. Click the Create a new collection (+) button at the bottom of the Collection list in the main Font Book window.

   or

   Choose File > New Collection (**Figure 25**), or press ⌃⌘N.

   An untitled collection appears in the Collection list with its name selected (**Figure 30**).

2. Enter a name for the collection, and press Return.

   The collection name appears in the list (**Figure 31**).

To add a font to a collection

1. In the Collection list, select All Fonts or the name of a library or collection that includes the font you want to add (**Figure 18**).

2. Locate the font in the Font list.

3. Drag the font from the Font list onto the name of the collection you want to add it to (**Figure 19**). When you release the button, the font is copied to that collection.

✔ Tips

- Dragging a font from one collection to another does not duplicate the font's files on your computer. It just adds a reference to the font to the collection.

- You can also use the Add Font command as discussed on the previous page to add a font to a selected collection. Doing so copies the font to the default library specified in Font Book Preferences (**Figure 13**) and adds it to the selected collection.

To remove a font from a library or collection

1. In the Collection list of the main Font Book window, select the name of the library or collection you want to modify.

2. In the Font list, select the font or typeface you want to remove.

3. Press ⌈Delete⌋, choose File > Delete "*Font Name*" family (**Figure 25**), or choose File > Delete "*Font Name*." A dialog like the one in **Figure 32** or **33** appears. Click Remove.

✔ Tips

■ What happens when you remove a font depends on whether the font was in a default library, a library you created, or a collection:

▲ Removing a font from one of Font Book's default libraries (**Figure 32**) removes it from Font Book and moves the font files to the Trash, thus deleting it from your computer.

▲ Removing a font from a library you created (**Figure 33**) removes the font from Font Book, thus making it unavailable for use in applications. The font remains in its folder on disk.

▲ Removing a font from a collection (**Figure 33**) removes it from that collection but does not remove it from Font Book, so it is still available for use in applications.

■ You may find it more convenient to deactivate a font than to delete it. I explain how on page 352.

■ Font Book warns you if you attempt to delete a font needed by the System for operation (**Figure 34**). If this dialog appears, I recommend you click Cancel and not remove the System font.

Figure 32 When you remove a font from a default library, a confirmation dialog like this one appears.

Figure 33 When you remove a font from a user library or collection, a confirmation dialog like this one appears.

Figure 34 When you attempt to remove a System font, Font Book warns you that the font might be needed.

Figure 35 A confirmation dialog like this appears when you delete a library or a collection.

To remove a library or collection

1. In the Collection list, select the library or collection you want to remove (**Figure 27**).

2. Press Delete, choose File > Delete "*Library Name*," or File > Delete "*Collection Name*."

3. Click Remove in the confirmation dialog that appears (**Figure 35**).

    The library or collection is removed.

✔ Tips

- Removing a library or a collection does not delete font files from disk.

- When you remove a library, its fonts are no longer available for use in applications. When you remove a collection, the collection name no longer appears in the Fonts panel, but the fonts it contains are still available for use in applications.

- You may find it more convenient to deactivate a library or collection than to delete it. I explain how on the next page.

- You cannot remove the default libraries that are installed with Font Book.

To disable a library or collection

1. In the Collection list, select the name of the library or collection you want to disable (**Figure 27**).

2. Choose Edit > Disable "*Collection Name*" (**Figure 36**) or press Shift ⌘ E.

   The library or collection is disabled and the word Off appears beside it in the Collection column (**Figure 37**).

✔ Tips

- When you disable a library, you disable all of its fonts (**Figure 37**).

- A disabled collection will not appear in the Fonts panel.

- If a font appears in only one collection and that collection is disabled, the font is also disabled.

To disable a font

1. In the Collection list, select the name of the library or collection containing the font you want to disable.

2. In the Font list, select the font or typeface you want to disable.

3. Choose Edit > Disable "*Font Name*" Family (**Figure 33**), Edit > Disable "*Font Name*," press Shift ⌘ D, or click the check box beneath the Font column.

4. In the confirmation dialog that appears (**Figure 38**), click Disable.

Figure 36
Font Book's Edit menu.

Enable button

Figure 37 The word *Off* appears beside a disabled library and all of its fonts.

Figure 38 You need to confirm that you want to disable a font.

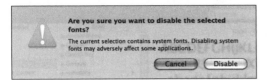

Figure 39 Font Book warns you when you try to disable a System font.

Figure 40 The Edit menu with a disabled font in a disabled library selected.

✔ Tips

■ When you disable a font in a collection, that font will not appear in the Font panel when the collection is selected. When you disable a font in a library, that font is not available for use in any application.

■ Font Book displays a dialog like the one in **Figure 36** when you try to disable a font that is used by the System.

To enable a library, collection, or font

1. In the Collection list, select the name of the disabled library or collection that you want to enable.

2. Choose Edit > Enable "*Library Name*" (**Figure 40**), choose Edit > "*Collection Name*," or press Shift ⌃ ⌘ E .

   The library or collection is enabled.

To enable a font

1. If the font is disabled in a collection, in the Collection list, select the collection the font is part of.

   or

   If the font is disabled in a library, in the Collection list, select the library the font is part of.

2. In the Font list, select the font or typeface that is disabled.

3. Choose Edit > Enable "*Font Name*" family (**Figure 40**), choose Edit > Enable "*Font Name*," press Shift ⌃ ⌘ D , or click the Enable button beneath the Font list (**Figure 37**). The font is enabled.

ENABLING LIBRARIES, COLLECTIONS, & FONTS

To resolve font conflicts

1. In the Collection list, select All Fonts.

2. Locate and select a font with a bullet character to the right of its name.

3. If necessary, click the triangle to the left of the font name to display its typefaces. One or more of them should have bullet characters beside them (**Figure 41**).

4. Choose Edit > Resolve Duplicates (**Figure 40**).

5. Font Book may display a dialog like the one in **Figure 42**. Click OK.

   Font Book disables one of the conflicting typefaces (**Figure 43**).

✔ Tips

- Font conflicts like the one in **Figure 41** are often caused when multiple copies of a font or typeface are installed in the same computer but in different places. Disabling one of the copies stops the conflict.

- If you prefer (and have the correct privileges), you can delete a duplicate typeface. Follow steps 1 through 3 above, select one of the duplicate typefaces, and press (Delete). Then click Remove in the confirmation dialog that appears.

- Keep in mind that if multiple users access your computer, disabling or deleting a conflicting font that is installed for the Computer (rather than for the User) may make that font unavailable for other users.

Figure 41 In this example, two copies of the Symbol Regular typeface have been installed.

Figure 42 Click OK in this dialog to disable duplicate typefaces and prevent conflicts.

Figure 43 Font Book disables the extra copies of the typeface.

Figure 44 The Font Validation window displays the fonts you validated, with icons to indicate minor or serious problems.

Figure 45 Clicking the disclosure triangles displays individual type faces and their validation status.

To validate a font

1. In the Collection list, select the library or collection containing the font you want to validate.

2. In the Font list, select the Font you want to validate.

3. Choose File > Validate Font (**Figure 25**).

   Font Book checks the font and display results in the Font Validation window (**Figure 44**).

4. Consult the results summary at the bottom of the Font Validation window.

5. To get detail about a minor or serious problem, click the triangle on the left end of the line displaying the problem icon (**Figure 45**).

6. When you are finished working with the Font Validation dialog, click its close button to dismiss it.

✔ Tips

- In step 2, you can select multiple fonts by holding down ⌘ and clicking each font you want to select.

- You can remove a problem font from within the Font Validation window. Simply turn on the check box beside the font you want to remove, click the Remove Checked button, and then click Remove in the confirmation dialog that appears (**Figure 32**).

- By default, Font Book automatically validates each font you install with it. That's why it's a good reason to use Font Book to install your fonts!

- The Font menu's Validate File command (**Figure 25**) displays an Open dialog you can use to validate a font file that is not installed on your computer.

VALIDATING FONTS

The Fonts Panel

The Fonts panel (**Figure 46**) offers a standard interface for formatting font characters in a document. This Mac OS X feature is fully integrated with Font Book, so the time you spend organizing your fonts there will help you be more productive when working with the Fonts panel.

In this part of the chapter, I explain how to use the Fonts panel to format text.

✔ Tip

■ This chapter looks at the Fonts panel as it appears in TextEdit, the text editor that comes with Mac OS X. I discuss TextEdit in detail in **Chapter 11**.

To open TextEdit's Fonts panel

With TextEdit active, choose Format > Font > Show Fonts (**Figure 47**) or press ⌘⌘T. The Fonts panel appears (**Figure 46**).

✔ Tips

■ The command to open the Fonts panel in other applications that support it is similar.

■ You can open Font Book from within the Fonts panel by choosing Manage Fonts from the shortcut menu (**Figure 48**).

■ To display a preview of font formatting in the Fonts panel, choose Show Preview from the shortcut menu (**Figure 48**). A pane appears at the top of the Fonts panel with a preview of the selected font settings (**Figure 49**).

Figure 46 TextEdit's Fonts panel.

Figure 47 Choose Show Fonts from the Font submenu under TextEdit's Format menu.

Figure 48
The Fonts panel's shortcut menu.

Figure 49 You can display a Preview area at the top of the Fonts panel.

Size box

Size list

Size slider

Figure 50 The Fonts panel offers three different ways to set the font size.

To apply basic font formatting

1. Open the Fonts panel (**Figure 46**).

2. Select a collection from the Collections list.

3. Select a font family from the Family list.

4. Select a style from the Typeface list.

5. Set the font size by entering a value in the Size box, selecting a size from the Size list, or dragging the Size slider up or down (**Figure 50**).

   The changes you make are applied to selected text or to text typed at the insertion point.

✔ Tips

- The styles that appear in the Typeface list vary depending on the font selected in the Family list. Some font families offer more styles than others.

- Oblique is similar to italic. Light, regular, medium, bold, and black refer to font weights or boldness.

- You can see a preview of what text looks like with the formatting applied in the Preview area of the Fonts panel (**Figure 49**).

APPLYING BASIC FONT FORMATTING

357

To apply font effects

Use the effects controls at the top of the Fonts panel window (**Figure 51**) to apply other font formatting options to selected text or start formatting at the insertion point:

◆ **Text Underline** offers four underline options: None, Single, Double, and Color. If you choose Color, you can use the Colors panel that appears (**Figure 52**) to set the underline color.

◆ **Text Strikethrough** offers four strike-through options: None, Single, Double, and Color. If you choose Color, you can use the Colors panel that appears (**Figure 52**) to set the strikethrough color.

◆ **Text Color** enables you to set the color of text. When you click this button, the Colors panel appears (**Figure 52**) so you can choose a color for text.

◆ **Document Color** enables you to set the color of the document background. When you click this button, the Colors panel appears (**Figure 52**) so you can choose a color for the entire document's background.

◆ **Text Shadow** adds a shadow to text characters (**Figure 53**).

◆ **Shadow Opacity** makes an applied shadow darker or lighter. Drag the slider to the right or left.

◆ **Shadow Blur** makes the shadow sharper or more blurry. Drag the slider to the right or left.

◆ **Shadow Offset** moves the shadow closer to or farther from the text. Drag the slider to the right or left.

◆ **Shadow Angle** changes the position of the shadow in relation to the text. (It's like moving the light source.) Drag the dial around to the desired angle.

Text Underline   *Text Color*   *Text Shadow*   *Shadow Blur*   *Shadow Angle*

Text Strikethrough   *Document Color*   *Shadow Opacity*   *Shadow Offset*

Figure 51 Along the top of the Fonts panel, you'll find a collection of effects menus, buttons, and controls.

Figure 52
The Colors panel enables you to select a color.

The Shadow Knows...

Figure 53 It's easy to apply a shadow to text characters.

✔ Tip

■ I tell you more about using the Colors panel on page 161.

Figure 54 The Character Palette, displaying characters by category.

Figure 55 Display the Character Palette by choosing Special Characters from TextEdit's Edit menu.

The Character Palette

The Character Palette (**Figure 54**) enables you to type any character in any language for which a font is installed in your computer, including Asian and Eastern European languages. It is especially useful for typing special characters, like mathematical symbols, arrows, and dingbats characters.

The Character Palette is available within some Mac OS X applications, including TextEdit. Once displayed, any character you click is inserted in the current document, at the insertion point.

✔ Tip

- Although you can enter foreign language characters into documents on your Macintosh, those characters may not appear properly when your documents are viewed on other computers.

To display the Character Palette

In TextEdit, choose Edit > Special Characters (**Figure 55**).

Or

In the Fonts panel, choose Characters from the shortcut menu (**Figure 48**).

✔ Tip

- You can also display the Character Palette by choosing Show Character Palette from the Input menu. I explain how to configure and use the Input menu on page 545.

THE CHARACTER PALETTE

To insert a character with the Character Palette

1. In a document window, position the insertion point where you want the character to appear.

2. Display the Character Palette (**Figure 54**).

3. Choose a character group from the View pop-up menu (**Figure 56**). The window may change to offer different options (**Figure 57**).

4. Click a button above the scrolling lists to view characters in a specific order.

5. Select one of the options in the left scrolling list.

6. Select one of the characters in the right scrolling list.

7. Click Insert. The character is inserted at the insertion point in your document.

✔ Tips

- To display information about the selected character, click the triangle beside Character Info to reveal it (**Figure 58**).

- To specify a font for the character, click the triangle beside Font Variation to display the character in multiple fonts (**Figure 58**). You can then click the character in the font you want.

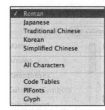

Figure 56
Use this pop-up menu to choose the characters to view.

Figure 57 When you choose an option from the View pop-up menu, the options in the Character Palette may change.

Figure 58 Clicking disclosure triangles expands the Character Palette to show more information and options.

Printing & Faxing

Printing & Faxing

On a Mac OS system, printing and faxing is handled by the operating system rather than individual applications. You choose the Print command in the application that created the document you want to print. Mac OS steps in, displaying the Print dialog and telling the application how to send information to the printer or fax modem. There are two main benefits to this:

◆ If you can print documents created with one application, you can probably print documents created with any application.

◆ The Page Setup and Print dialogs look very much the same in most applications.

This chapter covers most aspects of printing and faxing documents on a computer running Mac OS X.

To print (an overview)

1. If necessary, add your printer to the Printers list in the Print & Fax preferences pane.

2. Open the document that you want to print.

3. If necessary, set options in the Page Setup dialog, and click OK.

4. Set options in the Print dialog, and click Print.

Printer Drivers

A printer driver is software that Mac OS uses to communicate with a specific kind of printer. It contains information about the printer and instructions for using it. You can't open and read a printer driver, but your computer can.

There are basically two kinds of printers:

◆ A **PostScript** printer uses PostScript technology developed by Adobe Systems. Inside the printer is a *PostScript interpreter*, which can process PostScript language commands to print high-quality text and graphics. Examples of PostScript printers include most laser printers.

◆ A **non-PostScript** printer relies on the computer to send it all of the instructions it needs for printing text and graphics. It cannot process PostScript commands. Examples of non-PostScript printers include most inkjet or photo printers. Non-PostScript printers are generally more common for home and small business use, primarily because they are less expensive than PostScript printers. Their print quality is quite acceptable for most purposes.

A standard installation of Mac OS X 10.6 installs printer drivers for the printers it detects during installation. If you have an Internet connection, it checks to make sure you have the most up-to-date version of the installed printer drivers. It can also install printer drivers on the fly when you connect to a new printer.

When you buy a printer, it should come with a CD that includes its printer driver software; if your computer does not recognize your printer, you'll need to install this software to use it.

✔ Tips

■ If you need to manually install printer driver software for your printer, make sure it is Mac OS X compatible. If your printer did not come with Mac OS X-compatible printer software, you may be able to get it from the printer manufacturer's Web site.

■ If you do cannot install a printer driver for your printer, you may not be able to print.

Figure 1 The Print & Fax preferences pane before any printers have been added.

Figure 2 Directly connecting a printer automatically adds it to the Print & Fax preferences pane.

Using the Print & Fax Preferences Pane

Before you can print from a Mac OS X application, you must make a printer accessible to Mac OS X. You do this with the Print & Fax preferences pane (**Figure 1**).

Mac OS X is smart. If you connect a printer directly to your Mac and it has an appropriate driver installed, it automatically recognizes the printer and sets it as the default. However if Mac OS X does not recognize your printer or you want to use a printer accessible via a network, you must manually add the printer to the Print & Fax preferences pane.

The Print & Fax preferences pane enables you to perform the following tasks:

◆ Add printers and fax modems to the Printers list (**Figures 1** and **2**) that your Mac consults when printing or faxing.

◆ Set the default printer and paper size.

◆ Set printer options.

◆ Create printer pools so your print jobs go to whatever networked printer is available when you're ready to print.

✔ Tips

■ The Printer Setup Utility that was part of previous versions of Mac OS X is gone. Its functionality has been added to the Print & Fax preferences pane!

■ You only have to add a printer if it does not already appear in the Printers list (**Figures 1** and **2**). This needs to be done only once; Mac OS will remember all printers that you add.

To open the Print & Fax preferences pane

1. Choose Apple > System Preferences or click the System Preferences icon in the Dock.

2. In the System Preferences window that appears, click the Print & Fax icon.

   The Print & Fax preferences pane appears (**Figures 1** and 2).

✔ Tip

■ You can also open Print & Fax preferences pane by choosing Print & Fax Preferences from the Printer pop-up menu in the Print dialog (**Figure 28**).

To add a printer that is listed by default

1. If necessary, connect the printer you want to use with the computer and turn it on. If the printer appears in the Print & Fax preferences pane (**Figure 2**), you're done. You can skip the remaining steps.

2. Click the **+** button beneath the Printers list in the Print & Fax preferences pane (**Figures 1** and 2).

   A window like the one in **Figure 3** appears. It displays the printers your computer "sees" locally or on a network you are connected to.

3. If the printer you want to add appears in the list, select it (**Figure 4**).

   or

   If the printer you want to add does not appear in the list, skip the remaining steps and follow the instructions in the section titled "To add a printer that is not listed by default" on page 366.

Figure 3 Your Mac displays a list of the printers it "sees"—in this example, via USB connection and network printer sharing.

Figure 4 Select the printer you want to add. You can then set some options at the bottom of the window.

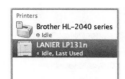

Figure 5
The printer appears in the Printers list.

Figure 6 In this example, I've added three printers and a fax modem.

4. If necessary, choose a driver from the Print Using pop-up menu at the bottom of the window.

5. Click Add.

6. If the printer's driver needs to be downloaded from the Internet, a confirmation dialog appears. Click Install. Then click Agree in any licensing agreement dialogs that appear.

7. The printer is added to the Printers list in the Print & Fax preferences pane (**Figure 5**). Repeat these steps for each printer or fax device you want to add.

✔ Tips

■ In step 3, if the printer you want to use does not appear in the list, double-check to make sure the printer is connected to your computer or network and turned on.

■ As indicated at the bottom of **Figure 4**, your Mac can often connect to the Internet and download a printer driver it needs.

■ In step 4, if you're not sure which driver to select, choose Auto Select and let Mac OS pick the driver for you based on what it learns from the printer.

ADDING PRINTERS

To add a printer that is not listed by default

1. Follow step 2 in the section titled "To add a printer that is listed by default" on page 364.

2. In the window's toolbar, click the button for the type of printer you want to add:

   ▲ **Fax (Figure 7)** lets you add an internal or external fax modem.

   ▲ **IP (Figure 8)** enables you to add a printer at a specific IP address.

   ▲ **Windows (Figure 9)** lets you add a printer connected to a Windows computer or Windows network.

3. Set options for the printer type and location.

4. Click Add. The printer is added to the Printers list (**Figure 6**).

✔ Tips

■ In step 3, it may be necessary to log in to a network to access certain types of networked printers.

Figures 7, 8, & 9 Clicking buttons at the top of the window enable you to add printers that don't appear by default.

Figure 10 You'll have to click Delete Printer to delete the selected printer.

✓ Last Printer Used

Brother HL–2040 series
Brother MFC–6490CW
HP Color LaserJet 2600n @ iMac
LANIER LP131n

Figure 11 Choose the name of a printer from the Default Printer pop-up menu.

✓ US Letter
US Legal
A4
A5
B5 JIS
B5
Envelope #10
Envelope DL
Tabloid
A3
Tabloid Extra
ROC 16K
Envelope Choukei 3
Super B/A3

Figure 12 Use this pop-up menu to choose a default paper size.

To delete a printer

1. In the Printer list, select the printer you want to delete (**Figure 6**).

2. Click the − button beneath the list.

3. Click Delete Printer in the confirmation dialog that appears (**Figure 10**).

   The printer is removed from the list.

✔ Tip

- You cannot print to a printer that you have deleted unless you re-add it.

To set the default printer

In the Print & Fax preferences pane, choose one of the printers from the Default Printer pop-up menu (**Figure 11**).

The word *Default* appears in the Printers list beneath the name of the printer you chose (**Figure 6**).

✔ Tips

- The default printer is the one that is automatically chosen when you open the Print dialog.

- If you choose Last Printer Used from the Default Printer pop-up menu (**Figure 11**), the last printer you used to print becomes the default printer. Thus, the default printer changes every time you choose a different printer for printing.

To set the default paper size

In the Print & Fax preferences pane, choose one of the paper sizes from the Default Paper Size in Page Setup pop-up menu (**Figure 12**).

✔ Tip

- The default paper size is the one that is automatically chosen when you open the Page Setup dialog.

To configure a printer

1. In the Printers list (**Figure 6**), select the printer you want to configure.

2. Click the Options & Supplies button.

3. Set options or review information in the three separate panes of the dialog that appears:

   ▲ **General** (**Figure 13**) enables you to set the printer's name and location and provides additional information about the printer's location and driver.

   ▲ **Driver** (**Figure 14**) enables you to set the printer driver and set printer-specific options (if available).

   ▲ **Supply Levels** (**Figure 15**) enables you to see the ink or toner levels for printers that can communicate this information to your computer. (None of mine can, so don't feel bad if this pane is blank for you, too.)

   ▲ **Utilities** may give you access to additional installed utilities to work with your printer. This option is only available for some printers.

4. Click OK to save your settings.

✔ Tips

■ It's not possible to show all configuration options for all printers. The instructions and illustrations here should be enough to get you started with your printer. Consult the manual that came with your printer for more information.

■ Clicking the Supplies button in the Supply Levels pane launches your Web browser and takes you to the Apple Store with a list of printer supplies for your printer.

Figure 13 General options include the name and location of the printer.

Figure 14 Driver options enable you to choose an installed driver and set printer-specific options.

Figure 15 For some printers—but not any of mine—the Supply Levels pane displays ink or toner levels.

CONFIGURING PRINTERS

Sharing Printers

If your Mac is connected to a network, you can add printers that are connected to other computers or network devices, as I discussed earlier in this chapter. You can also share your directly connected printers with other users on a network.

When you share a printer, your printer appears as an available printer to other network users. As long as your computer is turned on and connected to the network and your printer is turned on, other network users can print to your printer.

You can also create a printer *pool*, or group of shared printers. When you or another user prints to a printer pool, the document prints on the first available printer in the pool. This is especially helpful on a busy network when many users have access to just a handful of printers.

In this section, I explain how to share a printer connected to you computer. I also tell you how you can set up a printer pool that includes any printer that you have added to your Printers list (**Figure 6**).

✔ Tip

■ I tell you more about networking and sharing in **Chapter 20**.

To share a printer with other network users

1. In the Printers list (**Figure 6**), select the printer you want to share.

2. Turn on the Share this printer check box.

✔ Tips

■ After step 2, if a warning icon and message that printer sharing is turned off appears beneath the check box (**Figure 16**), click the Sharing Preferences button. Then turn on the Printer Sharing check box in the Service list of the Sharing preferences pane that appears (**Figure 17**).

■ You can also disable printer sharing for a specific printer and set up printing privileges in the Sharing preferences pane (**Figure 17**). I tell you more about sharing and privileges in **Chapter 20**.

To stop sharing a printer with other network users

1. In the Printers list (**Figure 6**), select the printer you want to share.

2. Turn off the Share this printer check box.

✔ Tip

■ You can also disable printer sharing for a specific printer in the Sharing preferences pane (**Figure 17**).

To disable all printer sharing

1. Choose Apple > System Preferences or click the System Preferences icon in the Dock.

2. Click the Sharing icon in the System Preferences window that appears.

3. In the Sharing preferences pane (**Figure 17**) turn off the Printer Sharing check box in the Service list.

Figure 16 In this example, the printer is set up for sharing but Printer Sharing has been disabled in the Sharing preferences pane.

Figure 17 Use the Sharing preferences pane to enable or disable printer sharing.

Figure 18 When you select multiple printers to include in a printer pool, the Create Printer Pool button appears.

Figure 19 Enter a name for the printer pool in this little dialog.

Figure 20 The printer pool you created appears in the Printers list.

To create a printer pool

1. In the Printer list, select the printers you want to include in the printer pool (**Figure 18**). To select more than one printer at a time, hold down ⌃ ⌘ while clicking the name of each one.

2. Click the Create Printer Pool button (**Figure 18**).

3. Enter a name for the printer pool in the Name box of the dialog that appears (**Figure 19**), and click OK.

   The name of the printer pool you created appears in the Printer list window (**Figure 20**) and in the Printer pop-up menu in Print dialogs (**Figure 28**).

✔ Tip

■ When you print to a printer pool, your computer automatically looks at each printer in the pool, in the order they are listed, and prints to the first one available.

To delete a printer pool

1. In the Printers list, select the printer pool you want to delete (**Figure 20**).

2. Click the − button beneath the list.

3. Click OK in the confirmation dialog that appears (**Figure 10**).

   The printer pool is removed from the list.

✔ Tip

■ Deleting a printer pool does not delete the printers it includes.

The Page Setup Dialog

The Page Setup dialog (**Figure 22**) lets you set page options prior to printing, including the printer the document should be formatted for, paper size, orientation, and scale.

To set Page Attributes

1. In the application you plan to print from, choose File > Page Setup (**Figure 21**) to display the Page Setup dialog.

2. If necessary, choose Page Attributes from the Settings pop-up menu to display Page Attributes options (**Figure 22**).

3. Set options as desired:

   ▲ To format the document for a specific printer, choose the printer from the Format For pop-up menu (**Figure 23**).

   ▲ To change the paper size, choose an option from the Paper Size pop-up menu (**Figure 24**).

   ▲ To change the page orientation, click the Orientation option you want.

   ▲ To change the print scale, enter a scaling percentage in the Scale box.

4. Click OK to save your settings and dismiss the Page Setup dialog.

✔ Tip

■ The Format For pop-up menu (**Figure 23**) should list all of the printers that appear in the Printers list of the Print & Fax preferences pane (**Figure 6**).

Figure 21
An application's File menu—such as this one from TextEdit—is home to the Page Setup and Print commands.

Figure 22 Here's the Page Setup dialog as it appears in TextEdit.

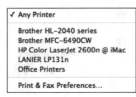

Figure 23
The Format For pop-up menu should include all printers and printer pools your computer knows about.

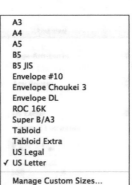

Figure 24
Choose a paper size for the current document from the Paper Size pop-up menu.

SETTING PAGE ATTRIBUTES

Click here to toggle between Print dialog sizes.

Figures 25 & 26 The Print dialog can have two different appearances: small (above) with limited options and large (below) with access to all options. You can toggle between the two versions by clicking the disclosure triangle button.

Setting Options in the Print Dialog

The Print dialog (**Figure** 25 or 26) enables you to set printing options and output the document to a printer, fax modem, or PDF file.

Like the Page Setup dialog, the Print dialog is a standard dialog, but two things can cause its appearance and options to vary:

◆ Print options vary depending on the selected printer.

◆ Additional options may be offered by specific applications.

The Print dialog offers two modes: a simple view with few options (**Figure** 25) and a detailed view with all options (**Figure** 26). Simply click a disclosure triangle to toggle from one view to the other.

This section explains how to set Print options available for most printers and applications.

✔ Tips

■ If your Print dialog includes options that are not covered here, consult the documentation that came with your printer.

■ For information about using Print options specific to an application, consult the documentation that came with the application.

■ Throughout this chapter, I work with the full version of the Print dialog (**Figure** 26).

To open the Print dialog

Choose File > Print (**Figure** 21), or press ⌘ P. The Print dialog appears (**Figure** 25 or 26).

THE PRINT DIALOG

To set basic printing options

On the top-right corner of the Print dialog
(**Figure 27**), set options as desired:

Figure 27 Set basic printing options in the top-right corner of the Print dialog.

◆ **Printer** (**Figure 28**) is the printer you
want to print to.

◆ **Presets** (**Figure 29**) is a set of predefined
options. I explain how to use this feature
later in this section.

◆ **Copies** is the number of copies to print.

◆ **Collated** prints multiple copies in collated sets.

◆ **Two-Sided** prints the pages for two-sided
printing. This option is only available if
your printer supports two-sided printing.

◆ **Pages** enables you to enter a range of
pages to print:

  ▲ **All** prints all pages in the document.

  ▲ **From** enables you to enter values in
  the From and to boxes to set a range
  of pages to print.

◆ **Paper Size** (**Figure 24**) is the size of paper
you want to print to.

◆ **Orientation** is the paper orientation for
printing: portrait (the default) or land-
scape.

Figure 28 The Printer menu includes all printers and fax modems you added to the Print & Fax preferences pane.

✔ Tips

■ The Printer pop-up menu (**Figure 28**)
should list all of the printers and fax
modems that appear in the Printers list
of the Print & Fax preferences pane
(**Figure 2**).

Figure 29 The Presets menu enables you to save or select predefined options.

■ Choosing Add Printer from the Printer
pop-up menu (**Figure 28**) opens the
dialog you can use to add a printer to the
Print & Fax preferences pane (**Figure 3**).
I explain how to add printers on page 364.

SETTING BASIC PRINTING OPTIONS

Figure 30
Use this pop-up menu to select the type of option you want to set.

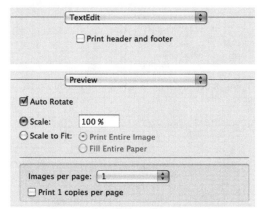

Figures 31 & 32 Application-specific settings vary from one application to another. In these examples are settings for TextEdit (top) and Preview (bottom).

Figure 33 Layout options control pages per sheet and related settings.

Figure 34 Color Matching options control how color-matching features work.

To set other options

1. In the lower-right corner of the Print dialog, choose an option from the pop-up menu at the divider line (**Figure 30**). Here are some of the possible options:

   ▲ *Application name* (**Figures 31** and **32**) displays application-specific options.

   ▲ **Layout** (**Figure 33**) enables you to set the number of pages per sheet, layout direction, border, two-sided printing, and reverse page orientation, which prints the pages in reverse order.

   ▲ **Color Matching** (**Figure 34**) enables you to set color-matching options.

   ▲ **Paper Handling** (**Figure 35**) enables you to specify which pages to print (all, even, or odd), set scaling options, and set the page order (normal or reverse).

   ▲ **Paper Feed** (**Figure 36**) enables you to specify whether paper will be fed automatically or manually.

Continued on next page...

Figure 35 Paper Handling options control which pages print, how they're scaled, and what order they print in.

Figure 36 Paper Feed options control how paper is fed into the printer.

Continued from previous page.

▲ **Cover Page (Figure 37)** enables you to set options for a cover page that can be printed before or after the document.

▲ **Scheduler (Figure 38)** enables you to schedule a print job for the future, put it on hold, and set a document's print priority.

▲ **Paper (Figure 39)**, **Color Options (Figure 40)**, **Print Options (Figure 41)**, and **Printer Features (Figure 42)** are examples of printer-specific options.

▲ **Summary** displays a summary of settings (**Figure 43**). You can click the disclosure triangles to show or hide each category of options.

2. Set options as desired in the bottom half of the Print dialog.

3. Repeat steps 1 and 2 for each group of options you want to set.

✔ Tips

■ Many of the options that appear in the lower half of the print dialog are printer-specific, so what you see may vary from what is shown in this book.

■ The Scheduler options' Priority setting determines when your print job will print when you send it to a printer that already has print jobs waiting in the queue.

■ I tell you about print queues, including how to work with print jobs that are on hold, on page 386.

■ The Reverse page order option is useful if your printer places documents face up in the printer tray when printed. But if printer does this, the Automatic option may ensure that pages print in the right order. Experiment with a short document and see for yourself!

Figure 37 Cover Page options enable you to print a cover page for the print job.

Figure 38 Scheduler options help you schedule print jobs.

Figure 39 Print Settings control general printer-specific options.

Figure 40 You can see a summary of settings in the Print dialog.

■ Some paper handling options may also be offered in application-specific print settings. For example, Microsoft Word enables you to print just odd or just even pages in its application-specific options.

Figure 41 Use this dialog to name a preset.

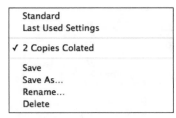

Figure 42 The preset you created is added to the Presets pop-up menu.

Figure 43 The Preset is automatically selected when you add it.

To save settings as a preset

1. In the Print dialog (**Figure 26**), choose Save As from the Presets pop-up menu (**Figure 29**). The Save Preset As dialog appears (**Figure 41**).

2. Enter a name for the settings in the Preset Name box.

3. Choose a Preset Available For option to specify whether it should be available for just the current printer or all printers.

4. Click OK.

The name you entered is added to the Presets menu (**Figure 42**) and chosen (**Figure 43**).

✔ Tip

■ It's a good idea to save settings if you often have to change the Print dialog's settings. This can save time when you need to print.

To save changes to preset settings

In the Print dialog (**Figure 36**), choose Save from the Presets pop-up menu (**Figure 42**). Your changes to the preset settings are saved.

To use preset settings

In the Print dialog (**Figure 26**), choose the name of the preset settings you want to use from the Presets pop-up menu (**Figure 42**).

All Print dialog settings are set according to the saved settings.

To delete a preset setting

1. In the Print dialog (**Figures 26**), choose the name of the preset settings you want to delete from the Presets pop-up menu (**Figure 42**).

2. Choose Delete from the Presets pop-up menu (**Figure 42**).

The preset setting is deleted.

SAVING SETTINGS AS PRESETS

Previewing Documents

The Print dialog includes a preview area that you can use to get a large thumbnail preview of each page of the document. This is a good way to see how a document will print before actually printing it.

✔ Tip

- You can also use the Print dialog's Open PDF in Preview command, which I discuss on page 380, to create a PDF of the document and open it in Preview. This gives you a full-sized version of the document to examine before printing. I tell you more about Preview on page 299.

To preview a document in the Print dialog

1. Set options as desired in the Print dialog's panes.

2. Look at the Preview area on the left side of the Print dialog to see what the first page looks like (**Figure 44**).

3. If the document has multiple pages, use the controls beneath the preview (**Figure 44**) to scroll through the document.

✔ Tip

- Some applications, such as Microsoft Word, include a Print Preview command. This displays a preview of the document from within the application and does not open the Print dialog.

First page Previous page   Next page Last page

Figure 44 You can view a "large thumbnail" preview of your document right in the Print dialog.

PREVIEWING DOCUMENTS

Figure 45 Use this pop-up menu to select an output option other than printing.

Saving Documents as PDF Files

PDF, which stands for *Portable Document Format*, is a standard file format that can be opened and read by Preview and Adobe Reader. PDF is a good format for distributing a formatted document when you're not sure what software the document's recipient has. Most computer users have some kind of PDF reader software; if they don't, they can download Adobe Reader for free.

The PDF menu in the Print dialog offers several options for saving a document as a PDF file (**Figure 45**):

◆ **Open PDF in Preview** opens the document as a PDF file in Preview. This is useful for seeing a full-sized preview of a document you plan to print.

◆ **Save as PDF** saves the document as a PDF file.

◆ **Save as PostScript** saves the document as a PostScript format file, which can then be sent to a PostScript output device.

◆ **Fax PDF** uses a fax modem to fax the document as a PDF.

◆ **Mail PDF** creates a PDF file of the document and attaches it to an e-mail message form.

◆ **Save as PDF-X** saves the document as a PDF-X file. This format is more compatible with print-production equipment.

◆ **Save PDF to iPhoto** saves the document as a PDF file and adds it to your iPhoto library. (You must have iPhoto installed to use this feature.)

◆ **Save PDF to Web Receipts Folder** saves the document as a PDF file in the Web Receipts folder in your Documents folder.

✔ Tip

■ The commands below the split line on the PDF menu (**Figure 45**) are PDF workflows created with AppleScript or Automator. I tell you more about Mac OS X's automation tools in **Chapter 24**.

SAVING DOCUMENTS AS PDF FILES

To save a document as a PDF file

1. Set options as desired in the Print dialog's panes.

2. Choose Save as PDF from the PDF menu (**Figure 45**).

3. In the Save dialog that appears (**Figure 46**), enter a name and select a disk location for the PDF file.

4. If desired, provide additional information about the file in the Title, Author, Subject, and Keywords boxes in the bottom part of the dialog.

5. To secure the document against unauthorized access or use, click the Security Options button. Then set options in the PDF Security Options dialog that appears (**Figure 47**) and click OK.

6. Click Save. The file is saved as a PDF file in the location you specified.

✔ Tips

- To open a file as a PDF before creating it, choose Open PDF in Preview from the PDF menu.

- As shown in **Figure 47**, you can use the PDF Security Options dialog to require separate passwords to Open the document or copy and print its content.

- The Save dialog is covered in **Chapter 10**.

Figure 46 Use this dialog to name and save a PDF file.

Figure 47 You can use options in this dialog to protect a PDF from unauthorized access, text copying, or printing.

SAVING DOCUMENTS AS PDF FILES

Sending & Receiving Faxes

You can fax documents from within the Print dialog. All you need is a fax modem that is listed in the Print & Fax dialog (**Figure 6**) and connected to a telephone line.

If desired, you can also use a fax modem to receive faxes at your computer.

To fax a document

1. Set options as desired in the Print dialog's panes.

2. Choose Fax PDF from the PDF menu (**Figure 45**).

   or

   Choose a fax modem from the Printer pop-up menu (**Figure 28**).

   The bottom half of the Print dialog changes to offer options for faxing the document (**Figure 48**).

3. Enter the name of the person you are faxing the document to in the To box. As you type, your computer attempts to match what you're typing to entries in your Address Book file (**Figure 49**). If you prefer, you can click the Addresses button to display a searchable Addresses window (**Figure 50**); double-click a fax number to enter it in the window.

4. If you need to dial a number to get a dial tone (like in an office or hotel) or a 1 for long distance, enter these numbers in the Dialing Prefix box.

5. To include a fax cover page, turn on the Use Cover page check box, type a subject in the Subject box, and type a message in the Message box.

Continued on next page...

Figure 48 Use the bottom-right corner of the Print dialog to set options for faxing a document.

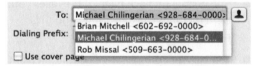

Figure 49 As you enter a recipient's name, your computer attempts to match it to Address Book entries.

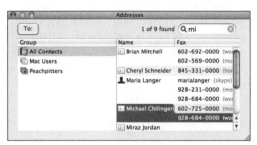

Figure 50 Another way to add a recipient is to use the searchable Addresses window. This is especially useful when a recipient has more than one fax number; double-click the one you want.

Continued from previous page.

6. **Click Fax.** A Print status dialog appears briefly as the document is spooled to the fax modem's queue. A moment later, the computer dials and sends the fax.

✔ Tips

- If you have multiple fax devices listed in the Print & Fax preferences pane (**Figure 6**), it's best to start the fax process by choosing the fax device from the Printer pop-up menu in step 2. This specifies which fax device you want to use.

- In step 3, you don't have to enter a name. Instead, just enter a fax phone number. You might find this quicker when sending a one-time fax to someone whose fax number is not in your Address Book.

- In step 3, you can enter multiple recipients in the To box. Separate each one with a comma (,).

- The header on each page of the faxes you send includes the date, time, and page number.

- You can set options for a fax modem from within the Print dialog. While a fax modem is chosen from the Printer menu, choose Fax Modem from the pop-up menu on the divider line in the bottom half of the Print dialog (**Figure 51**). Then set options for dialing, sound, and dial tone (**Figure 52**).

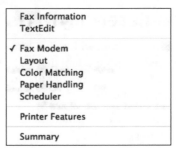

Figure 51 Choose Fax Modem from the pop-up menu to...

Figure 52 ...view and set fax modem options.

SENDING FAXES

Figure 53 In the Printers list, select the fax modem you want to use to receive faxes.

Figure 54 The Fax Status menu makes it easy to check on the status of a fax modem and to quickly open its preferences window.

Figure 55 Use this dialog to set options for receiving faxes.

Figure 56 Use this dialog to select a different folder in which to save incoming faxes.

To set up your computer to receive faxes

1. Open the Print & Fax preferences pane as discussed earlier on page 364.

2. In the Printers list, select a fax modem (**Figure 53**).

3. Enter your fax number in the Fax Number box. This information will appear at the top of every fax you send.

4. To display a fax status menu, turn on the Show fax status in menu bar check box. You can use this menu (**Figure 54**) to check the status of the fax modem and to access Print & Fax preferences.

5. Click the Receive Options button to open the fax preferences dialog (**Figure 55**).

6. Turn on the check box marked Receive faxes on this computer.

7. Set other options as desired:

   ▲ **Answer after** is the number of rings before the computer answers the phone.

   ▲ **Save To** enables you to choose a folder in which faxes should be saved. The options are Faxes and Shared Faxes, but you can choose Other Folder and use the dialog that appears (**Figure 56**) to choose a different folder.

   ▲ **Print To** tells your computer to print the fax on the printer you choose from the pop-up menu.

   ▲ **Email To** tells your computer to e-mail a copy of the fax to the address you enter in the box.

8. Click OK.

✔ Tip

■ To receive faxes, your computer must be turned on and awake and its modem must be connected to a telephone line.

SETTING UP TO RECEIVE FAXES

Printing Documents

As you've probably figured out, the Print dialog also enables you to send a document to a printer to be printed.

To print a document

1. Set options as desired in the Print dialog's panes.

2. Click Print.

   The print job is sent to the print queue, where it waits for its turn to be printed. A progress window appears as it is sent or spooled.

✔ Tips

- You can normally cancel a print job as it is being spooled to the print queue or printer by pressing ⌃⌘.. Any pages spooled before you press ⌃⌘., however, may be printed anyway.

- Canceling a print job that has already been spooled to a print queue is discussed on page 387.

Figure 57 Drag the printer from the list onto the desktop.

Figure 58
When you release the mouse button, a desktop printer icon appears for the printer.

Figure 59 Drag the document you want to print onto the desktop printer icon to print it.

Desktop Printers

Mac OS X's *desktop printers* feature enables you to create an icon for a printer you use frequently. Then, when you want to print a document on that printer, simply drag the document icon onto the printer icon.

To create a desktop printer

1. Open the Print & Fax preferences pane as discussed earlier on page 364.

2. Drag the icon for the printer you want to create a desktop printer for out of the window and onto the desktop (**Figure 57**). When you release the button, an alias icon for the printer appears on the desktop (**Figure 58**).

To print with a desktop printer

1. Drag the icon for the document you want to print onto the printer icon (**Figure 59**).

2. When you release the button, the document is sent to the printer's print queue and prints.

✔ Tips

■ You can drag any number of document icons onto the printer icon. They will all be spooled to the printer.

■ The Print dialog does not appear when you use a desktop printer.

Print Queues

A *print queue* is a list of documents or print jobs waiting to be printed. When you click the Print button to send a document to a printer, you're really sending it to the printer's queue, where it waits its turn to be printed.

You can open a printer's queue window to check the progress of print jobs that are printing; to stop printing; and to hold, resume, or cancel a specific print job.

✔ Tip

■ Although this section discusses printer queues, your fax modem also has a queue that works exactly the same way.

To open a printer's queue window

1. Open the Print & Fax preferences pane (**Figure 6**) as discussed on page 364.

2. In the Printers list, double-click the name of the printer you want to open the queue for.

Or

Double-click the desktop printer icon for a printer (**Figure 58**).

The printer's queue window opens (**Figure 60** or **61**).

✔ Tips

■ When a document is in a print queue, the icon for the printer that will print it appears in the Dock (**Figure 62**). Click the icon to view the printer's print queue.

■ Clicking the tiny button to the left of a document's status in the print queue displays a preview of the document (**Figure 63**).

Figure 60 A printer's queue window with no documents in the queue...

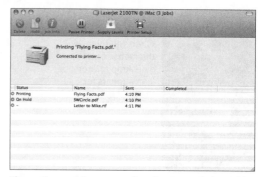

Figure 61 ...and the same printer's queue window with three documents in the queue: one printing, one on hold, and one waiting to be printed.

Figure 62 When print jobs are in a printer's queue or the print queue is open, an icon for the printer appears in the Dock.

Figure 63 Clicking a button in the Print Queue window displays a preview of the document.

Figure 64 The queue status appears in the queue window.

Figure 65 When you select a print job that is not on hold, the Delete and Hold buttons are active.

Figure 66 When you select a print job that is on hold, the Delete and Resume buttons are active.

To stop all print jobs

Click the Pause Printer button in the Print Queue window (**Figures 60** and **61**). Any printing stops and the words *Printer Paused* appear in the print queue window (**Figure 64**).

To restart print jobs

Click the Resume button in the Print Queue window (**Figure 64**). The next print job starts printing.

To hold a specific print job

1. In the printer's queue window (**Figure 61**), select the print job you want to hold.

2. Click the Hold button (**Figure 65**). *On Hold* appears in the Status column beside the job name in the queue window (**Figure 61**). If the job was printing, it stops and another queued job prints.

To resume a specific print job

1. In the printer's queue window (**Figure 61**), select the print job you want to resume.

2. Click the Resume button (**Figure 66**). *On Hold* disappears from the Status column beside the job name in the queue window. If no other jobs are printing, the job begins to print.

✔ Tip

- You can also use this technique to start printing a job that you scheduled using the Scheduler options in the Print dialog (**Figure 38**).

To cancel a specific print job

1. In the printer's queue window (**Figure 61**), select the print job you want to cancel.

2. Click the Delete button (**Figure 65** or **66**). The job is removed from the print queue. If it was printing, printing stops.

WORKING WITH PRINTERS & PRINT JOBS

The Finder's Print Command

The Finder's File menu also includes a Print command (**Figure 67**). This is a quick-and-dirty command for sending a selected document to the default printer, without even displaying the Print dialog.

✔ Tip

- The Finder's Print command works very much like the Print One command available in some applications.

To use the Finder's Print command

1. In a Finder window, select the document(s) you want to print.

2. Choose File > Print (**Figure 67**).

   If necessary, the application that created the document opens. The document is sent to the default printer and prints.

Figure 67 The Finder's Print command sends any selected document(s) to the default printer.

Connecting to the Internet

Connecting to the Internet

The Internet is a vast, worldwide network of computers that offers information, communication, online shopping, and entertainment for the whole family.

There are two ways to connect to the Internet:

◆ In a *direct* or *network* connection, your computer has a live, high-speed *broadband* connection to the Internet all the time. This is common for workplace computers on companywide networks. At home, cable modems and DSL offer direct connections.

◆ In a *modem* or *dial-up* connection, your computer uses a modem to dial in to a server, which gives it access to the Internet. This functionality is available to cell phone users utilizing *tethering* or *dial-up networking* (*DUN*). Access speed is generally slower than direct connections.

This chapter explains how to configure your system for a direct Internet connection and connect to the Internet.

✔ Tips

■ Internet connectivity is provided by *Internet service providers* or *ISP*s for a fee.

■ The *World Wide Web* is part of the Internet.

■ Your computer accesses the Internet via a TCP/IP connection. *TCP/IP* is a standard Internet *protocol*, or set of rules, for exchanging information.

■ **Chapter 19** covers using Internet applications to exchange e-mail, browse the Web, and participate in online chats.

■ DUN service and setup varies based on cell phone carrier and service offered. A complete discussion of DUN is beyond the scope of this book.

389

Using the Network Setup Assistant

The Network Setup Assistant steps you through the process of setting up an Internet connection using an AirPort wireless network, telephone modem, DSL modem, cable modem, or local area network with Ethernet connection.

The Network Setup Assistant is easy to use. Just get it started and provide basic information about your Internet connection. It automatically sets options in the Network preferences pane for your connection.

In this part of the chapter, I explain how to use the Network Setup Assistant to set up an Internet connection.

✔ Tips

- If you set up your Internet connection as part of the setup process discussed in **Chapter 1**, your computer should be ready to connect to the Internet and you can skip this chapter. But if you didn't set up your connection or if your Internet connection information has changed since setup, the Network Setup Assistant is a good way to configure your computer to connect to the Internet.

- The Network Setup Assistant groups all settings for a connection as a *location*. If your computer has more than one way to connect to the Internet, you can create a location for each method.

- Before you use the Network Setup Assistant to configure your computer for an Internet connection, make sure you have all the information you need to properly configure the options. You can get all of the information you need from your ISP or network administrator.

About This Mac
Software Update...
Mac OS X Software...

System Preferences...
Dock ▶
Recent Items ▶
Force Quit... ⌥⌘⎋
Sleep ⌥⌘⏏
Restart...
Shut Down...
Log Out Maria Langer... ⇧⌘Q

Figure 1
Choose System
Preferences from
the Apple menu.

Figure 2 The Network Preferences pane showing the status and basic settings for my AirPort connection.

Figure 3 This dialog appears when you click the Assist me button.

To launch the Network Setup Assistant

1. Choose Apple > System Preferences (**Figure 1**) or click the System Preferences icon in the Dock.

2. In the System Preferences window that appears, click the Network icon. Network preferences appears, displaying network status and connection information for one of your network interfaces (**Figure 2**).

3. Click the Assist me button at the bottom of the window.

4. A dialog like the one in **Figure 3** appears. Click the Assistant button.

   The Introduction screen of the Network Setup Assistant appears (**Figure 4**). Continue following the instructions in the appropriate section on the following pages to set up the type of connection you want.

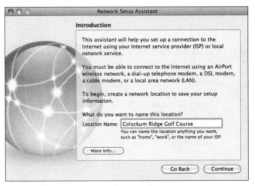

Figure 4 The Introduction screen of the Network Setup Assistant.

LAUNCHING THE NETWORK SETUP ASSISTANT

To set up an AirPort connection

1. In the Introduction screen of the Network Setup Assistant (**Figure 4**), enter a name for the connection in the Location Name box and click Continue.

2. In the How Do You Connect to the Internet? screen that appears next (**Figure 5**), select the I use AirPort to connect to the Internet wirelessly option. Click Continue.

3. In the Connect to an AirPort or Other Wireless Network screen (**Figure 6**), select the name of the wireless network you want to join and, if necessary, enter a password. Click Continue.

4. In the Ready to Connect? screen (**Figure 7**), click Continue.

5. Wait while the Network Setup Assistant configures your connection. When it's finished, it displays a Congratulations! screen like the one in **Figure 8**. Click Done.

✔ Tip

■ In step 3, if you want to connect to an existing wireless network that is not listed, select Other AirPort Network. Then enter the name of the network and your password in the boxes that appear (**Figure 9**) and click Continue.

Figure 5 Use this screen to indicate the type of connection you want to set up. The telephone modem option is gray because there's no modem connected to my computer.

Figure 6 Select the wireless network you want to connect to. In this case, the network I'm connecting to is not password protected, so no password box appears.

Figure 7 Click Continue in this screen to connect.

Figure 8 This screen confirms that you have successfully configured the connection.

Figure 9 If you want to connect to a network that is within range but not listed because of security settings, you can enter the network name and your password in this screen.

Figure 10 If you can't automatically connect with a cable modem, this screen appears so you can enter additional configuration information.

To set up a DSL or cable modem connection

1. In the Introduction screen of the Network Setup Assistant (**Figure 4**), enter a name for the connection in the Location Name box and click Continue.

2. In the How Do You Connect to the Internet? screen that appears (**Figure 5**), select the I use a DSL modem to connect the Internet or the I use a cable modem to connect to the Internet option. Click Continue.

3. In the Ready to Connect? screen, click Continue.

4. If you are unable to connect automatically, a screen like the one in **Figure 10** or 11 appears. Select the appropriate radio button and provide the required information. Click Continue.

5. If you choose More choices (**Figure 11**), an additional screen of options appears (**Figure 12**). Set options and click Continue.

6. A Congratulations! screen like the one in **Figure 8** appears. Click Done.

Figure 11 If you can't automatically connect with a DSL connection, this screen appears so you can enter additional configuration information...

Figure 12 ...or display more options for configuration.

393

To set up a LAN connection

1. In the Introduction screen of the Network Setup Assistant (**Figure 4**), enter a name for the connection in the Location Name box and click Continue.

2. In the How Do You Connect to the Internet? screen that appears next (**Figure 5**), select the I connect to my local area network (LAN) radio button. Click Continue.

3. In the Ready to Connect? screen, click Continue.

4. If you are unable to connect automatically, a screen like the one in **Figure 13** appears. Enter IP information for your connection and Click Continue.

5. A Congratulations! screen like the one in **Figure 8** appears. Click Done.

✔ Tip

■ You may need to consult your network administrator or ISP to get the information required to complete step 4. In most instances, however, you can skip that step because you'll be able to connect automatically.

Figure 13 If you have a static IP address, you can enter IP information in this screen.

Figure 14 Choose the Location you want to use from the Location submenu under the Apple menu.

Figure 15 You can choose a location from the Location pop-up menu in the Network preferences pane.

Working with Locations

If you've used the Network Setup Assistant to create one or more location settings, you can choose the one you want to use to connect to the Internet. You can also rename and remove locations. You do all this in the Network Preferences pane.

To choose a location

1. Choose Apple > Location to display a menu of configured locations (**Figure 14**).

2. Choose the location you want to use.

Or

1. Choose Apple > System Preferences (**Figure 1**) or click the System Preferences icon in the Dock.

2. In the System Preferences window that appears, click the Network icon. Network preferences appears, displaying network status and connection information for one of your network connections (**Figure 2**).

3. Choose the location you want to use from the Location pop-up menu (**Figure 15**).

4. Click Apply. The Network preferences pane changes to reflect your settings.

✔ Tip

- Automatic (**Figures 14** and **15**) is the default location setting. It senses the best connection option and chooses it for you.

To edit locations

1. In the Network preferences pane, choose Edit Locations from the Location pop-up menu (**Figure 15**). A dialog like the one in **Figure 16** appears. It lists all locations.

2. Select the location you want to work with.

3. Click one of the buttons or choose a pop-up menu option at the bottom of the dialog (**Figure 17**):

   ▲ + adds a new location setting.

   ▲ − removes the selected location setting.

   ▲ **Duplicate Location** makes a copy of the location and adds it to the list. You can rename the location, click Done, and then modify settings in the Network preferences pane to configure the new location based on settings for the one you duplicated.

   ▲ **Rename Location** puts an edit box around the location name (**Figure 18**) so you can rename it.

4. When you are finished working with locations, click Done.

To change a location's settings

1. In the Network preferences pane, choose the location you want to modify from the Location pop-up menu (**Figure 15**).

2. Make changes in the Network preferences pane as discussed in the section titled "Setting Internet Options in Network Preferences" starting on the next page.

3. Click Apply.

4. Choose System Preferences > Quit System Preferences or press ⌃⌘Q.

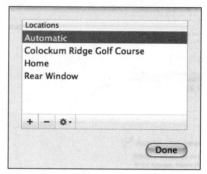

Figure 16 Use this dialog to edit locations.

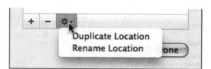

Figure 17 Clicking the pop-up menu's button displays two more commands for working with the selected location.

Figure 18 Choosing Rename Location puts an edit box around the location so you can rename it.

Setting Internet Options in Network Preferences

The Network pane of System Preferences displays information about your network connections (**Figure 2**) and enables you to manually configure your Internet connection options.

For each connection type, you can set basic options, such as the network you want to connect to for AirPort connections, login settings for DUN connections, and TCP/IP settings for Ethernet and FireWire connections. If you need to set more advanced options, you can click the Advanced button for your connection type and change settings in a series of connection-specific panes.

This part of the chapter explains how you can manually set Internet options in the Network preferences pane.

✔ Tips

- If all of this sounds confusing to you, don't mess with it. Instead, use the Network Setup Assistant, which I discuss earlier in this chapter, to set up a new connection with the correct settings.

- If your Internet configuration is working fine, don't change it! Internet connections follow one of the golden rules of computing: *If it ain't broke, don't fix it.*

- PPPoE, which stands for Point to Point Protocol over Ethernet, is a connection method used by some cable and DSL ISPs.

- Before you set Network preferences, make sure you have all the information you need to properly configure the options. You can get configuration information from your ISP or network administrator.

- I tell you more about networking in **Chapter 20**.

To open Network preferences

1. Choose Apple > System Preferences (**Figure 1**) or click the System Preferences icon in the Dock.

2. In the System Preferences window that appears, click the Network icon. Network preferences appears, displaying network status and connection information for one of your network interfaces (**Figure 2**).

3. Choose an option from the Location pop-up menu (**Figure 19**) to view options for the location setting you want to modify.

4. Select the interface type you want to change by clicking it in the list on the left side of the window (**Figure 23**):

   ▲ **AirPort** shows settings for your Air-Port connection to a base station or other AirPort network.

   ▲ **Internal Modem** or **External Modem** (not shown in **Figure 19**) shows the settings for a modem.

   ▲ **Bluetooth DUN** shows settings for connecting to a network via a Blue-tooth mobile phone.

   ▲ **Ethernet** shows the settings for the computer's Ethernet port.

   ▲ **FireWire** shows settings for a FireWire connection to another computer.

   Basic settings for the interface appear on the right side of the preferences pane (**Figure 2**).

✔ Tip

■ The options that appear in the interface type list (**Figure 19**) vary depending on your computer model and its features.

Figure 19
Select the interface you want to check or modify.

OPENING NETWORK PREFERENCES

Figure 20 Basic settings for an AirPort connection.

Figure 21 You can choose a different wireless network from the Network Name pop-up menu.

Figure 22 The AirPort menu enables you to choose a different network to connect to and access other network options.

To set basic configuration options for an AirPort connection

1. In the Network preferences pane, select AirPort in the interfaces list to display basic options (**Figure 20**).

2. To connect to a different network, choose an option from the Network Name pop-up menu. This menu lists all available networks (**Figure 21**).

3. If you want your computer to offer to join unknown networks when no known network is available, turn on the Ask to join new networks check box.

4. To access AirPort options from the menu bar, turn on the Show AirPort status in menu bar check box. You can use this menu (**Figure 22**) to find and connect to available wireless networks.

5. Click Apply to save your changes.

✔ Tips

■ You can disable your computer's AirPort connection by clicking the Turn AirPort Off button. This not only disconnects you from the Internet (if you're connected via AirPort), but disables all AirPort networking.

■ Turning on the Ask to join new networks check box in step 3 is especially useful on laptops, since it helps you find wireless networks at travel destinations.

■ The Network Name pop-up menu (**Figure 21**) and the AirPort status menu (**Figure 22**) also indicates whether a network is password protected and how strong its signal is. This is a new feature of Mac OS X 10.6.

To set basic configuration options for a Bluetooth DUN connection

1. In the Network preferences pane, select Bluetooth DUN in the interfaces list to display basic options (**Figure 23**).

2. Choose the configuration you want to modify from the Configuration pop-up menu.

3. Enter the dialup information provided by your cell phone carrier in the text boxes.

4. To test your connection, click the Connect button. After connecting, connection status should appear in the Status area (**Figure 24**). Click Disconnect if you do not want to remain connected to the Internet.

5. To access DUN options from the menu bar, turn on the Show modem status in menu bar check box. You can use this menu (**Figure 25**) to connect or disconnect via DUN.

6. Click Apply.

✔ Tips

■ The Bluetooth DUN option appears only if you have configured a Bluetooth device for DUN with your computer. When you set this up, you'll likely provide all the information shown in **Figure 23**; it isn't necessary to change these options unless your configuration information changes. I explain how to pair Bluetooth devices in **Chapter 20**.

■ The Configuration pop-up menu lists all dial-up accounts you have created. Chances are, you will have just one.

Figure 23 Here's what basic options for Bluetooth DUN might look like. These are the settings I use to connect my Macs to the Internet with my BlackBerry Storm.

Figure 24 When you're connected, status appears in the settings window.

Figure 25 The Modem Status menu offers access to DUN connection commands and display options.

Figure 26 Basic settings for an Ethernet connection.

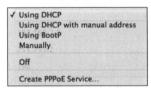

Figure 27
Use this menu to choose the kind of configuration settings you need to enter.

To set basic configuration options for Ethernet or FireWire connections

1. In the Network preferences pane, select Ethernet or FireWire in the interfaces list to display basic options (**Figure 26**).

2. Choose one of the options from the Configure pop-up menu (**Figure 27**). The option you select determines the appearance of the rest of the screen. **Figures 26** and **28** through **30** show examples.

3. If necessary, enter the appropriate IP addresses and domain names in the fields.

4. Click Apply.

✔ Tips

- Do not use the settings illustrated here. They will not work. Use the settings provided by your ISP or network administrator.

- DHCP is a type of network addressing system.

- If you're not sure which option to choose in step 2, ask your network administrator.

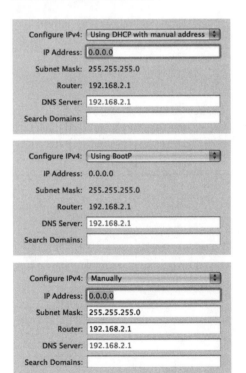

Figures 28, 29, & 30 Three examples of configuration options.

SETTING ETHERNET OR FIREWIRE OPTIONS

To set advanced connection options

1. In the Network preferences pane, select the interface you want to set advanced options for (**Figures 20, 23**, and **26**).

2. Click the Advanced button. A dialog of advanced options appears. A row of connection-specific buttons for categories of settings appears near the top of the dialog.

3. Click the button for the settings you want to change. You can see examples in **Figures** 31 through 33.

4. Set options as desired.

5. Repeat steps 3 and 4 for each category of setting you want to change.

6. Click OK to save your settings.

7. Back in the Network preferences pane, click Apply.

✖ Warning!

■ Incorrectly setting advanced options can prevent your computer from connecting to the Internet or your local area network. If you're not sure what to change, don't make any changes at all.

✔ Tips

■ A complete discussion of these settings is beyond the scope of this book. I recommend that you set up all Internet and Network connections with the Network Setup assistant discussed on page 390 and use the Network preference pane to make changes only when necessary.

■ If you're concerned about Internet security, be sure to consult the information about firewalls on page 529.

Figure 31 The advanced AirPort settings for an AirPort connection.

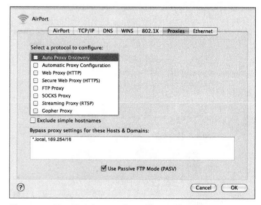

Figure 32 The Proxies settings for an AirPort connection; it looks and works very much the same for other kinds of connections.

Figure 33 The Modem settings for a Bluetooth DUN connection. It looks very much the same for an internal or external modem connection.

SETTING ADVANCED CONNECTION OPTIONS

Manually Connecting to an ISP

If you're connecting to an ISP via a modem or Bluetooth DUN connection, you'll need to manually connect and disconnect to the Internet. You can do this with the Network preferences pane or Modem Status menu.

✔ Tip

- If you have a network connection to the Internet—including a cable modem or DSL connection—you are always connected and can skip this section.

To connect with the Network preferences pane

1. In the Network preferences pane, select your Bluetooth DUN device or modem in the interfaces list (**Figure 23**).

2. If necessary, choose the configuration you want to connect with from the Configuration pop-up menu.

3. Click Connect.

   Your computer uses your device to dial in to your ISP's network and connect to the Internet. It displays the connection status in its Status area and the Connect button becomes a Disconnect button (**Figure 24**).

To disconnect with the Network preferences pane

1. If necessary, display the Network preferences pane settings for your Bluetooth DUN device or modem (**Figure 24**).

2. Click Disconnect. Your computer terminates its connection with your ISP's network.

MANUALLY CONNECTING & DISCONNECTING

To connect with the Modem Status menu

1. From the Modem Status menu, choose the modem connection you want to use to connect (**Figure 25**).

2. From the Modem Status menu, choose the Connect option at the top of the menu (**Figure 25**).

   Your computer uses your modem to dial into your ISP's network and connect to the Internet. It displays the connection time in the menu bar (**Figure 34**).

✔ Tip

■ To use the Modem Status menu, it must be enabled in the Network Preferences pane (**Figure 25**).

To disconnect with the Modem Status menu

Choose the Disconnect command at the top of the Modem Status menu while you are connected to the Internet (**Figure 35**). Your computer terminates its connection.

Time connected   *Bluetooth connection active*

Figure 34 When you're connected via Bluetooth DUN, you'll see indications on the Modem and Bluetooth menus on the menu bar (if they are displayed).

Figure 35 The Connect command turns into a Disconnect command while you're connected.

MANUALLY CONNECTING & DISCONNECTING

Internet
Applications

Internet Applications

Mac OS X includes three applications and an online service for interacting with the Internet:

◆ **Mail** is an *e-mail client* application. It enables you to exchange e-mail messages, create to do lists, and subscribe to RSS feeds.

◆ **iChat** is a *chat client* application. It enables you to exchange instant messages and conduct audio or video conferences with MobileMe, AIM, Google Talk, and Jabber users.

◆ **Safari** is a *Web browser* application. It enables you to browse Web sites, download files from FTP sites, and subscribe to RSS feeds.

◆ **MobileMe** (formerly known as .Mac) is an online service offered by Apple, Inc. It includes three features that integrate with Mac OS X: Sync, iDisk, and Back to My Mac.

This chapter provides brief instructions for using these tools—just enough to get you started. You can explore the other features on your own.

Continued on next page...

Continued from previous page.

✔ Tips

- To use these applications, your computer must have access to the Internet and be set up to use it. I explain how to configure your Mac for an Internet connection in **Chapter 18**.

- Mail and Safari are set as the default e-mail and Web browser applications.

- Firefox (www.firefox.com) and Opera (www.opera.com) are two other useful Web browsers. Although neither comes with Mac OS, they are both popular among Mac users.

To open an Internet application

Use one of the following techniques:

- ◆ Open the icon for the application in the Applications folder (**Figure 1**).

- ◆ Click the icon for the application in the Dock (**Figure 2**).

Figure 1 The Applications folder.

Figure 2 A Mac OS X 10.6 installation puts icons for Mail, Safari, and iChat in the Dock.

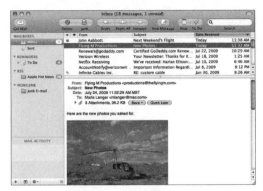

Figure 3 The Mail main window with an incoming message displayed.

Mail

Mail (**Figure 3**) is an e-mail client application. It enables you to send and receive e-mail messages using your Internet e-mail account.

Here's how it works. Imagine having a mailbox at the post office. As mail comes in, the postmaster sorts it into the boxes—including yours. To get your mail, you need to go to the post office to pick it up. While you're there, you're likely to drop off any letters you need to send.

E-mail works the same way. Your e-mail is delivered to your e-mail server—like the post office where your mailbox is. The server software (like the postmaster) sorts the mail into mailboxes. When your e-mail client software (Mail, in this case) connects to the server via the Internet, it picks up your incoming mail and sends any outgoing messages it has to send.

If you set up your Internet connection and provided MobileMe login information when you first configured Mac OS X, that information is automatically stored in Mail so it's ready to use. Just open Mail, and it automatically makes that virtual trip to the post office to get and send messages.

In this part of the chapter, I explain how to set up an e-mail account with Mail. I also explain how to compose, send, read, and retrieve e-mail messages.

✔ Tip

- If you don't have a MobileMe account set up on your Mac, when you first start Mail, it displays the first screen of the Welcome to Mail window, which looks very much like **Figure 5**. Follow steps 2 through 7 in the section titled "To set up an e-mail account" on page 408.

MAIL

To set up an e-mail account

1. If necessary, choose File > New Account (**Figure 4**) to display the first screen of the Mail setup.

2. A dialog like the one in **Figure 5** appears. Enter basic information for the account:
   - ▲ **Full Name** is your full name.
   - ▲ **Email Address** is your e-mail address.
   - ▲ **Password** is your e-mail account password.

3. Click Continue. If you created a MobileMe account, you're done. You can skip the remaining steps.

4. In the Incoming Mail Server dialog (**Figure 6**), enter information for your incoming mail server and click Continue.
   - ▲ **Account Type** is the type of account. Your options are POP, IMAP, Exchange 2007, and Exchange IMAP.
   - ▲ **Description** is an optional description for the account.
   - ▲ **Incoming Mail Server** is the domain name or IP address of your incoming mail server.
   - ▲ **User Name** is your user ID on the mail server.
   - ▲ **Password** is your password on the mail server.
   - ▲ **Also set up** (not shown) offers check boxes to set up Address Book contacts and iCal calendars. This option is only available for Exchange 2007 accounts.
   - ▲ **Outlook Web Access Server** (not shown) is the domain name or IP address of the Outlook server for Web access to e-mail. This option is only available for Exchange IMAP accounts.

Figure 4 Mail's File menu.

Figure 5 Start by providing basic information about the account.

Figure 6 For most account types, you'll have to enter information about your incoming mail server.

Figure 7 For most types of e-mail accounts, you'll also have to provide outgoing mail server info.

Figure 8 Mail displays a summary of the account information it has confirmed.

Figure 9 The new account is added to Mail and any waiting for that account is fetched from the server. (You know you're in trouble when you're writing a book and the only incoming e-mail is from editors at two different publishing companies.)

5. In the Outgoing Mail Server dialog (**Figure 7**), enter information for your outgoing mail server and click Continue.

▲ **Description** is an optional description for the server.

▲ **Outgoing Mail Server** is the domain name or IP address of your outgoing mail server. You can choose a server from the drop-down list or enter information for a different server. If you turn on the Use only this server check box, the server you enter or select is the only one that can be used with the account.

▲ **Use Authentication** tells Mail to send your user name and password when sending mail. This is required by most mail servers. If you turn on this check box, be sure to enter your account user name and password in the boxes below it.

6. When Mail has verified all information you entered, it displays the results in an Account Summary window (**Figure 8**). Make sure the Take account online check box is turned on. Then click Create.

The new account is added to Mail's Accounts list and appears as an Inbox item in the main Mail window (**Figure 9**). Mail fetches whatever mail is waiting in that account.

Continued on next page...

SETTING UP E-MAIL ACCOUNTS

✔ Tips

- You only have to set up an e-mail account once. Mail will remember all of your settings.

- Your ISP or network administrator can provide all of the important information you need to set up an e-mail account, including the account name, password, and mail servers.

- Do not fill in forms using the information shown in figures here to set up an account. It will not work.

- If a dialog like the one in **Figure 10** appears after step 5, chances are, you've entered incorrect server information. Click Cancel and double-check your entries in the Outgoing Mail Server screen (**Figure 7**). If everything looks right and your Internet connection is functioning, you might want to contact your ISP for assistance.

- If Mail can't verify the identity of a mail server, it may display a dialog like the one in **Figure 11**. You have several choices to proceed:

  - ▲ **Show Certificate** displays the certificate and additional information for the server (**Figure 12**).

  - ▲ **Cancel** aborts the attempt to connect with the server.

  - ▲ **Connect** connects with the server despite the problem.

- You cannot use the outgoing mail server for a MobileMe account to send e-mail messages for an account with another ISP. The MobileMe outgoing mail server only works with MobileMe accounts. Outgoing or SMTP server information should be provided by your ISP.

Figure 10 This dialog appears if you've entered incorrect information in the Outgoing Mail Server screen.

Figure 11 A dialog like this appears if Mail can't verify the identity of a mail server.

Figure 12 You can view a certificate for a server to learn more about what Mail doesn't like about it.

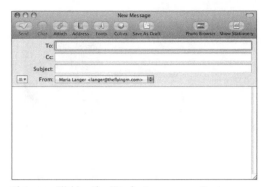

Figure 13 Clicking the New button opens a New Message window like this one.

Figure 14 When you begin to type in a name, Mail tries to match it to entries in Address Book.

Figure 15 You can also use an Addresses window to enter a recipient's e-mail address.

Figure 16 Here's a short message ready to be sent.

To create & send a message

1. Click the New Message button at the top of the main Mail window (**Figure** 3). The New Message window appears (**Figure 13**).

2. Use one of the following techniques to enter the recipient's address in the To box:
   - ▲ Type the recipient's e-mail address.
   - ▲ If the recipient is someone in your Address Book file or someone you have received an e-mail message from in the past, enter the person's name. As you type, Mail attempts to match the name (**Figure 14**). Click the correct entry. (Address Book is covered in **Chapter 12**.)
   - ▲ Click the Address button. Use the searchable Addresses window that appears (**Figure 15**) to locate the recipient's name and double-click it.

3. Repeat step 2 to add additional names. When you are finished, press [Tab] twice.

4. Enter a subject for the message in the Subject field, and press [Tab].

5. If you have more than one e-mail address, choose the address you want to use to send the message from the From pop-up menu. For some types of accounts, you may also have to select an outgoing mail server from a menu that appears beside it.

6. Type your message in the large box at the bottom of the window. When you are finished, the window might look like the one in **Figure 16**.

7. Click the Send button. The message window closes and Mail sends the message.

CREATING & SENDING MESSAGES

To perform message-related tasks with toolbar buttons

1. Follow steps 1 through 5 on the previous page to prepare a new mail message.

2. Click the toolbar button (**Figure 13**) for the task you want to perform:

   ▲ **Send** sends the message, as discussed on the previous page.

   ▲ **Chat** initiates an iChat session with the message addressee.

   ▲ **Attach** displays a standard Open dialog (**Figure 17**). Locate and select a file you want to attach and then click Choose File.

   ▲ **Address** displays a searchable Address Book window, as discussed on the previous page.

   ▲ **Fonts** displays the Fonts panel (**Figure 18**), which you can use to format text in the body of the message.

   ▲ **Colors** displays the Colors panel (**Figure 19**), which you can use to apply color to text in the body of the message.

   ▲ **Save As Draft** saves the message in the Drafts folder without sending it. You can later open, modify, and send it.

   ▲ **Photo Browser** gives you access to your iPhoto (if installed) and Photo Booth libraries so you can attach photos to your message.

   ▲ **Show Stationery** displays a gallery of stationery templates above the message form (**Figure 20**). Select a category in the left column and then click to select the stationery you want to use (**Figure 21**). The stationery's formatting fills the message body area. Replace sample text and/or images (**Figure 22**) with your content to complete the message (**Figure 23**).

Figure 17 Use this dialog to attach a file to a message.

Figure 18 You can use the Fonts panel to format selected text in the body of a message.

Figure 19
The Color panel makes it possible to apply color formatting to selected text.

Figure 20 Clicking the Show Stationery button displays a gallery of templates you can use in your message.

Figure 21 The stationery you select appears in the message body.

Figure 22 Once you've selected a template, you can replace sample content such as images and text with your own content. In this example, I'm dragging an image icon onto one of the stationery's image drop zones.

✔ Tips

■ The Chat button is only available if the addressee is online and you have his buddy information set up in iChat or Address Book.

■ Attached images and one-page PDFs appear as images in mail messages. Other types of files appear as icons.

■ You can also attach a file by simply dragging its icon into the message window.

■ I tell you about iChat later in this chapter, the Fonts panel in **Chapters 11** and **16**, and the Colors panel in **Chapter 8**.

Figure 23 Here's an example of what the beginning of a message created with stationery might look like.

To retrieve e-mail messages

1. Click the Get Mail button at the top of the main window (**Figure 3**).

2. Mail accesses the Internet and then connects to your e-mail server and downloads messages waiting for you. Incoming messages appear in a list when you select the Inbox in the Mailboxes column (**Figure 3**).

✔ Tips

- A blue bullet character appears beside each unread e-mail message (**Figure 3**).

- Messages that Mail thinks are junk mail are colored brown. You can set junk mail filtering options in the Junk Mail preferences window (**Figure 24**). Choose Mail > Preferences and click the Junk Mail button to get started. You'll find that Mail's junk mail filter can weed out at least 75 percent of the spam that you get.

- Mail automatically creates a separate in-box for each e-mail account. Click an in-box to see only the messages for that e-mail address.

- You can configure Mail to have multiple mailboxes to organize your incoming e-mail more effectively. Use commands under the Mailbox menu to create and customize mailboxes.

Figure 24 Mail's Junk Mail preferences window enables you to set options that weed out junk mail messages.

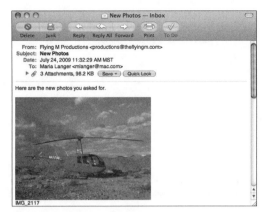

Figure 25 Double-click a message to open it in its own window.

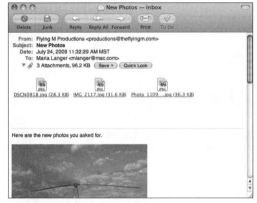

Figure 26 Clicking the Attachments triangle displays icons for attachments. In this example, five JPEG image files are attached.

Figure 27 The Save menu enables you to save all attachments or a specific attachment.

To read a message

1. Click the message that you want to read. It appears in the bottom half of the main Mail window (**Figure 3**).

2. Read the message.

✔ Tips

- You can also double-click a message to display it in its own message window (**Figure 25**).

- To view a list of message attachments (when present), click the triangle beside the paper clip icon in the message header. The header expands to show icons for each attachment (**Figure 26**). To save attachments, click the Save button to display a menu (**Figure 27**) and choose the desired option. A Save As dialog appears so you select a location to save the file(s).

- If a message includes photos, you can click the Quick Look button to display a slide show of all photos, one at a time (**Figure 28**).

Figure 28 You can use the Quick Look feature to view attachments as a slide show.

READING MESSAGES

To reply to a message

1. Click the Reply or Reply All button at the top of the window. A preaddressed message window with the entire message quoted appears (**Figure 29**).

2. Type your reply, in the message body.

3. Click Send.

✔ Tip

■ The Reply button addresses the reply to the person who sent you the message. The Reply All button addresses the reply to the person who sent you the message and sends a copy of the message to all other recipients.

To forward a message

1. Click the Forward button at the top of the window. A copy of the message appears in a new message form (**Figure 30**).

2. Enter the e-mail address of the person you want to forward the message to in the To box.

3. If desired, enter a message at the top of the message body.

4. Click Send.

To add a message's sender to Address Book

1. Select (**Figure 3**) or open (**Figure 25**) the message sent by the sender you want to add.

2. Choose Message > Add Sender to Address Book or press Shift ⌃ ⌘ Y.

   Mail adds the person's name and e-mail address to Address Book's entries. You can open Address Book and add additional information for the record as desired.

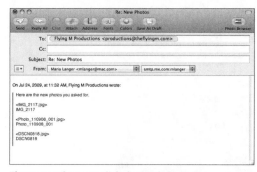

Figure 29 When you click the Reply button, a preaddressed message window appears.

Figure 30 A forwarded message includes the entire message and any attachments.

Figure 31 Selected text in an e-mail message...

Figure 32 ...can form the basis of a to-do item.

Figure 33 To-do items created in Mail appear in iCal.

Figure 34
You can even set options for a to-do item you create in Mail.

Figure 35
A clickable link in the to-do item's details makes it easy to open the e-mail message linked to it.

To create a to-do item from an e-mail message

1. Display the e-mail message you want to base the to-do item on.

2. Select any text you want to appear in the to-do item (**Figure 31**).

3. Choose File > New To Do (**Figure 4**), or press Option ⌃ ⌘ Y. The text you selected is copied to a to-do item form at the top of the e-mail message (**Figure 32**).

4. If desired, edit the text of the to-do item.

   The to-do item appears in the list of To Do Items in iCal (**Figure 33**).

✔ Tip

■ You can use the To Do Options menu (**Figure 34**) to set additional options for the to-do item, including the due date, alarm, priority, and calendar.

■ Creating a to-do item like this automatically links it to the e-mail message where you created it. You can click the Show in Mail link in the to-do item's details in iCal (**Figure 35**) to quickly open the linked e-mail message.

■ To-do items also appear in Mail. Select the To Do item under Reminders in Mail's sidebar to display them (**Figure 36**).

■ I discuss iCal starting on page 246.

Figure 36 Mail also maintains a list of to-do items.

To create an event from an e-mail message

1. Display the e-mail message with date or time information for the event you want to create.

2. Point to the date or time. A pop-up menu outline appears around the information (**Figure 37**).

3. Click the triangle to display the menu and choose Create New iCal Event. (**Figure 38**).

4. A new event form appears with some information already filled in (**Figure 39**).

5. Edit the form's fields to display the information you want to include in the event. When you're finished, it might look something like **Figure 40**.

6. Click Add to iCal. The event is added to iCal with the settings you specified (**Figure 41**).

✔ Tips

- Creating an event like this automatically links it to the e-mail message where you created it. You can click the Show in Mail link in the event's details in iCal (**Figure 42**) to quickly open the linked e-mail message.

- I discuss iCal starting on page 246.

Figure 37 When you point to a date or time in an e-mail message, the outline for a pop-up menu appears.

Figure 38 Click to display a menu of options for the date or time.

Figure 39 A partially completed form like this appears.

Figure 40 Edit the information in the form so it shows what you want.

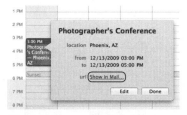

Figure 42 The event is linked to the e-mail message.

Figure 41 The event is added to iCal.

Figure 43 Use this dialog to add a feed that has already been added as a Safari bookmark.

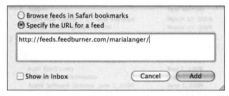

Figure 44 You could also enter the URL for a feed.

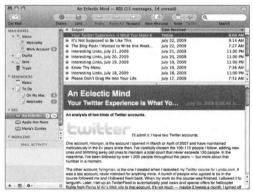

Figure 45 You can read RSS feeds right in the Mail window.

To add an RSS feed

1. Choose File > Add RSS Feeds (**Figure** 4) to display a dialog like the one in **Figure** 43.

2. To add a feed from a Safari bookmark, select Browse feeds in Safari Bookmarks and turn on check boxes for the bookmarks you want to add (**Figure** 43). Then click Add.

   or

   To add a feed by typing its URL, select Specify a custom feed URL and enter the URL in the edit box that appears (**Figure** 44). Then click Add.

   The feeds are added under RSS in the column on the right side of the main Mail window (**Figure** 45).

✔ Tip

- I tell you more about RSS later in this chapter, in my discussion of Safari.

To read RSS feeds in Mail

1. In the main Mail window, click the name of the feed you want to read under RSS in the column on the left side of the window.

2. In the list of feed posts in the top half of the window, click the post you want to read.

   The post's content appears in the bottom half of the window (**Figure** 45).

✔ Tip

- Feed content is treated similarly to e-mail messages in Mail. Unread posts are marked with a blue bullet, you can forward posts via e-mail, and you can delete posts using the Delete button or by pressing Delete.

READING RSS FEEDS IN MAIL

iChat

iChat enables you to conduct live chats or audio or video conferences with MobileMe (or .Mac), AIM (AOL Instant Messenger), Jabber, and Google Talk users.

Here's how it works. The first time you open iChat, you configure it with your chat account information, as well as the information for your buddies who use compatible chat networks. Then, while you're connected to the Internet with iChat running, iChat does two things:

◆ It tells the network that you're available to receive instant messages and participate in chats.

◆ It tells you when your buddies are online and available to receive instant messages and participate in chats.

When a buddy is available, sending him an instant message is as easy as clicking a button and typing what you want to say. If more than one buddy is available, you can open a chat window and invite them to participate together.

iChat also includes audio and video conferencing features. If you have a microphone or a compatible video camera (including Apple's iSight camera), you can have live audio or video chats with your buddies.

In this part of the chapter, I explain how to configure iChat for your account, set up an iChat buddy list, invite a buddy to a chat, and participate in text or video chats.

✔ Tips

■ To use iChat, you must have a MobileMe, AIM, Jabber, or Google Talk account. To use the AV features, you must have a microphone (for audio only) or compatible video camera (for audio and video) and a fast Internet connection.

■ iChat's audio and video features work with built-in iSight cameras as well as the old FireWire iSight cameras.

Figure 46 The Welcome to iChat screen tells you a little about iChat.

Figure 47 Use this screen to enter information about your iChat account.

Figure 48
Be sure to choose the right account type from this pop-up menu.

Figure 49 Use this screen to request encrypted chat.

To set up iChat

1. Open iChat as discussed earlier in this chapter.

2. Read the information in the Welcome to iChat screen that appears, (**Figure 46**) and click Continue.

3. In the Account Setup screen (**Figure 47**), choose an Account Type from the pop-up menu (**Figure 48**) and then enter your account information. The information you need to add varies depending on your account type. Then click Continue.

4. If you have a MobileMe account, a screen like the one in **Figure 49** appears, asking if you want to enable iChat encryption. If you turn on the check box, after you click Continue another screen confirms your encryption request. Click Continue.

5. Read the information in the Conclusion screen and click Done.

   A Buddy List window with a "Connecting" message appears next. After a moment, the window expands to list your buddies and their online status (**Figure 50**).

✔ Tips

■ In step 3, if you don't have a chat account, click the Get an iChat Account button. This launches your Web browser and displays a site where you can sign up for a free MobileMe iChat screen name.

■ To use iChat encryption, you and the person you are chatting with must have paid MobileMe accounts.

■ The type of account you create determines which Buddy List appears. For example, if you have a MobileMe account, you'll see the AIM Buddy List (**Figure 50**); if you have a Google Talk account, you'll see the Jabber Buddy List.

SETTING UP ICHAT

421

To add a buddy

1. Choose Add Buddy from the **+** button menu at the bottom of the Buddy List window (**Figure 51**).

   or

   Choose Buddies > Add Buddy, or press Shift ⌃ ⌘ A.

2. A dialog like the one in **Figure 52** appears. Fill in the form with information about your buddy's account, including account name and type, group to add the buddy to, and his first and last name.

3. Click Add. The buddy is added to the Buddy List window (**Figure 53**).

✔ Tips

- The Buddy List automatically includes contacts for which you have provided AIM information in Address Book, as well as buddies you may have added while using any previous version of iChat.

- You can add as many buddies as you like to your buddy list.

- A buddy's online status and audio or video capabilities is indicated in the buddy list with a color-coded bullet and phone or camera icons. **Figures 50** and **53** show some examples.

To remove a buddy

1. Select the name of the buddy you want to remove.

2. Press Delete.

3. Click OK in the confirmation dialog that appears.

Figure 50
The Buddy List displays all your iChat buddies, organized by online status.

Figure 51 Choose Add Buddy from the menu at the bottom of the Buddy List window.

Figure 52 Fill in this form with buddy information.

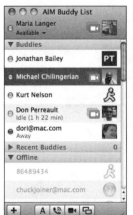

Figure 53
The contact is added to your Buddy List. In this example, it's my husband, who is online.

Start a Text Chat

Start a Video Chat

Start an Audio Chat

Start Screen Sharing

Figure 54 Buttons at the bottom of the Buddy List.

To conduct a text chat

1. In the Buddy List, select the name of a buddy who is available for chatting (**Figure 53**).

2. Click the Start a Text Chat button at the bottom of the Buddy List window (**Figure 54**). A window like the one in **Figure 55** appears.

3. Enter your message in the box at the bottom of the window. As you type, a "cloud" appears beside your icon to indicate that you're writing something (**Figure 56**).

4. Press [Return]. The comment appears in the top half of the window beside your icon (**Figure 57**).

5. Wait for your buddy to answer. His comments appear in the top half of the window beside his icon (**Figure 58**).

6. Repeat steps 3 through 5 to continue your instant message conversation in the window. **Figure 59** shows an example of a conversation between me and my husband—his first ever chat!

Figure 55
A window like this appears when you initiate a chat.

Figure 56
Type your comment at the bottom of the window. A "cloud" appears by your icon to indicate that you're typing.

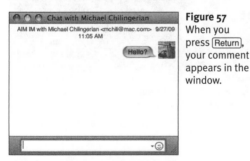

Figure 57
When you press [Return], your comment appears in the window.

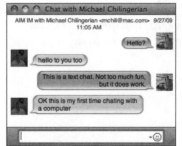

Figure 58
The start of a conversation.

Figure 59
The conversation continues.

CONDUCTING TEXT CHATS

To conduct a video chat

1. In the Buddy List, select the name of a buddy who is available for video chatting (**Figure 53**).

2. Click the Start a Video Chat button at the bottom of the Buddy List window (**Figure 54**). A window like the one in **Figure 60** appears.

3. Wait until your buddy responds. When he accepts the chat, the window changes to show his live image, with yours in a small box (**Figure 61**).

4. Talk!

Figure 60 Here's what you'll look like on your buddy's screen when he responds. (Less than seven days until we go to press. How can I be smiling?)

✔ Tips

- Audio chats work a lot like video chats—but without the picture.

- To conduct a video chat, both you and your buddy must have video capabilities. Look for a camera icon beside a buddy's name (**Figures 50** and **53**).

- Video chats work best when both parties are accessing the Internet at speeds of 256 Kbps or faster. You will notice an annoying time delay and some image distortions if you access at slow speeds.

- You can use the Effects button at the bottom of the window to apply a special effect to your image. I tell you more about effects in my coverage of Photo Booth on page 295.

Figure 61 When the buddy appears, start talking. (This is my husband, Mike.)

To end a chat

Click the close button in the chat window (**Figures 59 and 61**). Be sure to say "Bye" first!

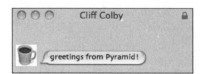

Figure 62 A chat invitation appears in a little window like this.

Figure 63 Click the window to expand it.

Figure 64 Enter your message in the bottom of the window.

Figure 65 When you accept a chat, the window expands so you can read and write messages.

To respond to a text chat invitation

1. When another iChat user invites you to a text chat, his message appears in a window on your desktop (**Figure 62**). Click the window to display an Instant Message window (**Figure 63**).

2. To accept the invitation, enter a message in the box at the bottom of the window (**Figure 64**) and click Accept or press Return. The message appears in the main window, which expands to display the chat (**Figure 65**).

   or

   To decline the invitation, click the Decline button or click the window's close button. The Instant Message window disappears.

   or

   To prevent the person from ever bothering you again with an invitation, click the Block button. Then click Block in the confirmation dialog that appears (**Figure 66**). The Instant Message window disappears.

Figure 66 Click Block in this dialog to prevent an annoying person from bothering you. (No, Cliff is not annoying; I clicked Cancel.)

RESPONDING TO TEXT CHAT INVITATIONS

To respond to a video chat invitation

1. When another iChat user invites you to a video chat, an invitation window like the one in **Figure 67** appears and iChat makes a phone ringing sound. Click the window to display a Video Chat window (**Figure 68**).

2. To accept the invitation, click Accept or press ⌐Return⌐. iChat establishes a connection with the caller and the window changes to show his live image, with yours in a small box (**Figure 69**). Start talking!

   or

   To decline the invitation, click the Decline button or click the window's close button. The Video Chat window disappears.

   or

   To respond with a text message, click Text Reply. Then use the text chat window that appears (**Figure 55**) to conduct a text chat with your buddy.

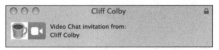

Figure 67 When you get a video chat invitation, you'll hear the sound of a ringing phone and a dialog like this appears.

Figure 68 Use one of the buttons at the bottom of the window to respond to the invitation.

Figure 69 When you accept an invitation, the caller's face appears and you can start talking. (This is my editor, Cliff, ordering lunch at the Pyramid Brewery. He told me he ordered root beer, but I think it was just a dark brew of the real thing.)

Figure 70 Drag the icon into the iChat window.

Figure 71 A view of the file appears in the iChat window.

Figure 72 Here's Jodene, sharing a photo of herself in the local coffee shop.

To share files with iChat Theater

1. Enter into a video chat with a buddy.

2. Drag the icon for the file you want to share from a Finder window to the video chat window.

3. Two hot areas appear on the chat window screen. Drag the icon onto the one labeled *Share with iChat Theater* (**Figure 70**).

4. The screen changes to display a preview of the file with a smaller image of your buddy (**Figure 71**). You can continue chatting.

✔ Tips

■ To cancel iChat Theater without ending the chat, click the close button that appears when you point to the shared picture.

■ **Figure 72** shows what iChat Theater looks like when you're on the receiving end of an image file.

■ If you share a file that doesn't have a preview—for example, a compressed file—the icon for that file appears in the window.

■ Dragging a file icon onto the Send to *Buddy Name* area of the screen (**Figure 70**), sends the file as a download to your buddy.

SHARING FILES WITH iCHAT THEATER

To share screens with another iChat user

1. In the Buddy List, select the name of a buddy who is available for video chatting.

2. Click the Start Screen Sharing button at the bottom of the Buddy List window (**Figure 54**) to display a menu with two options (**Figure 73**):

   ▲ **Share My Screen with** *Buddy Name* offers to share your screen with the buddy.

   ▲ **Ask to Share** *Buddy Name***'s Screen** asks your buddy if you can share his screen.

3. A dialog like the one in **Figure 74** appears while your request is sent to your buddy. If he accepts the request, one of two things happen:

   ▲ If you offered to share your screen, the dialog disappears. A blinking red icon in the menu bar indicates that your screen is being shared (**Figure 75**).

   ▲ If you requested to share your buddy's screen, your screen collapses into a large thumbnail image and your buddy's screen takes its place (**Figure 76**). You can click the thumbnail to return to your screen temporarily while sharing screens.

✔ Tips

■ When you share your screen, your buddy can not only see what you see onscreen but can control your computer. Use this feature with care!

■ To end screen sharing, choose End Screen Sharing from the blinking iChat menu in the menu bar (**Figure 75**).

Figure 73 The Start Screen Sharing button is really a menu with two options for sharing screens.

Figure 74 This window appears while you buddy to answer your request.

This blinking icon is a menu

Figure 75 When you share your screen, the only indication is the blinking red icon on the menu bar.

Figure 76 When you share someone else's screen, a thumbnail appears in your window so you can switch back to your screen.

Mouse pointer when pointing to a clickable link

RSS feed button

Figure 77 When you launch Safari, it displays the default Home page.

Figure 78 Clicking the link in **Figure 77** displays this page.

Figure 79 You can change the default Home page and other settings in Safari's preferences window.

Safari

Safari is a Web browser application. It enables you to view, or *browse,* pages on the World Wide Web.

A *Web page* is a window full of formatted text and graphics (**Figures 77** and **78**). You move from page to page by clicking text or graphic links or by opening *URLs* (*uniform resource locators*) for specific Web pages. These two methods of navigating the World Wide Web can open a whole universe of useful or interesting information.

✔ Tips

■ Safari supports *RSS* (*Really Simple Syndication*) feeds. RSS makes it possible to scan articles from several Web sites in one browser window, be notified when a Web site has new articles, and search specific Web sites for terms. I tell you how to get started using RSS later in this section.

■ You can easily identify a link by pointing to it; the mouse pointer turns into a pointing finger (**Figure 77**).

■ You can change the default home page by specifying a different page's URL in Safari's General preferences (**Figure 79**). Choose Safari > Preferences and click the General button to get started.

To follow a link

1. Position the mouse pointer on a text or graphic link. The mouse pointer turns into a pointing finger (**Figure 77**).

2. Click. After a moment, the page or other location for the link you clicked will appear (**Figure 78**).

To view a specific URL

Enter the URL in the address box (**Figure 80**), and press [Return] or [Enter].

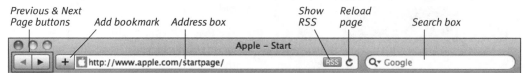

Previous & Next Page buttons   Add bookmark   Address box   Show RSS   Reload page   Search box

Figure 80 The top of the Safari window offers a number of buttons and fields for working with Web pages.

To bookmark a page

1. Display the Web page that you want to create a bookmark for.

2. Click the Add bookmark for the current page button (**Figure 80**), choose Bookmarks > Add Bookmark, or press [⌘][D].

3. In the dialog that appears (**Figure 81**), enter a name for the bookmark in the box, choose a location for it from the pop-up menu, and click Add.

   The bookmark is added to the location you specified: the bookmarks bar (**Figure 82**) or the Bookmarks menu (**Figure 83**).

Figure 81
Use this dialog to set bookmark options.

Figure 82 In this example, I added a bookmark for my Home page to the bookmarks bar...

✔ Tips

■ Once a page has been added to the Bookmarks menu, you can display it by selecting its name from the menu.

■ The sync feature of MobileMe, which I discuss on page 435, can synchronize Safari bookmarks between computers.

Figure 83
...and also to the Bookmarks menu.

To display a grid of your top sites

Choose History > Show Top Sites or press [Shift][⌘][1]. A page with thumbnail images of your most frequently visited Web pages appears. You can click a thumbnail to go to that page.

✔ Tip

■ The first time you open Safari, The Top Sites window (**Figure 84**) appears.

Figure 84 Safari keeps track of your favorite Web pages and can display clickable thumbnail images in a grid like this.

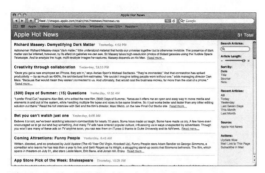

Figure 85 The RSS feed for the page in **Figure 74**.

Figure 86 The RSS feed for my personal site and blog. I use WordPress software and FeedBurner to automatically create a custom RSS feed of all new content.

Figure 87 Choosing View All RSS Articles from the Bookmarks Bar submenu displayed this page on July 25, 2009.

To access an RSS feed

Click the RSS button that appears in the address bar (**Figure 80**).

Or

Enter the URL for an RSS feed in the address bar and press Return.

Or

On a Web page, click the link for an RSS feed.

The page changes to RSS feed format (**Figures 85** and **86**).

✔ Tips

- RSS feeds are sometimes referred to as XML feeds.

- If Safari can find an RSS feed for a site you are viewing, it automatically displays an RSS button in the address bar (**Figure 80**).

- You can find RSS feeds already bookmarked in Safari by choosing Bookmarks > Bookmarks Bar > View All RSS Articles. **Figure 87** shows what the feed page looked like on the day I viewed it.

- You can return to the regular Web page view for an RSS feed by clicking the RSS button in the address bar again.

BROWSING RSS FEEDS

MobileMe's Web-Based Features

Apple's MobileMe online service, which can be found at www.me.com, offers a wide range of features for Mac users:

◆ **Mail** (**Figure 88**) gives you an e-mail address in the .me (or .mac for legacy users) domain that can be accessed via Apple's Mail software, any other e-mail client software, or a Web browser.

◆ **Contacts** (**Figure 89**) puts all your Address Book entries on your MobileMe account, where you can access them from any computer.

◆ **Calendar** (**Figure 90**) puts all your iCal events and to-do items on your MobileMe account, where you can access them from any computer.

◆ **Gallery** (**Figure 91**) enables you to put photos and movies on the Web where they can be shared with others.

◆ **iDisk** (**Figure 92**) gives you access to the contents of your iDisk from any computer.

There are two levels of membership:

◆ **Trial Membership** lets you work with MobileMe features for 60 days. Not all features are available to trial members, but the price is right: It's free!

◆ **Full Membership** gives you full access to all MobileMe features. When this book went to press, the annual fee was $99.95 per year, but you can often get a membership at a discount when you purchase a new Mac.

Because MobileMe's Web-based features are not part of Mac OS X, this book does not cover them in detail. Instead, I urge you to visit MobileMe and explore them on your own.

Figures 88, 89, 90, 91, & 92 MobileMe makes it possible to access your data on the Web.

Using MobileMe with Mac OS X

What can be useful to many Mac users are the MobileMe features that are fully integrated with Mac OS X:

◆ **Sync** enables you to synchronize information on your Mac with MobileMe and any other Mac that has access to the Internet. This makes it easy, for example, to synchronize iCal calendars, Address Book contacts, and Safari bookmarks between a desktop Mac and a laptop.

◆ **iDisk** gives you 20 GB of hard disk space on Apple's server. You can use this space to save or share files, host Web sites and photo galleries, and store backups.

◆ **Back to My Mac** makes it possible to access your computer for file and screen sharing from other Macs with Back to My Mac enabled. This can come in handy the next time you realize that you forgot to copy an important file to your laptop before hitting the road.

This part of the chapter explains how to set MobileMe options and use these features with Mac OS X.

✔ Tip

■ In order to use MobileMe features with Mac OS X, you must become either a Trial or Full member. To join, visit www.me.com and click the Join Now link or button on the Home page.

To sign in to a MobileMe account

1. Choose Apple > System Preferences, or click the System Preferences icon in the Dock (**Figure 2**).

2. In the System Preferences window that appears, click the MobileMe icon to display MobileMe preferences (**Figure 93** or **94**).

3. If the MobileMe preferences pane looks like **Figure 93**, continue following these steps.

   or

   If the MobileMe preferences pane looks like **Figure 94**, you're already set up to use MobileMe. You can skip the remaining steps.

4. Enter your MobileMe Member Name and Password in the appropriate boxes (**Figure 93**).

5. If necessary, click Sign In.

6. After a moment, the window should change so it indicates that you're logged in and provide information about your account status (**Figure 94**).

✔ Tips

■ Once you're signed in to MobileMe from your computer (**Figure 94**) you can sign out by clicking the Sign Out button. But in most instances, that should not be necessary.

■ If you are not signed in to your MobileMe account, you cannot access MobileMe's integrated features, including Sync, iDisk, and Back to My Mac.

Figure 93 Use this screen to sign in to your MobileMe account so you can access its features from within Mac OS X.

Figure 94 If the Account pane of the MobileMe preferences pane looks like this, you're already logged in.

MobileMe Sync

MobileMe's Sync feature enables you to automatically synchronize selected data on your Macintosh with MobileMe and any other Mac that has access to the Internet.

You can synchronize the following types of data:

◆ Safari Bookmarks

◆ iCal Calendars

◆ Address Book Contacts

◆ Dashboard Widgets

◆ Dock Items

◆ Keychains

◆ Mail Accounts

◆ Mail Rules, Signatures, and Smart Mailboxes

◆ Notes

◆ System Preferences

There are three main benefits to using MobileMe Sync:

◆ Syncing to MobileMe is a good way to back up your data. You can always restore your computer's settings from the data on MobileMe in the event of a hard disk crash or other serious problem.

◆ Syncing makes it possible to consistently set up multiple computers. This is great feature for people who have multiple Macs, such as a desktop Mac and a laptop Mac.

◆ Syncing is an easy way to copy data from one Mac to a new or recently reconfigured one.

MOBILEME SYNC

To enable & configure MobileMe Sync

1. Choose Apple > System Preferences or click the System Preferences icon in the Dock (**Figure 2**).

2. In the System Preferences window that appears, click the MobileMe icon to display MobileMe preferences.

3. Click the Sync button to display options (**Figure 95**).

4. Turn on the Synchronize with MobileMe check box.

5. Choose an option from the pop-up menu:

   ▲ **Automatically** synchronizes when the data has changed.

   ▲ **Every Hour**, **Every Day**, or **Every Week** synchronizes periodically.

   ▲ **Manually** requires that you initiate a synchronization.

6. Turn on the check box beside each item you want to synchronize with MobileMe.

7. To add a Sync menu to the menu bar (**Figure 96**) turn on the Show status in menu bar check box.

8. Click the Sync Now button.

9. A dialog like the one in **Figure 97** may appear. Choose an option from the pop-up menu and click Sync:

   ▲ **Merge all data** merges whatever data is on your computer with the data stored on your MobileMe account.

   ▲ **Replace data on computer** replaces the data on your computer with the data stored on your MobileMe account.

   ▲ **Replace all data on MobileMe** replaces whatever data is stored on your MobileMe account with the data on your computer.

Figure 95 The Sync panel of the MobileMe preferences pane lets you enable and configure syncing.

Figure 96 You can add a Sync menu to the menu bar.

Figure 97 The first time you sync, a dialog like this may appear, asking how you want to sync the data.

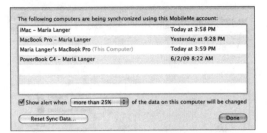

Figure 98 You can see a list of all computers that will be synchronized with MobileMe. (I have entirely too many laptops.)

10. Wait while all data is synchronized. When synchronization is complete, the sync date appears in the Sync panel of the MobileMe preferences pane.

✔ Tips

■ Enabling this feature by following step 2 automatically registers your computer with the MobileMe server. If you have more than one computer, you can see a list of registered computers by clicking the Advanced button in the Sync panel (**Figure 95**). The computers in this list (**Figure 98**) are the ones that will be synchronized with MobileMe.

■ If you choose Manual in step 3, you must click the Sync Now button in the Sync panel of the MobileMe preferences pane (**Figure 95**) or choose Sync Now from the Sync menu (**Figure 96**) every time you want to synchronize data.

■ In step 7, the dialog in **Figure 97** may appear more than once the first time you perform a synchronization.

To disable MobileMe synchronization

1. In the MobileMe preferences pane, click the Sync button to display its options (**Figure 95**).

2. Turn off the Synchronize with MobileMe check box.

iDisk

iDisk is 20 GB of private hard disk space on an Apple Internet server that you can use to store files and publish a Web site. But rather than deal with complex FTP software to access your iDisk space, Apple gives you access from within the Finder's Sidebar (**Figure 99**) and within Open and Save dialogs. Best of all, you manage files in your iDisk storage space just like you manage files on any other mounted volume.

Your iDisk storage space (**Figure 99**) is preorganized into folders, just like your Mac OS X Home folder:

◆ **Documents** is for storing documents. This folder is completely private; only you have access to it.

◆ **Desktop** is your iDisk's Desktop folder—which is just like the Desktop folder for your Mac account.

◆ **Music**, **Pictures**, and **Movies** are for storing various types of media.

◆ **Public** is for storing files you want to share with others. This folder can only be opened by a MobileMe member who knows your member name.

◆ **Sites** is for storing Web pages that you want to publish on the World Wide Web. iWeb, which is part of Apple's iLife suite of software, can store Web pages here. You can also create Web pages with another authoring tool and publish them by placing them in this folder.

◆ **Groups** is for accessing content stored using the old .Mac groups feature, which has been discontinued in MobileMe.

◆ **Shared** (not shown) appears on the iDisks of members of a Family Pack account. It contains files that can be shared by all account members.

Figure 99 The contents of an iDisk Home folder.

◆ **Backup** is for data files that have been backed up using the Backup application. It is a read-only folder, so you cannot manually add anything to it. This folder may not appear until you use Backup.

◆ **Software** is a read-only folder maintained by Apple Computer. It may contain applications that might interest you. The contents of this folder do not count toward the disk space iDisk allows you.

◆ **Library** is for storing support files used by MobileMe features. You cannot change the contents of this folder.

This part of the chapter tells you how you can access your iDisk from your computer.

✔ Tips

■ iDisk is a great place to store secondary backups of important files. Your iDisk storage space is an excellent off-premises backup for added protection against data loss. As a MobileMe member, you can automate this process with the Backup application, which you can find in the Software folder on your iDisk.

■ You can purchase additional iDisk space from Apple if you need it.

■ Technically, the 20 GB of disk space that comes with a MobileMe account is split between Mail and iDisk. You can set the amount of space allocated to each feature by logging in to the MobileMe Web site and setting preferences there.

■ I cover file management operations such as copying and deleting files in **Chapters 2 through 4**.

■ Your iDisk home folder (**Figure 99**) also includes a text file called About your iDisk, which has more information about iDisk. You can open this file with TextEdit.

iDisk

To set iDisk preferences

1. Choose Apple > System Preferences, or click the System Preferences icon in the Dock (**Figure 2**).

2. In the System Preferences window that appears, click the MobileMe icon to display MobileMe preferences.

3. Click the iDisk button to display options (**Figure 100**).

4. To buy more iDisk storage space, click the Upgrade Storage button. Your computer's default Web browser opens and displays a log in page for the MobileMe Web site. Follow the instructions that appear onscreen to complete the transaction. The storage space is made available to you almost immediately.

5. Set options to control Public folder access:
   ▲ **Allow others to write files in your public folder** tells MobileMe to allow others to both read and write to files in your Public folder.
   ▲ **Password-protect your public folder** enables you to set a password that users must enter to access your Public folder. When you turn on this option, a password dialog appears (**Figure 101**). Enter the same password twice, and click OK.

6. To copy the contents of your iDisk storage space to your computer's hard disk, click the Start button. You can then choose one of the Update options (**Figure 102**):
   ▲ **Automatically** syncs your iDisk and its local copy when you connect to the Internet.
   ▲ **Manually** requires you to initiate a synchronization.

Figure 100 The iDisk panel of the MobileMe preferences pane.

Figure 101 Use this dialog to set a password for your public folder.

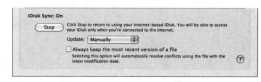

Figure 102 When you turn iDisk Syncing on, you can set options to control how it works.

Figure 103 When your iDisk is being synchronized, a spinning icon appears in the sidebar and a progress bar appears at the bottom of the window.

Figure 104 You can use commands on the Action pop-up menu to control syncing.

✔ Tips

- Creating a copy of your iDisk on your computer is a great way to quickly access most iDisk items, even when you're not connected to the Internet.

- Turning on the Always keep the most recent version of a file check box at the bottom of the iDisk panel (**Figure 100**), automatically ensures that your iDisk contains latest version of a file.

- When your iDisk is being synchronized, spinning arrows appear beside the iDisk icon in the Sidebar and a progress bar appears at the bottom of the window (**Figure 103**).

- The first time your computer syncs with iDisk can take some time. You can continue working with your computer while the sync is in progress.

- When you create a copy of your iDisk, your entire iDisk is not copied to your computer. Instead, your computer makes aliases to the Backup, Library, and Software folders, which can be rather large and which cannot be modified by you anyway.

- You can use commands on the Action pop-up menu (**Figure 104**) to control syncing when your iDisk is selected in the Sidebar.

- You can change the password you set up in step 5 by clicking the Set Password button (**Figure 100**).

To open your iDisk storage space from the Finder

Use one of the following techniques:

◆ Click the iDisk icon in the Sidebar (**Figure 103**).

◆ Choose Go > iDisk > My iDisk (**Figure 105**) or press [Shift] [⌘] [I].

A Finder window with your iDisk contents appears (**Figure 103**), and an iDisk icon appears on the desktop (**Figure 106**).

✔ Tip

■ The status bar of the Finder window (**Figure 103**) tells you how much space is left in your iDisk storage space. To display the status bar, make sure the window is active and then choose View > Show Status Bar.

To open another user's iDisk

1. Choose Go > iDisk > Other User's iDisk (**Figure 105**).

2. In the Connect to iDisk dialog that appears (**Figure 107**), enter the user's MobileMe member name and password to open the iDisk. Then click Connect.

   A window displaying the contents of the user's iDisk appears and an icon for that iDisk appears on the desktop (**Figure 106**).

To open a user's Public folder

1. Choose Go > iDisk > Other User's Public Folder (**Figure 105**).

2. In the Connect to iDisk Public Folder dialog that appears (**Figure 108**), enter the MobileMe member name and click Connect.

Figure 105
The iDisk submenu under the Finder's Go menu.

Figure 106
Icons for connected iDisks can appear on your desktop (depending on how Finder preferences are set).

Figure 107 Use this dialog to enter the MobileMe member name and password for the iDisk to connect to.

Figure 108 Use this dialog to enter the member's name.

Figure 109 If a public folder is password-protected, a dialog like this appears.

Figure 110 Click iDisk in the Save dialog's sidebar to open the iDisk folder.

Figure 111 Click iDisk in the Open dialog's sidebar to access folders and files stored on your iDisk.

3. If the Public folder is password-protected, a dialog like the one in **Figure 109** appears. Enter the password to access the folder, and click OK.

   A window displaying the contents of the user's Public folder appears and an icon for that folder appears as a volume on the desktop (**Figure 106**).

To save a file to iDisk from within an application

1. Choose File > Save As to display the Save dialog.

2. If necessary, click the triangle beside the Save As box to display the Sidebar and file locations (**Figure 110**).

3. In the Sidebar, click iDisk and choose a location on iDisk in which to save the file.

4. Enter a name for the file in the Save As box.

5. Click Save. The file is saved to the folder you selected in your iDisk storage space.

To open a file on iDisk from within an application

1. Choose File > Open to display the Open dialog.

2. In the Sidebar, click iDisk (**Figure 111**) and choose the folder in which the file you want to open resides.

3. In the list of files, select the file you want to open.

4. Click Open. The file is opened in a document window.

Back to My Mac

Back to My Mac makes it possible for you to access any of your Macs at home from any Mac with an Internet connection. In fact, the computers appear right in the Shared section of the sidebar.

✔ Tips

- To use Back to My Mac, each computer you want to connect to must be running Mac OS X 10.5 or later.

- Back to My Mac requires a router that supports NAT Port Mapping Protocol (NAT-PMP) or Universal Plug and Play (UPnP). AirPort base stations, including Time Capsule, support NAT.

To enable Back to My Mac

1. Choose Apple > System Preferences or click the System Preferences icon in the Dock (**Figure 2**).

2. In the System Preferences window that appears, click the MobileMe icon to display MobileMe preferences.

3. Click the Back to My Mac button to display options (**Figure 112**).

4. Click the Start button.

✔ Tips

- You must enable Back to My Mac on each computer you plan to use it with.

- To use file sharing or screen sharing via Back to My Mac, you must enable sharing preferences. I explain how in **Chapter 20**.

- Accessing another computer via Back to My Mac is the same as accessing via local area network. I tell you more about networking in **Chapter 20**.

Figure 112 The Back to My Mac panel of the MobileMe preferences pane.

Networking

Networking

Networking uses wired or wireless connections and network protocols to link your computer to others on a network. Once connected, you can share files, access e-mail, and run special network applications on server computers.

This chapter looks at peer-to-peer networking, which uses the built-in features of Mac OS X to connect to other computers for sharing. It explains how to configure an AirPort base station for use as a networking tool. It also covers some of the advanced network configuration tools available as Mac OS X utilities.

✔ Tips

- A discussion of Mac OS X Server, which is designed to meet the demands of large workgroups and corporate intranets, is beyond the scope of this book.

- This chapter touches only briefly on using networks to connect to the Internet. Connecting to the Internet is discussed in detail in **Chapter 18**.

Network Interfaces

Mac OS computer support the following types of network interfaces:

- **AirPort** is Apple's *wireless* or, *Wi-Fi*, networking technology. Through AirPort, your Mac can join wireless networks. AirPort Extreme, can handle 802.11n connections as well as those using the 802.11a, b, or g specifications. This makes it fast and highly compatible with other wireless networks.

- **Ethernet** is a network connection method that uses Ethernet cables to connect to the Ethernet ports of computers and network printers. Additional hardware such as routers and hubs may be needed, depending on the network setup and device. Ethernet was perhaps the most common form of networking until recently, when the benefits of wireless networking—no wires!—started providing a real alternative.

- **Bluetooth** is wireless technology that is designed for short-range (less than 30 feet) connections between devices. Although Bluetooth is commonly used to connect to input peripherals such as a keyboard or mouse, it's also a viable way to connect between computers or hand-held computing devices such as smart phones.

- **FireWire**, which is also known as IEEE 1394, is Apple's peripheral standard. It's an extremely fast connection method that is commonly used to connect external hard disks and to transfer data from video cameras to computers. FireWire can also be used to attach two computers for networking purposes using IP over FireWire.

Figure 1 The Network preferences pane showing status information for an AirPort connection. Connection status for each type of connection appears in the column on the left side of the window. In this illustration, information for an AirPort connection is shown.

◆ **Modem**, which can be internal or external, can establish a connection between two computers over a phone line. This older technology is used primarily for Internet connections when higher-speed alternatives are not available or desired.

You can check the status of a network interface or add additional interfaces in the Network preferences pane (**Figure 1**).

✔ Tips

■ I tell you briefly about using Bluetooth with cellphone for dial-up networking (DUN) in **Chapter 18**.

■ Other network technologies supported by Mac OS X 10.6 include VPN, PPPoE, and 6 to 4. A discussion of these technologies is beyond the scope of this book.

■ Network hardware configuration details involving hubs and routers are far beyond the scope of this book. If you need help setting up a complex network, refer to a detailed networking reference or contact a network consultant.

To check network status

1. Choose Apple > System Preferences or click the System Preferences icon in the Dock.

2. In the System Preferences window that appears, click the Network icon.

3. Get general status information in the column on the left side of the window (**Figure 1**).

4. To get details about the status and settings for a specific connection, select it in the list on the left side of the window. Details appear in the right side of the window (**Figure 1**).

✔ Tip

■ You can set advanced options for a selected interface by clicking the Advanced button near the bottom of the Network preferences pane window. I tell you about some of the advanced options in **Chapter 18**.

AirPort

AirPort is Apple's wireless local area network technology. It enables your computer to connect to a network or the Internet via radio waves instead of wires. As this book was being written, all new Macintosh computers came with AirPort Extreme functionality pre-installed.

In addition to the AirPort capabilities of your computer, Apple offers three different types of AirPort devices:

◆ **AirPort Extreme Base Station** is an external device that works as a router to share an incoming Internet connection, printer, and external hard disk with other computers.

◆ **Time Capsule** is an AirPort Extreme Base Station with a built-in hard disk. It's designed for use with the Time Machine feature for automated backup, but it can also be used for a centralized storage space for network users.

◆ **AirPort Express Base Station** is an external device that can connect to a network via Ethernet or can extend an existing AirPort network. It also has the ability to receive data from iTunes on an AirPort-equipped Mac to play music on compatible stereo speakers.

Mac OS X includes AirPort Utility (**Figure 2**), which enables you to configure an AirPort device for networking: This part of the chapter explains how to configure a two kinds of AirPort base stations: a Time Capsule and an AirPort Express. It also tells you how you can connect to an AirPort network with an AirPort-equipped Mac.

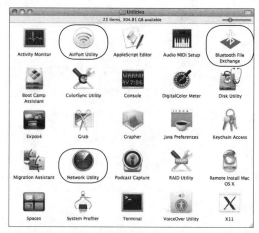

Figure 2 The Utilities folder includes a number of applications for working with networks.

✔ Tips

■ An AirPort network can include multiple base stations and AirPort-equipped computers.

■ You can learn more about AirPort devices and networking at Apple's Web site, www.apple.com/wifi/.

■ I tell you more about connecting to the Internet in **Chapter 18**.

Figure 3 In this example, AirPort Utility found two unconfigured base stations: an AirPort Express and a brand new Time Capsule.

Figure 4 You need to switch a base station's network to configure it.

Figure 5 In this screen, enter a name and password for the Time Capsule.

To create a Time Capsule network

1. Open the icon for the AirPort Utility application in the Utilities folder (**Figure 2**) inside the Applications folder. AirPort Utility uses your computer's AirPort wireless capabilities to scan for AirPort Base stations and Time Capsules and displays a list of the ones it finds on the left is of its window (**Figure 3**).

2. Select the Time Capsule you want to configure and click Continue.

3. If a dialog like the one in **Figure 4** appears, click Switch.

4. AirPort Utility scans the Time Capsule for current settings and displays a screen like the one in **Figure 5**. Set options.

    ▲ **Time Capsule Name** is the name you want to assign to the Time Capsule.

    ▲ **Time Capsule Password** and **Verify Password** is the same password for the Time Capsule, entered twice. You'll need this password to make changes to the Time Capsule configuration in the future.

    ▲ **Remember this password in my keychain** automatically creates a keychain item for the Time Capsule password.

    ▲ **Use a different password to secure disks** enables you to specify a different password to protect the data on disks inside and connected to the Time Capsule.

5. Click Continue:

Continued on next page...

CREATING A TIME CAPSULE NETWORK

Continued from previous page.

6. The next screen (**Figure 6**) asks what you want to do:

   ▲ **I want to create a new wireless network** uses the Time Capsule to create a wireless network. Choose this option to continue following instructions here.

   ▲ **I want to replace an existing base station or wireless router with Time Capsule** enables you to swap out another wireless router with the Time Capsule.

   ▲ **I want Time Capsule to join my current network** adds the Time Capsule to an existing network, thus extending the network's reach and adding the devices connected to Time Capsule to the network.

7. Click Continue.

8. The next screen (**Figure 7**) enables you to set network name and security options:

   ▲ **Wireless Network Name** is the name of the network. If you have multiple networks, you may want to give it a name related to its location or use.

   ▲ You have two security options: **WPA/WPA2 Personal** password-protects your network so no one can join it without a password. If you choose this option, enter a password of 8 to 63 characters in both boxes. **No security** leaves your network open so anyone can join it without a password.

9. Click Continue.

Figure 6 AirPort Utility offers three main options for configuring a base station.

Figure 7 Use this screen to give your network a name and select a security option.

CREATING A TIME CAPSULE NETWORK

Figure 8 Tell Time Capsule how it'll get its IP address.

Figure 9 If you connect using Bridge Mode, you'll need to set TCP/IP information.

This configuration will cause your Time Capsule's status light to blink amber. Are you sure you want to continue?

Click Ignore to prevent your Time Capsule's status light from blinking amber for this problem.

Skip   Cancel   Ignore

Figure 10 AirPort Utility warns you when it's going to blink some lights. That's okay; ignore it.

---

10. In the next screen, select the method your Time Capsule gets its IP address (**Figure 8**). The method you choose depends on what your ISP requires. Your options are:

    ▲ **Bridge Mode** is for a base station that will be using an IP address assigned by another device.

    ▲ **Share a single IP address using DHCP and NAT** is for a base station that will be assigning IP addresses to the computers that connect to it.

11. Click Continue. What happens next depends on the option you selected in **Figure 8**.

    ▲ If you chose Bridge Mode, a screen like the one in **Figure 9** appears. Set options to match the information you received from your ISP. Click Continue and skip ahead to step 16.

    ▲ If you chose Share a single IP address using DHCP and NAT, a dialog like the one in **Figure 10** appears. Click Ignore and continue with step 12.

12. A screen offering to create a guest network may appear next (**Figure 11**). This makes it possible for other people to utilize your Internet connection without being able to access the computers on the network. To enable this feature, turn on the check box, enter a name for the guest network, set security options, and if necessary, enter the same password in each password box.

13. Click Continue.

Continued on next page...

CREATING A TIME CAPSULE NETWORK

Continued from previous page.

14. In the next screen (**Figure 12**), indicate how you use DHCP.

   ▲ **I connect to the Internet with a DSL or cable modem using DHCP** uses the DHCP information you receive from your Internet connection to set IP addresses for the computers on your network.

   ▲ **I do not use DHCP** disables IP address sharing on your network.

15. Click Continue.

16. Next, you're asked if you want to set up Time Machine to back up your computer (**Figure 13**). If you choose yes, you'll be prompted as part of the setup to configure Time Machine.

17. Click Continue.

18. A summary of your settings appears (**Figure 14**). Click Update.

19. A dialog like the one in **Figure 15** appears. Click Continue.

20. The Time Capsule restarts. When it's finished, it appears in AirPort Utility's list of base stations with a green bullet beside it and the name you specified (**Figure 16**). Click Quit.

Figure 11 You may be able to set up a guest network.

Figure 12 Specify how you use DHCP.

Figure 13 Indicate whether you want to set up Time Machine.

CREATING A TIME CAPSULE NETWORK

Figure 14 A summary of your settings appears near the end of the configuration process. You can always click Go Back to make changes.

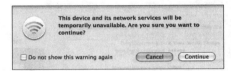

Figure 15 AirPort Utility warns you that the network services will be temporarily disrupted. Click Continue.

Figure 16 When configuration is complete, the Time Capsule appears in the list with the name you gave it and a green bullet indicating that it is connected.

✔ Tips

- It's not possible to show in this book every single combination of configuration option. Instead, I've done my best to show the configuration options you're most likely to use for your setup.

- If you're not sure how to set an option in a configuration screen, consult your ISP.

- If a firmware update for your base station is available, a dialog or notification in the AirPort Utility window may appear to tell you. Follow onscreen instructions to install any updates that area available.

- The Time Capsule and network passwords are for different things. The Time Capsule password controls access to the Time Capsule configuration. The network password controls access to the network by wireless users.

- If you are the only user of your AirPort network, it's OK to have the same password for the network as the Time Capsule. But if multiple users will be using the network, you should assign a different password to the base station to prevent other users from changing base station settings.

CREATING A TIME CAPSULE NETWORK

To create an AirPort Express network

1. Open the icon for the AirPort Utility application in the Utilities folder (**Figure** 2) inside the Applications folder. AirPort Utility uses your computer's AirPort wireless card to scan for AirPort Base stations and Time Capsules and displays a list of the ones it finds on the left is of its window (**Figure 3**).

2. Select the AirPort Express you want to configure and click Continue.

3. If a dialog like the one in **Figure 4** appears, click Switch.

4. AirPort Utility scans the AirPort Express for current settings and displays a screen like the one in **Figure 17**. Set options.

   ▲ **AirPort Express Name** is the name you want to assign to the AirPort Express.

   ▲ **AirPort Express Password** and **Verify Password** is the same password for the AirPort Express, entered twice. You'll need this password to make changes to the AirPort Express configuration in the future.

   ▲ **Remember this password in my keychain** automatically creates a keychain item for the AirPort Express password.

5. Click Continue:

6. The next screen (**Figure 18**) asks what you want to do:

   ▲ **I want to create a new wireless network** uses the AirPort Express to create a wireless network. Choose this option to continue following instructions here.

Figure 17 In this screen, enter a name and password for the AirPort Express.

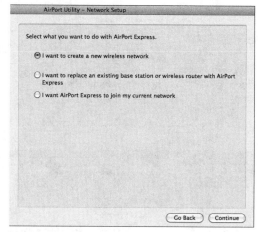

Figure 18 AirPort Utility offers three main options for configuring a base station.

Figure 19 There are three security options for AirPort Express base stations.

Figure 20 Specify how you use DHCP.

▲ **I want to replace an existing base station or wireless router with Air-Port Express** enables you to swap out another wireless router with the AirPort Express.

▲ **I want AirPort Express to join my current network** adds the AirPort Express to an existing network, thus extending the network's reach and adding the devices connected to AirPort Express to the network.

7. Click Continue.

8. Next, enter a name and set security options for the network (**Figure 19**). There are three security options:

   ▲ **WPA/WPA2 Personal** is a much more secure security method that only works with computers that support WPA and WPA2. If you choose this option, enter a password of 8 to 63 characters in both boxes.

   ▲ **WEP** is an older and less secure security method. If you choose this option, enter a password of exactly 13 characters in both boxes.

   ▲ **No security** does not secure the network at all. Anyone within range can connect.

9. Click Continue.

10. In the next screen (**Figure 20**), indicate how you use DHCP.

   ▲ **I connect to the Internet with a DSL or cable modem using DHCP** uses the DHCP information you receive from your Internet connection to set IP addresses for the computers on your network.

   ▲ **I do not use DHCP** disables IP address sharing on your network.

Continued on next page...

CREATING AN AIRPORT EXPRESS NETWORK

Continued from previous page.

11. Click Continue.

12. A summary of your settings appears (**Figure 21**). Click Update.

13. A dialog like the one in **Figure 15** appears. Click Continue.

14. The base station restarts. When it's finished, it appears in AirPort Utility's list of base stations with a green bullet beside it and the name you specified (**Figure 22**). Click Quit.

✔ Tips

■ It's not possible to show in this book every single combination of configuration options. Instead, I've done my best to show the configuration options you're most likely to use for your setup.

■ If you're not sure how to set an option in a configuration screen, consult your ISP.

■ If a firmware update for your base station is available, a dialog or notification in the AirPort Utility window may appear to tell you. Follow onscreen instructions to install any updates that area available.

■ The base station and network passwords are for different things. The base station password controls access to the base station configuration. The network password controls access to the network by wireless users.

■ If you are the only user of your AirPort network, it's OK to have the same password for the network as the base station. But if multiple users will be using the network, you should assign a different password to the base station to prevent other users from changing settings.

Figure 21 Near the end of the configuration process, AirPort Utility displays a summary of the options you've set. You can always click the Go Back button to change settings before applying them to the base station.

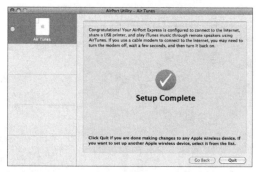

Figure 22 When setup is complete, you'll know it.

Figure 23 Select the base station you want to configure—in this example, it's a Time Capsule.

Figure 24 The AirPort Summary pane summarizes all AirPort settings.

Figure 25 The Internet Connection pane displays Internet configuration settings.

To manually set AirPort base station options

1. Open the icon for the AirPort Utility application in the Utilities folder (**Figure 2**) inside the Applications folder. AirPort Utility uses your computer's AirPort wireless capabilities to scan for AirPort Base stations and Time Capsules and displays a list of the ones it finds on the left is of its window (**Figure 23**).

2. Select the base station you want to configure and click the Manual Setup button.

3. If necessary, enter the base station password when prompted.

4. The manual configurations window appears. It offers up to five categories of options. Click a button at the top of the window to display and set options in a variety of panels:

   ▲ **AirPort** includes basic AirPort options. **Figure 24** shows the Summary pane for AirPort options.

   ▲ **Internet** displays Internet configuration options. **Figure 25** shows the Internet Connection panel.

   ▲ **Printers** shows printers connected to the base station (**Figure 26**).

   ▲ **Disks** shows disks connected to the base station (**Figure 27**) and enables you to set file sharing options for AirPort Disks.

   ▲ **Advanced** (**Figure 28**) includes a number of advanced networking options.

5. Repeat step 4 for each screen of options you want to change.

6. Click update to save your changes to the base station and restart it.

Continued on next page...

MANUALLY SETTING AIRPORT OPTIONS

Continued from previous page.

✔ Tips

- The manual configuration options offered by AirPort Utility are advanced and powerful. Do not make changes to these options unless you know what you're doing or you may inadvertently disable your network.

- Want more advanced information about setting up an AirPort network? Consult the Apple documentation that can be downloaded from support.apple.com/manuals/airport/.

Figure 26 If a printer is attached, it's listed in the Printers pane.

Figure 27 In this example, the Time Capsule's internal hard disk (Data) and an external USB disk (Red Drive) are both accessible to network users.

Figure 28 Advanced options are for networking power users who can understand what all the options are for.

Figure 29 The AirPort Status menu enables you to connect to available networks, create your own, or quickly open Network Preferences.

Figure 30 If the network you want to join isn't listed in the menu, you can use this dialog to join it—if you know its name and security information.

Figure 31 Use this dialog to create a computer-to-computer network.

Figure 32
Here's the AirPort Status menu with a computer-to-computer network created. Note how the menu icon changes.

To use the AirPort status menu

Choose commands on the AirPort status menu (**Figure 29**) to perform the following tasks:

◆ **Turn AirPort Off** disables AirPort on your computer. This option turns into a Turn Airport On command when AirPort is off.

◆ *Network Name* connects you to that network. If multiple networks are within range, all of them will appear on the menu, along with a padlock icon if secured and a signal strength indicator icon.

◆ **Join Other Network** displays a dialog like the one in **Figure 30**, which you can use to join a network that doesn't appear on the AirPort Status menu. Enter the name of the network and its password (if necessary) and click Join.

◆ **Create Network** displays a dialog like the one in **Figure 31**, which you can use to create a network between your computer and another AirPort-equipped computer. When you click OK in this dialog, the new network appears on the menu (**Figure 32**) on your computer, as well as on other computers in range. Choose the new network on both computers to connect. When you're finished using the network, choose Disconnect.

◆ **Open Network Preferences** opens the Network Preferences pane (**Figure 1**) so you can check or change AirPort settings.

Continued on next page...

Continued from previous page.

✔ Tips

■ To use the AirPort Status menu (**Figure 29**), it must be enabled. You can enable it in the Network preferences pane when your AirPort interface is selected (**Figure 1**).

■ Wondering how to connect to the Wi-Fi network in a coffee shop or cafe with your laptop? Use the AirPort Status menu. It will automatically display all open networks. Just select the network you want to join to connect. You can also join a secure network if you have a password.

■ The number of curves in the AirPort status menu's icon indicates the signal strength. The more curves, the stronger the signal.

■ If the base station has a dial-up connection to the Internet, a Connect command will also appear on this menu. Use this command to connect to the Internet.

Figure 33 In this example, I've connected my iMac to the MacBook Pro running Snow Leopard. Internet sharing from the iMac makes Internet available to the MacBook Pro, which automatically senses the connection and uses it. Can't get much easier than that!

FireWire

Although FireWire can be used to connect two computers for networking, it isn't often used that way. Instead, it's more often used to exchange information between two Macs when transferring configuration information as part of a Mac OS X installation (as mentioned in **Chapter 1**) or to use one computer's hard disk in target disk mode. And, of course, it's most often used to connect peripheral devices, including hard disks and digital video cameras.

There's not much to say about connecting two computers for networking via FireWire. It's pretty straightforward. Just connect a FireWire cable to each computer's FireWire port. If there's no other network connection, your Mac will use the FireWire cable to make one (**Figure 30**).

✔ Tips

- If you want to share an Internet connection over FireWire, be sure to set up Internet sharing. I explain how later in this chapter.

- Using a FireWire connection to transfer configuration information or to set up a disk in target disk mode is beyond the scope of this book. If you need to use either of these features, you can learn more on Apple's Web site.

FireWire

Ethernet

Despite the rush to connect without wires, Ethernet is still a familiar and widely used networking option, especially in business environments and in places where network administrators see Wi-Fi as a security challenge.

A simple Ethernet connection involves stringing an Ethernet cable between the Ethernet port—which looks like a big fat telephone port—on two computers. A more complex setup involves hubs and routers.

Once a Mac is connected to an Ethernet network (**Figure 34**), it knows it and takes advantage of all that network has to offer, including Internet and printer sharing, if available.

✔ Tips

■ Apple's AirPort Extreme and Time Capsule base stations, which are discussed on page 448, offer three Ethernet ports for connecting computers and other devices that do not have wireless capabilities.

■ A discussion of Ethernet hubs and routers is far beyond the scope of this book.

Figure 34 In this example, I've disabled or disconnected all other connections except a direct connection with an Ethernet cable to my iMac, which is sharing an Internet connection via Ethernet. The two computers can share not only an Internet connection (provided by an AirPort base station) but files.

Bluetooth

Bluetooth is a very short-range—30 feet or less—wireless networking technology. It enables you to connect Bluetooth-enabled computers, personal digital assistants (PDAs), and mobile phones to each other. It also lets you connect Bluetooth-enabled input devices, such as a mouse or keyboard, to your Mac.

Mac OS X includes two tools for working with Bluetooth:

◆ **Bluetooth** preferences pane, which is available if your computer is Bluetooth enabled, allows you to configure Bluetooth and set up Bluetooth devices with the Bluetooth Setup Assistant.

◆ **Bluetooth File Exchange** enables you to send files from one Bluetooth device to another or browse files on another Bluetooth-enabled computer.

This part of the chapter explains how to configure and use Bluetooth to exchange files between two computers, as well as how to pair a Bluetooth mouse with your Mac. Although this chapter does not go into specifics about using other devices, it should be enough to get you started using your Bluetooth device with Mac OS X.

✔ Tips

■ You can learn more about Bluetooth technology at www.bluetooth.com.

■ Don't confuse Bluetooth with AirPort. AirPort makes it possible for an AirPort-enabled computer to connect to and exchange information on an AirPort network. Bluetooth enables your computer to exchange information with a single Bluetooth-enabled device.

■ For detailed information about using your Bluetooth-enabled device with Mac OS X, consult the documentation that came with the device.

To set Bluetooth preferences

1. Choose Apple > System Preferences, or click the System Preferences icon in the Dock.

2. In the System Preferences window that appears (**Figure 35**), click the Bluetooth icon to display basic Bluetooth preferences (**Figure 36**).

3. Set options as desired:

   ▲ **On** turns Bluetooth on. As you've probably guessed, Bluetooth must be turned on for your computer to communicate with Bluetooth devices. But you might want to turn it off to conserve power or comply with airline regulations when using your laptop on a plane.

   ▲ **Discoverable** enables other Bluetooth devices to find your computer. You should enable this option when setting up other devices with your computer.

   ▲ **Show Bluetooth status in the menu bar** displays the Bluetooth status menu (**Figure 37**).

4. Click the Advanced button in the Bluetooth preferences pane to display additional options (**Figure 38**). Set options as desired and click OK:

   ▲ **Open Bluetooth Setup Assistant at startup when no input device is present** tells your computer to launch the Bluetooth Setup Assistant if no keyboard or mouse is connected; this assumes that you're going to set up a Bluetooth input device.

   ▲ **Allow Bluetooth devices to wake this computer** makes it possible for a Bluetooth device to wake the computer. This option is not supported by all computer models.

Figure 35 If you have it, Bluetooth shows up under Hardware in System Preferences.

Figure 36 The Bluetooth preferences pane, before any devices have been added.

Figure 37 The Bluetooth menu offers options for working with Bluetooth devices. This menu shows four devices added.

Figure 38 Set advanced Bluetooth options in this dialog.

▲ **Prompt for all incoming audio requests** displays an alert when an audio device, such as Bluetooth headphones, attempt to connect to the computer.

▲ **Share my internet connection with other Bluetooth devices** enables a Bluetooth device such as a mobile phone to access the Internet using your computer's Internet connection.

▲ **Serial ports that devices use to connect to this computer** enables you to add serial port information for devices you will connect via Bluetooth. You normally will not need to make changes to this list unless instructed by a device's installation manual.

5. Close the Bluetooth preferences window to save your settings.

✔ Tip

■ The Bluetooth icon only appears in System Preferences (**Figure 35**) if your computer has Bluetooth built in or Bluetooth is available via a connected adapter.

To pair devices with the Bluetooth Setup Assistant

1. Choose Apple > System Preferences, or click the System Preferences icon in the Dock.

2. In the System Preferences window that appears (**Figure 35**), click the Bluetooth icon to display basic Bluetooth preferences (**Figure 36**).

3. Click the Set Up New Device button. The Bluetooth Setup Assistant launches. It scans the area for Bluetooth devices and lists them in the Welcome window (**Figure 39**).

4. Select the device you want to work with and click Continue.

5. If the device has an input method (for example, a cell phone or keyboard), the next screen displays a passkey and provides instructions (**Figure 40**). If the device you want to configure has a screen (such as a cell phone or computer) it should display a message prompting you to enter the passkey (**Figure 41**). Either way, enter the passkey and press Return or click Pair.

6. A Conclusion screen appears next (**Figure 42**). To set up another device, click the Set Up Another Device button and follow steps 3 though 5 above. Otherwise, click Quit.

   The paired device appears in the Devices list in the Bluetooth preferences pane (**Figure 43**).

Figure 39 The Bluetooth Setup Assistant lists Bluetooth devices that are not already paired and connected.

Figure 40 The Bluetooth Setup Assistant may display a pairing passkey to enter in the other device.

Figure 41 This dialog appears onscreen when another device attempts to pair with your computer.

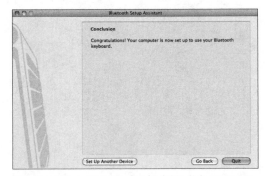

Figure 42 When pairing is finished this dialog appears.

PAIRING BLUETOOTH DEVICES

Figure 43 Here are four devices successfully paired with my MacBook Pro: an iMac, a wireless keyboard, a wireless mouse, and a BlackBerry Storm smartphone.

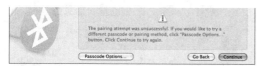

Figure 44 If you can't type in the right passkey quickly enough, the Bluetooth Setup Assistant tells you...

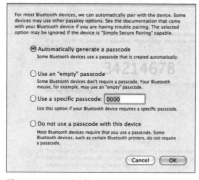

Figure 45 ...and offers additional options.

Figure 46 You can use the Action pop-up menu to work with a selected device.

✔ Tips

- Some devices have predefined passkeys. If you aren't told the passkey for a pairing and need one, consult the device's manual for more information.

- If you're not prompted for a passkey at all, you can skip step 5.

- To add or remove a device, use the + and – buttons at the bottom of the Bluetooth preferences pane (**Figure 43**).

- If you cannot successfully enter a passkey within the time allotted by the Bluetooth Setup Assistant, a note appears at the bottom of the screen (**Figure 44**). You can click the Passcode options button to display a dialog with other options (**Figure 45**), including the option to pair with an "empty" passcode or make up your own.

- You can rename a Bluetooth device in the Bluetooth preferences pane (**Figure 43**). Simply select the device and choose Rename from the Action pop-up menu beneath the list (**Figure 46**). Enter a new name for the device in the dialog that appears and click OK.

- You can set options for a Bluetooth keyboard or mouse in the Keyboard or Mouse preferences panes, which I discuss in **Chapter 23**.

To transfer a file from one Bluetooth device to another

1. If necessary, enable Bluetooth sharing as discussed in the section titled "To enable Bluetooth Sharing" on page 477.

2. Open the Bluetooth File Exchange icon in the Utilities folder (**Figure 2**) inside the Applications folder.

3. The Select File to Send dialog should appear automatically (**Figure 47**). If it does not, choose File > Send File to display it.

4. Use the dialog to locate and select the file you want to send and then click Send.

5. A Send File dialog appears (**Figure 48**). In the Device list, select the device you want to send the file to and click Send.

6. A dialog like the one in **Figure 49** appears while your computer waits for the device to accept the file. On the device, you'll see an Incoming File Transfer message (**Figure 50**). Click Accept.

7. Wait while the file is transferred. You'll see a progress dialog on the sending Mac (**Figure 51**); one will also appear on the receiving device (**Figure 52**).

   When the file has been transferred, the device displays a dialog with information about it (**Figure 53**).

Figure 47 Use this dialog to select the file to send.

Figure 48 Then use this dialog to choose the device you want to send the file to.

Figure 49 This dialog appears while your computer waits for the device to accept the file.

Figure 50 You'll see a dialog like this on the device when your computer tries to send a file.

Figure 51 A progress dialog on your computer enables you to see transfer status.

Figure 52 You can also check progress on the receiving end.

Figure 53 A dialog like this appears on the device when the file has been received.

Figure 54 You can also use commands on the Bluetooth Status menu to initiate a file transfer.

✔ Tips

■ If the Bluetooth status menu is displayed (**Figure 37**), you can initiate a file transfer to a specific device by choosing Send File from the submenu for the device you want to send to (**Figure 54**). You can then skip steps 2, 3, and 5.

■ In step 4, you can select multiple files by holding down ⌘ while clicking each one.

■ In step 6, you can turn on the Accept all check box (**Figure 50**) to receive all files without giving you an opportunity to accept or decline.

■ You can click the magnifying glass button in the Incoming File Transfer window (**Figure 53**) to open the folder where the file has been saved.

To use the Bluetooth status menu

Choose commands on the Bluetooth status menu (**Figure 37**) to perform the following tasks:

◆ **Turn Bluetooth Off** disables Bluetooth on your computer.

◆ **Discoverable** enables other Bluetooth devices to easily find your computer.

◆ **Send File** launches Bluetooth File Exchange so you can send a file to a Bluetooth device. I explain how to send files in the section titled "To transfer a file from one Bluetooth device to another" on page 468.

◆ **Browse Device** launches Bluetooth File Exchange and displays a dialog like the one in **Figure 48**. Select the device you want to browse and click the Browse button. A Browsing window with the contents of the folder set up for Bluetooth browsing appears (**Figure 55**).

◆ *Device Name* displays a submenu for the device similar to the one in **Figure 54**. Each menu offers options that are appropriate for the device.

◆ **Set up Bluetooth Device** launches the Bluetooth Setup Assistant, which I discuss on page 466, so you can set up a Bluetooth device.

◆ **Open Bluetooth Preferences** opens the Bluetooth preferences pane (**Figure 43**).

✔ Tips

■ The Bluetooth status menu only appears if the Show Bluetooth status in the menu bar option is turned on in the Bluetooth preferences pane (**Figure 43**).

■ I explain how to set up a computer for Bluetooth sharing on page 477.

Figure 55 The Browsing window enables you to browse the contents of another computer's hard disk via Bluetooth. Bluetooth sharing must be set up on the other computer to use this feature.

Figure 56 The Sharing preferences pane with no services enabled.

Sharing Services

To share files, printers, Internet connection, or other services with other network users, you must set options in the Sharing preferences pane (**Figure 56**). Sharing lets you name your computer, enable sharing for specific services, and control how other users can access your computer.

As shown in **Figure 56**, the Sharing preferences pane includes the following services:

◆ **DVD or CD Sharing** enables other network users to use your computer's CD or DVD drive from their computer.

◆ **Screen Sharing** enables users of other computers to view and control your computer over the network. This is handy for providing support to novice users.

◆ **File Sharing** enables other network users to access files on your computer.

◆ **Printer Sharing**, which I discuss in **Chapter 17**, enables other network users to print or fax documents with your printers or fax modems.

◆ **Scanner Sharing** enables other network users to scan documents with your scanners.

◆ **Web Sharing** makes it possible for other network users to view Web pages stored in the Sites folder of your Home folder.

◆ **Remote Login** enables other network users to access your computer using Secure Shell (**SSH**) and Unix.

◆ **Remote Management** enables other network users to operate your computer using Apple Remote Desktop, a software package available for an additional fee from Apple Inc.

Continued on next page...

SHARING SERVICES

Continued from previous page.

◆ **Remote Apple Events** makes it possible for other network computers to send Apple Events to your computer. Apple Events are scripting commands that perform specific tasks.

◆ **Xgrid Sharing** allows Xgrid controllers on the network to connect to your computer and distribute tasks for your computer to perform.

◆ **Internet Sharing** enables you to share an Internet connection with other network users.

◆ **Bluetooth Sharing** enables you to set options for how other computers can share files with your computer via Bluetooth.

To enable a sharing service, simply turn on its check box. You can then set options in the area to the right of the list. To disable a sharing service, turn off its check box.

This part of the chapter explains how to set sharing options for the following services: File Sharing, Internet Sharing, and Bluetooth Sharing.

✔ Tips

■ Printer sharing is discussed in **Chapter 17**. A discussion of the remaining sharing services is beyond the scope of this book.

■ Unless your computer is part of a big network and managed by a system administrator, its extremely unlikely that you'll need to enable Remote Login, Remote Management, Remote Apple Events, or Xgrid Sharing. Leave these options turned off unless you know that you'll need to use them.

✖ Warning!

■ If your computer is on a large network, consult the system administrator before changing any sharing configuration options.

SHARING SERVICES

Figure 57 You can change the local hostname for your computer in this dialog.

To open Sharing preferences

1. Choose Apple > System Preferences, or click the System Preferences icon in the Dock.

2. In the System Preferences window that appears, click the Sharing icon to display the Sharing preferences pane (**Figure 56**).

To set the computer's identity

Enter a name in the Computer Name text box (**Figure 53**).

✔ Tips

- Your computer name is not the same as your hard disk name.

- If your computer is on a large network, give your computer a name that can easily distinguish it from others on the network. Ask your system administrator; there may be organization-wide computer naming conventions that you need to follow.

- If desired, you can change the identifier for your computer on the local subnet. Click the Edit button in the Sharing preferences pane (**Figure 53**) to display a dialog like the one in **Figure 54** and enter a new name in the Local Hostname text box. The name you enter cannot include spaces and must end in *.local*, which cannot be changed. Click OK.

OPENING SHARING PREFS, SETTING IDENTITY

To enable file sharing

1. Open Sharing Preferences (**Figure 56**).

2. Turn on the File Sharing check box (**Figure 58**).

3. To specify folders to share, click the **+** button beneath the Shared Folders list. Then use the dialog that appears (**Figure 59**) to locate and select the folder you want to share. Click Add to add it to the list of folders (**Figure 60**).

4. To specify users who can access a folder, select the folder you want to set access for and click the + button under the Users column. Then use the dialog that appears (**Figure 61**) to select an existing account from Users & Groups or your Address Book. Or click the New Person button and use the New Person dialog (**Figure 62**) to add a new user account. The additional user is added to the Users list (**Figure 63**). You'll need to repeat this step for each folder you want to add users for.

5. To set permissions for a user, select the user name and choose an option from the pop-up menu that appears beside his name (**Figure 64**). Repeat this process for each user for each folder as desired.

6. To set more advanced options, click the Options button. Then set options in the dialog that appears (**Figure 65**) to enable the different connection methods, and click Done.

Figure 58 Turn on the File Sharing check box and set file sharing options.

Figure 59 Use a dialog like this to select additional folders to share.

Figure 60 The folder you selected is added to the Shared Folders list.

Figure 61 Use this dialog to add an existing user account.

Figure 62 Or use this dialog to create a new account on the fly.

Figure 63 In this example, I added two users for the Pictures folder.

Figure 64 Set user permissions by choosing an option for the user from a pop-up menu.

Figure 65 You can use this dialog to enable various file sharing connection methods. Normally, just AFP is enabled. In this example, I've also enabled SMB for a user account so a Windows user can share files.

✔ Tips

■ Be default, your Public folder is always set up to be shared.

■ I tell you more about users, groups, and permissions later in this chapter.

■ To share files with Windows users, you must follow step 6 and enable SMB. Be sure to enable the Windows users' names in the bottom half of the dialog (**Figure 65**) and enter their passwords when prompted.

To enable Internet Sharing

1. Open Sharing Preferences (**Figure 56**).

2. Select the Internet Sharing option in the Service list (**Figure 66**).

3. Choose the source of your computer's Internet connection from the Share your connection from pop-up menu (**Figure 67**).

4. Turn on the check box for each port in the To computers using list to indicate how you want to distribute your Internet connection.

5. Turn on the Internet Sharing check box in the Services list.

6. A confirmation dialog like the one in **Figure 68** may appear. Click Start.

   The Sharing preferences pane indicates that Internet sharing is enabled and how your preferences are set (**Figure 69**).

✔ Tips

- To make changes to Internet Sharing options, you must first turn off the Internet Sharing check box in the Services list.

- Internet sharing enables you to share your existing Internet connection with another computer. If you do not have an Internet connection, you can use a connection shared by another network user. Use the Network preferences pane to choose the interface on which the shared connection is available to you. I discuss the Network preferences pane near the beginning of this chapter.

- When you share an Internet connection, the total connection speed is divided among the active connections. So, for example, if two computers are actively sharing a 1.5 Mbps DSL connection with you, the average speed of each connection will only be about 0.5 Mbps.

Figure 66 Internet Sharing options in the Sharing preferences pane.

Figure 67 The options on this menu vary depending on your system setup.

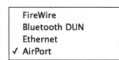

Figure 68 Click Start in this dialog if it appears.

Figure 69 When Internet sharing is enabled, the options become gray. You cannot change them unless you disable Internet Sharing.

Figure 70 Bluetooth Sharing settings help you protect your data from unauthorized access.

To enable Bluetooth Sharing

1. Open Sharing Preferences (**Figure 55**).

2. Turn on the check box for Bluetooth Sharing in the Service list (**Figure 70**).

3. Set options on the right side of the Sharing preferences pane:

   ▲ **When receiving items** lets you specify what your computer should do when receiving items from a Bluetooth device. Your options are Accept and Save, Accept and Open, Ask What to Do, and Never Allow. If you turn on the **Require pairing** option, your computer must be paired with the other device before receiving items.

   ▲ **Folder for accepted items** enables you to select a folder to store items you receive from a Bluetooth device. Choose Other from this pop-up menu to use a dialog to select a folder other than Downloads.

   ▲ **When other devices browse** enables you to specify what your computer should do when a Bluetooth device attempts to browse files on your disk. Your options are Always Allow, Ask What to Do, and Never Allow. If you turn on the **Require pairing** option, your computer must be paired with the other device before it can browse your computer.

   ▲ **Folder others can browse** enables you to choose the folder a Bluetooth device can browse. Choose Other from this pop-up menu to use a dialog to select a folder other than Public.

✔ Tip

■ Clicking the Bluetooth Preferences button in the Sharing preferences pane opens the Bluetooth Preferences pane (**Figure 43**).

✖ Warning!

■ If you've enabled Bluetooth sharing on a laptop that you often use in public places, be careful how you set these options! If you set an option to Always Allow an operation without pairing, you are allowing unauthorized access to your computer's files.

Users, Groups, & Privileges

Network file sharing access is determined by the users and groups set up for the computer, as well as the privileges settings for each file or its enclosing folder.

✔ Tip

- The concept of users, groups, and privileges is also referred to as *permissions*.

Users & Groups

Each person who connects to a computer (other than with Guest access) is considered a *user*. Each user has his own user name or ID and a password. User names are set up by the computer's system administrator, using the Accounts preferences pane. The password is also assigned by the system administrator, but in most cases, it can be changed by the user in the Accounts preferences pane when logged in to his account. This enhances security.

Each user can belong to one or more groups. A *group* is one or more users who have the same privileges. Some groups are set up automatically by Mac OS X when you install it and add users with the Accounts preferences pane. A system administrator can also add groups with the Accounts preferences pane.

✔ Tip

- Setting up users and using the Accounts preferences pane is discussed in detail in **Chapter 21**. Setting up groups is beyond the scope of this book.

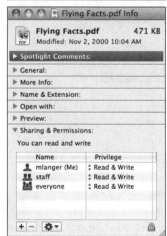

**Figures
71, 72, & 73**
Privileges settings in the Info window for the Applications folder (top), Public folder (middle), and a document (bottom).

Privileges

Each file or folder can be assigned a set of privileges. Privileges determine who has access to a file and how it can be accessed.

There are four possible privileges settings:

◆ **Read & Write** privileges allow the user to open and save files.

◆ **Read only** privileges allow the user to open files but not save files.

◆ **Write only** (**Drop Box**) privileges allow the user to save files but not open them.

◆ **No Access** means the user can neither open nor save files.

Privileges can be set for three categories of users:

◆ **Owner** is the user or group who can access and set access privileges for the item. In Mac OS X, the owner can be you (if it's your computer and you set it up), system, or admin.

◆ **Group** is a group that has access to the item.

◆ **Everyone** is everyone else on the network, including users logged in as Guest.

✔ Tip

■ You can check or set an item's privileges in the Sharing & Permissions area of the Info window for the item (**Figures 71, 72, and 73**).

To set an item's permissions

1. Select the icon for the item you want to change permissions for.

2. Choose File > Get Info or press ⌃⌘I to display the Info window.

3. If necessary, click the triangle beside Sharing & Permissions to display permissions information (**Figures 71**, **72**, and **73**).

4. If the padlock icon at the bottom of the window indicates that settings are locked, click it. Then enter an administrator name and password in the dialog that appears (**Figure 74**) and click OK.

5. To add specific user or group privileges, click the + button under the Name column. Then use the dialog that appears (**Figure 61**) to select an existing account from Users & Groups or your Address Book. Or click the New Person button and use the New Person dialog (**Figure 62**) to add a new user account. The additional user is added to the Name list.

6. To set permissions for a user or group, choose an option from the pop-up menu that appears beside its name (**Figure 75**).

7. If the item is a folder, you can choose Apply to enclosed items from the Action menu at the bottom of the window (**Figure 76**) to apply the settings to all folders within it.

8. Close the window to save your changes.

✔ Tips

- You cannot change privileges for an item if you are not the owner (**Figure 71**) unless you have an administrator password.

- The Write only (Drop Box) privilege is only available for folders and disks.

Figure 74 Use this dialog to prove that you have the authority to make changes to privileges.

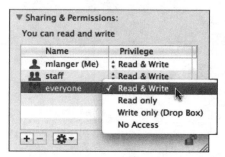

Figure 75 Choose a permission option from the Privilege pop-up menu for a name.

Figure 76 Choose Apply to enclosed items to apply the settings to all items within a folder.

- The privileges you assign to one category of users will affect which privileges can be assigned to another category of user. For example, if you make a folder Read only for Everyone, you can only make the same folder Read & Write or Read only for the Group and Owner.

SETTING PERMISSIONS

Go	
Back	⌘[
Forward	⌘]
Enclosing Folder	⌘↑
🖥 Computer	⇧⌘C
🏠 Home	⇧⌘H
🖼 Desktop	⇧⌘D
🌐 Network	⇧⌘K
💾 iDisk	▶
🅰 Applications	⇧⌘A
📄 Documents	⇧⌘O
🔧 Utilities	⇧⌘U
Recent Folders	▶
Go to Folder...	⇧⌘G
Connect to Server...	⌘K

Figure 77
The Go menu.

Figure 78 The network browser displays icons for all of the servers available via network.

Connecting to Another Computer for File Sharing

Once network and sharing options have been set up for sharing, you can connect to another computer and access its files. Mac OS X offers two ways to do this:

◆ The Go menu's Connect to Server command (**Figure 77**) prompts you to enter the address of the server you want to connect to. You enter a user name and password to connect, choose the volume you want to access, and display its contents in Finder windows.

◆ The network browser enables you to browse the computers on the network—from the Finder (**Figure 78**) and from within Open and Save dialogs. You open an alias for another computer and you're prompted for a user name and password. Enter login information, choose a volume, and work with the files just as if they were on your computer.

The main difference between these two methods is that the Connect to Server command makes it possible to connect to servers that are not listed in the network browser.

The next few pages provide instructions for connecting to other computers using both methods, along with some tips for speeding up the process in the future.

✔ Tips

■ I tell you about mounting volumes in **Chapter 6**.

■ Mac OS X's networking features refer to network-accessible computers as *servers*.

■ To mount a server volume, you must have access as a user or guest. I tell you how to set up accounts in **Chapter 21**.

To use the network browser

1. Choose Go > Network (**Figure 81**), or press ⟨Shift⟩⟨⌥⟩⟨⌘⟩⟨K⟩. The Network window opens, displaying the servers you have access to (**Figure 78**).

2. To connect to a server as a guest, double-click its icon or click its name in the sidebar. Folders guests have access to appear in the server's window (**Figure 79**). Use these folders as you would any other Finder item. Skip the remaining steps.

   or

   To connect to a server with a registered user account, select the server's icon in the sidebar. Then click Connect As in the connection bar near the top of the window (**Figure 79**).

3. A dialog like the one in **Figure 80** appears. Enter a user name and password that is recognized by the server and click Connect.

4. Folder icons for the available volumes appear in the window (**Figure 81**). Use these folders as you would any other Finder item.

✔ Tips

- If guest access is disabled, you will not be able to connect as a guest, or, if you can connect, you will not have access to any items.

- When you are connected to a server using a registered user account and have accessed a volume, an eject button appears beside the server name in the sidebar (**Figure 82**). Click the button to disconnect from the server.

- In step 3, turning on the Remember this password in my keychain check box enables you to log in in the future without entering your password.

Figure 79 Connecting as a guest is as easy as double-clicking an icon.

Figure 80 To log in, enter your user name and password in this dialog.

Figure 81 When you connect to a server with a registered user account, you see and open the volumes and folders your account gives you access to.

USING THE NETWORK BROWSER

Figure 82
An eject button appears beside any shared item for which you have accessed disks.

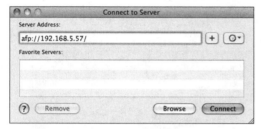

Figure 83 Enter the address of the server you want to connect to.

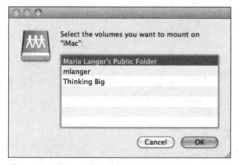

Figure 84 Choose the volume you want to mount.

Figure 85 In this example, I've saved two server addresses as favorites, but I can also choose a recently opened server from the Recent Server menu.

To use the Connect to Server command

1. In the Finder, choose Go > Connect to Server (**Figure 77**), or press ⌃⌘K.

2. In the Connect to Server dialog that appears (**Figure 83**), enter the network address of the server you want to connect to.

3. Click Connect.

4. A dialog like the one in **Figure 80** appears. Enter a user name and password that is recognized by the server and click Connect.

5. A dialog displays the volumes available for access (**Figure 84**). Select the volume(s) you want to mount and click OK.

   The name of the server appears in the Shared area of the sidebar with an eject button beside it (**Figure 82**). You can open the volume you selected like any other disk to work with its contents.

✔ Tips

■ You can specify a server address by IP or server name. This information appears in the Sharing preferences pane when File Sharing is enabled and selected (**Figure 58**).

■ After step 2, you can click the **+** button to add the server address to the Favorite Servers list in the Connect to Server dialog (**Figure 85**). You can then access a favorite server by double-clicking its address in the list.

■ In step 2, to open a recently opened server, choose its address from the Recent Servers pop-up menu (**Figure 85**).

■ I discuss mounting volumes in **Chapter 6**.

USING THE CONNECT TO SERVER COMMAND

To change your password on the server

1. Follow the steps earlier in this section to display a login dialog like the one in **Figure 80**.

2. Select the Registered User option and enter your user name in the Name box.

3. Choose Change Password from the Action menu in the bottom left corner of the dialog (**Figure 86**) to display a dialog like the one in **Figure 87**.

4. Enter your current password in the Old Password box.

5. Enter a new password in the New Password and Verify boxes.

6. Click Change Password.

7. To continue connecting to the server, in the login window (**Figure 80**), enter your new password in the Password box and click Connect.

Figure 86 Choose Change Password from the Action pop-up menu in the server login dialog.

Figure 87 Enter old and new passwords in this dialog and click Change Password.

Figure 88 Use the Info pane to get information about a network interface.

Figure 89 Use the Netstat pane to get network performance statistics.

Figure 90 Use the Ping pane to "ping" another computer on the network or Internet.

Figure 91 Use the Lookup pane to get the IP address for a specific domain name.

Network Utility

Network Utility, which can be found in the Utilities folder (**Figure 2**) in your Applications folder, is an information-gathering tool to help you learn more about and troubleshoot a network. Its features are made available in eight tabs:

◆ **Info** (**Figure 88**) provides general information about the network interfaces.

◆ **Netstat** (**Figure 89**) enables you to review network performance statistics.

◆ **Ping** (**Figure 90**) enables you to test your computer's access to specific domains or IP addresses.

◆ **Lookup** (**Figure 91**) uses a domain name server to convert between IP addresses and domain names.

◆ **Traceroute** (**Figure 92**) traces the route from your computer to another IP address or domain.

◆ **Whois** (**Figure 93**) uses a whois server to get information about the owner and IP address of a specific domain name.

◆ **Finger** (**Figure 94**) gets information about a person based on his e-mail address.

◆ **Port Scan** (**Figure 95**) scans a specific IP address for active ports.

Continued on next page...

Figure 92 Use the Traceroute pane to trace the routing between your computer and another IP address.

✔ Tips

- The tools within Network Utility are used primarily for troubleshooting network problems and getting information about specific users or systems.

- Many of these utilities are designed to work with the Internet and require Internet access.

- In this day and age of increased privacy and security, you'll find that Finger (**Figure 94**) and Port Scan (**Figure 95**) are seldom successful in getting information about a person or server.

To use Network Utility

1. Open Network Utility in the Utilities folder (**Figure 2**) in your Applications folder.

2. Click the button for the utility you want to use (**Figures 88** through **95**).

3. Enter the domain name, IP address, or e-mail address you want to check.

4. Click the button to start the scan process. (The name of the button varies from one utility to another.)

   The results appear in the scrolling list at the bottom of the Network Utility window (**Figures 88** through **95**).

Figure 93 Use the Whois pane to look up information about a domain name.

Figure 94 You can try to use Finger to look up information about a person based on his e-mail address.

Figure 95 Use the Port Scan pane to check for active ports on an IP address or domain.

Multiple Users

Multiple Users

Mac OS X is designed to be a multiple-user system. This means that different individuals can log in and use a Mac OS X computer.

Each user can install his own applications, configure his own desktop, and save his own documents. User files and setup is kept private. When each user logs in to the computer with his account, he can access only the files that belong to him or are shared.

Mac OS X makes it easy to set up a guest account for friends and family members you may want to allow temporary access to your computer. It also enhances parental controls, which help shield young computer users from certain content while protecting your computer from being accidentally reconfigured by a novice user.

In this chapter, I discuss the multiple user features of Mac OS X.

✔ Tips

- Using a multiple-user operating system doesn't mean that you can't keep your computer all to yourself. You can set up just one user—you.

- **Chapter 3** provides some additional information about how Mac OS X's directory structure is set up to account for multiple users.

Configuring Mac OS X for Multiple Users

In order to take advantage of the multiple users feature of Mac OS X, you need to set up user accounts.

The Mac OS X Setup Assistant, which I discuss in **Chapter 1**, does part of the setup for you. Immediately after you install Mac OS X, the Setup Assistant prompts you for information to set up the Admin user.

If you are your computer's only user, you're finished setting up users. But if additional people—coworkers, friends, or family members—will be using your computer, it's in your best interest to set up a separate user account for each one. You can then specify what each user is allowed to do on the computer. You do all this with the Accounts preferences pane (**Figure 2**).

In this section, I explain how to add, modify, set capabilities for, and delete user accounts.

✔ Tips

- I tell you more about accessing another user's folders and files on page 510.

- You also use the Accounts preferences pane to modify settings for your own account and to set up Login Options and Login Items, as I discuss later in this chapter.

Figure 1
Choose System
Preferences from
the Apple menu.

Figure 2 The Accounts preferences pane with the Admin user selected.

Figure 3 Use the Authenticate dialog to unlock Accounts preferences, if necessary.

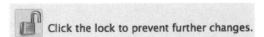

Figure 4 The lock icon looks unlocked when Accounts preferences are unlocked for editing.

To open & unlock the Accounts preferences pane

1. Choose Apple > System Preferences (**Figure 1**) or click the System Preferences icon in the Dock.

2. In the System Preferences window that appears, click the Accounts icon to display the Accounts preferences pane (**Figure 2**).

3. If the lock icon in the bottom-left corner of the window appears locked, click it. An authentication dialog like the one in **Figure 3** appears.

4. Enter an administrator name and password in the appropriate boxes and click OK. The padlock unlocks (**Figure 4**) and the Accounts preferences pane is ready for editing.

✔ Tips

- In step 4, if you are the person who set up the computer, you are the administrator and can use your own name and password to authenticate.

- If your name and password do not work in step 4, ask the system administrator to assist you with the changes you need to make.

To activate the guest account

1. In the list of users on the left side of the Accounts preferences pane, select the Guest Account (**Figure 5**).

2. Set options on the right side of the window to specify how guests can access the computer:

   ▲ **Allow guests to log in to this computer** enables the guest account for login. This makes it possible for a guest user to access your computer's applications and temporarily store files in a Guest user folder on your hard disk.

   ▲ **Allow guests to connect to shared folders** enables guest users to login to your computer via a network connection to access the contents of shared folders. This option is turned on by default.

Figure 5 Guest account settings in the Accounts preferences pane.

✔ Tips

- Files created or saved to a Guest account user folder are deleted when the Guest logs out. If you expect a user to regularly login to your computer, you might find it more convenient to set up a regular account for that user.

- If you turn on the Allow guests to log in to this computer check box in step 2, you can also turn on the Enable parental controls check box. I explain parental controls on page 497.

- The guest account cannot be used to log in to your computer from a remote location.

- You can disable guest access to your computer by turning off both check boxes for the guest account in the Accounts preferences window (**Figure 5**).

- I tell you about file sharing in **Chapter 20**.

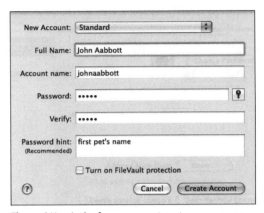

Figure 6 Here's the form you use to set up a new user account, with example information entered.

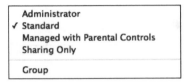

Figure 7 Use this pop-up menu to choose a type of account.

To add a new user

1. In the Accounts preferences pane (**Figure 5**), click the **+** button at the bottom of the accounts list to display a blank new user dialog (**Figure 6**).

2. Choose the type of account you want to create from the New Account pop-up menu (**Figure 7**):

   ▲ **Administrator** is an account that has full administrative access over the computer.

   ▲ **Standard** is a normal user account with regular privileges.

   ▲ **Managed with Parental Controls** is an account with limited access and privileges, as set up with parental controls.

   ▲ **Sharing Only** is an account for file sharing only. A user with this kind of account cannot log in to your computer to access its applications.

   ▲ **Group** enables you to create a group for multiple users. I tell you more about creating and using groups on page 478. If you choose this option, you can skip steps 3 through 7 below.

3. Enter the name of the user in the Full Name box.

4. Enter a account name for the user in the Account name box. This name, which is often a shorter variation of the user's full name, should be in lowercase characters and should not include spaces.

5. Enter a password for the user in the Password and Verify boxes. The password should be at least six characters long.

Continued on next page...

ADDING NEW USERS

Continued from previous page.

6. If desired, enter a hint for the password in the Password hint box.

7. To secure the user's account with File-Vault, check the Turn on FileVault protection check box. I tell you about FileVault on page 525.

8. Click Create Account. The new account appears in the list of accounts on the left side of the Accounts preferences pane (**Figure 8**).

   A folder for the new user appears in the Users folder on your hard disk (**Figure 11**).

✖ Warning!

- Only give Administrator privileges to individuals you trust and who have a good understanding of how Mac OS X works. An Administrator has access to the entire computer and can make changes that lock you out or prevent the computer from working properly.

✔ Tips

- In step 5, you can use the Password Assistant to generate a random password. Click the key button beside the Password box to display the Password Assistant (**Figure 10**), choose an option from the Type pop-up menu, drag the slider to modify the password length, and consider the password that appears in the Suggestion box.

- After step 8, a dialog like the one in **Figure 11** may appear, asking if you want to turn off automatic login. Click the button for the option you prefer; I tell you about automatic login on page 506.

Figure 8 A new user account.

Figure 9 A new folder appears in the Users folder.

Figure 10
The Password Assistant helps you come up with a secure password that you might even be able to remember.

Figure 11 If automatic login is turned on when you create a new user account, a dialog like this appears so you can turn it off, if you like.

Figure 12 Use this dialog to change a user's password.

To modify an existing user's settings

1. In the accounts list of the Accounts preferences pane, select the name of the account you want to modify (**Figure 8**).

2. Make changes as desired on the left side of the window:

   ▲ **Reset Password** displays a dialog like the one in **Figure 12** for the user. Enter a new password twice and change the password hint, if necessary. Then click Reset Password.

   ▲ **Full Name** is the user's name.

   ▲ **MobileMe User Name** is the user's account name on Apple's MobileMe service. Entering this information will enable the user to access his MobileMe account and iDisk from the computer.

   ▲ **Allow user to administer this computer** gives the user administrator privileges.

   ▲ **Enable parental controls** lets you limit access based on the parental controls feature, which I discuss on page 497.

✔ Tips

■ Resetting a user's password does not change his login password for his Keychain. I tell you more about Keychain Access on page 514.

■ You cannot modify a user's account settings while he is logged in using fast user switching. I tell you about fast user switching on page 508.

■ I tell you about MobileMe and iDisk in **Chapter 19**.

To change a user's picture

1. In the Accounts preferences pane, click to select the name of the user you want to change the picture for (**Figure 6**).

2. Click the picture well to display a menu of pictures (**Figure 13**).

3. Choose a new picture.

    or

    Choose Edit Picture to display an image dialog. Then drag the icon for an image from a Finder window into the image area (**Figure 14**). You can drag the image into position and drag the slider to zoom the image in or out to frame it (**Figure 15**). Then click Set.

4. The picture changes to the image you selected or inserted (**Figure 16**).

✔ Tips

- You could also skip steps 2 and 3 above and simply drag an image from a Finder window to the image well for the user (**Figure 17**). The image window appears so you can zoom and properly frame the image as desired (**Figure 16**). Click Set to save it.

- A user's picture appears in his Address Book card, the Login screen, and as his default iChat picture.

Figure 13 Clicking the image well displays a menu of available pictures.

Figure 14 Drag an image file's into the image dialog.

Figure 15 Use the image window to adjust and frame the portion of the picture you want to use.

Figure 17 Or you can just drag an image file's icon onto the image well for the user.

Figure 16 The new picture appears for the user's account.

Figure 18 Login items in the Accounts preferences pane.

Figure 19 One way to add an item to the Login items list is to drag it in from a Finder window.

Figure 20 You can use a dialog like this one to locate, select, and add a startup item.

To specify login items

1. In the Accounts preferences pane, click to select the name of the account you logged in with. Normally, this will be your account, but if you want to set login items for another user, you must log in with that user's account.

2. Click the Login Items button to display its options (**Figure 18**).

3. To add a startup item, drag its icon into the list (**Figure 19**) or click the + button at the bottom of the list and use the dialog sheet that appears (**Figure 20**) to locate, select, and open the item. The item you dragged or selected appears in the list.

   or

   To remove an item from the list, click to select it and then click the − button at the bottom of the list. The item disappears from the list.

4. To automatically hide an item when it launches, turn on the Hide check box beside it.

✔ Tips

- *Login items* are applications, documents, folders, or other items that are automatically opened when you log in or start up the computer.

- Each user can change his own login items, unless his account has Parental Controls enabled. I discuss Parental Controls on page 497.

To delete a user account

1. In the Accounts preferences pane, select the name of the user you want to delete.

2. Click the — button at the bottom of the accounts list.

3. A dialog like the one in **Figure 21** appears. It offers three options for dealing with the user's Home folder:

   ▲ **Save the home folder in a disk image** saves the contents of the user's Home folder in a disk image file in the Deleted Users folder (**Figure 22**). The file can be opened, if necessary, to extract files.

   ▲ **Do not change the home folder** leaves the Home folder in the Users folder, without making any changes to it.

   ▲ **Delete the home folder** removes the user's Home folder from the hard disk.

4. Click OK to delete the user.

✔ Tip

■ When you delete a user's account, he can no longer log in to the computer and access his files.

Figure 21 Mac OS X offers three options for dealing with a deleted user's Home folder.

Figure 22 If you save a user's Home folder as a disk image, it's stored in the Deleted Users folder inside the Users folder.

Parental Controls

Parental controls enable you to limit an account's access to computer features. Designed to help parents protect their children from certain content and activities, it can also be used to limit a user to certain applications, activities, and usage times. In addition, it can keep a log of a user's activities for later review.

Parental controls are broken down into five groups of settings:

◆ **System** (**Figure 26**) control what applications and tasks the user can access. It also allows you to enable Simple Finder, which is a greatly simplified version of the Finder for novice users.

◆ **Content** (**Figure 29**) enables you to control access to certain Dictionary words and Web sites.

◆ **Mail & iChat** (**Figure 32**) limits who the user can e-mail and instant message with.

◆ **Time Limits** (**Figure 35**) enables you to set the amount of time on weekdays and weekends the user can use the computer and to prevent the user from using the computer at certain times of the day or night.

◆ **Logs** (**Figure 36**) lets you view activity logs for the user's access.

In this section, I'll explain how to open the Parental Controls preferences pane and activate parental controls for a user account. I'll also discuss the available settings you can assign to a user's account.

PARENTAL CONTROLS

To open & unlock the Parental Controls preferences pane

1. Choose Apple > System Preferences to open the System Preferences window.

2. Click the Parental Controls icon to display the Parental Controls preferences pane (**Figure 23**).

3. If the lock icon in the bottom-left corner of the window appears locked, click it. An authentication dialog like the one in **Figure 3** appears.

4. Enter an administrator name and password in the appropriate boxes and click OK. The padlock unlocks (**Figure 4**) and the Parental Controls preferences pane is ready for editing.

✔ Tips

- Another way to open the Parental Controls preferences pane is to click the Open Parental Controls button in the Accounts preferences pane when a user account is selected (**Figure 8**).

- In step 4, if you are the person who set up the computer, you are the administrator and can use your own name and password to authenticate.

- Authentication is required, in part, to prevent other users from modifying their own settings—or yours!

Figure 23 The Parental Controls preferences pane looks like this when you first open it.

Figure 24 Parental controls are disabled for this user.

Figure 25 Disable parental controls by turning off the Enable parental controls check box in the Accounts preferences pane for the user.

To enable parental controls for a user account

1. In the Parental Controls preferences pane, select the user you want to enable parental controls for (**Figure 24**).

2. Click the Enable Parental Controls button. Parental controls settings appear (refer to **Figure 26** on the next page).

✔ Tips

■ You cannot set parental controls for a user with administrator privileges.

■ You can also enable parental controls by turning on the check box beside Enable Parental Controls in the user's account settings in the Accounts preferences pane (**Figure 25**).

■ If parental controls settings for the user appear after step 1 (refer to **Figure 26** on the next page), parental controls are already enabled for that user.

■ The Manage parental controls from another computer option in the Parental Controls preferences pane (**Figure 24**) enables a user on a networked computer running Mac OS X 10.5 or later to log in to the computer and set parental control options. A discussion of this feature is beyond the scope of this book.

To disable parental controls for a user account

1. Follow the instructions in the section titled "To open & unlock the Accounts preferences pane" on page 489.

2. Select the account you want to disable parental controls for (**Figure 25**).

3. Uncheck the Enable parental controls check box.

ENABLING & DISABLING PARENTAL CONTROLS

To limit a user's access to applications & system functions

1. In the Parental Controls preferences pane, click to select the name of the user you want to set access limitations for.

2. Click the System button (**Figure 26**).

3. Set options as desired:

   ▲ **Use Simple Finder** enables Simple Finder for the user.

   ▲ **Only allow selected applications** enables you to disable applications you do not want the user to access.

   ▲ **Check the applications to allow** enables you to specify which applications the user can access. Toggle check boxes in the list. You can click the disclosure triangle to the left of a category to display the individual applications within it. This option is only available if either the Use Simple Finder or Only allow selected applications check box is turned on.

   ▲ **Can administer printers** enables the user to change printer settings, add printers, and remove printers.

   ▲ **Can burn CDs and DVDs** enables the user to copy data, music, or other material to disc.

   ▲ **Can change password** enables the user to change his password.

   ▲ **Can modify the Dock** enables the user to add or remove Dock items for his user account.

Figure 26 The System options in the Parental Controls preferences pane.

Figure 27 Simple Finder is just that—a simple version of the Finder.

Figure 28 If a user attempts to open an application he does not have access to, he'll see a dialog like this.

✔ Tips

■ Simple Finder (**Figure 27**), as the name suggests, is a highly simplified version of the Finder. Designed for users with little or no knowledge of computers, it offers a safe, highly controlled environment for kids and novices. If you want to try Simple Finder, create a new user with Simple Finder enabled, then log in as that user. If you've been using a Mac for more than a few years, I guarantee you'll go nuts in about five minutes. (I didn't even last two.)

■ If a user attempts to access an application he does not have access to, a dialog like the one in **Figure 28** appears. If you click the Always Allow or Allow Once button, an authentication dialog like the one in **Figure 3** appears. You'll need to enter an administrator's name and password to continue.

To limit access to content

1. In the Parental Controls preferences pane, click to select the name of the user you want to set access limitations for.

2. Click the Content button (**Figure 29**).

3. To hide "bad words" in Mac OS X's dictionary, turn on the **Hide profanity in Dictionary** check box.

4. To set Web site restrictions, select one of the three Website Restrictions options:

   ▲ **Allow unrestricted access to websites** does not apply restrictions.

   ▲ **Try to limit access to adult websites automatically** uses a built-in filter to prevent access to adult content Web sites. If you select this option, you can click the Customize button to create and maintain a list of Web sites the user can and can't access (**Figure 30**). Just use the + and − buttons beneath each list to add or remove URLs.

   ▲ **Allow access to only these websites** displays a list of Web sites that the user can access (**Figure 31**). These are the *only* sites the user can access. Use the + and − buttons beneath the list to add or remove bookmarks.

✔ Tips

■ The Hide profanity in Dictionary check box setting does not affect non-Apple application dictionaries, like the one that comes with Microsoft Word.

■ Customizing the content filter does not prevent access to content not listed in the dialog. For example, given the settings in **Figure 30**, if the user attempted to access my Web site (www.marialanger.com), he would not be stopped, since the site is not forbidden and has no objectionable content. (Well, at least *I* don't think so.)

Figure 29 You can use Content options to limit access to certain content on your computer or the Web.

Figure 30 You can customize the content filter by adding sites that are allowed and forbidden.

Figure 31 You can also prevent a user from visiting any site except those you allow.

Figure 32 Use the Mail & iChat settings to specify who the user can exchange e-mail and chat with.

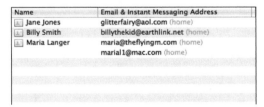

Figure 33 You can use a dialog like this to specify who the user can exchange e-mail or instant messages with.

Figure 34 Here's an example of a list of permitted e-mail addresses and instant message addresses.

To limit access to e-mail & chat

1. In the Parental Controls preferences pane, click to select the name of the user you want to set access limitations for.

2. Click the Mail & iChat button (**Figure 32**).

3. Turn on the check box for the application you want to limit:

   ▲ **Limit Mail** restricts the e-mail addresses the user can exchange e-mail with.

   ▲ **Limit iChat** restricts the instant messaging addresses the user can enter into a chat session with.

4. If you checked either of the options in step 3, build a list of the allowed e-mail or instant messaging addresses in the list below. Click the + button and use the form that appears to add people. As shown in **Figure 33**, you can add e-mail and instant messaging addresses for each person. If you turn on the Add person to my address book check box, the record is added to your Address Book file. **Figure 34** shows an example of what a short list of allowed addresses might look like.

5. To receive an e-mail message from anyone not on the list who attempts to e-mail the user, turn on the Send permission requests to check box and enter your e-mail address in the box beside it. This makes it possible to see who is trying to send e-mail to the user and what that e-mail contains.

✔ Tip

■ Parental Controls for Mail and iChat are a good way to prevent your children from getting e-mail from or chatting with people you don't know.

To limit a user's time on the computer

1. In the Parental Controls preferences pane, click to select the name of the user you want to set access limitations for.

2. Click the Time Limits button (**Figure 35**).

3. To limit the amount of time the user can spend on the computer on weekdays, turn on the Weekday time limits check box and use the slider to set the amount of time.

4. To limit the amount of time the user can spend on the computer on weekends, turn on the Weekend time limits check box and use the slider to set the amount of time.

5. To prevent the user from using the computer at certain hours of the day or night, turn on the School nights or Weekend check box (or both) and set the start and end times that the computer *cannot* be used.

✔ Tip

■ Although this feature is designed to limit the time a child spends on a computer, I sometimes wish someone would set it for me!

Figure 35 Use the Time Limits options to limit the amount of time—and the time of day—the user works with the computer.

Figure 36 You can use the log feature of parental controls to see what your bundle of joy has been up to.

Today
✓ One week
One month
Three months
Six months
One year
All

Figure 37 Choose a reporting period from this pop-up menu.

To review access logs for a user

1. In the Parental Controls preferences pane, click to select the name of the user you want to set access limitations for.

2. Click the Logs button (**Figure 36**).

3. Set options at the top of the window to determine how logs are displayed:

   ▲ **Show activity for** (**Figure 37**) enables you to specify the amount of time the logs should cover.

   ▲ **Group by** enables you to choose how you want the report content grouped: by Website, Application, or Contact or by Date.

4. In the Log Collections list, click the log you want to view. Its content appears in the Logs list. As shown in Figure 36, you can click disclosure triangles to display more information about items.

5. To open an item in the log, select it and click the Open button at the bottom of the window.

6. To allow or restrict a site, application, or contact, select the item in the log and click the Restrict or Allow button at the bottom of the window. (The button that appears varies based on what is selected.)

✔ Tip

■ Although it seems sneaky, it's a good idea to review this information periodically to see what your children have been doing with the computer.

REVIEWING ACCESS LOGS

Login Options

Login Options determine how the computer's login functions work. How you set these options will vary depending on how many users are set up for the computer and what features you want to enable.

For example, if you're the only person who ever uses your computer, you might want to enable automatic login disable fast user switching. This is how Mac OS X is set up by default. But if your computer has multiple users and one of them has a vision impairment, you might want to disable automatic login, enable VoiceOver for the login window, and enable fast user switching.

In this section, I explain what each of the Login Options are and how you can set them.

✔ Tip

- Although I consider myself somewhat of a screenshot expert (there are over 2,000 shots in this book alone), I could not figure out a way to take a screenshot of a main login window. Sorry!

To set Login Options

1. Follow the instructions in the section titled "To open & unlock the Accounts preferences pane" on page 489.

2. Click the Login Options button at the bottom of the accounts list. Login options appear on the right side of the window (**Figure 38**).

3. Set options as desired:

   ▲ **Automatic login** (**Figure 39**) enables you to choose a user account for the computer to automatically log in to when you start the computer. To disable this feature, choose Disabled.

Figure 38 The Login Options window enables you to specify options for the login window and related features.

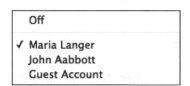

Figure 39 Choose a user account for the automatic login feature—or choose Disabled to turn it off.

```
✓ Name
  Short name
  Icon
```

Figure 40 Use this menu to determine what should appear in the menu bar when fast user switching is enabled.

✔ Tips

- The login window option to display Name and password is more secure than a List of users because it requires unauthorized users to know both a valid user name and the corresponding password.

- With the automatic login feature enabled, the login window will not appear when you start the computer.

- I tell you more about the Input menu on page 545 and VoiceOver on page 591.

▲ **Display login window as** lets you select how the Login window should appear: as a list of users or as blank fields for user name and password.

▲ **Show the Restart, Sleep, and Shut Down buttons** displays these buttons in the login window, making it possible to do any of these things without logging into the computer.

▲ **Show input menu in login window** displays the input menu, which a user can use to choose a different keyboard layout for logging in and using the computer. This may be useful in a multilingual workplace.

▲ **Show password hints** displays a password hint in the login window if the user has unsuccessfully attempted to log in three times.

▲ **Use VoiceOver in the login window** activates the VoiceOver feature of Mac OS to audibly name each item in the login window as a user points to it.

▲ **Show fast user switching menu as** makes it possible to switch user accounts without logging out of the currently active account. If you turn on this option, use the pop-up menu (**Figure 40**) to determine what should display on the far right end of the menu bar: name, short name, or icon of the user who is logged in. I explain how to use fast user switching on the next page.

▲ **Network Account Server** enables you to join or edit connection information for a network account server. This is an advanced feature of Mac OS X that is beyond the scope of this book.

SETTING LOGIN OPTIONS

Fast User Switching

Fast user switching enables one user to log in and use the computer without another user logging out.

The main benefit to this is that it's fast—hence the name. You don't need to close all open documents and quit all applications for another user to access his account. That means you don't have to reopen all those documents and applications when he's done and you can continue using the machine.

✔ Tip

■ Before you can use fast user switching, you must enable it. You can learn how in the section titled "To set login options" on the previous two pages.

To use fast user switching

1. With the computer turned on and a user already logged in, choose a user account from the menu at the far right end of the menu bar (**Figure 41**).

2. In the Login window that appears (**Figure 42**), enter the account password and click Log In.

   The screen changes (using a cool, rotating cube graphic effect) to the account you logged in to.

✔ Tip

■ The user menu (**Figure 41**) indicates each user's status:

   ▲ A user name that cannot be selected (Maria Langer in **Figure 41**) is the active user.

   ▲ A white check mark in an orange circle appears beside the name of any user who is logged in.

   ▲ You must always enter a password to switch to another account.

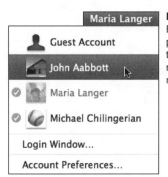

Figure 41
Fast user switching puts a menu like this one on the far right end of the menu bar.

Figure 42 A login window appears on the current user's screen to allow a different user to log in.

Figure 43 The Users folder includes a Shared folder and a Home folder for each account.

Figure 44 Your Home folder contains a number of pre-defined folders for organizing and storing your files.

Figure 45 The Home folder in **Figure 44** when viewed by another user.

The folder "Documents" can't be opened because you don't have permission to see its contents.

OK

Figure 46 A dialog like this one appears if you try to open another user's private folder.

The Home Folder

Mac OS X creates a Home folder for each user account in the Users folder (**Figure 43**), with the user's short name as the folder name. The icon for the folder appears as a house for the user who is currently logged in and as a regular folder for all other users. Each user's Home folder contains folders for storing his files (**Figure 44**):

◆ **Desktop** contains all items (other than mounted disks) on the user's desktop.

◆ **Documents** is the default file location for document files.

◆ **Movies**, **Music**, and **Pictures** are for storing video, audio, and image files.

◆ **Sites** is for the user's Web site, which can be put online with the Personal Web Sharing feature.

◆ **Library**, which is maintained by Mac OS X for you, is for storing various preferences files.

◆ **Public** is for storing shared files.

◆ **Applications**, when present, is for storing applications installed by the user for his private use.

✔ Tips

■ You can quickly open your Home folder by clicking the name of your Home folder in the Sidebar.

■ Although a user can open another user's Home folder, he can only open the Public and Sites folders within that user's Home folder; all other folders are locked (**Figure 45**). A dialog like the one in **Figure 46** appears if you attempt to open a locked folder.

Sharing Files with Other Users

Mac OS X offers several ways for multiple users of the same computer to share files with each other:

- The Shared folder in the Users folder (**Figure 43**) offers read/write access to all users.

- The Public folder in each user's Home folder (**Figure 44**) offers read access to all users.

- The Drop Box folder in each user's Public folder (**Figure 47**) offers write access to all users.

✔ Tips

- Read access for a folder enables users to open files in that folder. Write access for a folder enables users to save files into that folder.

- File sharing over a network is covered in **Chapter 20**.

To make a file accessible to all other users

Place the file in the Shared folder in the Users folder (**Figure 43**).

Or

Place the file in the Public folder in your Home folder (**Figure 44**).

✔ Tip

- If your computer is managed by a system administrator, check to see where the administrator prefers public files to be stored.

Figure 47 Each user's Public folder contains a Drop Box folder for accepting incoming files.

Figure 48 When you drag a file into a Drop Box folder, a dialog like this appears.

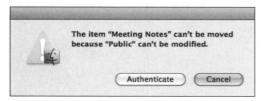

Figure 49 You can't place files into another user's Public folder or any other locked folder...

Figure 50 ...unless you're an administrator.

To make a file accessible to a specific user

1. Drag the file's icon onto the Drop Box folder icon inside the Public folder in the user's Home folder (**Figure 47**).

2. A dialog like the one in **Figure 48** appears. Click OK. The file moves into the Public folder.

✔ Tips

■ When you drag a file into a Drop Box folder, the file is moved—not copied— there. You cannot open a Drop Box folder to remove its contents. If you need to keep a copy of the file, hold down Option while dragging the file into the Drop Box folder to place a copy of the file there. You can then continue working with the original.

■ To use the Drop Box, be sure to drag the file icon onto the Drop Box folder icon. If you drag an icon into the Public folder, a dialog like the one in **Figure 49** appears, telling you that you can't modify the Public folder. You can click the Authenticate button and enter an administrator password in the Authenticate dialog (**Figure 50**) to override this warning and put the file there anyway.

Security
Features

22

Security Features

Mac OS X has a number of security features you can use to keep your files private or make it easier to access online content:

◆ **Keychain Access** enables you to securely store passwords for accessing applications, servers, and Internet locations.

◆ **General Security preferences** enable you to set additional security-enhancing options.

◆ **FileVault** encrypts the contents of your Home folder so it can't be read by hackers.

◆ **Firewall** protects your computer from unauthorized network or Internet access.

In this chapter, I discuss the security features of Mac OS X.

✔ Tip

■ Mac OS X's multiple user accounts feature uses a login feature that protects files from access by other computer users. I discuss multiple user features in **Chapter 21**.

Keychain Access

The Keychain Access feature offers users a way to store passwords for accessing password-protected applications, servers, and Internet locations. Each user's keychain is automatically unlocked when he logs in to the computer, so the passwords it contains are available when they are needed to access secured files and sites.

✔ Tips

- Mac OS X automatically creates a keychain for each user. This is the default, or *login*, keychain.

- Keychain Access only works with applications that are keychain-aware.

- You can also use your keychain to store other private information, such as credit card numbers and bank personal identification numbers (PINs).

To open Keychain Access

Open the Keychain Access icon in the Utilities folder inside the Applications folder (**Figure 1**).

The keychain window for your default keychain appears (**Figure 2**). It lists all of the items in your keychain.

Figure 1 You can find Keychain Access in the Utilities folder inside the Applications folder.

Figure 2 The Keychain window for a default keychain.

Figure 3 This example shows the login dialog for accessing another computer on the network.

Figure 4 The item is added to your keychain.

To add a keychain item when accessing a secure application, server, or Internet location

1. Follow your normal procedure for accessing the secure item.

2. Enter your password when prompted (**Figure 3**).

3. Turn on the Remember password in keychain check box (**Figure 3**). (In some applications, you may have to click an Options button to see it.)

4. Finish accessing the secure item. When you open Keychain Access, you'll see that the password has been added to your keychain (**Figure 4**).

✔ Tips

- The exact steps for adding a keychain when accessing a secure item vary based on the item you are accessing and the software you are using to access it.

- It is not necessary to open Keychain Access to verify the existence of a keychain item after adding it. In fact, you may never need to open Keychain Access at all.

ADDING KEYCHAIN ITEMS AUTOMATICALLY

To add a password item manually

1. In Keychain Access (**Figure 2**), click the +
   button beneath the list of keychain items,
   choose File > New Password Item (**Figure
   5**), or press ⌃⌘N to display a dialog like
   the one in **Figure 6**.

2. Enter an identifying name or Internet
   URL for the item in the Keychain Item
   Name box.

3. Enter the user ID or account name or
   number for the item in the Account
   Name box.

4. Enter the password for the item in the
   Password box.

5. Click Add. The new item is added to your
   keychain.

✔ Tips

- If you turn on the Show Typing check box
  in the dialog (**Figure 6**), the password you
  enter will appear as text rather than as
  bullets. You may want to use this option
  to be sure that you're typing the password
  correctly, since you only enter it once.

- If you need a random password, you can
  click the key button in the dialog (**Figure
  6**) to open the Password Assistant window
  (**Figure 7**), choose an option from the
  Type pop-up menu, drag the slider to
  modify the password length, and consider the password that appears in the
  Suggestion box. If you don't like that one,
  you can click the triangle beside the
  suggested password to display a menu of
  others.

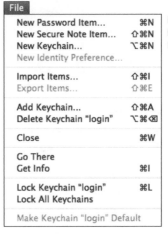

Figure 5
Keychain Access's
File menu.

Figure 6 Use this dialog to manually enter password
information.

Figure 7 You can use the Password Assistant
window to come up with a secure password.

Figure 8 Use this dialog to create a secure note in Keychain Access.

Figure 9 You must click Delete in this dialog to delete a keychain item.

To add a secure note

1. In Keychain Access (**Figure 2**), choose File > New Secure Note Item (**Figure 5**) or press [Shift][⌃][⌘][N] to display a dialog like the one in **Figure 8**.

2. Enter an identifying name for the note in the Keychain Item Name box.

3. Enter the note in the Note box.

4. Click Add. The new item is added to your keychain.

✔ Tip

■ You might find this feature handy for storing information you sometimes need to access while at your computer, such as social security, bank account, and credit card numbers.

To delete a keychain item

1. In Keychain Access (**Figure 2**), select the keychain item you want to remove.

2. Press [Delete].

3. A confirmation dialog like the one in **Figure 9** appears. Click Delete.

    The item is removed from the keychain.

✔ Tip

■ Removing a keychain item does not prevent you from accessing an item. It just prevents you from accessing it without entering a password.

To get general information about a keychain item

1. In Keychain Access (**Figure** 2) select the keychain item you want to learn about.

2. Click the i button at the bottom of the keychain item list. A window with information about the keychain item appears.

3. If necessary, click the Attributes button to show general information about the item (**Figures 10** and **11**).

4. To see the item password, turn on the Show password check box (**Figure 10**).

   or

   To see a note, turn on the Show note check box (**Figure 11**).

5. When you are finished working with keychain information, click the window's close box to dismiss it.

✔ Tips

■ You can also see information about an item by double-clicking the item in the Keychain Access window.

■ In step 4, if you turn on the Show password (**Figure 10**) or Show note (**Figure 11**) check box, a dialog like the one in **Figure 12** may appear. To see the password or note, you must enter the keychain password (your user password, for the default keychain) and click the Allow or Always Allow button.

Figure 10 The Attributes pane of the Keychain Access window for a keychain with a password selected.

Figure 11 The Attributes pane of the Keychain Access window for a password with a password selected.

Figure 12 This dialog appears when you try to view the password or note in a keychain item.

GETTING KEYCHAIN ITEM INFORMATION

Figure 13 Access control information for a keychain item.

Figure 14 When an application that does not have permission to use a keychain item wants to use it, it displays a dialog like this.

Figure 15 Use a standard Open dialog like this to add applications to the list of allowed applications.

Figure 16 You must enter a password in this dialog to change Access Control settings.

To set Access Control options

1. In Keychain Access (**Figure** 2), select the keychain item you want to set Access Control options for.

2. Click the i button at the bottom of the keychain item list. A dialog with information about the keychain item appears.

3. Click the Access Control button (**Figure 13**).

4. Select an access option:

   ▲ **Allow all applications to access this item** enables any application to access the item, without displaying a confirmation dialog. If you choose this option, skip ahead to step 7.

   ▲ **Confirm before allowing access** displays a confirmation dialog for each application that attempts to access the item (**Figure 14**). To specify whether the dialog should include a password prompt (**Figure 12**), toggle the Ask for Keychain password check box.

5. If desired, use the + and – buttons in the window to modify the list of applications that can access the item without displaying the confirmation dialog:

   ▲ + displays a dialog sheet like the one in **Figure 15**, which you can use to locate and choose an application to add to the list.

   ▲ – removes a selected application from the list.

6. Click Save.

7. A dialog like the one in **Figure 16** appears. Enter the keychain password in the box and click Allow to save the change.

8. Click the window's close box to dismiss it.

SETTING ACCESS CONTROL OPTIONS

To use a keychain item

1. Follow your normal procedure for accessing the secure item.

2. If Access Control settings are set up to allow access to the item without confirmation, the item opens without displaying any dialog.

    or

    If Access Control settings are set up to require a confirmation, a dialog like the one in **Figure 12** or **14** appears. Enter a password (if necessary; **Figure 16**) and click a button:

    ▲ **Always Allow** enables the keychain to open the item and adds the item to the Access Control application list so the dialog does not appear again.

    ▲ **Deny** prevents use of the keychain item. You will have to manually enter a password to access the secure item.

    ▲ **Allow** enables the keychain to open the item this time.

✔ Tips

■ The only reason I can think of for denying access with a keychain is if you have another user name and password you want to use.

■ If a keychain item does not exist for the secure item, you'll have to go through the usual procedure for accessing the item.

Figure 17 Enter a name for your new keychain and click Create.

Figure 18 Enter the same password for the new keychain in both boxes of this dialog.

Figure 19 Your new keychain appears in the keychain list.

To create a new keychain

1. In Keychain Access, choose File > New Keychain (**Figure 5**) or press Option ⌃ ⌘ N.

2. Enter a name for the keychain in the New Keychain dialog that appears (**Figure 17**) and click Create.

3. The New Keychain Password dialog appears (**Figure 18**). Enter the same password in each box and click OK.

✔ Tips

■ If you're an organization nut, you may want to use multiple keychains to organize passwords for different purposes. Otherwise, one keychain should be enough for you. (It is for me.)

■ In step 2, although you can specify a different location to save the new keychain, it's a good idea to save it in the default location, the Keychains folder.

■ In step 3, you can click the key button to use the Password Assistant (**Figure 6**) to help you come up with a secure password. I tell you about the Password Assistant on page 516.

To view a different keychain

1. In Keychain Access, if necessary, click the Show Keychains button at the bottom of the Category list to display the Keychains list.

2. Select the keychain you want to view (**Figure 19**).

✔ Tip

■ As shown in **Figure 19**, your computer creates and maintains other keychains that are used by the system.

To unlock a keychain

1. Open Keychain Access, and, if necessary, click the Show Keychains button in the bottom-left corner of the window to display the Keychain list (**Figure 19**).

2. Select the keychain you want to unlock.

3. Click the padlock button at the top of the Keychain Access window.

4. A password dialog appears (**Figure 20**). Enter the password for the keychain and click OK. The icon beside the keychain name changes so it looks unlocked.

✔ Tips

■ The password for the login keychain Mac OS X automatically creates for you is the same as your login password.

■ By unlocking a keychain, you make its passwords available for use by applications as set in the keychain's access controls.

To lock a keychain

1. Open Keychain Access, and, if necessary, click the Show Keychains button in the bottom-left corner of the window to display the Keychain list (**Figure 19**).

2. Select the keychain you want to lock.

3. Click the padlock button at the top of the Keychain Access window. The icon beside the keychain name changes to look locked.

✔ Tips

■ When a keychain is locked, if you try to open a secure item for which you have a keychain item, a password dialog appears (**Figure 20**). Enter your keychain password and click OK to unlock the keychain and use it.

■ To quickly lock all keychains, choose File > Lock All Keychains (**Figure 5**).

Figure 20 Use a dialog like this to unlock a keychain.

Figure 21
Choose System Preferences from the Apple menu.

Figure 22 The General options of the Security preferences pane.

General Security Options

Mac OS X has a number of general security options that you can use to make your computer more secure. Some of these options are especially useful in workplace environments, where your computer may be left unattended while turned on. You can find and set these options in the General panel of the Security Preferences pane.

✔ Tip

- You must be logged in as an administrator to make changes to General security options.

To set system security options

1. Choose Apple > System Preferences (**Figure 21**) or click the System Preferences icon in the Dock.

2. Click the Security icon to display the Security preferences pane.

3. If necessary, click the General button to display General security preferences (**Figure 22**).

4. Set options as desired:

   ▲ **Require password after sleep or screen saver begins** displays an authentication dialog when you wake your computer or deactivate the screen saver. If you enable this option, choose a time period from the pop-up menu; your options range from immediately to 4 hours.

   ▲ **Disable automatic login** turns off the automatic login feature.

   ▲ **Require password to unlock each System Preferences pane** displays an authentication dialog before any user can modify any System preferences pane.

Continued on next page...

Continued from previous page.

▲ **Log out after *n* minutes of inactivity** automatically logs out a user when he has been inactive for the number of minutes you specify.

▲ **Use secure virtual memory** encrypts the invisible virtual memory file your computer maintains while running.

▲ **Disable Location Services** turns off the location services feature that enables your computer to determine its location based on access to wireless signals.

▲ **Disable remote control infrared receiver** prevents the computer from responding to a signal sent by an Apple remote control device.

✔ Tips

■ Not all Macintosh models can be accessed with an Apple remote. If your computer does not support this feature, the Disable remote control infrared receiver option will not appear among the General security options.

■ I tell you about the automatic login feature on page 506 and about System preferences in **Chapter 23**.

Figure 23 You set up FileVault in the FileVault pane of the Security preferences pane.

FileVault

FileVault enables you to encrypt your Home folder using Advanced Encryption Standard 128-bit (AES-128) encryption. This makes it virtually impossible for any hacker to access the files in your Home folder. Best of all, it's all done quickly and transparently—files are decrypted automatically when you log in and encrypted again when you log out.

Setting up FileVault is a two-step process. First, enable FileVault by setting a master password for the computer. Next, turn on FileVault for your user account. You do both of these things in the FileVault pane of the Security preferences pane. In this section, I show you how.

✔ Tips

■ I say "virtually impossible" above because I don't believe that anything is really impossible. But this comes pretty close—certainly close enough for most people!

■ If you're worried about someone recovering one of your deleted files, use the Secure Empty Trash command when you empty the Trash. I tell you more about deleting files on page 57.

To set a FileVault master password

1. Make sure all other users are logged off.

2. Log in with an administrator account.

3. Choose Apple > System Preferences (**Figure 21**) or click the System Preferences icon in the Dock.

4. Click the Security icon to display the Security preferences pane.

5. Click the FileVault button to display its options (**Figure 23**).

6. Click Set Master Password.

7. In the dialog that appears (**Figure 24**), enter the same password in the top two boxes. Then enter a password hint in the bottom box and click OK.

   The Security preferences pane indicates that a master password has been set (**Figure 25**).

✔ Tips

- By setting a master password, you make it possible for users to use the FileVault feature. You do not, however, enable it for any particular account.

- The master password is used as a "safety net" to help users who have forgotten their account password. After trying unsuccessfully to log in three times, you can click the Forgot Password button and enter the master password when prompted to reaccess your account.

- In step 7, you can click the key button to use the Password Assistant (**Figure 6**) to help you come up with a secure password. I tell you about the Password Assistant on page 516.

Figure 24 Use this dialog to set up a master password for the entire computer.

Figure 25 When a master password has been set, the FileVault pane of the Security preferences pane tells you.

Figure 26 Use this dialog to change the master password.

- In step 7, don't forget to enter a password hint that will help you remember the master password. If you forget the master password, you or other users could be locked out of your Home folder forever.

- To change the Master Password, follow steps 1 through 5, then click the Change button (**Figure 25**) to display the Change Master Password dialog (**Figure 26**). Enter the current password in the top box and the new password and hint in the next three boxes. Click OK.

- Once you enter a master password, you cannot remove it.

Figure 27 To turn on FileVault for your account, enter your password in this dialog.

Figure 28 A dialog like this explains what happens when you turn on FileVault and offers two options.

To protect your Home folder with FileVault

1. Log in to your account.

2. Choose Apple > System Preferences (**Figure 21**).

3. Click the Security icon to display the Security preferences pane.

4. Click the FileVault button to display its options (**Figure 23**).

5. Click Turn On FileVault.

6. A dialog like the one in **Figure 27** appears. Enter your account password and click OK.

7. A dialog like the one in **Figure 28** appears next. Read it carefully!

8. To automatically use the Secure Empty Trash feature each time you delete a file and empty the Trash, turn on the Use secure erase check box. I tell you more about this feature on page 60.

9. Click the Turn On FileVault button.

   You are logged out and a FileVault window appears. It shows encryption progress and may display an estimate of how long it will take to finish.

10. When the encryption process is done, a Login window appears. Log in to your account.

    From that point forward, every time you open a file in your Home folder, your computer decrypts it before displaying it. When you close a file, your computer encrypts it.

✔ Tips

■ The initial encryption process can be time consuming, depending on how many files are in your Home folder.

■ You cannot use the automatic login feature to log in a user with FileVault enabled. I tell you about the automatic log in feature on page 506.

To turn off FileVault

1. Log in to your account.

2. Choose Apple > System Preferences (**Figure 21**).

3. Click the Security icon to display the Security preferences pane.

4. Click the FileVault button to display its options.

5. Click Turn Off FileVault.

6. A dialog like the one in **Figure 27** appears. Enter your account password and click OK.

7. A dialog explaining what will happen next appears. Click the Turn Off FileVault button.

   You are logged out and a FileVault window appears. It shows decryption progress and may display an estimate of how long it will take to finish.

8. When the decryption process is done, a Login window appears. Log in to your account.

Figure 29 The default settings of the Firewall options of the Security preferences pane.

Figure 30 When the firewall is enabled, the Start button turns into a Stop button.

Firewall

A *firewall* is software that protects your computer from unauthorized access via a network or Internet connection. This helps prevent hackers from gaining access to your computer.

When you enable a firewall, it blocks your computer's networking *ports* from incoming traffic. You open up only the ports you need to exchange information with various Mac OS networking services, such as Personal File Sharing or iTunes Music Sharing.

In this part of the chapter, I explain how to enable the firewall feature of Mac OS X.

✔ Tips

- If your computer never connects to the Internet and is not part of a network, there's no benefit to using the firewall feature.

- Mac OS X's firewall feature works hand-in-hand with its sharing services. I discuss sharing services in **Chapter 20**.

- I tell you more about the Internet in **Chapter 18** and networking in **Chapter 20**.

To enable the firewall

1. Choose Apple > System Preferences (**Figure 21**) or click the System Preferences icon in the Dock.

2. Click the Security icon to display the Security preferences pane.

3. If necessary, click the Firewall button to display Firewall preferences (**Figure 29**).

4. Click the Start button. The window changes to indicate that the firewall is On and a Stop button appears (**Figure 30**).

SETTING FIREWALL OPTIONS

To set advanced firewall options

1. Follow the instructions on the previous page to open Firewall preferences (**Figure 29**) and, if necessary, enable the firewall.

2. Click the Advanced button to display advanced options (**Figure 31**).

3. Set options as desired:

   ▲ **Block all incoming connections** does not allow any outside connections to your computer.

   ▲ To limit incoming connections to specific services and applications click the + button and use the standard Open dialog that appears to locate, select, and add applications. The Block all incoming connections check box must be turned off to set this option.

   ▲ **Automatically allow signed software to receive incoming connections** allows connections for software and services with a valid certificate of authority.

   ▲ **Enable stealth mode** prevents your computer from responding to access attempts, making it appear as if your computer does not exist.

4. Click OK.

✔ Tip

■ In step 3, if you allow only certain applications and services, active services will automatically be added based on your choices in the Sharing preferences pane. I tell you about sharing services in **Chapter 20**.

Figure 31 There are two advanced firewall options.

System Preferences

Figure 1 The System Preferences window, with icons for all panes displayed.

System Preferences

One of the great things about Mac OS is the way it can be customized to look and work the way you want it to. Many customization options can be set within the System Preferences application (**Figure 1**). That's where you'll find a variety of preferences panes, each containing settings for a part of Mac OS.

System Preferences panes are organized into four categories:

◆ **Personal** preferences panes enable you to set options to customize various Mac OS X appearance and operation options for personal tastes. This chapter covers Language & Text.

◆ **Hardware** preferences panes control settings for various hardware devices. This chapter covers Displays, Energy Saver, Keyboard, Mouse, Trackpad (which only appears on a computer with a trackpad), and Sound.

◆ **Internet & Network** preferences panes enable you to set options related to Internet and network connections.

◆ **System** preferences panes control various aspects of your computer's operation. This chapter covers Date & Time, Software Update, Speech, Startup Disk, and Universal Access.

Continued on next page...

Continued from previous page.

✔ Tip

- Other Preferences panes are covered elsewhere in this book:
  - ▲ Spotlight, in **Chapter 5**.
  - ▲ CDs & DVDs, and Time Machine in **Chapter 6**.
  - ▲ Appearance, Desktop & Screen Saver, and Dock, in **Chapter 8**.
  - ▲ Exposé & Spaces, in **Chapter 9**.
  - ▲ MobileMe, in **Chapters 12** and **19**.
  - ▲ Print & Fax, in **Chapter 17**.
  - ▲ Network, in **Chapters 18** and **20**.
  - ▲ Bluetooth (which appears only if your computer has Bluetooth capabilities) and Sharing, in **Chapter 20**.
  - ▲ Accounts and Parental Controls, in **Chapter 21**.
  - ▲ Security, in **Chapter 22**.

To open System Preferences

Choose Apple > System Preferences (**Figure 2**) or click the System Preferences icon in the Dock. The System Preferences window appears (**Figure 1**).

To open a preferences pane

Click the icon for the pane you want to display.

Or

Choose the name of the pane you want to display from the View menu (**Figure 3**).

Figure 2
To open System Preferences, choose System Preferences from the Apple menu.

Figure 3
The View menu lists all of the System Preferences panes.

Figure 4 System Preferences pane icons can also be displayed alphabetically.

Figure 5 You can search System Preferences to find the preferences pane you need to perform a task.

Figure 6 The System Preferences menu.

To show all preferences pane icons

Choose a command from the System Preferences' View menu (**Figure 3**):

◆ **Show All Preferences** (⌘L) displays all preferences pane icons.

◆ **Organize by Categories** displays all icons organized by category (**Figure 1**).

◆ **Organize Alphabetically** displays all icons organized alphabetically by name (**Figure 4**).

Or

Click the Show All button in the toolbar of the System Preferences window (**Figures 1 and 4**).

To find a preference pane by task or topic

1. Enter a search word or phrase in the search box in the upper-right corner of the System Preferences window. Three things happen (**Figure 5**):

   ▲ The window gets dark.

   ▲ Icons for related preference panes are highlighted.

   ▲ A menu of possible topics appears.

2. Select a topic from the menu.

   or

   Click a highlighted icon.

   The appropriate preference pane opens.

To quit System Preferences

Use one of the following techniques:

◆ Choose System Preferences > Quit System Preferences (**Figure 6**).

◆ Press ⌘Q.

◆ Click the System Preferences window's close button.

Date & Time

The Date & Time preferences pane includes three panes for setting the system time and clock options:

◆ **Date & Time** (**Figure 7**) enables you to automatically or manually set the date and time.

◆ **Time Zone** (**Figure 10**) enables you to set your time zone.

◆ **Clock** (**Figure 12**) enables you to set options for the appearance of the clock.

To set the date & time

1. In the Date & Time preferences pane, click the Date & Time button (**Figure 7**).

2. To set the date and time automatically, turn on the Set data and time automatically check box. Then choose the closest time server from the drop-down list (**Figure 8**).

    or

    To set the date and time manually, turn off the Set date and time automatically check box. Then click the numbers you want to change in the date and time boxes and enter new values (**Figure 9**) or click in the calendar and clock images to set the correct values. Click Save to save your settings.

✔ Tips

■ With the network time server feature enabled, your computer will use its Internet connection to periodically get the date and time from a time server and update the system clock automatically. This ensures that your computer's clock is always correct.

Figure 7 The Date & Time pane of the Date & Time preferences pane.

Figure 8 The drop-down list includes the time servers all over the world.

Figure 9 Click the part of the date that you want to change, then use the arrow buttons to change the value.

■ You can't manually change the date or time if you have enabled the network time server feature; I tell you more about that on the next page.

Figure 10 The Time Zone pane of the Date & Time preferences pane, with a time zone selected.

Figure 11 In this example, my Mac is smart enough to know that I'm not really in the Phoenix area this summer but in Quincy, WA, which is close to Yakima.

Figure 12 The Closest City drop-down list only displays cities in or near the currently selected time zone.

To set the time zone

1. In the Date & Time preferences pane, click the Time Zone button (**Figure 10**).

2. To automatically set the time zone, turn on the Set time zone automatically using current location check box. Then wait while your computer sets your time zone based on your current location (**Figure 11**).

   or

   To manually set the time zone, turn off the Set time zone automatically using current location check box. Then click your approximate location on the map. A white bar indicates the time zone area (**Figure 10**). Choose the name of a city in your time zone from the Closest City drop-down list beneath the map (**Figure 11**).

✔ Tips

- An Internet connection is required to automatically set your time zone. This feature uses Mac OS X 10.6's location services capabilities.

- When manually setting the time zone, only those cities in or near the white bar on the map are listed in the drop-down list (**Figure 12**). If a nearby city does not appear, make sure you clicked the correct area in the map.

- It's a good idea to choose the correct time zone, since Mac OS uses this information with the network time server (if utilized) and to properly change the clock for daylight saving time.

To set clock options

1. In the Date & Time preferences pane, click the Clock button (**Figure 13**).

2. To enable the clock, turn on the Show date and time in menu bar check box.

3. Select a View as radio button:

   ▲ **Digital** displays the date and time with letters and numbers.

   ▲ **Analog** displays the time on an analog clock (**Figure 14**). If you choose this option, skip step 4.

4. Toggle check boxes to customize the clock's appearance:

   ▲ **Display the time with seconds** displays the seconds as part of the time.

   ▲ **Flash the time separators** blinks the colon(s) in the time every second.

   ▲ **Use a 24-hour clock** displays the time as a 24-hour (rather than 12-hour) clock.

   ▲ **Show AM/PM** displays AM or PM after the time.

   ▲ **Show the day of the week** displays the three-letter abbreviation for the day of the week before the time.

   ▲ Show date displays the date before the time.

5. To instruct your computer to vocally announce the time periodically, turn on the Announce the time check box and choose a frequency option from the pop-up menu: On the hour, On the half hour, or On the quarter hour.

✔ Tips

■ The menu bar clock is also a menu that displays the full date and time and offers options for changing the clock display (**Figure 15**).

Figure 13 The Clock pane of the Date & Time preferences pane.

Figure 14 If you have good eyesight, you might prefer an analog clock.

Figure 15 The menu bar clock is also a menu.

Figure 16 You can customize the computer's clock voice by setting options in this dialog.

■ Clicking the Customize Voice button in step 5 displays a dialog you can use to set options for the time speaking voice (**Figure 16**).

Figure 17 The Display pane of the Displays preferences pane for a 13-inch MacBook Pro.

Figure 18 A MacBook Pro display set to 800 x 600...

Figure 19 ...and the same display set to 1280 x 800.

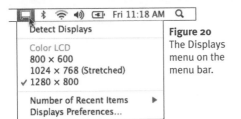

Figure 20 The Displays menu on the menu bar.

Displays

The Displays preferences pane enables you to set the resolution, colors, and other settings for your monitor. Settings are organized into panes; this section covers the Display (**Figure 17**) and Color (**Figure 21**) panes.

✔ Tip

■ The options that are available in the Displays preferences pane vary depending on your computer and monitor. The options shown in this chapter are for a 13-inch MacBook Pro.

To set basic display options

1. In the Displays preferences pane, click the Display button (**Figure 17**).

2. Set options as desired:

   ▲ **Resolutions** control the number of pixels that appear on screen. The higher the resolution, the more pixels appear on screen. This makes the screen contents smaller, but shows more, as shown in **Figures 18** and **19**.

   ▲ **Show displays in menu bar** displays a menu of recently used display settings in the menu bar (**Figure 20**).

   ▲ **Brightness** lets you adjust the display's brightness by dragging a slider.

   ▲ **Automatically adjust brightness as ambient light changes** adjusts brightness based on the brightness of your workspace. This option is only available on computers that support it.

SETTING DISPLAY OPTIONS

To set display color profile

1. In the Displays preferences pane, click the Color button (**Figure 21**).

2. Select one of the Display Profiles.

✔ Tips

- To limit the selection of color profiles to just those designed to work with your display, turn on the Show profiles for this display only check box.

- You can view the technical details of a selected color profile (**Figure 22**) by clicking the Open Profile button.

- Color profiles is an advanced feature of Mac OS. It works with ColorSync technology to display colors onscreen as they will appear when printed. I tell you about the ColorSync Utility on page 575.

- Clicking the Calibrate button in the Color tab of the Displays preferences pane opens the Display Calibrator Assistant, which you can use to fine-tune color options for your display. A discussion of the Display Calibrator Assistant is beyond the scope of this book.

Figure 21 The Color pane of the Displays preferences pane for a MacBook Pro.

Figure 22 You can view the details for a color profile in a window like this.

Figure 23 The Energy Saver preferences pane, as it appears on an iMac.

Figure 24 The Battery pane of the Energy Saver preferences pane on a MacBook Pro.

Figure 25 The Power Adapter pane of the Energy Saver preferences pane on a MacBook Pro.

Energy Saver

The Energy Saver preference pane (**Figures 23, 24,** and **25**) enables you to specify settings that can reduce the amount of power your computer uses when idle.

✔ Tips

■ Energy Saver settings are especially important for laptop users running on battery power.

■ The appearance of and options in the Energy Saver preferences pane vary depending on your computer.

To set Energy Saver options

1. In the Energy Saver preferences pane, click the Sleep button to display its options (**Figure 23**).

2. On a laptop Mac, click the button at the top of the preferences pane to indicate whether you want to set options for Battery or Power Adapter operations.

3. To set the amount of inactive time before the computer sleeps, drag the Computer sleep slider to the right or left.

4. To set the amount of inactive time before the display sleeps, drag the Display sleep to the left or right. (You cannot set display sleep for longer than computer sleep.)

5. Toggle check boxes to set additional options as desired:

   ▲ **Put the hard disk(s) to sleep when possible** tells your computer to put the hard disk to sleep when it isn't needed.

   ▲ **Wake for network access** wakes the computer from computer sleep when it detects a Wake-on-LAN packet.

Continued on next page...

SETTING ENERGY SAVER OPTIONS

Continued from previous page.

▲ **Allow power button to put the computer to sleep** enables you to invoke computer sleep by pressing the computer's power button.

▲ **Slightly dim the display when using this power source** reduces the brightness of the display when on battery power.

▲ **Automatically reduce the brightness of the display before display sleep** dims the screen a short while before the display sleeps. You can use this as a sort of warning signal that the display will sleep shortly.

▲ **Start up automatically after a power failure** automatically restarts the computer when power is restored after a power failure.

6. To display battery status as a menu on a laptop's menu bar (**Figure 26**), turn on the Show battery status on the menu bar check box.

✔ Tips

■ To wake a sleeping display, press any key. A sleeping hard disk wakes automatically when it needs to.

■ If your computer is being used as a server, it's important to turn on the Start up automatically check box. This ensures that the computer is running whenever possible.

Figure 26 The Battery Status menu offers battery information and a command to open Energy Saver.

Figure 27 Use the options in this dialog to schedule automatic startup and shutdown days and times.

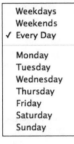

Figure 28
Use this pop-up menu to specify the days you want to start up or shut down the computer automatically.

Figure 29
Automatically sleep, restart, or shut down the computer.

Figure 30 At scheduled shutdown time, your Mac displays a 10-minute warning.

To schedule start up & shut down

1. In the Energy Saver preferences pane, click the Schedule button to display its options (**Figure 27**).

2. To set automatic startup, turn on the top check box. Then choose an option from the pop-up menu (**Figure 28**) and enter a time beside it.

3. To set automatic sleep, restart, or shut down, turn on the second check box, choose options from the pop-up menus beside it (**Figures 28** and **29**), and enter a time beside them.

✔ Tip

■ Your computer will give you a 10-minute warning for a scheduled shutdown. When the warning dialog appears (**Figure 30**), you can choose to cancel the shutdown, shut down immediately, or just wrap up your work and let the computer shut down when it's ready.

Language & Text

The Language & Text preferences pane enables you to set options that control how Mac OS X works in an environment where U.S. English is not the primary language or multiple languages are used.

International preferences are broken down into four different categories: Language (**Figure 31**), Text (**Figure 35**), Formats (**Figure 41**), and Input Sources (**Figure 45**).

✔ Tip

■ The Language & Text preferences pane was known as the International preferences pane in previous versions of Mac OS X.

To set preferred language options

1. In the Language & Text preferences pane, click the Language button (**Figure 31**).

2. To set the preferred order for languages to appear in application menus and dialogs, drag languages up or down in the Languages list (**Figure 32**).

3. To set sort order for text, choose an option from the Order for sorted lists pop-up menu.

✔ Tips

■ You can edit the Languages list. Click the Edit List button in the Language pane (**Figure 31**) to display a dialog like the one in **Figure 33**. Turn on the check boxes beside each language you want to include in the list and click OK.

■ The changes you make to the Languages list in step 2 take effect in the Finder the next time you restart or log in. Changes take effect in applications (**Figure 34**) the next time you open them.

Figure 31 The Language pane of the Language & Text preferences pane.

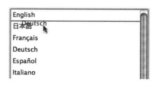

Figure 32 Change the preferred language order by dragging a language up or down in the list.

Figure 33 Turn on check boxes for the languages you want to include in the Languages list.

Figure 34 Changing an application's language is as easy as dragging the language to the top of the list. Here's TextEdit in Spanish.

SETTING LANGUAGE OPTIONS

Figure 35 The Text options of the Language & Text preferences pane.

Figure 36 You can add a text substitution pair to the bottom of the Symbol and Text Substitution list.

Figure 37
Use this pop-up menu to choose the primary language for spelling checks in Apple applications.

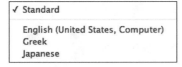

Figure 38
The Word Break pop-up menu.

To set text substitution options

1. In the Language & Text preferences pane, click the Text button (**Figure 35**).

2. In the Symbol and Text Substitution list, toggle check boxes to enable the automatic substitutions you want.

3. To add a new substitution to the list, click the + button at the bottom of the list and, in the new line that appears (**Figure 36**) enter the text you want to replace as well as the text you want to replace it with.

4. Choose options from the pop-up menu on the right side of the preferences pane as desired:

   ▲ **Spelling (Figure 37)** is the language you want to use for spelling checks in your document.

   ▲ **Word Break (Figure 38)** determines how a word is selected when double-clicked. Choose your language style.

   ▲ **Smart Quotes** enables you to specify how quote characters should be displayed. Choose options for double (**Figure 39**) and single (**Figure 40**) quotes.

✔ Tip

■ Text substitution, which is new in Mac OS X 10.6 Snow Leopard, controls automatic text substitution options available in several Apple applications, including TextEdit, iCal, and iMovie.

✔ "abc"
„abc"
„abc"
"abc"
« abc »
«abc»
»abc«
"abc"

Figures 39 & 40
The two Smart Quotes pop-up menus.

✔ 'abc'
‚abc'
‚abc'
'abc'
‹ abc ›
‹abc›
›abc‹
'abc'

To set the date, time, & number formats

1. In the Language & Text preferences pane, click the Formats button (**Figure 41**).

2. Choose an option from the Region pop-up menu.

3. To customize the date or time format, click the Customize button in the appropriate area of the dialog. In the dialogs that appear (**Figures 42** or **43**), use the pop-up menu to specify which format you want to customize, then drag elements into the edit area to set the format. Repeat this process for each format you want to customize and click OK.

4. Use the Calendar and First day of week pop-up menu to set additional calendar options as desired.

5. To customize the number format, click the Customize button in the Numbers area of the dialog and set options in the dialog that appears (**Figure 44**). Click OK.

6. To change the currency format, choose an option from the Currency pop-up menu.

7. To change the measurement unit, choose an option from the Measurement Units pop-up menu.

✔ Tips

- Changes in this pane affect how dates, times, and numbers are displayed throughout Mac OS X and applications.

- The sample dates, times, and numbers in the Formats pane (**Figure 35**) show the effect of your changes.

Figure 41 The Formats pane of the Language & Text preferences pane.

Figure 42 Use this dialog to customize the date format, ...

Figure 43 ...this dialog to customize the time format, ...

Figure 44 ...and this dialog to customize the number format.

Figure 45 The Input Menu pane of the Language & Text preferences pane.

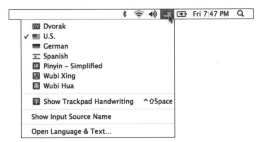

Figure 46 An input menu appears on the menu bar with all of the language options you selected.

To create & customize an input menu

1. In the Language & Text preferences pane, click the Input Sources button (**Figure 45**).

2. Turn on the check boxes beside each input method or keyboard layout you may want to use with Mac OS X. If more than one item is selected, an Input menu appears on the menu bar (**Figure 46**).

3. Select one of the Input source options to determine whether you use the same input method in all documents or allow a different one for each document.

4. To toggle the display of the input menu, set the Show input menu in menu bar check box.

✔ Tips

■   To switch from one keyboard or input method to another, select an item from the Input menu (**Figure 46**) or press ⌘ ⌘ Option Spacebar to cycle through all options on the menu, one at a time.

■   The Input menu may also automatically appear on the menu bar when you use the Special Characters command in an application.

■   A discussion of Mac OS X 10.6's new features for entering characters in complex languages such as Chinese is far beyond the scope of this book. If you need to use these features, you can find more information in Mac Help. Enter the search phrase *input method* to get started.

Keyboard

The Keyboard preferences pane enables you to customize the way the keyboard works. Options can be set in up to five panes, depending on your computer model, its capabilities, and the attached devices:

◆ **Keyboard** (**Figure 47**) enables you to set keyboard functionality options, such as key repeat rate.

◆ **Keyboard Shortcuts** (**Figure 49**) enables you to view and assign shortcuts for application menu commands.

✔ Tips

■ The appearance of the Keyboard preferences pane varies depending on the type of computer and keyboard you are using. It's impossible to show all versions of this preference pane. The illustrations here are for a MacBook Pro.

■ To use a Bluetooth keyboard with your Mac, it must be *paired*. I explain how to pair Bluetooth devices on page 466.

■ In previous versions of Mac OS, the Keyboard, Mouse, and Trackpad were combined into one multipaneled preferences pane. The Mouse and Trackpad preferences panes are covered later in this chapter.

Figure 47 The Keyboard options for a MacBook Pro includes options you won't find on a standard keyboard.

KEYBOARD

Figure 48 The Keyboard & Character Viewer menu enables you to access the Character Viewer and Keyboard Viewer palettes.

Figure 49 You can use the Character Viewer palette to insert special characters into a document.

Figure 50 The Keyboard Viewer palette displays your current keyboard layout and offers clickable keys to enter characters.

To set keyboard options

1. In the Keyboard & Mouse preferences pane, click the Keyboard button (**Figure 40**).

2. Set options as desired:
   - ▲ **Key Repeat Rate** sets how fast a key repeats when held down.
   - ▲ **Delay Until Repeat** sets how long a key must be pressed before it starts to repeat.

3. Set additional options, if available, for a keyboard:
   - ▲ **Use all F1, F2, etc. keys as standard function keys** takes away special functionality for these keys, such as brightness and volume control, and requires you to press [Fn] with those keys for the same functionality.
   - ▲ **Illuminate keyboard in low light conditions** turns on backlighting for your keyboard in low light conditions. (Keep in mind that this can reduce battery life.)
   - ▲ **Turn off when computer is not used for** lets you specify, with a slider, how long before keyboard lighting should be turned off when the computer is idle.
   - ▲ **Show Keyboard & Character Viewer in menu bar** displays a menu like the one in **Figure 48**, which you can use to display the Character Viewer (**Figure 49**) and Keyboard Viewer (**Figure 50**) palettes. These palettes enable you to enter characters into Mac OS applications by clicking a palette button.

Continued on next page...

SETTING KEYBOARD OPTIONS

Continued from previous page.

4. To change the behavior of modifier keys such as ⌘ ⌘, Option, and Control, click the Modifier Keys button. In the dialog that appears (**Figure 49**), use the pop-up menus to set the action you want each key to perform and click OK.

✔ Tips

■ The options that appear in the Keyboard preferences panel vary depending on the keyboard(s) accessible by your Mac.

■ Key Repeat settings are especially useful for heavy-handed typists.

■ I tell you more about using the Character palette on page 359.

■ Why you'd want to change the behavior of modifier keys is beyond me. It would make a good April Fool's joke, though.

Figure 51 You can use this dialog to change the behavior of modifier keys. If you have more than one keyboard, be sure to select the one you want to configure from the Select Keyboard pop-up menu before settings options and clicking OK.

Figure 52 The Keyboard Shortcuts pane of the Keyboard preferences pane.

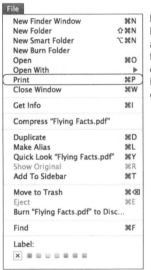

Figure 53 In this example, I've added a shortcut key for the Finder's Print command. (Don't know why Apple didn't include one.)

✔ Tips

■ You cannot remove or change Mac OS X keyboard shortcuts. You can, however, remove or change the keyboard shortcuts you add.

■ When you add a keyboard shortcut for a menu command, the shortcut appears on the menu (**Figure 53**).

To customize keyboard shortcuts

1. In the Keyboard preferences pane, click the Keyboard Shortcuts button (**Figure 52**).

2. In the list on the left side of the window, select the category or type of shortcut key you want to change.

3. To turn a shortcut on or off, toggle its check box in the list on the right side of the window.

4. Add or modify custom shortcuts in the list on the right side of the window:

   ▲ To add a shortcut, click the + button at the bottom of the list. Then set options in the dialog that appears (**Figure 53**) to specify the application, menu command, and keyboard shortcut you want to add.

   ▲ To change a shortcut, select the shortcut you want to change and press a new keyboard shortcut combination.

   ▲ To remove a shortcut, select the shortcut you want to add and click the – button at the bottom of the list.

5. To set the way the [Tab] key highlights items in windows and dialogs, select one of the two options at the bottom of the preferences pane: **Text boxes and lists only** or **All controls**.

■ You can also use the Keyboard Shortcuts pane to learn about shortcuts available in the Finder and other applications that do not appear on menus. The ones listed under Keyboard & Text Input are especially interesting and you may find them useful.

Mouse

The Mouse preferences pane (**Figure 54**) enables you to set mouse functionality options, such as scroll speed and button assignment.

✔ Tip

■ The appearance of the Mouse preferences pane varies depending on the type of mouse connected to your Macintosh.

To set mouse options

1. Open the Mouse preferences pane (**Figure 54**).

2. Use sliders at the top of the pane to set speed options:

   ▲ **Tracking** is the speed of the pointer movement on your screen.

   ▲ **Double-Click** is the amount of time between each click of a double-click.

   ▲ **Scrolling** is how scroll wheel or ball movements are translated to window scrolling.

3. Use pop-up menus (**Figure 55**) to assign actions to each mouse button.

4. Select an option from the scrolling pop-up menu (**Figure 56**) to determine how the scroll bar scrolls window contents.

5. To use the scroll ball to zoom instead of scroll, turn on the **Zoom using scroll ball while holding** check box and choose a key from the drop-down list. With this option enabled, you can click the Options button to display additional settings for zooming with the scroll ball (**Figure 57**).

✔ Tip

■ If you choose Other from any of the button pop-up menus (**Figure 47**), you can assign that button to an application.

Figure 54 The Mouse preferences pane for a wired Mighty Mouse.

Figure 55 Use this pop-up menu to set the functionality of each of the Mighty Mouse's buttons.

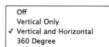

Figure 56 Indicate how you want the scroll ball to scroll.

Figure 57 Use this dialog to fine-tune the way scroll ball zooming works.

Figure 58 The Trackpad preferences pane for a circa 2006 15-inch MacBook Pro...

Figure 59 ...and the Trackpad preferences pane for a 2009 13-inch MacBook Pro. (The things I'm willing to do to get screen shots is amazing.)

Trackpad

The Trackpad preferences pane (**Figures 58 and 59**), which is only available on computers with a trackpad (such as a MacBook or MacBook Pro), enables you to set trackpad functionality options, such as tracking speed and trackpad gestures.

✔ Tips

- As shown in **Figures 58** and **59**, the options that appear in the Trackpad preferences pane vary depending on the computer model.

- On a MacBook or MacBook Pro that supports multi-touch gestures, you can point to one of the gestures in the list to view a short video demonstration of how it works in the video pane beside it (**Figure 59**). Try a few—they're fun!

To set trackpad options

1. Open the Trackpad preferences pane (**Figures 58** and **59**).

2. Use the sliders to set general speed options:
   - ▲ **Tracking Speed** is the speed of the pointer movement on your screen.
   - ▲ **Double-Click Speed** is the amount of time between each click of a double-click.
   - ▲ **Scrolling Speed** is how trackpad movements are translated to window scrolling.

3. Toggle check boxes and set menu options as desired to configure gestures compatible with your computer's trackpad.

4. To prevent your computer from interpreting accidental brushes against your trackpad as input, turn on the **Ignore accidental trackpad input** check box (**Figure 58**).

SETTING TRACKPAD OPTIONS

Software Update

The Software Update preferences pane (**Figure 60**) enables you to configure the Mac OS software update feature. This program uses your Internet connection to check Apple's servers for updates to your Apple software—including Mac OS and other installed Apple applications and utilities. If updates are found, it enables you to download and install them.

✔ Tip

■ You must have an Internet connection to update Mac OS X software with this feature.

To set automatic update options

1. In the Software Update preferences pane, click the Scheduled Check button (**Figure 60**).

3. Turn on the Check for updates check box.

4. Use the pop-up menu to specify how often your computer should check for updates: Daily, Weekly, or Monthly.

5. To automatically download important updates without asking you, turn on the check box labeled Download important updates automatically.

✔ Tip

■ When your computer checks for updates and finds one or more, it displays a window like the one in **Figure 61**. Follow the instructions on the next page to install software or dismiss the window.

Figure 60 The Software Update options of the Software Update preferences pane.

Figure 61 A dialog like this appears when there's new software to install.

SETTING AUTOMATIC UPDATE OPTIONS

Figure 62 Your computer uses its Internet connection to check for updates.

Figure 63 A list of available updates appears in the window.

Figure 64 If a dialog like this appears, you'll need to enter an administrator's name and password to complete the installation.

To manually check for updates

1. In the Scheduled Check panel of the Software Update preferences pane (**Figure 60**), click Check Now.

   Your computer connects to the Internet and checks Apple's servers for updates (**Figure 62**).

2. When the check is complete, if updates are available, a Software Update window like the one in **Figure 61** appears. Follow the instructions in the next section to install the updates.

To install updates

1. In the Software Update window (**Figure 61**), click the Show Details button.

2. The window expands to display a list of available updates (**Figure 63**). You have two options:

   ▲ **Not Now** temporarily ignores the updates and dismisses the dialog. You'll be reminded about the updates the next time Software Update automatically runs. Skip the remaining steps.

   ▲ **Install _n_ item(s)** installs the items checked off in the list. Before clicking this button be sure to deselect any items you don't want to install.

3. An authentication dialog like the one shown in **Figure 64** may appear. Enter an administrator name and password and click OK.

4. If a License Agreement window appears, read the license agreement (or at least pretend to) and click Agree.

Continued on next page...

INSTALLING SOFTWARE UPDATES

Continued from previous page.

5. If you'll need to restart your computer after installing the software, a dialog like the one in **Figure 65** appears. Click Restart.

6. Wait while your computer downloads (if necessary) and installs the update from Apple's server. If your computer does not need to be restarted, you can continue working with it until the installation is complete.

7. When Software Update is finished installing software, it either restarts your computer or displays a dialog telling you that the installation is complete. If the dialog appears, click OK.

✔ Tips

- You can learn about an update before you install it by selecting it in the top half of the Software Update window to display a description in the bottom half of the window (**Figure 63**).

- If you don't install a listed update, it will appear in the Software Update window (**Figure 63**) again the next time you check for updates. To remove it from the list without installing it, select it and choose Update > Ignore Update and then click OK in the confirmation dialog that appears.

- To view a log of installed updates, click the Installed Updates panel of the Software Update preferences pane (**Figure 66**).

Figure 65 If the software update requires that you restart your computer, you'll have to click Restart in this dialog to complete the installation.

Figure 66 The Installed Updates pane of the Software Update preferences pane shows a log of recent software update installations.

Figure 67 The Sound Effects panel of the Sound preferences pane on an older 15-inch MacBook Pro (which has two audio ports)...

Figure 68 ...and on a new 13-inch MacBook Pro (which has only one audio port).

Figure 69
You can use the Sound menu in the menu bar to adjust system sound levels.

Sound

The Sound preferences pane enables you to set options to control the system and alert sounds, output device, and input device Sound settings can be change in three panels:

◆ **Sound Effects** (**Figures 67** and **68**) lets you set options for alert sounds and sound effects.

◆ **Output** (**Figure 70**) allows you to set the output device and balance.

◆ **Input** (**Figure 71**) enables you to set the input device and volume.

✔ Tip

■ The options that appear in the Sound preferences pane vary depending on your computer and connected audio devices.

To set system volume

1. Display any panel of the Sound preferences pane (**Figure 67, 68, 70,** or **71**).

2. On a Mac with only one audio port (such as the 13-inch MacBook Pro illustrated in **Figure 68**), select an option from the Use audio port for pop-up menu to determine whether the audio port is used for Sound Input or Sound Output.

3. Set options in the bottom of the window:

▲ **Output volume** is the overall output volume for all sounds. Drag the slider to the left or right. Each time you move and release the slider in step 2, an alert sounds so you can hear a sample of your change.

▲ **Mute** keeps your computer quiet.

▲ **Show volume in menu bar** displays a sound volume menu in the menu bar (**Figure 69**).

SETTING SYSTEM SOUND VOLUME

To set sound effects options

1. In the Sound preferences pane, click the Sound Effects button (**Figures 67** and **68**).

2. To set the alert sound, select one of the options in the scrolling list.

3. Set other options as desired:

   ▲ **Play sound effects through** enables you to set the output device for alert and sound effect sounds. (This option may not be accessible if your computer has only one output device.)

   ▲ **Alert volume** is the volume of alert sounds. Drag the slider to the left or right.

   ▲ **Play user interface sound effects** plays sound effects for different system events, such as dragging an icon to the Trash or completing a copy operation.

   ▲ **Play feedback when volume is changed** enables you to hear the volume each time you change it.

   ▲ **Play Front Row sound effects** plays sound effects associated with using Front Row. (This option is only available on computers that support Front Row.)

✔ Tips

■ With the Play feedback when volume is changed check box turned on, each time you move and release the slider or select a different alert sound, an alert sounds so you can hear a sample of your change.

■ Alert volume depends partly on the main volume setting, which is discussed on the previous page. An alert sound cannot be louder than the main sound.

■ I tell you about Front Row on page 265.

Figure 70 The Output pane of the Sound preferences pane shows all attached output devices.

Figure 71 The Input pane of the Sound preferences pane shows all attached sound input devices.

To set output device options

1. In the Sound preferences pane, click the Output button (**Figure 70**).

2. To set the output device, select one of the options in the scrolling list.

3. To set the speaker balance for the selected device, drag the Balance slider to the left or right.

✔ Tip

- Each time you move and release the slider, an alert sounds so you can hear a sample of your change.

To set input device options

1. In the Sound preferences pane, click the Input button (**Figure 71**).

2. To set the input device, select one of the options in the scrolling list.

3. To set the input volume for the selected device, drag the Input volume slider to the left or right. The further to the right you drag the slider, the more sensitive the microphone will be. You can test this by watching the Input Level bars as you speak or make sounds.

4. To filter out ambient sounds, turn on the Use ambient noise reduction check box. (This option is only available for some input devices.)

✔ Tip

- Input device and volume are especially important if you plan to use Mac OS X's speech recognition features. I discuss speech recognition next.

Speech

Mac OS X's Speech preferences pane includes two groups of options:

◆ **Speech Recognition** (**Figure 72**) lets you enable and configure speech recognition features.

◆ **Text to Speech** (**Figure 83**) allows you to set the default system voice and enable and configure talking alerts and other spoken items.

In this section, I explain how to set up and use these features.

✔ Tips

■ Speech recognition requires a sound input device, such as a built-in or external microphone or iSight camera.

■ The speech recognition feature works best in a relatively quiet work environment.

To enable & configure speech recognition

1. In the Speech preferences pane, click the Speech Recognition button (**Figure 72**).

2. Select the On radio button.

3. A dialog may appear with instructions for using Spoken Commands (**Figure 73**). If this is your first time using this feature, read the contents of the dialog and click Continue to dismiss it.

   The round Feedback window appears (**Figure 74**).

4. If necessary, click the Settings button to display its options (**Figure 72**).

Figure 72 The Settings options for Speech Recognition in the Speech preferences pane.

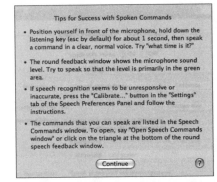

Figure 73 This dialog provides brief instructions for using Apple's Spoken Commands feature.

Figure 74
The Feedback window.

Figure 75 Use this dialog to enter a new listening key.

Figure 76 This pop-up menu enables you to specify how the keyword should be used for listening.

Figure 77 The Commands options for Speech Recognition in the Speech preferences pane.

5. Set options and click buttons as desired:

   ▲ **Microphone** is your sound input device.

   ▲ **Listening Key** is the keyboard key you must press to either listen to spoken commands or toggle listening on or off. By default, the key is [Esc]. To change the key, click the Change Key button, enter a new key in the dialog that appears (**Figure 75**), and click OK.

   ▲ **Listening Method** enables you to select how you want your Mac to listen for commands. Listen only while key is pressed requires you to press the listening key to listen. Listen continuously with keyword tells the computer to listen all the time. If you select this option, you can choose an option from the Keyword is pop-up menu (**Figure 76**) and enter a keyword for your computer to recognize commands.

   ▲ **Upon Recognition** instructs your computer how to acknowledge that it has heard the command. Speak command acknowledgement tells your computer to repeat the command. Play this sound enables you to choose a sound for acknowledgement.

6. Click the Commands button to display its options (**Figure 77**).

7. Turn on the check box beside each command set you want your computer to recognize.

Continued on next page...

Continued from previous page.

✔ Tips

- An external microphone—especially one on a headset—will work more reliably than a built-in microphone, such as the one on the front of the computer.

- Clicking the Calibrate button in the Settings pane (**Figure 72**) displays a dialog like the one in **Figure 78**, which you can use to test and adjust microphone volume.

- For best results, either set the Listening method to Listen only while key is pressed or require the computer name before each spoken command. Otherwise, your computer could interpret background noise and conversations as commands.

- The description of a command set appears in the Commands pane when you select the command set in the list (**Figure 77**).

- You can set options for some command sets. Select the command set in the Commands pane (**Figure 77**) and click the Configure button. A dialog appears with options you can set (**Figure 79**).

- Clicking the Open Speakable Items Folder button in the Commands pane (**Figure 77**) opens a Finder window that includes all Speakable Items commands Mac OS X can recognize (**Figure 80**).

- Each user has his or her own Speakable Items folder, which can be found at /Users/*username*/Library/Speech/ Speakable Items.

Figure 78 This dialog enables you to test and adjust the microphone volume.

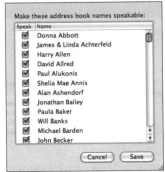

Figure 79 This example shows how you can configure the Address Book command set to recognize just certain people in your Address Book.

Figure 80 The contents of the Speakable Items folder.

Figure 81
When your computer recognizes a spoken command, the command appears above the Feedback window.

Figure 82
When a command has feedback, the response appears beneath the Feedback window.

✔ Tips

- The Speakable Items folder (**Figure 80**) contains preprogrammed Speakable Items. Each file corresponds to a command. Say the file name to issue the command.

- The Application Speakable Items folder inside the Speakable Items folder (**Figure 80**) contains Speakable Items commands that work in specific applications.

- If it is not possible to execute a command, nothing will happen after the command appears above the Feedback window. For example, if you use the "Close this window" command and no window is active, nothing will happen.

To use Speakable Items

1. If your computer is configured to listen with a listening key, hold down the listening key and speak the command you want your computer to perform.

   or

   If your computer is configured to listen continuously, speak the command you want your computer to perform. If the keyword is required before or after the command, be sure to include it.

2. If your computer understands the command, it will acknowledge it with voice and/or sound and the command will appear above the Feedback window (**Figure 81**). The command is executed (if possible).

   or

   If your computer did not understand the command, nothing happens. Wait a moment and try again.

- If the command you issued results in feedback (for example, the "What Time Is It?" command) and you set up speech recognition to speak feedback, your computer displays (**Figure 82**) and speaks the results of the command.

- To add a Speakable Item, use AppleScript to create a script for the command. Save the script as a compiled script in the appropriate location in the Speakable Items folder. Be sure to name the script with the words you want to use to issue the command. AppleScript is discussed briefly in **Chapter 24**.

To set Text to Speech options

1. In the Speech preferences pane, click the Text to Speech button (**Figure 83**).

2. Select one of the voices in the System Voice list (**Figure 84**).

3. To change the speed at which the voice speaks, use the Speaking Rate slider.

4. To test the settings, click the Play button.

5. To speak alerts, turn on the Announce when alerts are displayed check box. Then click the Set Alert Options button, set options in the dialog that appears (**Figure 85**), and click OK:

   ▲ **Voice** enables you to choose the System Voice or another voice.

   ▲ **Phrase (Figure 86)** is text that should be spoken before the alert.

   ▲ **Delay** is the amount of time that should elapse between when the dialog appears and the alert is spoken. Use the slider to set the delay.

6. To get a verbal alert when an application needs your attention, turn on the Announce when application requires your attention check box. (Normally, the icon for an application needing attention bounces in the Dock.)

7. To have your computer speak selected text, turn on the Speak selected text when the key is pressed check box. Then use the dialog sheet that appears (**Figure 87**) to press the keystroke you want to use to speak or stop speaking selected text and click OK. You can change the keystroke by clicking the Set Key button to display this dialog sheet again.

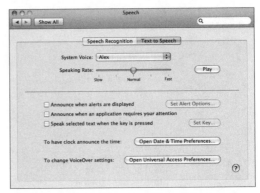

Figure 83 The Text to Speech options of the Speech preferences pane.

Figure 84 Mac OS X comes preconfigured with a number of voices. Choose Show More Voices to expand this menu's options.

Figure 85 Use this dialog to set options for the way your computer speaks alert items.

Figure 86 As this pop-up menu indicates, your computer can be very polite when it tells you about alerts.

Figure 87 Use this dialog to specify a keystroke that will speak or stop speaking selected items.

Figure 88 You can customize the way your computer alerts you by editing the Alert Phrases it uses.

✔ Tips

■ As you try some of the voices, you'll see that the novelty voices are more fun than practical.

■ The settings you make in the Text to Speech pane affect any application that can speak text.

■ In step 5, you can choose Edit Phrase List from the Phrase pop-up menu (**Figure 86**) to display the Alert Phrases dialog (**Figure 88**). Click the Add or Remove buttons to add a new phrase or remove a selected one. When you're finished, click OK to save your changes.

■ To speak the time, click the Open Date & Time Preferences button. This displays the Date & Time preferences pane. Click the Clock button and set Announce the time options (**Figure 16**). I tell you about the Date & Time preferences pane earlier on page 534.

■ To change VoiceOver settings, click the Open Universal Access Preferences button. This displays the Seeing options of the Universal Access preferences pane (**Figure 91**) which I discuss briefly on page 566. I tell you about VoiceOver on page 591.

SETTING TEXT TO SPEECH OPTIONS

Startup Disk

The Startup Disk preferences pane (**Figure 89**) enables you to select a startup disk and, if desired, restart your computer. You might find this helpful if you want to start your computer under Windows using Boot Camp or from a bootable CD or DVD disc, such as a Mac OS installer disc.

Mac OS X's Target Disk Mode feature makes it possible for your computer's hard disk to be used as an external hard disk when connected to another computer via FireWire cable. You can enable this option in the Startup Disk preferences pane, too.

✔ Tips

- I tell you briefly about Boot Camp in **Chapter 24**.

- To decide "on the fly" which startup disk to use, hold down the (Option) key at startup to display icons for each startup disk. Click the disk you want and then press (Return) complete the startup process from the disk you selected.

- Holding down the (Control) key while a bootable disc is inserted in your computer usually starts the computer from the System folder on that disc.

- A discussion of the Network Startup feature, which works with Mac OS X Server and its NetBoot service, is beyond the scope of this book.

Figure 89 In this example, a hard disk and a bootable DVD are available to start the computer.

Figure 90 This dialog appears when you prepare to restart your computer in Target Disk Mode.

To select a startup disk

1. Display the Startup Disk preferences pane (**Figure 89**).

2. Click the icon for the startup disk you want to use.

3. To immediately restart your computer, click the Restart button.

   or

   Quit System Preferences.

✔ Tip

■ If you do not immediately restart your computer with the new startup disk selected, that disk will be used the next time you restart or start up.

To use target disk mode

1. Use a FireWire cable to connect your computer to another computer.

2. In the Startup Disk preferences pane (**Figure 89**), click Target Disk Mode.

3. Read the information in the dialog sheet that appears (**Figure 90**).

4. Click Restart.

✔ Tips

■ When you're finished using your computer in target disk mode, press its power button.

■ Your computer must have a FireWire port to utilize target disk mode.

SETTING STARTUP DISK, TARGET DISK MODE

Universal Access

The Universal Access preferences pane enables you to set options for making your computer easier to use by people with disabilities.

Universal Access's features can be set in four different tabs:

◆ **Seeing** (**Figure 91**) enables you to set options for people with visual disabilities.

◆ **Hearing** (**Figure 92**) allows you to set options for people with aural disabilities.

◆ **Keyboard** (**Figure 93**) lets you set options for people who have difficulty using the keyboard.

◆ **Mouse** or **Mouse & Trackpad** (**Figure 94**) enables you to set options for people who have difficulty using the mouse.

A complete discussion of Universal Access is beyond the scope of this book. If you have a need to use these features, explore them on your own. You can click the Help (**?**) button in a panel to get detailed information about its options.

Figures 91, 92, 93, & 94 The four panels of the Universal Access preferences pane—Seeing, Hearing, Keyboard, and Mouse & Keyboard—enable you to set up your Mac so it's easier to use by people with disabilities.

Figure 95 When a preferences pane is unlocked, the padlock icon at the bottom of its window looks unlocked.

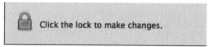

Figure 96 When a preferences pane is locked, the padlock icon at the bottom of its window looks locked.

Figure 97 Enter an administrator's user name and password in a dialog like this to unlock the preferences pane.

Locking Preference Settings

Many preferences panes include a lock button that enables you to lock the settings. Locking a preferences pane's settings prevent them from being changed accidentally or by users who do not have administrative privileges.

To lock a preferences pane

Click the lock button at the bottom of a preferences pane window (**Figure 95**).

The button changes so that the icon within it looks like a locked padlock (**Figure 96**).

To unlock a preferences pane

1. Click the lock button at the bottom of a locked preferences pane window (**Figure 96**).

2. Enter an administrator's name and password in the Authenticate dialog that appears (**Figure 97**) and click OK.

The button changes so that the icon within it looks like an unlocked padlock (**Figure 95**).

LOCKING & UNLOCKING PREFERENCES PANES

567

Mac OS Utilities

Figure 1 The Utilities folder contains a bunch of utility applications for working with your computer and files.

Mac OS Utilities

The Utilities folder inside the Applications folder **(Figure 1)** includes a number of utility applications you can use to work with your computer and its files.

This chapter covers the following utilities:

◆ **Activity Monitor** displays information about your computer CPU's workload.

◆ **AppleScript Editor** enables you to write and edit AppleScripts for automating tasks.

◆ **Audio MIDI Setup** enables you to set options for audio and MIDI devices connected to your Macintosh.

◆ **Boot Camp Assistant** makes it possible to install and run Windows on your Macintosh.

◆ **ColorSync Utility** enables you to check and repair ColorSync profiles and to assign profiles to hardware devices.

◆ **Console** displays technical messages from the system software and applications.

◆ **DigitalColor Meter** enables you to measure and translate colors on your display.

◆ **Grab** enables you to capture screen images and save them as image files.

Continued on next page...

Continued from previous page.

◆ **Grapher** lets you create static or animated graphs of formulas.

◆ **Migration Assistant** enables you to transfer data from another Mac.

◆ **System Profiler** provides information about your Mac's installed software and hardware.

◆ **Terminal** offers an interface for accessing Unix and entering command-line instructions.

◆ **VoiceOver Utility** enables you to configure the VoiceOver feature of Mac OS X.

This chapter also explores Automator and one of the less-used features of Mac OS X: Application Services.

✔ Tips

■ This chapter does not provide in depth discussions of each of these applications. Instead, it introduces you to them and provides enough information for you to get started using them.

■ This chapter does not cover the following utilities, which are discussed elsewhere in this book:

  ▲ AirPort Utility, Bluetooth File Exchange, and Network Utility, in **Chapter 20**.

  ▲ Disk Utility, in **Chapter 6**.

  ▲ Exposé and Spaces, in **Chapter 9**.

  ▲ Keychain Access, in **Chapter 22**.

■ Coverage of Java Preferences, Podcast Capture, RAID Utility, Remote Install Mac OS X, and X11 is beyond the scope of this book.

UTILITIES

Figure 2 The Activity Monitor window shows a list of all processes running on your computer.

Figure 3
Use this pop-up menu to choose the type of processes to display.

Figures 4, 5, 6, & 7 The bottom half of the Activity Monitor window can show System Memory, Disk Activity, Disk Usage, and Network information.

Activity Monitor

Activity Monitor enables you to get information about the various processes running on your computer. It also displays, in graphical format, CPU activity, memory usage, and disk and network statistics. You may find this information helpful if you are a programmer or network administrator or you are trying to troubleshoot a computer problem.

✔ Tip

■ A *process* is a running program that performs a task.

To monitor computer activity

1. Open the Activity Monitor icon in the Utilities folder (**Figure 1**). The Activity Monitor window appears (**Figure 2**).

2. To view only specific types of processes, choose an option from the pop-up menu at the top of the window (**Figure 3**). The list of processes in the top half of the window changes accordingly.

3. Click a button at the bottom of the window to view other information:

   ▲ **CPU** (**Figure 2**) displays CPU activity.

   ▲ **System Memory** (**Figure 4**) displays RAM usage.

   ▲ **Disk Activity** (**Figure 5**) displays disk access activity.

   ▲ **Disk Usage** (**Figure 6**) displays free and utilized disk space. Use the pop-up menu to choose other available disks.

   ▲ **Network** (**Figure 7**) displays network activity.

✔ Tip

■ To sort processes in the Activity Monitor window (**Figure 2**), click the column you want to sort by. You can reverse the sort order by clicking the same column again.

To display other monitor windows

Choose an option from the Window menu or its Floating CPU Window submenu (**Figure 8**):

◆ **Activity Monitor** displays the Activity Monitor window (**Figure 2**).

◆ **CPU Usage** displays a graphical representation of current CPU usage (**Figure 9**).

◆ **CPU History** displays a window with a chart of CPU usage over time (**Figure 10**).

◆ **Floating CPU Window** submenu commands (**Figure 8**) display a horizontal or vertical bar with a graphical representation of current CPU usage.

Or

Choose an option from the View menu's Dock Icon submenu (**Figure 11**). These commands display graphical representations of usage and activity in the Dock. **Figure 12** shows an example of the Dock with a Network Usage display icon.

✔ Tips

■ You can use the Update Frequency submenu under the Monitor menu to change how often monitor windows are updated.

■ As shown in **Figures 9**, **10**, and **12**, if your computer has multiple processors, it will display a separate graph for each one.

Figure 8 The Window menu and its Floating CPU Window submenu.

Figure 9
This tiny window displays a live, graphical representation of current CPU usage.

Figure 10 This window displays CPU usage over time. (Looks a bit like a pair of city skylines, doesn't it?)

Figure 11 The Dock Icon submenu offers options for displaying computer activity information in the Dock.

Figure 12 Activity Monitor can display activity graphs, such as Network Usage, as an icon in the Dock.

Figure 13 The Audio Devices window of Audio MIDI Setup.

Figure 14 The MIDI Studio window of Audio MIDI Setup, before any devices have been added.

Audio MIDI Setup

Audio MIDI Setup lets you configure audio and MIDI devices for use with a MIDI music system. It offers two windows of settings:

◆ **Audio Devices** (**Figure 13**) enables you to configure input and output devices, including internal and external microphones and speakers.

◆ **MIDI Studio** (**Figure 14**) enables you to configure MIDI devices, such as MIDI keyboards and other instruments, that are connected to your Macintosh.

This section provides a quick overview of Audio MIDI Setup.

✔ Tips

■ If you don't use MIDI devices with your Macintosh, you probably won't ever need to use Audio MIDI Setup.

■ Make sure drivers or other software required to use your MIDI device is installed before setting options.

To configure audio devices

1. Open the Audio MIDI Setup icon in the Utilities folder (**Figure 1**).

2. If necessary, choose Window > Show Audio Window to display the Audio Devices window (**Figure 13**).

3. In the list of devices on the left side of the window, select the device you want to configure.

4. Set options as desired in the appropriate pane on the right side of the window.

5. Repeat steps 3 and 4 for each device you want to configure.

CONFIGURING AUDIO DEVICES

573

To configure a MIDI setup

1. Connect your MIDI interface device to your computer as instructed in its documentation and turn it on.

2. Open the Audio MIDI Setup icon in the Utilities folder (**Figure 1**).

3. If necessary, choose Window > Show MIDI Window to display the MIDI Studio window (**Figure 14**).

4. Click the Add Device button. A new external device icon appears in the window (**Figure 15**).

5. Double-click the new external device icon to display a Properties window like the one in **Figure 16**.

6. Enter information about the device in the appropriate boxes. You may be able to use the pop-up menus to select a Manufacturer and Model. Click Apply to save your settings.

7. To enter port information, click the Ports button to display Ports options (**Figure 17**). Be sure to click Apply to save your settings.

8. Close the device's properties window.

9. Repeat steps 4 through 8 for each device you want to add.

✔ Tips

- Your MIDI devices may appear automatically in step 3, depending on how they are connected.

- Don't change the default settings for a device unless you know what you're doing! Consult the documentation that came with the device if you need help.

Figure 15
An icon like this appears when you click the Add Device button.

Figure 16 Use this dialog to enter information about your MIDI device.

Figure 17 The Ports pane enables you to enter port information for the device.

CONFIGURING A MIDI SETUP

Boot Camp Assistant

Boot Camp is an Apple technology that makes it possible to run Windows on your Intel-based Macintosh computer. Once installed and configured, you can *boot*, or start, your Macintosh in either Mac OS X or Windows and use the software you have installed for the system you've booted.

Boot Camp Assistant is a utility application that installs the software you need to use Boot Camp. You run it once, install Boot Camp and Windows, and shouldn't have to run it again.

Boot Camp has some very specific requirements:

◆ Mac OS X 10.6 or later.

◆ A USB keyboard and mouse or a built-in keyboard and trackpad.

◆ A built-in or compatible external optical disc drive.

◆ A Mac OS X 10.6 installation disc.

◆ At least 10 GB of free hard disk space. Note that you cannot install Boot Camp on a partitioned hard disk.

◆ Windows XP Home or Professional with Service Pack 2 or Windows Vista. Boot Camp does *not* include Windows; it must be purchased separately.

Although this chapter doesn't provide step-by-step instructions for installing and using Boot Camp, it does explain how you can get illustrated instructions prepared by Apple.

✔ Tips

■ We were unable to test BootCamp with Windows 7 before this book went to press.

■ A discussion of Windows is beyond the scope of this book. I highly recommend Peachpit Press's *Visual QuickStart Guides* for the Windows version you prefer.

To print a Boot Camp installation & setup guide

1. Open the Boot Camp Assistant icon in the Utilities folder (**Figure 1**). The Boot Camp Assistant's window and Introduction screen appears (**Figure 18**).

2. Click the Print Installation & Setup Guide button.

3. In the Page Setup dialog that appears (**Figure 19**), set options for your printer and click OK.

4. In the Print dialog that appears (**Figure 20**), set options for your printer and click Print.

   A 14-page illustrated document is printed. It includes complete instructions for installing and using Boot Camp.

✔ Tips

■ To print, you must have a printer set up for use with your Mac. I tell you about Printing in **Chapter 17**.

■ If you'd rather save paper, you can save the document as a PDF. In step 4, choose Save as PDF from the PDF menu, set options for the PDF in the dialog that appears, and click Save. I tell you about saving documents as PDFs on page 380.

Figure 18 The Installation screen of the Boot Camp Assistant.

Figure 19 Use this page Setup dialog to set options for printing.

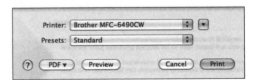

Figure 20 Use a Print dialog to send the guide to the printer or create a PDF.

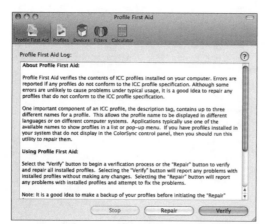

Figure 21 When you first display the Profile First Aid pane of the ColorSync Utility, a window full of instructions appears.

Figure 22 Here's what the results of a profile repair might look like after repairing a profile.

ColorSync Utility

ColorSync is an industry-standard technology that helps designers match the colors they see onscreen to those in devices such as scanners, printers, and imagesetters. For the average user, color matching may not be very important, but for a designer who works with color, correct reproduction makes it possible to complete complex projects on time and within budget.

In this section, I explain how to use the ColorSync utility to check ColorSync profiles and view profiles and devices.

✔ Tip

- A complete discussion of ColorSync is far beyond the scope of this book. To learn more about ColorSync features and settings, visit www.apple.com/colorsync.

To verify or repair ColorSync profiles

1. Open the ColorSync Utility icon in the Utilities folder (**Figure 1**).

2. In the window that appears, click the Profile First Aid icon (**Figure 21**).

3. Click Verify to check all installed profiles for errors.

   or

   Click Repair to repair any errors in installed profiles.

   ColorSync Utility checks or repairs installed profiles. When it's finished, it displays results in its window (**Figure 22**).

✔ Tip

- Use this feature to check or fix ColorSync Profiles if you notice a difference between what you see on your monitor and what you see on printed documents.

To view lists of installed profiles, registered devices, & available filters

1. Open the ColorSync Utility icon in the Utilities folder (**Figure 1**).

2. Click an icon in the ColorSync Utility window's toolbar:

   ▲ **Profiles** displays a list of installed ColorSync profiles (**Figure 23**).

   ▲ **Devices** displays a list of registered ColorSync devices (**Figure 24**).

   ▲ **Filters** displays a list of available ColorSync filters (**Figure 25**).

3. If necessary, click triangles beside a folder pathname to view a list of the items in the folder (**Figures 23** and **24**) or settings for the item (**Figure 25**).

✔ Tips

■ A registered device is one that is recognized by the system software and has a ColorSync profile assigned to it.

■ Clicking the name of a profile or device displays information about it in the right side of the window, as shown in **Figures 23** and **24**.

■ You can change a device's profile by choosing an option from the Current Profile pop-up menu when the item is displayed (**Figure 24**).

■ The filters that are installed with Mac OS X are locked and cannot be changed.

Figure 23 The Profiles pane displays a list of all installed profiles. Click a profile to learn more about it.

Figure 24 The Devices pane displays a list of all registered devices. Click a device to learn more about it.

Figure 25 The Filters pane lists available filters.

VIEWING PROFILES, DEVICES, & FILTERS

Figure 26 This example shows a conversion from a Generic RGB profile to the profile for my MacBook Pro's display.

Figure 27 You can click the magnifying glass icon and use a special cross-hairs pointer to get the color value of any pixel on the screen.

To convert color values

1. Open the ColorSync Utility icon in the Utilities folder (**Figure 1**).

2. In the ColorSync Utility window that appears, click the Calculator icon (**Figure 26**).

3. On the left side of the window, use the pop-up menus to set the color space or profile you are converting from.

4. Use the sliders on the left side of the window to enter color values.

5. On the right side of the window, use the pop-up menus to set the color space or profile you are converting to.

    The converted color values appear on the right side of the window (**Figure 26**).

✔ Tip

■ To find the color value for a pixel on your screen, click the magnifying glass icon to change the mouse pointer into a magnified cross-hairs pointer (**Figure 27**). Click the pixel you want to get the color values for to insert the values on the left side of the screen. This feature is similar in functionality to DigitalColor Meter, which I discuss a little later in this chapter.

To modify an image

1. Open the ColorSync Utility icon in the Utilities folder (**Figure 1**) to open Color-Sync Utility.

2. Choose File > Open, or press ⌘O.

3. Use the Standard Open dialog that appears (**Figure 28**) to locate, select, and open an image file. The photo opens in its own window (**Figure 29**).

4. Use toolbar buttons and the pop-up menus at the bottom of the window to set options for the image. The appearance of the image changes accordingly.

5. When you're finished setting options, click Apply.

6. To save the image with the changes applied, choose File > Save As or press Shift⌘S.

7. Set options in the Save As dialog that appears (**Figure 30**) and click Save.

✔ Tips

- I explain how to use the Open and Save As dialogs in **Chapter 10**.

- In step 4, if you set an option with the middle pop-up menu and don't like the results, choose None from that menu to revert back to the last time you clicked Apply.

- In step 7, you can use the Format pop-up menu to choose from a number of popular image file formats (**Figure 31**).

Figure 28 Use a standard Open dialog to locate, select, and open an image to work with.

Figure 29 The image appears in its own window.

Figure 30 Use a standard Save As dialog to save the modified image.

Figure 31 ColorSync Utility supports most popular image file formats.

Figure 32 The Console Messages window displays messages recorded by Mac OS and its applications. What may look like a bunch of gibberish to you and me can help a programmer or troubleshooter debug a Mac.

Figure 33 Use a standard Save As dialog to save the contents of the currently displayed window as a text file that can be shared with troubleshooters.

Console

The Console application enables you to read messages from Mac OS X system software and applications. You might find this useful if you are a programmer or are troubleshooting a problem. (If not, you'll probably think it looks like a bunch of gibberish.)

To view system messages

1. Open the Console icon in the Utilities folder (**Figure 1**).

2. The Console Messages window appears (**Figure 32**). Scroll through its contents to read messages.

✔ Tips

■ The most recent entries appear at the end of the document.

■ You can choose File > Open System Log to display the system.log window, which displays only messages from Mac OS.

■ You can click the Clear Display button in the Console Messages window (**Figure 32**) to erase the contents of the window and start a fresh log.

To save a copy of the log

1. Choose File > Save a Copy As or press ⇧ ⌘ S.

2. Use the standard Save As window that appears (**Figure 33**) to save the contents of the currently displayed window as a plain text file.

✔ Tip

■ Following these steps makes it possible to send a copy of your console.log or system.log file to someone helping you to troubleshoot a problem on your Mac.

VIEWING SYSTEM MESSAGES WITH CONSOLE

DigitalColor Meter

The DigitalColor Meter (**Figure 31**) enables you to measure colors that appear on your display as RGB, CIE, or Tristimulus values. This makes it possible to precisely record or duplicate colors that appear onscreen.

✔ Tip

■ A discussion of color technology is far beyond the scope of this book. To learn more about how your Mac can work with colors, visit the ColorSync page on Apple's Web site, www.apple.com/colorsync/.

To measure color values

1. Open the DigitalColor Meter icon in the Utilities folder (**Figure 1**) to display the DigitalColor Meter window (**Figure 34**).

2. Point to the color onscreen that you want to measure. Its values appear in the right side of the DigitalColor Meter window (**Figure 34**).

3. If desired, choose a different option from the pop-up menu above the measurements (**Figure 35**). The value display changes to convert values to that measuring system (**Figure 36**).

Figure 34 The DigitalColor Meter can tell you the color of any area onscreen—in this case, one of the pixels in its icon.

Figure 35 Choose an option to determine the system or units of the color measurement.

Figure 36 Choosing a different color measurement option from the pop-up menu changes the way the color values appear.

Image

Lock Position	⌘L
Lock X	⌘X
Lock Y	⌘Y
Copy Image	⌘C
Save as TIFF...	⌘S

Figure 37 Use the Image menu to work with the sample.

Color

Hold Color	⇧⌘H
Copy Color as Text	⇧⌘C
Copy Color as Image	⌥⌘C

Figure 38 Use the Color menu to work with sampled colors.

Figure 39 By changing the aperture setting, you can sample more pixels. DigitalColor Meter automatically computes the average.

✔ Tips

■ You can use commands under the Image menu (**Figure 37**) to work with the color sample image that appears in Digital-Color Meter's window:

▲ Lock Position (⌘L) prevents the image from moving.

▲ Lock X (⌘X) allows only vertical changes in the color sample.

▲ Lock Y (⌘Y) allows only horizontal change in the color sample area.

▲ Copy Image (⌘C) copies the color sample image to the clipboard.

▲ Save as TIFF (⌘S) saves the color sample image as a TIFF file.

■ You can use commands under the Color menu (**Figure 38**) to work with a selected color. For best results, either use the command's shortcut key or choose Image > Lock Position (**Figure 37**) before using the Color menu's commands.

▲ **Hold Color** (Shift ⌘H) saves the color in the sample well until you choose the Hold Color command again.

▲ **Copy Color as Text** (Shift ⌘C) copies the color information to the clipboard, where it can be pasted into other applications.

▲ **Copy Color as Image** (Option ⌘C) copies the color information as a color sample to the clipboard, where it can be pasted into other applications.

■ You can change the amount of color that is sampled by dragging the Aperture Size slider to the right or left (**Figure 39**). A large aperture size will average the colors within it.

Grab

Grab is an application that can capture screen shots of Mac OS X and its applications. You tell Grab to capture what appears on your screen, and it creates a TIFF file. You can then view the TIFF file with Preview or any application capable of opening TIFFs.

✔ Tips

- You might find screen shots useful for documenting software—or for writing books like this one.

- Although Grab is a handy screen shot utility, it isn't the best available for Mac OS X. Snapz Pro X, a shareware program from Ambrosia Software, is far better. If you take a lot of screen shots, be sure to check it out at www.ambrosiasw.com.

To create a screen shot

1. Set up the screen so it shows what you want to capture.

2. Open the Grab icon in the Utilities folder (**Figure 1**).

   or

   If Grab is already running, click its icon on the Dock (**Figure 40**) to make it active.

3. Choose an option from the Capture menu (**Figure 41**) or press its corresponding shortcut key:

   ▲ **Selection** (Shift ⌃ ⌘ A) enables you to capture a portion of the screen. When you choose this option, the Selection Grab dialog (**Figure 42**) appears. Use the mouse pointer to drag a box around the portion of the screen you want to capture (**Figure 43**). Release the mouse button to capture the screen.

Figure 40 If Grab is already running, click its icon in the Dock to make it active.

Figure 41 Grab's Capture menu.

Figure 42 The Selection Grab dialog includes instructions for selecting a portion of the screen.

Figure 43 Use the mouse to drag a red rectangle around the portion of the screen you want to capture.

Figure 44 The Window Grab dialog tells you how to capture a window.

Figure 45 The Screen Grab dialog provides instructions for capturing the entire screen.

Figure 46 The Timed Screen Grab dialog includes a button to start the 10-second screen grab timer.

Figure 47 The image you capture—in this case, the icons selected in **Figure 43**— appears in a preview window.

File	
Close	⌘W
Save	⌘S
Save As...	⇧⌘S
Page Setup...	⇧⌘P
Print...	⌘P

Figure 48
Grab's File menu.

▲ **Window** (Shift ⌃ ⌘ W) enables you to capture a window. When you choose this option, the Window Grab dialog (**Figure 44**) appears. Click the Choose Window button, then click the window you want to capture.

▲ **Screen** (⌃ ⌘ Z) enables you to capture the entire screen. When you choose this option, the Screen Grab dialog (**Figure 45**) appears. Click outside the dialog to capture the screen.

▲ **Timed Screen** (Shift ⌃ ⌘ Z) enables you to capture the entire screen after a ten-second delay. When you choose this option, the Timed Screen Grab dialog (**Figure 46**) appears. Click the Start Timer button, then activate the program you want to capture and arrange onscreen elements as desired. In ten seconds, the screen is captured.

4. Grab makes a camera shutter sound as it captures the screen. The image appears in an untitled document window (**Figure 47**).

5. If you are satisfied with the screen shot, choose File > Save (**Figure 48**) or press ⌃ ⌘ S and use the Save As dialog that appears to save it as a file on disk.

or

If you are not satisfied with the screen shot, choose File > Close (**Figure 48**) or press ⌃ ⌘ W to close the window. In the Close dialog, click Don't Save.

✔ Tip

■ You can create screen shots without Grab. Press Shift ⌃ ⌘ 4 or Shift ⌃ ⌘ 4 to capture the entire screen or a portion of the screen that you select. The screen shot is automatically saved on the desktop as a PNG image file.

Grapher

Grapher is a charting tool that can create static and dynamic 2-D and 3-D graphs based on formulas.

I won't pretend to be an expert on Grapher because I'm not. Sure, I can tell you how to use it, but I can't tell you how it works to create all the cool graphs it can create. In fact, if you have a need for a tool like Grapher, you probably know a lot more about its use than I do. But in this section, I explain how to get started using it so you can experiment on your own.

✔ Tip

■ Grapher's predecessor, Graphing Calculator, has a fascinating history that might interest you if you like Apple trivia. To learn more about how and why it was written, fire up your Web browser and visit www.pacifict.com/story/.

Figure 49 The first step to graphing a formula is to choose a graph type in the New Graph dialog.

Figure 50 An untitled document for a 3-D graph.

Figure 51 Grapher can create 3-D graphs like this one.

Figure 52 You may find it easier to enter complex formulas with the Equation Editor.

Figure 53
Grapher's File menu offers commands you can use with completed graphs.

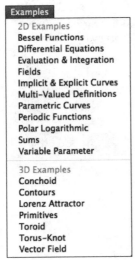

Figure 54
The Examples menu lists a bunch of cool sample graphs.

To graph a formula

1. Open the Grapher icon in the Utilities folder (**Figure 1**).

2. If necessary, choose File > New or press ⌘N to display the New Graph dialog (**Figure 49**).

3. Click a button near the top of the dialog to list either 2D or 3D document types.

4. In the list on the left side of the dialog, select the type of document you want. A preview appears in the right side of the dialog (**Figure 49**).

5. Click Choose. An untitled window with an empty graph appears (**Figure 50**).

6. Type the formula you want to chart in the box at the top of the window.

7. Press Return. The formula's graph appears in the window and the formula is added to the Definitions list (**Figure 51**).

8. If desired, repeat steps 6 and 7 to add other formulas to the graph.

✔ Tips

- Grapher's Equation Palette (**Figure 52**) makes it a bit easier to enter complex formulas. To display it, choose Window > Show Equation Palette or press Shift ⌘E.

- Once you've created a graph, you can save or print it using commands under the File menu (**Figure 53**). I tell you about saving files in Chapter 7 and printing in Chapter 12.

- Want to see some cool examples? Check out a few options under the Examples menu (**Figure 54**).

GRAPHING FORMULAS

Migration Assistant

Migration Assistant enables you to copy user information three ways:

◆ **From another Mac** enables you to transfer user information from another Mac to the one you're working on.

◆ **From a Time Machine backup or another disk** enables you to transfer user information from a Time Machine backup or from another disk containing a user folder.

◆ **To another Mac** enables you to transfer user information from the Mac you're working on to another Mac.

This makes it possible to transfer your information from an old Mac to a new one, restore user information with Time Machine, or add user accounts from or to another Mac.

The Migration Assistant is very easy to use. It provides clear instructions for completing every step and walks you through the process of copying user information. Simply double-click its icon to get started and follow the prompts. **Figures 55** and **56** show examples of the first two screens you'll encounter.

✔ Tips

■ The Mac OS X Setup Assistant may automatically perform the same tasks as the Migration Assistant, depending on your answers to questions during setup. I discuss the Mac OS X Setup Assistant in **Chapter 1**.

■ The Migration Assistant requires that you authenticate as an Administrator when using it. This prevents unauthorized users from adding accounts to the computer.

■ Most users will never need to use the Migration Assistant after completing the setup process for a Mac.

■ I cover Time Machine on page 122.

Figure 55 The first screen of the Migration Assistant gives you a good idea of the kind of assistance it provides.

Figure 56 The Migration Assistant can copy user account information from three different sources.

Figure 57
Clicking the More Info button in this window launches System Profiler.

Figures 58, 59, & 60 Three examples of the information System Profiler can provide about your system.

System Profiler

The System Profiler application provides information about your computer's hardware, software, network, and logs. This information can come in handy when you are troubleshooting problems or just need to know more about the hardware and software installed on your computer.

✔ Tip

- Clicking the More Info button in the About This Mac window (**Figure 57**) launches System Profiler.

To view system information

1. Open the System Profiler icon in the Utilities folder (**Figure 1**).

2. In the Contents list of the System Profiler window, click the type of information you want to view (**Figures 58** through **60**).

3. The information appears in the window.

✔ Tips

- You can click a triangle to the left of an item in any System Profiler window to display or hide detailed information.

- Clicking an item in the top-right portion of a System Profiler window displays details about that item (**Figures 59** and **60** show examples).

- You can use the File menu's Save and Print commands to save or print the information that appears in System Profiler. You might find this handy if you need to document your system's current configuration for troubleshooting or backup purposes.

Terminal

Terminal is an application that enables you to enter command line instructions into your Mac. These instructions are interpreted by Unix, the operating system beneath Mac OS X. This makes it possible to modify your Mac's internal settings with Unix and run Unix applications.

✔ Tips

- Don't know anything about Unix? Then you'd probably want to steer clear of Terminal. Typing an incorrect command into Terminal can render your Mac useless.

- A discussion of Unix is beyond the scope of this book. However, you can find a PDF containing the Unix chapter of the Tiger edition of this book at the book's companion Web site, www.mariasguides.com/2007/10/27/mac-os-x-tiger-unix-chapter/.

To use Terminal

1. Double-click the Terminal icon in the Utilities folder (**Figure 1**). A Terminal window with a *shell* prompt appears (**Figure 61**).

2. Use your keyboard to enter commands into terminal. Press ⟨Return⟩ to send each command to Unix.

   The results of your commands appear in the Terminal window (**Figure 62**)

✔ Tip

- The shell prompt shown in **Figures 61** and **62** (Maria-Langers-MacBook-Pro: ~mlanger$) includes the following components:

  ▲ *Computer name* is the name of the computer you're logged in to.

Figure 61 When you open Terminal, it displays a command line prompt.

Figure 62 Here's a simple example of Terminal in action. I entered the ls command to get a list of the contents in the currently active directory—my Home folder. (Aren't you glad you don't have to deal with this regularly?)

  ▲ *Directory* is the current directory. ~ (the tilde character) is Unix shorthand for your home directory.

  ▲ *User name* is your user name, which, in this example, is mlanger.

  ▲ $ is the end of the prompt.

Figures 63, 64, 65, & 66 Some of VoiceOver Utility's configuration panes.

VoiceOver Utility

VoiceOver is a built-in screen reader that helps visually impaired people use their computers. Once configured, VoiceOver enables you to hear descriptions of everything onscreen, move around the screen, select items, and read and manipulate text.

A complete discussion of VoiceOver is beyond the scope of this book. However, in this section, I introduce you to VoiceOver Utility, the application you use to configure VoiceOver.

✔ Tips

- VoiceOver can be enabled or disabled in the Universal Access preferences pane, which I discuss on page 566.

- To learn more about configuring and using VoiceOver, open VoiceOver Utility and choose Help > VoiceOver Help. Then follow the links to get the information you need.

To configure VoiceOver

1. Open the VoiceOver Utility icon in the Utilities folder (**Figure 1**).

2. The VoiceOver Utility window appears. Click buttons to set options in each of nine categories:

   ▲ **General (Figure 63)** lets you set the greeting and how portable preferences are used.

   ▲ **Verbosity (Figures 64 and 65)** includes four panes of settings that control how much speaking VoiceOver does.

   ▲ **Speech (Figure 66)** enables you to select the default voice and voices for various types of spoken text.

Continued on next page...

Continued from previous page.

▲ **Navigation (Figure 67)** controls how VoiceOver moves and tracks the cursor and text selections.

▲ **Web (Figure 68)** controls how Voice-Over works with your Web browser.

▲ **Sound** enables you to set sound-related preferences.

▲ **Visuals (Figure 69)** enables you to set the size of the VoiceOver cursor and menu magnification, as well as configure the Caption Panel.

▲ **Commanders (Figure 70)** enables you to map commands to the trackpad, numeric keypad, or keyboard.

▲ **Braille** lets you set the way Braille display works.

3. Choose VoiceOver Utility > Quit Voice-Over Utility, or press ⌃⌘Q, to save your settings.

Figures 67, 68, 69, & 70 Here are some more of VoiceOver Utility's configuration panes. As you can see, VoiceOver is highly configurable!

Figure 71 Here's one of the example Automator workflows; it goes online and displays all the latest movie trailers from Apple's Web site in Safari windows.

Figure 72 This AppleScript converts image files dropped into a folder into TIFF format and saves a copy.

✔ Tip

■ You can find a PDF containing the Automation Tools chapter of the Leopard edition of this book at the book's companion Web site, www.mariasguides.com/2009/10/01/mac-os-x-leopard-automation-chapter/.

Automation Tools

Computers are supposed to make our lives easier, right? They can—if we "teach" them to perform repetitive tasks automatically.

For example, when I start work in the morning, I start my computer and launch the applications I use every day: Mail, iCal, iTunes, InDesign, and Photoshop. I check my e-mail, delete the junk mail, and start playing one of my iTunes playlists. Then I open the folders and documents I'm working on: book chapters and the folder in which I store the chapter's files. When I'm done with a book's chapter, I save it as a PDF file, create an archive of the chapter's folder, and upload it all to my publisher's FTP site. There are many repetitive tasks here—tasks my computer has been trained to do automatically at my request. This saves me time—let's face it: My Mac can do things a lot faster than I can.

Mac OS X includes two tools for automating repetitive tasks:

◆ **Automator** (**Figure 71**) enables you to build workflows that automate tasks in multiple applications—all without knowing a single line of programming code. You can find Automator in the Applications folder on your hard disk.

◆ **AppleScript** (**Figure 72**) is a scripting language that enables you to automate tasks and extend the functionality of Mac OS. You use AppleScript Editor to create and edit scripts and save them in a variety of formats—including formats that work with Automator. You can find Apple-Script Editor in the Utilities folder on your hard disk (**Figure 1**).

A discussion of these two automation tools is beyond the scope of this book. But once you've mastered the basics of Mac OS, why not experiment with them on your own?

Application Services

Some Mac OS X applications provide services that enable you to use content from one application with another. The content can include text, graphics, or movies. For example, the services for Mail and Safari (among others) are available from within TextEdit (**Figure 73**)—this means you can use Mail to send selected text as an e-mail message or Safari to quickly open a selected URL.

Although these application services have been available in Mac OS X since its original release, Mac OS X 10.6 adds the ability to specify which application services can appear on the Services submenu.

✔ Tip

- You can easily see which application will provide a service on the menu by looking at the icon to the left of a command name.

To use application services

1. If necessary, selected text, an image, or a file.

2. Display the Services submenu under the application menu (**Figure 73**).

3. Choose the command you want.

To specify commands to appear on the Services submenu

1. Choose Services Preferences from the Services submenu under the application menu (**Figure 73**). The Services list appears in the Keyboard Shortcuts pane of the Keyboard Preferences pane (**Figure 74**).

2. Toggle check boxes to enable or disable the commands that can appear.

3. Close the window to save your settings.

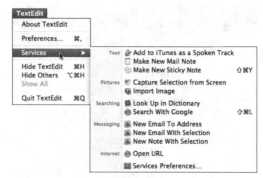

Figure 73 The services for Mail, Safari, and other applications are supported by TextEdit, giving you access to other application features from within TextEdit.

Figure 74 You can toggle check boxes here to determine which commands can appear on the Services submenu.

✔ Tip

- The Services menu only displays those options that can be used in the current applications, given the current selection.

Getting Help

Getting Help

Mac OS offers two basic ways to get additional information and answers to questions as you work with your computer:

- ◆ **Help Tags** identify screen items as you point to them. This help feature is supported by many (but not all) applications.

- ◆ **Mac Help** uses Mac OS X's Help Viewer to provide information about using Mac OS and its applications. This Help feature, which is accessible through commands on the Help menu, is searchable and includes clickable links to information.

This chapter explains how to get help when you need it.

✔ Tip

- ■ You can find additional support for Mac OS, as well as Apple hardware and software, on Apple's Support Web site, www.apple.com/support/. I tell you about using Safari to browse content on the Internet on page 429.

Help Tags

Help Tags identify screen elements that you point to by providing information in small yellow boxes (**Figures 1**, **2**, and **3**).

✔ Tip

- ■ Help Tags are especially useful when first starting out with a new software application. Pointing at various interface elements and reading Help Tags is a great way to start learning about how an application works.

To use Help Tags

Point to an item for which you want more information. If a Help Tag is available for the item, it appears after a moment (**Figures 1**, **2**, and **3**).

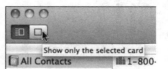

Figure 1 A Help Tag in the Address Book main window, ...

Figure 2 ...in a TextEdit document window, ...

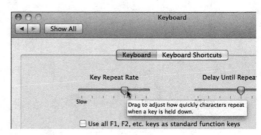

Figure 3 ...and in a System Preferences pane window.

Mac Help

Mac Help uses Mac OS X's Help Viewer to display information about Mac OS or a specific application. It includes several features that enable you to find information—and use it—quickly:

◆ **Main Help window** usually provides clickable links to introductory information and a table of contents or list of featured topics.

◆ **Search feature** enables you to search for topics containing specific words or phrases.

◆ **Related Topics links** enable you to move from one topic to a related topic.

◆ **Application links** enable you to open an application referenced by a help topic.

◆ **Online information links** enable you to get the latest information from Apple's Web site.

✔ Tips

■ Although this feature's generic name is Mac Help, help windows normally display the name of the application that Mac Help is displayed for.

■ If you are connected to the Internet when you access Mac Help, the most up-to-date help information automatically appears, downloaded from Apple's servers on the Internet.

MAC HELP

To open Mac Help

Choose Help > *Application Name* Help
(**Figures 4**, **5**, and **6**).

Or

Click the Help button in a window or dialog
in which it appears.

The main Help window appears (**Figures 7**, **8**,
and **9**).

✔ Tip

■ You can only have one Help window open
at a time. If the Help window is open for
one application and you choose the Help
command for another application, the
second application's Help opens in the
same window.

Figures 4, 5, & 6 The Help command on Help menus
for Finder (top), Address Book (middle), and TextEdit
(bottom).

Figures 7, 8, & 9 The main Help windows for Finder (top), Address Book (left), and TextEdit (right).

Figure 10
You can choose an application from this menu to display the application's help.

Figure 11 Clicking the "Network, share, and go online" link in Mac Help's main Help window (**Figure 8**) displays this Help window.

Figure 12 Clicking the "About AirPort" link in the Network, share, and go online window (**Figure 11**) displays this window.

To open Help for another application

1. Point to the Home button on the Help window's toolbar.

2. Click the button and hold it down until a menu of applications appears (**Figure 10**).

3. Choose the application you want to display help for. Help for the application you chose appears in the Help window.

✔ Tips

- The Home button's menu of applications makes it possible for you to open an application's help without opening the application itself.

- An application may not be listed on the Help window's menu (**Figure 10**) until you've used that application or have accessed its Help window.

To browse Mac Help

1. Click a link in a Help window. The window's contents change to view information about the item you clicked (**Figure 11**).

2. Continue clicking links to view related information (**Figure 12**).

✔ Tips

- Links in Mac Help normally appear in blue type.

- You can backtrack through topics you have viewed by clicking the back button in the toolbar (**Figure 11** or 12).

BROWSING MAC HELP

To search Help

1. Enter a search word, phrase, or question in the entry field at the top of the Help window (**Figure 13**) and press Return.

   After a moment, a Search Results window appears (**Figure 14**).

2. Double-click a topic in the search results list. The topic's information appears in the window (**Figure 15**).

✔ Tips

- As shown in **Figure 14**, search results can include Help Topics that reside in the Mac OS Help system on your computer as well as Support Articles that your Mac can retrieve from Apple's support site if you have an Internet connection.

- You can also enter a search word or phrase in the Help menu's Search text field (**Figure 17**) to see instant results. Simply click one of the search results in the menu to quickly display information about that item.

- You can use the Search field's menu (**Figure 16**) to specify what should be searched.

Figure 16 Typing a search word or phrase into the Help menu's search field may be the fastest way to find help about a specific topic.

Figure 13 Enter a search word or phrase in the Search box.

Figure 14 Search results appear in order of relevance.

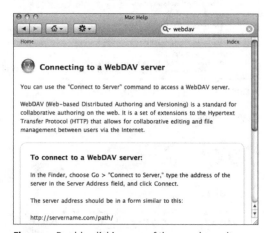

Figure 15 Double-clicking one of the search results displays the related information.

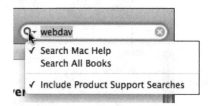

Figure 17 The Search box has a menu of options for what should be searched.

SEARCHING HELP

Figure 18 The Help menu in iTunes offers a number of commands for getting
onscreen help from within iTunes.

*Help
button*

Figure 19 The Help button that
appears within many Apple
applications is a button with a
question mark on it.

Application Help

Many applications include extensive
onscreen help. The help features of various
applications may look and work differently,
so it's impossible to cover them in detail here.
Most onscreen help features, however, are
intuitive and easy to use.

✔ Tips

- Some applications, such as the Microsoft
  Office suite of products, include an entire
  onscreen manual that is searchable and
  printable.

- Not all applications include onscreen
  help. If you can't locate an onscreen help
  feature for an application, check the
  documentation that came with the
  application to see if it has one and how
  you can access it.

To access an application's onscreen help

Choose a command from the Help menu
within the application (**Figure 18**).

Or

Click a Help button within a dialog
(**Figure 19**).

Help & Troubleshooting Advice

Here's some advice for getting help with and troubleshooting problems.

◆ **Join a Macintosh user group.** Joining a user group and attending meetings is probably the most cost-effective way to learn about your computer and get help. You can find a users' group near you by consulting the Apple User Group Web site, www.apple.com/usergroups/.

◆ **Attend free seminars at your local Apple Store.** You can learn more about Apple Stores and see a calendar of upcoming events at a store near you at www.apple.com/retail/.

◆ **Visit Apple's Web site.** If you have access to the Web, you can find a wealth of information about your computer online. Start at www.apple.com/support/ (**Figure 20**) and search for the information you need.

◆ **Visit the Web sites for the companies that develop the applications you use most.** A regular visit to these sites can keep you up to date on updates and upgrades to keep your software running smoothly. These sites can also provide technical support for problems you encounter while using the software. Learn the URLs for these sites by consulting the documentation that came with the software.

◆ **Visit Web sites that offer troubleshooting information.** MacFixIt (www.macfixit.com), MacInTouch (www.macintouch.com), The Unofficial Apple Weblog (www.tuaw.com), and Mac OS X Hints (www.osxhints.com) are four excellent resources.

Figure 20 Apple's Support site includes a wealth of information about all Apple products—both hardware and software.

◆ **Read Macintosh magazines.** Several magazines, each geared toward a different level of user, can help you learn about your computer: *Macworld* is the most popular. Be careful of PC-centric magazines; the majority of the information they provide will not apply to your Macintosh.

Menus & Keyboard Equivalents

A

Menus & Keyboard Equivalents

This appendix illustrates all of Mac OS X's Finder menus and provides a list of corresponding keyboard equivalents.

To use a keyboard equivalent, hold down the modifier key (usually ⌘) while pressing the keyboard key for the command.

Menus and keyboard commands are discussed in detail in **Chapter 2**.

Apple Menu

Option ⌘ D	Dock > Turn Hiding On/Off
Option ⌘ Esc	Force Quit
Option ⌘ ⏏	Sleep
Shift ⌘ Q	Log Out

Finder Menu

⌘ ,	Preferences
Shift ⌘ Delete	Empty Trash
⌘ H	Hide Finder
Option ⌘ H	Hide Others

```
┌─────────────────────────────────┐
│ Finder                          │
├─────────────────────────────────┤
│ About Finder                    │
│                                 │
│ Preferences...            ⌘,    │
│                                 │
│ Empty Trash...         ⇧⌘⌫     │
│ Secure Empty Trash...           │
│                                 │
│ Services                   ▶    │
│                                 │
│ Hide Finder               ⌘H    │
│ Hide Others              ⌥⌘H    │
│ Show All                        │
└─────────────────────────────────┘
```

File Menu

⌘ N	New Finder Window
Shift ⌘ N	New Folder
Option ⌘ N	New Smart Folder
⌘ O	Open
Option ⌘ O	Open and Close Window
Control ⌘ O	Open in New Window
⌘ W	Close Window
Option ⌘ W	Close All
⌘ I	Get Info
Option ⌘ I	Show Inspector
Control ⌘ I	Get Summary Info
⌘ D	Duplicate
⌘ L	Make Alias
⌘ Y	Quick Look
Option ⌘ Y	Slideshow
⌘ R	Show Original
⌘ T	Add To Sidebar
Shift ⌘ T	Add to Dock
⌘ Delete	Move to Trash
⌘ E	Eject
⌘ F	Find
Shift ⌘ F	Find by Name

```
┌─────────────────────────────────┐
│ File                            │
├─────────────────────────────────┤
│ New Finder Window         ⌘N    │
│ New Folder               ⇧⌘N    │
│ New Smart Folder         ⌥⌘N    │
│ New Burn Folder                 │
│ Open                      ⌘O    │
│ Open With                  ▶    │
│ Print                           │
│ Close Window              ⌘W    │
│                                 │
│ Get Info                  ⌘I    │
│                                 │
│ Compress "Letter to Cliff"      │
│                                 │
│ Duplicate                 ⌘D    │
│ Make Alias                ⌘L    │
│ Quick Look "Letter to Cliff" ⌘Y │
│ Show Original             ⌘R    │
│ Add To Sidebar            ⌘T    │
│                                 │
│ Move to Trash            ⌘⌫    │
│ Eject                     ⌘E    │
│ Burn "Letter to Cliff" to Disc...│
│                                 │
│ Find                      ⌘F    │
│                                 │
│ Label:                          │
│ ☒ ■ ■ ■ ■ ■ ■ ■               │
└─────────────────────────────────┘
```

```
┌─────────────────────────┐
│ Edit                    │
├─────────────────────────┤
│ Undo            ⌘Z       │
│ Redo          ⇧⌘Z        │
│                         │
│ Cut             ⌘X       │
│ Copy            ⌘C       │
│ Paste           ⌘V       │
│ Select All      ⌘A       │
│                         │
│ Show Clipboard          │
│                         │
│ Special Characters...   │
└─────────────────────────┘
```

Edit Menu

⌘Z	Undo
Shift ⌘Z	Redo
⌘X	Cut
⌘C	Copy
⌘V	Paste
⌘A	Select All
Option ⌘A	Deselect All

```
┌─────────────────────────┐
│ View                    │
├─────────────────────────┤
│ ✓ as Icons      ⌘1       │
│ as List         ⌘2       │
│ as Columns      ⌘3       │
│ as Cover Flow   ⌘4       │
│                         │
│ Clean Up Selection      │
│ Arrange By           ▶  │
│                         │
│ Show Path Bar           │
│ Hide Status Bar         │
│ Hide Sidebar      ⌥⌘S    │
│                         │
│ Hide Toolbar      ⌥⌘T    │
│ Customize Toolbar...     │
│                         │
│ Show View Options   ⌘J   │
└─────────────────────────┘
```

View Menu

⌘1	as Icons
⌘2	as List
⌘3	as Columns
⌘4	as Cover Flow
Control ⌘1	Arrange By Name
Control ⌘2	Arrange By Date Modified
Control ⌘3	Arrange By Date Created
Control ⌘4	Arrange By Size
Control ⌘5	Arrange By Kind
Control ⌘6	Arrange By Label
Option ⌘S	Show/Hide Sidebar
Option ⌘T	Show/Hide Toolbar
⌘J	Show/Hide View Options

EDIT & VIEW MENUS

605

Go Menu

⌃ ⌘ [	Back
⌃ ⌘]	Forward
⌃ ⌘ ↑	Enclosing Folder
Shift ⌃ ⌘ ↑	Select Startup Disk on Desktop
Control ⌃ ⌘ ↑	Enclosing Folder in New Window
Shift ⌃ ⌘ C	Computer
Shift ⌃ ⌘ H	Home
Shift ⌃ ⌘ D	Desktop
Shift ⌃ ⌘ K	Network
Shift ⌃ ⌘ I	My iDisk
Shift ⌃ ⌘ A	Applications
Shift ⌃ ⌘ U	Utilities
Shift ⌃ ⌘ O	Documents
Shift ⌃ ⌘ G	Go to Folder
⌃ ⌘ K	Connect to Server

Window Menu

⌃ ⌘ M	Minimize
Option ⌃ ⌘ M	Minimize All
⌃ ⌘ `	Cycle Through Windows

Help Menu

Shift ⌃ ⌘ /	Display Mac Help menu

Index

INDEX

INDEX

INDEX

INDEX

ISBN: 0-321-63493-4 • $59.99

ISBN: 0-321-63500-0 • $59.99

ISBN: 0-321-63501-9 • $59.99

AdobePress

Introducing the Learn by Video Series

As the official training for the Adobe Certified Associate exam, the new Learn by Video series teaches users not only the fundamentals of Adobe software, but also how to use the programs to create effective forms of visual, web and rich media communication.

Learn by Video offers between 14 to 19 hours of high quality video training, produced by video2brain and presented by their experienced trainers, as well as lesson files, assessment quizzes and review materials. The DVD is bundled with a printed book that provides supplemental information as well as a guide to the video topics.

14-19 hours of high-quality video training

Tutorials-to-Go! Transfer selected movies to your iPhone, iPod, or compatible cell phone

Table of Contents never more than a click away

Watch-and-Work mode shrinks the video into a small window while you work in the software

Video player remembers which movie you watched last

Lesson files are included on the DVD

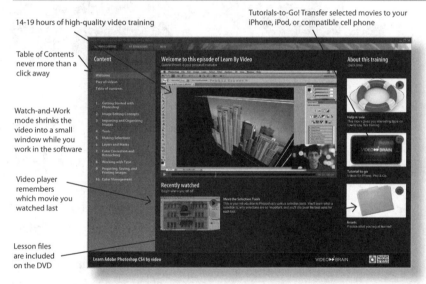

About video2brain

video2brain produces high-quality video training for software, photography, and programming topics. They have been commissioned by Adobe to produce many of the videos included on adobetv.com. Their videos feature top-notch instructors and stellar production values, and often employ innovative custom-built interfaces.

For more information and to view the series trailer go to
www.adobepress.com/learnbyvideo